Love and Despair

Love and Despair

HOW CATHOLIC ACTIVISM SHAPED POLITICS
AND THE COUNTERCULTURE
IN MODERN MEXICO

Jaime M. Pensado

UNIVERSITY OF CALIFORNIA PRESS

University of California Press
Oakland, California

© 2023 by Jaime M. Pensado

Library of Congress Cataloging-in-Publication Data

Names: Pensado, Jaime M., 1972– author.
Title: Love and despair : how Catholic activism shaped politics and the
   counterculture in modern Mexico / Jaime M. Pensado.
Description: Oakland, California : University of California Press, [2023] |
   Includes bibliographical references and index.
Identifiers: LCCN 2022055646 (print) | LCCN 2022055647 (ebook) |
   ISBN 9780520392953 (cloth) | ISBN 9780520392960 (paperback) |
   ISBN 9780520392977 (epub)
Subjects: LCSH: Catholics—Political activity—Mexico—History—
   20th century. | Youth in motion pictures. | Mexico—History—
   20th century.
Classification: LCC BX1482.2 .P46 2023 (print) | LCC BX1482.2 (ebook) |
   DDC 266/.20972—dc23/eng/20230316
LC record available at https://lccn.loc.gov/2022055646
LC ebook record available at https://lccn.loc.gov/2022055647

Manufactured in the United States of America

32   31   30   29   28   27   26   25   24   23
10   9   8   7   6   5   4   3   2   1

Para Jenny, Maité y Andrés
Los amo

CONTENTS

ILLUSTRATIONS

TABLE

FIGURES

ABBREVIATIONS

CECRUN   Centro Crítico Universitario (Critical University Center)

CELAM   Consejo Episcopal Latinoamericano (Latin American Episcopal Council)

CENCOS   Centro Nacional de Comunicación Social (National Center of Social Communications)

CIDOC   Centro Intercultural de Documentación (Intercultural Center of Documentation)

CUC   Centro Universitario Cultural (University Cultural Center)

CUEC   Centro Universitario de Estudios Cinematograficos (University Center for Cinematographic Studies)

DFS   Dirección Federal de Seguridad (Directorate of Federal Security)

JCFM   Juventud Católica Femenina Mexicana (Mexican Female Catholic Youth)

JECI   Juenesse Etudiante Catholique Internationale (International Young Catholic Students)

MEP   Movimiento Estudiantil Profesional (Movement of Professional Students)

MIEC   Mouvement International des Etudiants Catholiques (International Movement of Catholic Students)

MURO	Movimiento Universitario de Renovación Orientadora (University Movement of Renovated Orientation)
OCIC	Organisation Catholique Internationale du Cinema (International Catholic Cinema Office)
PAN	Partido de Acción Nacional (National Action Party)
PRI	Partido Revolucionario Institucional (Institutional Revolutionary Party)
SpP	Sacerdotes para el Pueblo (Priests for the People)
UFEC	Unión Femenina de Estudiantes Católicas (Women's Union of Catholic Students)
UIA	Universidad Ibero-Americana (Ibero-American University)
UNAM	Universidad Nacional Autónoma de México (National Autonomous University of Mexico)
UNEC	Unión Nacional de Estudiantes Católicos (National Catholic Student Union)

ACKNOWLEDGMENTS

My interest in Catholicism began with the research I conducted for my book *Rebel Mexico: Student Unrest and Authoritarian Political Culture during the Long Sixties* (2013). It continued in various papers in which I explored the conservative and progressive wings of the Mexican church. I thank Julia Young, Stephen Andes, Gema Kloppe-Santamaría, and Luis Herrán Ávila for their remarkable comments and support on these first publications.

While teaching at the University of Notre Dame, my research interests turned to youth activism, the counterculture, and state repression within the broader Catholic world of the Global Sixties. This approach took me to several archives and libraries in the United States, Europe, and Latin America thanks to the generous grants that I received from the Kellogg Institute for International Studies. I also benefited from financial support provided by the Institute for Scholarship in the Liberal Arts (ISLA), the Institute for Latino Studies (ILS), and the Department of History. I am equally grateful to the Notre Dame Institute for Advanced Studies (NDIAS) for its residential fellowship. These various entities provided me with rich intellectual spaces to share my ideas and receive instructive feedback from interdisciplinary scholars and friends. I am particularly grateful to Brad Gregory, Darren Dochuk, Thomas Kselman, David Lantigua, Lorena García Mourelle, Israel García Solares, Denisa Jashari, Vanesa Miseres, Rebecca McKenna, Aleida García Aguirre, Peter Casarella, Adela Cedillo, Nicolás Dip, Denisse Cejudo, Mario Santiago Jiménez, Allert Brown-Gort, Denise Wright, Victor Maqque, and Fr. Bob Pelton for their engagement with my work. I am also grateful for the invaluable conversations that I shared in other universities with so many admirable colleagues, including, among many others, Elena Poniatowska, Jean

Meyer, Soledad Loaeza, Matthew Butler, Gerd-Rainer Horn, Pablo Ben, José Ángel Hernández, and Isabella Cosse.

I want to thank those who accepted my invitation to travel to Notre Dame to present their work at the "1968 in Europe and Latin America" and "Confronting Mexico's Dirty War" workshops, in 2016 and 2018, respectively. My conversations with the participants further validated the importance of taking religion seriously in our understanding of the radicalism of the Cold War era, and I am particularly grateful for the rich interactions that I had with Wil Pansters, Valeria Manzano, Vania Markarian, Alan Shane Dillingham, Sandra Mendiola García, and Massimo De Giuseppe.

I owe a special debt of gratitude to Enrique Ochoa, who has been an amazing friend and an admirable mentor for more than twenty years. I am extremely grateful for his valuable comments on various sections of the manuscript and for his support in organizing the 1968 workshop at Notre Dame. I also extend my admiration to Ted Beatty and thank him for his immeasurable guidance.

I am very much indebted to Eric Zolov and Mary Kay Vaughan, who read an early version of the manuscript and provided feedback and detailed suggestions for improvement. I thank them for their generosity, thoughtful questions, perceptive critiques, and close readings of my arguments. I am also grateful to Eric for the support he has given me over the years. I benefited tremendously from the conversations that we shared.

At the University of California Press, I am grateful to Kate Marshall, who expressed enthusiasm for publishing my book; to the press's Latin Americanist reader who approved the final version of the manuscript; and to Enrique Ochoa-Kaup and Sheila Berg, whose thoughtful editorial recommendations made this a more coherent book.

I also benefited from myriad discussions with many talented graduate students, and I am most grateful to Ryne Clos, Robert Palermo, Carla Villanueva, Noe Pliego Campos, Jorge Iván Puma Crespo, and Aitor Valdesogo. Their support, patience, and intellectual rigor gave me focus and hope during challenging times. I also thank José Guzmán Dominguez, who located key sources in the Catholic University Archives.

My sister, Mari Carmen, transcribed some of my documents and provided immense support during my stays in Mexico City. I am grateful for her unconditional love. I also acknowledge the amazing support of my mom, Marina Valero, and I thank her for introducing me to the fascinating world of Mexican films when I was just a child. I examine some of these films in the book.

My interviews and long conversations with priests took place over several years and were of foremost importance in my understanding of the modern history of Catholic Mexico. I am particularly thankful to the Jesuit Jesús García and to the director of the Mexican Social Secretariat, Manuel Velázquez. They explained the comprehensive histories of the progressive tendencies of Catholicism and provided me with keen analyses of state repression in Mexico, as did Rafael Reygadas, a former Marist priest who shared intimate details of his life with me. The same is true of the Claretian priest Enrique Marroquín. Our delightful conversation in Guadalajara had a profound influence on my understanding of the counterculture. My interviews with him were extraordinarily rich in detail. My long conversations with the Spanish Dominican friar Laudelino Cuetos were also detailed and rewarding, and I am particularly grateful for the full access that he gave me to the archives of the Centro Universitario Cultural. With sources from this university parish, I was able to establish key contacts with Catholic students who had attended the National Autonomous University of Mexico (UNAM) during the Sixties.

I thank Tim Matovina for his support at Notre Dame and for facilitating my meeting with the Peruvian Fr. Gustavo Gutiérrez, a leading figure in Latin American liberation theology. My conversation with Father Gutiérrez was extraordinarily informative, enjoyable, inspiring, and humbling. I thank him for his time, amazing memory, and advice.

I am grateful to Jorge Bermeo for his generosity in introducing me to key leaders of the National Action Party (PAN) and the youth wings of Catholic Action. He kindly arranged meetings with Diego Zavala, Mercedes Gómez del Campo, and former members of the Corporation of Mexican Students. With his guidance I was also fortunate to have separate conversations with former activists of the Movimiento Estudiantil Profesional (MEP). They encouraged me to adopt a continental approach in my study of Catholic activism, and like Ana María Bidegain, they urged me to pay attention to the important role of women in the lay movements of the Sixties. I had equally rewarding conversations with Eufemia Belén Almanza Villarreal and Héctor Torres González. I thank them and those who preferred to remain anonymous for sharing delicate descriptions of their past with me.

Dozens of people working at the Catholic Action, archdiocese, surveillance, university, and film archives in Mexico City and countless archivists and librarians provided me with assistance in the United States, Europe, and South America. At the Hesburgh Library at the University of Notre Dame, I am particularly grateful to Erika Hosselkus for locating rare documents and films and to Jean McManus for introducing me to the rich collections of Catholic pamphlets and specialized documents. My special thanks also go to Pablo and Dario, who welcomed me with open arms to the Centro Leonidas Proaño in Quito, Ecuador. They gave me full access to work with the rich archives of the Latin American Secretariat of Pax Romana and took care of me when I got sick.

I would also like to draw attention to my friend Romina Robles Ruvalcaba. I learned of her tragic death as I began writing these acknowledgments. She was close to our family and very much admired by everyone who knew her. I am grateful for her beautiful friendship, kind spirit, and great sense of humor. She always expressed enthusiasm for my work and provided our family with tremendous love and kindness. We will keep her in our hearts forever.

Jenny and our beautiful children, Maité and Andrés, deserve my hardiest gratitude. I dedicate this book to them and to the incredible love that we share. Los admiro y adoro para siempre.

Introduction

The Argentine leader of the Cuban Revolution, Ernesto "Che" Guevara, proclaimed in 1965, "The true revolutionary is guided by strong feelings of love. It is impossible to think of an authentic revolutionary without this quality." The Colombian priest Camilo Torres comparably concluded before joining the guerrilla forces that same year, "Revolution is . . . the way to obtain a government that will feed the hungry, clothe the naked and teach the unschooled. Revolution . . . will carry out works . . . of love for one's fellows." For both of these Latin American revolutionaries, love was to be expressed in practical and concrete action, and it could not fully exist in an exploitative capitalist system. To make an alternative system "efficacious," it was imperative to create what they respectively called a "new man" and an "integrated man." The Brazilian bishop Hélder Câmara agreed, but in his call for liberation, he strongly condemned armed struggle, insisting that "without justice and love," peace will always be a great "illusion." Similarly, the Brazilian educator Paulo Freire described the rebellions of the oppressed as "gestures of love," and the Peruvian theologian Gustavo Gutiérrez noted that "love must guide the process of liberation." Prioritizing the pacifist and most utopian elements of the counterculture, the Beatles comparably noted in their 1967 single, "All you need is love."[1]

From the perspective of progressive Catholics who came of age in Latin America during the 1960s, love represented the opposite of disinterest. While selfishness created a repressive world without scruples, love encouraged individuals to identify with those around them in self-sacrifice and service, free of personal gain. They contended that if individuals worked collectively they could foster the values needed to improve a society capable of guaranteeing freedom, economic equity, and democracy. Only unselfish love had the potential to break the walls of fear, conceit, envy, corruption, and greed that kept people alienated and subjugated to authoritarian leaders. Through the practice of love as action, selfishness could be overcome. Only then would the soul blossom with strength, the humanities triumph over alienating philosophies, justice be guaranteed, and the possibility of creating a holistic society be materialized.[2]

In this book I examine these divergent notions of love as differently conceived by self-defined Catholics who became invested in youth activism and the counterculture from the postwar period (1945–ca. 1955) to the Global Sixties (ca. 1956–ca. 1976; hereafter referred to as the Sixties), including priests, university students, journalists, intellectuals, and filmmakers. Like the famous revolutionaries of the era, these figures spoke of love in an effort to create an inclusive world. But in the repressive context of these years, they were not always successful. They often faced a sense of despair in the form of disillusionment, alienation, suicidal frustration, perceived madness, co-optation, censorship, political disenfranchisement, social marginalization, and state violence. In this sense, Mexico did not represent an exceptional country in the Latin American region. It too witnessed a violent period of repression, economic exploitation, and authoritarianism that dramatically undermined the utopian aspirations of the Cold War era.

Progressive Catholics who welcomed a dialogue with divergent expressions of modernity during these years effectively called for countercultural change. This was evident in the emergence of an increasingly less conservative society that overwhelmingly rejected the socialist utopia of militant activists but proved more receptive to the less dramatic and everyday cultural changes that the nation experienced with secularization, including the liberation of sexuality, the questioning of traditional notions of gender, the emergence of innovative expressions of spirituality, and the rejection of authoritarianism.

The demand for radical change originated also among a small group of priests concerned with the most pressing problems of the world. They drew from encyclicals, sociological studies, Marxist texts, dependency theory, and religious documents on social teaching to ameliorate the lives of the oppressed. Their impact was significant, as evidenced in the proliferation of religious activists in grassroots base communities and political institutions. The same was true of Catholic journalists, university students, intellectuals, and filmmakers who were instrumental in bridging the gaps between the secular and religious worlds.

The political and cultural changes that came with the participation of these actors were compelling but mostly moderate, selective, and gradual. They often took place outside the realm of social movements and were primarily evident in new magazines designed for a rising middle class; in sociological discussions on poverty, marginality, development, and reproductive politics; in national and international conferences that spoke of Catholic youth as the vanguard of continental change; and in cultural shifts depicted in cinema, everyday interactions, shifting notions of gender roles, intergenerational relationships, and transnational networks and solidarity. Moreover, they frequently happened apart from the strict binaries of "Left" and "Right" and beyond the hegemony of the United States, which all too often have dominated the narratives of the Latin American Cold War but are not always useful in describing the activism that characterized the Sixties.[3] Rather, the demands for change were often simultaneously expressed in both progressive and conservative language, mostly independent of secular actors and in ordinary and less radical fashion but emblematic of "the internationalization and politicization of everyday life."[4]

In understanding the particularities of the political and countercultural challenges to the status quo during the Sixties, it is crucial to see the church as a heterogeneous institution, not as inherently irreconcilable with modernity, as often depicted in the liberal scholarship and the official state narratives that have monopolized the history of modern Mexico, but rather as a crucial player in the secularization of a nation with multiple internal schisms. It is also imperative to take into consideration the reformist movements of the earlier postwar years in the broader Latin American and European contexts.[5] This period gave rise to a new concept of liberation and paved the way for a new generation of activists, artists, and intellectuals who radicalized in the Sixties, not strictly in response to political events, but also in relation to innovative expressions of culture and Catholicism.[6]

LIBERATION AND THE NEW LEFT:
FROM THE POSTWAR ERA TO THE SIXTIES

The postwar years witnessed the emergence of a new understanding of the modern world. This coincided with the expansion of the welfare system, the consolidation of a growing middle class, the "discovery" of youth as a new political actor with purchasing power, and the politicization of social movements caught between optimistic aspirations for change and authoritarian politics. At the center of this tension emerged an innovative sense of liberation embraced by a new generation of Latin Americans who called for hemispheric unity.[7]

Their efforts reflected concerns about momentous contemporary world events that had a profound impact on their universities. These included the anticolonial wars in Algeria and Indochina; the rise of military dictatorships in Guatemala, Nicaragua, and the Dominican Republic; the "iron fist" following the Hungarian insurrection; and the Chinese and Cuban Revolutions. Asserting their ideological positions in the incipient language of the Cold War and favorably responding to the ideas of self-determination and peaceful coexistence in the Third World, as originally conceived during the Bandung Conference of 1955 in Indonesia, the new generation portrayed itself as the "vanguard" of Latin America's future and participated in key international conferences to further their cause.

Without question, the multiple meanings of "liberation" echoed during these years were overwhelmingly political. For example, the term served as part of an innovative language of dissent and an egalitarian ethos that young student activists embraced to confront capitalism and imperialism as well as the reformism, authoritarian structure, and corporatist apparatus of an older Left.[8] But liberation meant something countercultural and spiritual as well. It encompassed styles of dress, sexual mores, intergenerational relationships, educational norms, defiant hedonism, literary genres, musical tastes, and religious beliefs.[9]

Not immune to the rebellious ethos of the era, young Catholics across Latin America embraced the concept of liberation, and while some rejected the paternalistic notions of charity and the Eurocentric language of social justice that had shaped their activism in earlier decades, others forged concrete alliances with Europeans who became interested in the anti-imperialist movements of Latin America. Both pushed for innovative and more Latin Americanized notions of political and countercultural action. With time, these were often framed as concrete acts of love that demanded greater participation in social movements, a critical pedagogy, *concientización* (personal and social transformation), the creation of new spaces of debate and cultural production, and the fruition of a productive dialogue with the "New Left." The latter term referred to "a movement of movements" that proliferated across the Americas and Western Europe during the Sixties.[10]

In the broader Catholic world of Latin America, the New Left peaked in the aftermath of the Bandung Conference (1955), the Soviet invasion of Hungary (1956), the Cuban Revolution (1959), the Second Vatican Council (1962–65), and the rise of military dictatorships (1964) in the region. It was followed by the irreverence, politics of fun, and erotic energy of the counterculture and a more open engagement with the sexual revolution. It reached violent overtones of despair, first with the state repression of the late 1960s and early 1970s and then with the waning years of an "economic miracle" that that had brought steady prosperity to urban centers since the postwar period. It concluded with innovative expressions of armed struggle, the crumbling of the welfare state and the rise of its neoliberal alternative, and the commercialization and excess of defiant nonconformity.[11]

In postwar Mexico, the language of liberation and the call for concrete acts of love challenged but did not entirely defy the traditional status of Catholicism. While the geopolitical conflict of the Cold War had just started to grow in intensity and the nation consolidated its collaboration with the United States, the church reinforced its relationship with the Institutional Revolutionary Party (PRI), founded in 1946. The PRI government solidified its authoritarian structures with the support of conservatives, including those who made up the majority of ecclesiastical authorities. In this context, the Catholic hierarchy partially restored the social and political influence that it had maintained before the Mexican Revolution (1910–1920s).[12] It supported new lay organizations in the peasant, labor, and student sectors that actively discouraged the radicalism of the Cristero past, when militant peasants in the late 1920s had waged a violent war in the name of "Christ the King" against the secular and anticlerical state. Moreover, the anticommunist propaganda coming from Rome promoted a new wave of religious affiliation that overlapped with the repression the government unleashed on those who questioned the authority of the PRI.[13]

The renewed moral authority among the conservative middle class turned young laypeople, both men and women, into key actors.[14] During the Sixties, they defied the conservatism of the past. These challenges derived from multiple individuals and were manifested at different levels of political and cultural engagement. A push for religious pluralism and a greater dialogue with modernity, social action, political tolerance, innovative artistic expression, and the liberation of sexuality questioned the hierarchical structure of the ecclesiastical authorities and shaped the ways a new generation of young people understood their changing religious identities. Many redefined their Catholicism not exclusively in relation to the poor, as it is often assumed in the scholarship, but also in reference to the anticolonial, humanist, reformist, autonomist, existentialist, cinematic, and countercultural movements of this period.

The early Catholic movements of the postwar period demanded a democratic nation, but they ultimately fell short in transforming the authoritarian ethos that continued to characterize Mexico in the decades that followed. When their leaders failed to achieve the utopian expectations of the era, or when they were repressed and their ideas co-opted, marginalized, and commercialized, the liberating hope of love often turned into despair. In making these arguments, I examine innovative spaces that opened across the nation in response to the most significant social, cultural, ideological, theological, and political changes that characterized the broader Cold War period but that have received little attention from historians.[15] In agreement with the historians Odd Arne Westad and Tanya Harmer, I examine the Cold War "as a conceptual framework for explaining a wider twentieth century struggle between different visions of modernity."[16] With an emphasis on film and cinematic representations of Catholicism as an analytical window into the past, moreover, I draw specific attention to the changing notions of and divergent responses to youth activism, state repression, and the counterculture during the Sixties.

I understand the Sixties as a unique period of student radicalization and nonconformity of youth that expanded from the mid-1950s to the mid-1970s. These years were characterized by accelerated secularization, rapid urbanization, and the commercialization of the entertainment industry. It is a unique era that witnessed the waning of economic growth and what the historian Mary Kay Vaughan has called "the domestication of violent masculinity."[17] In addition, it is a period that experienced a peak in the growth of the middle class and a rising critique of authoritarianism, patriarchal authority, and traditional notions of Catholicism that allowed for the possibility of dialogue between Marxism and Christianity. As the Chilean historian David Fernández has argued, it was in the Sixties when this dialogue was "brought into the open for debate and as part of everyday life." Catholics embraced the Left, "not as something tacked on to their Christianity, but as a socio-political choice illuminated by faith."[18] Similarly, European and US historians have noted, for example, that this was "a period of decisive change in the religious history of the Western world." As the British historian Hugh McLeod has explained, the "main novelty was that those who rejected [or questioned] Christianity were increasingly ready to say so loudly and openly."[19] These voices emerged with support from Catholics who frequently saw themselves as modern, progressive, countercultural, even revolutionary actors. Yet while a minority of them conceived it as impossible to find effective acts of love in a capitalist society during the Sixties, others—the overwhelming majority— proved more flexible. For the most radical of these actors, the evolution of the Cuban Revolution served as a litmus test. Many initially sympathized with the humanist and anti-imperialist language of its leaders, but most eventually disapproved of their relationship with the Soviets, which in agreement with a significant sector of the New Left they overwhelmingly saw as totalitarian.[20]

The importance of Che Guevara and his radical ideology certainly loomed in the background and influenced the Catholicism of a group of activists and intellectuals. Yet the martyred leader of the Cuban Revolution represented only one of a larger number of figures who shaped the youthful activism and countercultural movements of the Cold War era. Rising generations of Catholics forged alliances with leaders of the National Action Party (PAN), lay activists who welcomed the social programs of the Mexican Social Secretariat, and intellectuals in the Christian Democratic movement. In addition, they found inspiration in an array of international figures participating in the progressive dioceses of Cuernavaca and traveling across Mexico who benefited from their friendship with the radical bishop Sergio Méndez Arceo; in new combative voices in journalism calling for a democratic nation; in filmmakers, novelists, and artists who welcomed a dialogue with religion; and in ordinary national and foreign priests representing various religious orders.

In their individual attempts at building a tolerant church and challenging the authoritarianism of the governing elite, these figures understood their respective movements in the transnational world in which competing forms of Catholicism operated. For inspiration they often looked to Freire, Câmara, Gutiérrez, Torres, and the Beatles but also to less famous figures in film, academia, journalism, international organizations, and countercultural movements of the era. In forging national and at times international alliances and framing their participation in their respective movements as an act of love, they called on Catholic youth to improve the lives of the oppressed, empower the politically disenfranchised majority, engage in a productive dialogue with modernity, explore the aesthetics and artistic expressions of the counterculture, shed light on the perceived alienation of the era, question traditional notions of gender, and challenge the conservative ideology and language of the government and ecclesiastical authorities.

In *Love and Despair* I see ultraconservatives as influential figures who interpreted the Sixties as a chaotic period of anarchy and immorality in need of law and order. But I primarily pay attention to those who saw themselves as modern, apolitical, liberal, progressive, countercultural, and leftist and who often sympathized with the revolutionary figures of the era and frequently expressed the need to create an "integrated man." To paraphrase Camilo Torres, these new actors were expected to reject paternalistic notions of charity and could no longer afford to be satisfied simply with receiving the sacraments.[21] While some accepted the spirit of sacrifice in creating real structural changes and were presumed to bring together the natural and the supernatural, others saw the need to forge new ways of engaging in the most inspirational movements of the time. Many remained hopeful of the church; others left it altogether.

The polarizing and shifting ideas that unfolded from love and despair in the broader context of the Cold War shaped Catholic youth and the authorities who responded to their activism. While a minority saw the existence of reciprocal love and liberation exclusively in the creation of a socialist society, the overwhelming majority instead found themselves and their respective movements in the middle. For them, a better world was possible in the capitalist society that solidified in the postwar period. But as the Beatles and others noted in relation to the counterculture, true liberation and genuine love were unthinkable in a selfish world that prioritized the repressive minority. These revolutionary ideas resonated throughout the Sixties, but it was in 1968 that they reached a pivotal moment across Latin America.[22]

LOVE AND DESPAIR IN THE AFTERMATH OF VATICAN II

The Latin American Episcopal Council (CELAM) meeting in Medellín, Colombia, in August 1968 called for the Christian community to embrace the perspectives of the marginalized sectors of society and the colonized world. The participants concluded that the developmentalist projects of the imperialist North had only intensified dependency and exploitation in the Global South. Solidarity with the poor could guarantee true liberation of the oppressed in the name of love. The origins of this "preferential option for the poor" dated to the mid-1950s with the creation of CELAM and the growing presence of the laity in social and political movements.[23]

Progressive Christianity expanded across the continent in the aftermath of Vatican II with the publication of four documents of social teaching that were instrumental in the radicalization of Catholics across the world: *Mater et magistra* (Mother and Teacher, 1961); *Pacem in terris* (Peace on Earth, 1963); *Gaudium et spes* (Joy and Hope, 1965); and *Populorum progressio* (Development of Peoples, 1967).[24] While the encyclical *Mater et magistra* demanded government intervention in the economy in the hope of correcting economic injustices, *Pacem in terris* called on the modern world to embrace peace, dignity, and the universal common good as concrete gestures of love. This language first emerged in response to the rising threat of technological warfare that intensified with the Cuban Missile Crisis of 1962 (when the United States and the Soviet Union came close to a nuclear war) and resonated across the world with greater intensity with the acceleration of the Vietnam War from 1964 to 1973. In Latin America, these latter years coincided with the state terror that the United States facilitated with its National Security Doctrine in the region.[25]

Formerly known as the "Pastoral Constitution on the Church and the Modern World," *Gaudium et spes* evolved into the most important document on social teaching and *aggiornamento*. This Italian term refers to the broader effort to bring the church up to date in a productive dialogue with modernity. The document demanded closer interaction and cooperation with the entire human family, not exclusively among Catholics, but also with those of different faiths and nonreligious points of view.[26] These included individuals who saw the arts and the counterculture as genuine forms of liberation, as I argue in the book, as well as those who saw value in Marxist texts. *Gaudium et spes* welcomed the "signs of the times," whereby the church and lay activists were asked to "recognize and understand the world in which we live, its explanations, its longings, and its dramatic characteristics."[27] More assertively than the first two encyclicals, it prioritized the common good, solidarity, human dignity, justice, the poor, and human rights.

But it was *Populorum progressio* that proved to be more radical in its message and interpretation.[28] Written by Pope Paul VI in March 1967—the same time the delegates at the 1966 Tricontinental conference published Che Guevara's call for "two, three, many Vietnams"—the encyclical denounced the legacy of colonialism, which was evident in the growing economic gap between the North and the Global South. Its tone was suspicious of liberal capitalism, and while it demanded the consolidation of peace through justice, it simultaneously called for fundamental changes on behalf of the impoverished masses of the Third World. It rejected Guevara's argument that hatred was necessary to defeat imperialism and the historical legacies of colonialism and instead prioritized love as a catalyst of change.[29]

The liberating language of *Populorum progressio* resonated during the Medellín conference, where a group of progressive priests made the radical statement that revolutionary violence was justified when all other paths to defeat tyranny had otherwise been exhausted.[30] Most priests and lay activists in Latin America disagreed with this interpretation. In their rejection of armed struggle, they instead drew inspiration from the nonviolence of love, as evident in the critical pedagogy of Paulo Freire and in the building of Christian base communities that expanded across the continent in the late Sixties.[31]

Of equal importance in the radicalization of Latin American Catholicism was the Revision of Life method of "seeing, judging, and acting." The appeal of this three-pronged method to university students coincided with the 1955 conference in Bandung, where a group of Asian and African intellectuals demanded self-determination, peaceful coexistence, and an end to racism within the developing countries and accused the imperialist nations of their exploitation. The method asked Catholics to "see" the reality of underdevelopment, "judge" it using religious texts, and "act" to ameliorate the lives of the oppressed.[32]

In Mexico, the preferential option for the poor was initially framed as an interactive dialogue between "faith and development" during the First National Congress of Theology, held in November 1969. The more than seven hundred participants discussed the future and particularities of the country's own liberationist movement.[33] But as evident in the various case studies examined in this book, "liberation" proved a highly contentious term. Equally contentious was the exact role the church and lay activists should play in solving the most desperate problems of the era, including rampant socioeconomic inequalities, discrimination, exploitation, and state violence.

Representing the most radical camp was a small group of priests who demanded a closer relationship with the nation's youth, welcomed collaboration with university student activists, opened a dialogue with Marxism, and concluded that true love for humanity could not fully exist in a capitalist society. This conclusion was first voiced in the aftermath of the

Tlatelolco massacre, a pivotal moment of despair when an undetermined number of people were killed and imprisoned on October 2, 1968, at the hands of the government of Gustavo Díaz Ordaz (1964–70). A small but assertive group of activists, intellectuals, journalists, filmmakers, and priests grew disillusioned with a national church that overwhelmingly supported the authoritarian PRI.

The diminishing aspirations of love only grew louder in the aftermath of a second student massacre. This time an undetermined number of people were killed during a student protest at the orders of the more deceitful presidential administration of Luis Echeverría (1970–76) on the bloody day of Corpus Christi, June 10, 1971. A small number of radical Catholics saw no other option but to pick up arms and interpreted the democratic opening of the president as a farce that was mostly designed to co-opt those who continued to criticize the regime. The majority of progressive Catholics strongly disagreed with the militancy of the era and instead framed their dissatisfaction with liberal capitalism in reference to the dignity and love of the human person.[34] Others abandoned Catholicism, the church, and their engagement with the political world.

But the sense of despair that defined the radicalism of the era and brought an end to the utopian language of the Sixties did not exclusively emerge in response to state repression. It was further evident in the alienation of youth and the rampant consumerism of the era, the commercialization and co-optation of the counterculture, the excess of defiant nonconformity, the limitations of liberation, and the moral panic that emboldened those on the Far Right.

Vitalized by the legacy of the Cristero Rebellion, ultraconservative Catholics who disapproved of the reforms of Vatican II saw the Sixties as a moment ripe for radical action, yet one mostly characterized by despair, in the form of ideological distortion, social chaos, anarchy, nihilism, immorality, and debauchery. For them, and the "silent majority" that provided tacit support for the repressive regimes of the Latin American region, the sexual revolution was just as detrimental to the nation as the rise of Marxism.[35] Their progressive counterparts disagreed with this interpretation and instead saw the cultural manifestations of youth radicalism as "signs of the times," in the language of *Gaudium et spes*. In valuing the importance of ecumenism, they welcomed a dialogue with the neo-humanist thinkers of the era, who saw relevance in existentialism, psychoanalysis, feminism, and the arts. The writings of Teilhard de Chardin, Marcuse, Sartre, and De Beauvoir were of foremost importance, but so were the European films of Buñuel, Pasolini, and Fellini (among others who addressed the concerns of the Sixties with a Christian ethos). The same was true of religious texts that more favorably addressed the topic of entertainment (like the encyclical *Miranda prorsus*, 1957) and welcomed a conversation with sexuality and Eastern religions. Among them was the *Dutch Catechism*, a widely read book published in Spanish in 1966 that challenged traditional views on marriage, virtue, contraception, and gender first found in *Casti connnubii* (Of Chaste Wedlock, 1930) and later reinstated in *Humane vitae* (Of Human Life, 1968). To understand these divergent religious interpretations of the Sixties, it is crucial to provide an overview of the scholarship of the counterculture with attention to Catholicism.

THE WRITING OF *LA ONDA* IN CATHOLIC MEXICO

Nearly half of the population in Mexico was eighteen years old or younger in the mid-Sixties.[36] The marketing, entertainment, and mass media industries took notice of their potential for consumption, and so did intellectuals, journalists, scholars, government leaders, and ecclesiastical authorities who instead became concerned about their erratic countercultural attitudes and alleged immorality. For example, in a series of columns published in 1968 in the cultural pages of the national newspaper *Heraldo* and in the Catholic magazine *Señal*, journalists and intellectuals provided radiographies of the nation's middle-class youth that alluded to their potential political power but expressed dissatisfaction with their rebellious language, style, and behavior.[37]

Sociological, psychological, and psychoanalytic studies and novels soon followed.[38] Not too different from the columns published in the press, this scholarship saw the innovative phenomenon of the counterculture as symptomatic of a national moment in crisis. While some authors expressed concern that Mexican youth were imitating their American counterparts, others pointed to their novel expressions of rebellion as a structural consequence associated with an underdeveloped country experiencing a rapid transition to modernity. The literary critic Margo Glantz represented the latter position with her anthology, *Onda y escritura en México* (1971). For her, the radical novels of *la onda* (the wave) not only foreshadowed the obscenity, libertine sexuality, and rock lyrics that largely shaped the counterculture but also represented a temporary fad that lacked the enduring quality, eloquent prose, and nationalist narratives of *la escritura* (pure writing). Similarly, in *Días de guardar* (1970), the chronicler and intellectual of Mexico's New Left, Carlos Monsiváis, mocked la onda as a colonized version of the US hippie movement and dismissed it as a failed attempt at legitimate social change.[39]

New studies were published that rejected the crisis, fad, and colonized theses and instead set out to define the counterculture from the perspective of young people. This scholarship did not see the counterculture with apprehension but as a genuine protest of liberation. Of particular importance were *Hippies: Expresión de una crisis* (1968), by the American beat poet and co-creator of the bilingual magazine *Corno emplumado/Plumed Horn*, Margaret Randall; the short article "Cuál es la onda" (1974) by José Agustín, the leading figure in countercultural literature; and the original study on the *xipitecas* (Mexican hippies), *La contracultura como protesta* (1975), by the Claretian priest Enrique Marroquín.

The original manuscript of Randall's volume was translated into Spanish by the Mexican painter Felipe Ehrenberg. It set out to explain the multifaceted aspects of the counterculture in the United States. According to the book, the term "hippie" was first coined in 1965 in San Francisco, California, to denote a new, up-to-date attitude toward life. But the roots of the movement went back to the postwar years. This was evident in the hipster radicalism in Black communities, as well as in the aggressive beat poetry and rebellious rock music in white American cities. Both were responses to the alienation of youth that paralleled the civil rights protests and the burgeoning language and institutions of repression that simultaneously developed with the Cold War. For Randall, the hippies had planted the seeds for a consciousness-raising movement of liberation that demanded a tolerant society.[40]

Agustín made similar arguments in his description of la onda. He traced the popularity of the concept to the mid-1960s as primarily used among affluent youth in Mexico City to describe their sexual awakening and shared dissatisfaction with the authoritarianism of the era, as well as their mutual taste in music, literature, style, fashion, slang, joy, and humor. Within three years la onda had developed into a full-blown but far from homogeneous movement mostly present in Mexico's largest urban centers, Mexico City, Guadalajara, Monterrey, and Tijuana. The movement lacked a coherent ideology but shared a collective attitude toward life, primarily based on the utopian aspirations of peace and love, which Agustín framed in relation to mutual respect for diversity and artistic innovation.[41] As in the United

States, la onda was eventually associated with the effervescence, spontaneity, irreverence, and erotic qualities found in rock music; in the new and more liberating appreciation of sexuality; and in the rising consumption of psychedelic drugs. However, by the end of the decade, the government, ecclesiastical authorities, and ultraconservatives saw the movement strictly as deviant hedonism with foreign and immoral tendencies that had to be subdued. Those on the Left made similar arguments but without calling for its repression.[42] But state violence and commercialism ultimately undermined its most utopian elements of liberation, reaching a peak at the Avándaro rock festival in 1971, when nearly a quarter of a million young people gathered in Valle de Bravo in the state of Mexico to listen to the nation's most important rock bands.

The bohemian priest Enrique Marroquín (a central player in this book) was present at the Avándaro festival. His 1971–72 columns in Mexico's *Rolling Stone* magazine, *Piedra Rodante*, provided him with the opportunity to explore the preliminary arguments that he eventually presented in *La contracultura como protesta* (1975). In the preface, Agustín described his pioneering book as "one of the first attempts in our country to shed light on the complexity" of la onda.[43] In his efforts to highlight the particularities of the xipiteca movement, Marroquín refused to describe the counterculture as irrational, chaotic, ingenuine, or fashionable but saw its essence as an internal revolution that brought attention to what he called a "lost Mexico." This was a world composed of rich but repressed Indigenous traditions that faced rapid destruction of the natural environment. In making this argument, he reflected on his Catholic faith and placed la onda in conversation with existentialists, Marxist and Orientalist philosophers, anthropologists, sociologists, musicologists, and medical scientists specializing in the consumption of drugs.

The second half of the 1970s and the decades of the 1980s and 1990s saw little academic interest in the topic. Mexican scholars interested in youth culture found *La contracultura como protesta* irrelevant and instead drew inspiration from the Chicago School of sociology and the Birmingham School of subcultural studies to describe the style and resistance of lumpen *chavos banda*, or young punks, mostly residing on the outskirts of Mexico City and Guadalajara.[44] For their part, historians of modern Mexico did not see the need to contribute to this scholarship. They remained indifferent to examining the phenomenon of the counterculture and instead limited their interest to youth culture strictly in relation to the 1968 student movement, with important contributions during the twentieth and thirtieth commemorations of the Tlatelolco massacre.

This drastically changed with the publication of *Refried Elvis: The Rise of the Mexican Counterculture* in 1999 by the historian Eric Zolov on the emergence, co-optation, and repression of la onda. Zolov provided a rich cultural analysis of the hegemony of the PRI and encouraged future historians of the postwar period to take full advantage of popular culture as a serious academic resource. He interpreted la onda as an emblematic movement of what he later called the "New Left," with roots in the 1950s. Rooted in a mixture of national and international rock music, slang, literature, and fashion, it allowed for the emergence of a "critical cultural consciousness." Moreover, la onda was an unprecedented challenge to a "hegemonic value system grounded in patriarchy and heroic nationalism." He convincingly concluded, in agreement with Marroquín, that the xipitecas found innovative ways of expressing national identity that challenged "the dominant ideology of state-sponsored nationalism." They questioned *buenas costumbres* (proper, honorable, and correct Catholic behavior), while the significance of their movement "lay precisely in its capacity to resist authority by reconstituting an imaginary community apart from the state yet tied to the nation." Like Marroquín, Zolov dated the apex of la onda to 1971 and pointed to the state repression and co-optation that intensified in the aftermath of the Avándaro festival, the specific event that marked the demise of the movement.[45]

More recently, historians of the Sixties have expanded on the work of Zolov to describe the shared values and distinct qualities of the counterculture in Latin America. Of particular importance is the work on Brazil by Christopher Dunn. In *Contracultura: Alternative Arts and Social Transformation in Authoritarian Brazil* (2016), Dunn drew a distinction between the United States, Western Europe, and Latin America. While the counterculture thrived in the United States mostly in relation to the celebration of individualism and youth disgruntlement with modern industrial society, Dunn argued, in Europe it often developed ties to the Left. Moreover, while in the United States the counterculture initially grew in the aftermath of the Civil Rights movement and quickly radicalized in response to the Vietnam War, in Latin America it evolved mostly in reaction to the traditional norms of Catholicism and political authoritarianism.[46] Yet, as others have argued for the cases of Uruguay, Argentina, and Chile, each country developed its particular countercultural movement. For example, whereas in Montevideo and Buenos Aires the militant Left saw no contradiction in aligning itself with young activists who welcomed rock music, in Santiago the radical government of Salvador Allende followed the path taken in Havana and saw the broader countercultural movement as a threat to its socialist revolution. For Chilean Marxists, the historian Patrick Barr-Melej explains, the emphasis that the counterculture placed on personal freedom "negated the imperative of social consciousness." It said little about class struggle and "evicted the egoism of capitalism." Hence the alleged threat of the counterculture was evident not only in what young people did "but also in what they did not do."[47]

In Mexico, liberals and conservatives similarly saw the counterculture with trepidation, and just as in Argentina, Uruguay, and Brazil, government authorities repressed it. But, as Marroquín and Zolov argue, what largely distinguished la onda was its close proximity to the United States and the influence of its interaction with the nation's Indigenous people. Not too different from the cases of El Salvador and Chile, moreover, the particularities of the counterculture were its interrelated connection to Catholicism and new, more esoteric, expressions of religion.[48] This was also true in the United States, where a reinterpretation of Christianity significantly shaped the central tenets of "peace and love" that influenced the hippie movement.[49]

The work of the historians Mary Kay Vaughan, Isabella Cosse, Valeria Manzano, Lessie Jo Frazier, Deborah Cohen, Alfonso Salgado, and Victoria Langland on the shifting notions of gender and sexuality during the Sixties is important to understanding the counterculture in Latin America. As they have convincingly argued, what largely distinguished the region during this period was not only the militant radicalism of the era but also the consolidation of a middle class that called for change in the authoritarian and corrupt policies of the state as well as those of society.[50] These challenges brought about new—more liberating—expressions of gender and sexuality, as well as an innovative existentialist view of the arts in which innovative articulations of love rooted in a Christian ethos often measured political commitment. In the countercultural sensibility of the Sixties, Saldago explains, young people understood love as crucial to achieving happiness, and many associated it with "universal fraternity and solidarity."[51] These aspirations were evident in the "feminization of male sensibility," as Vaughan argues, as well as in the consumption of drugs and a neo-humanist view of a world threatened by an increasing sense of despair that materialism made more apparent.[52] This rebellion was further manifested in the celebration of new notions of "free love" defined by a more relaxed attitude toward sex that questioned female virtue as historically associated with passivity and virginity.[53]

But as the Sixties came to signify a new period of the relaxation of sexual mores, it simultaneously marked an era characterized by a direct reaction to such liberation.[54] For example, by 1968 the birth control pill was available in many pharmacies in most urban centers in Mexico, but traditional notions of virtue, beauty (mostly defined according to the white phenotype), motherhood, and domesticity remained strong. That same year the encyclical *Humanae vitae* rejected contraception and reaffirmed the importance of married love between a man and a woman. In most Catholic spaces, moreover, flirting, promiscuity, the independence of women, birth control, and homosexuality remained taboo. Only at the end of the era did a new generation of feminists call on other women to enjoy sexual pleasure (i.e., the right to have an orgasm), experiment with their bodies, question the myth of motherhood, and challenge the sanctity of marriage. A demand to legalize abortion also emerged during this period, but abortion remained criminalized and absolutely prohibited by the ecclesiastical authorities.[55] Similar condemnation was expressed in response to the slow but steady growth of the gay liberation movement in the 1970s.[56]

Love and Despair expands on the scholarship on the Latin American counterculture in an effort to bring greater attention to the intriguing ways in which Catholicism interacted with, responded to, and shaped the significance of la onda in Cold War Mexico. While Dunn is correct to suggest that the counterculture mostly evolved in reaction to the conservative moral structure imposed by the church, the individual cases examined in this book show the multiple ways in which religious authorities and lay Catholics looked to the progressive language of Vatican II to make sense of the counterculture and in so doing also contributed to its reception, consumption, and radicalism.

SOURCES AND OVERVIEW

Love and Despair is divided into introductory, political, and countercultural parts, each containing thematic chapters. Meant to stand on their own but brought together by a common set of actors, networks, and concerns, the chapters examine a distinct Catholic movement and are developed around the lives of one or a few individuals: student activists, novelists, intellectuals, filmmakers, journalists, priests, conservatives, leftist militants, and self-described atheists. All felt compelled to engage in the political movements and artistic production that touched on the importance of religion, film, youth activism, and the counterculture.

These personal stories provide us with collective biographies of three overlapping generations of key and mostly overlooked players: one coming of age in the aftermath of the Cristero Rebellion; a second, in the conservative environment following World War II; and a third, in the radical student movements of the Sixties. As cultural historians of the Sixties have convincingly argued, biographies "can bring insight in the socializing, educational experience that produced [the] subjectivities of a generation."[57] The individual actors illustrate the transnational emphasis of the book, as many of them traveled to Europe and throughout Latin America before they settled and became active in Mexico, and others continued to move across the world as they became leading figures in their respective movements. It is this constant mobility that largely shaped their Catholic identity, their individual understandings of politics, their involvement in the counterculture, and their self-described gestures of love. As the historian Victoria Langland has convincingly argued in her essay on the transnational connections of the Global Sixties, "Actors in various places imagined themselves to be a part of particular global communities, and these aspirational connections to a much hoped-for global vanguard animated and propelled their decisions and actions."[58]

This book relies on oral interviews that I conducted over several years. Nearly all of them developed from casual conversations with former Catholic activists, ranging from prominent leaders of Mexican Catholic Action and the PAN to leftist players, including those who joined opposition parties and figures who engaged in guerrilla activities.[59] I also interviewed priests representing the Jesuit, Dominican, Marist, and Claretian orders. Oral history is always messy and problematic and does not always coincide with the ideological position of the interviewer. But as James Wilkie convincingly argued in his pioneering work during the 1960s and others have demonstrated more recently, there is great value in what people say to the historian. Based on real events, these self-representations of the past are often richer in detail than written sources. If read against the grain of printed and visual sources, they effectively highlight the role culture played in social movements. They allow the historian to give voice to those who have been silenced in the scholarship and bring to the fore those who have been overshadowed in social movements by hegemonic players, including scholars of Mexico, who, in agreement with the official narratives of the state, have overwhelmingly viewed the history of the nation almost exclusively through a secular lens.

From the margins of official interpretations of history, their memories point to contradictions and complexities of their respective political and cultural movements.[60]

I place my oral interviews in conversation with hundreds of original documents from ecclesiastical, private, university, and government archives and libraries in Mexico, the United States, Germany, Belgium, Ecuador, Chile, Argentina, Peru, and Colombia. The overwhelming majority of these sources have not been used by historians and thus point to individuals who have been left out of the official narrative of modern Mexican history. Among others, these documents include correspondence, student manifestos, religious newspapers, influential but largely ignored Catholic magazines, rare books, encyclicals, local ecclesiastical documents, and university papers. Of particular significance are my findings in the Dominican, Catholic Action, Intercultural Center of Documentation (CIDOC), film, and archdiocese archives in Mexico City; as well as the Latin American Secretariat collection in Quito and Lima; the Pax Romana collections at Notre Dame and the Catholic University; the International Catholic Cinema Office (OCIC) documents at the KADOC Documentation and Research Centre on Religion, Culture and Society in Louvain, Belgium; and the Adveniat sources in Essen, Germany.

In addition, I examined more than eighty films—B-movies (low budget/commercial), avant-garde, experimental, and countercultural—from Mexico, Europe, and the United States (see the appendixes at the end of the book) that touched on youth rebellion, the counterculture, and Catholicism. As the Spanish historian Jorge Pérez has argued, cinematic pictures provide rich windows into the interface between modernity and religion and test preconceived assumptions about the alleged demise of religious practices in modern societies. I placed films in conversation with other artistic expressions of the era, including scripts, plays, and novels, in order to examine the significance of Catholicism. Like Pérez, I approach these sources, "not from a theological point of view," as I am also "not qualified" to do so, "but rather as a sociopolitical force and cultural determinant" in the transformation of Mexican society, from the conservative 1950s to the peak of la onda in the late Sixties.[61] In addition, these sources provide a rare look at the ways in which influential filmmakers expressed their changing understandings of Catholicism as the post-1940 government improved its relationship with the church largely in response to the rapid urbanization, hedonistic modernity, sexual liberation, and increasing political and cultural radicalism that characterized this era. Not all the films analyzed in the book reached a mass audience. They overwhelmingly represented the perspective of male subjects, and most were disliked by the critics, but they provide additional evidence of the shifting notions of love and despair that compelled so many young people, filmmakers, and Catholic intellectuals to engage in political action and countercultural defiance that pushed others to demand law and order.

Last, in an effort to consider the point of view of the state and those who sympathized with the governing elite, I also rely on national newspapers and government reports of espionage (primarily written by the Directorate of Federal Security [DFS]). Although frequently rich in detail, these documents often reveal a poor understanding of Catholicism, which largely coincides with the secular historiographical interpretations of modern Mexico. They almost always describe the church as monolithic, caricature the multiple Catholic movements that proliferated during the postwar era as strictly reactionary, and make little effort to explain how and why young religious activists engaged in dialogue with modernity outside the realm of student politics, with little attention to culture. These reports are crucial, nonetheless, as they provide important information on the intricate relationship between the church and the state that, in addition to the Cristero-centered focus, has also dominated the discussion of religion in Mexico during the Cold War. In addition, they shed light on a progressive Catholicism and a secular Left that mostly operated independent of each other, although both groups attempted to solidify a dialogue between Marxism and Christianity during the Sixties.

I conclude the book with a discussion of *Una alma pura* (1964). Written by the renowned novelist Carlos Fuentes and directed by the young filmmaker Juan Ibáñez, the short film successfully depicts the alienation and sense of despair that marked the frustration when utopian aspirations of radical change could not be met. I place this fascinating picture in the broader context of Sixties counterculture and explain its relevance to the central arguments that I make to our understanding of modern Mexico.

PART ONE

Modernity and Youth

ONE

Beauty, Cinema, and Female Youth Rebellion

The renewed moral authority of the middle class turned laywomen into influential actors during the 1950s. These years marked the apex of traditional Catholicism, when Mexican Catholic Action grew exponentially to include more than four hundred thousand active members. Of these, more than 80 percent were women. In addition to taking part in moralizing campaigns and defining what was "proper" in the public sphere, the female leadership of Catholic Action played a crucial role in convincing other sectors of society to exercise their civic rights and religious duties.[1] Of particular importance was the Mexican Female Catholic Youth (JCFM) and its magazine, *Juventud*. Founded in the late 1920s by Sofía del Valle for single women between the ages of fifteen and thirty-five, the organization mushroomed from only eight original members in 1929 to more than one hundred thousand in the late 1950s.[2]

The JCFM organized influential campaigns to combat several evils that religious authorities associated with the precipitous transformation of Mexico from a rural to a more urbanized nation that paralleled the context of the Cold War. In its publications, Catholic Action warned that the lack of moral support and guidance, combined with the rampant consumerism of the period, had contributed to making youth vulnerable to losing its path in foreign ideologies. Initially, these alleged threats were posed by Protestantism and by what religious leaders identified as the new faces of postrevolutionary liberalism, including but not limited to secularism, materialism, existentialism, the excesses of capitalism, and especially communism.

But as Valentina Torres Septién has shown, fear was not limited exclusively to the world of politics.[3] These years were further marked by an increasing unease with what many government and religious authorities saw as the importation of "youth rebelliousness without a cause," which, according to them, young people imitated, especially after the screenings of Hollywood films starring a new generation of actors who openly flaunted their sexuality and celebrated innovative forms of hedonism on the big screen.[4] However, Mexican Catholic Action did not construct a totally reactionary movement wholeheartedly condemning the cinematic representations of youth rebelliousness. Rather, in taking the transnational story of Emma Ziegler and the pages of *Juventud* as evidence, this chapter argues that the new voices affiliated with the church created new spaces conducive to the proper understanding of the modernity and hedonism typical of the youth rebelliousness of the period. The lay leadership drew inspiration from papal encyclicals and from documents on motion pictures that included guidelines written by the International Catholic Cinema Office (OCIC) in Europe and Latin America. The liberal language of this organization often clashed with the conservative tone used by the League of Mexican Decency. Founded in 1934, the League was effectively active until the mid-1950s.

But the document that most closely defined Emma Ziegler's path through her cinematic movement was *Miranda prorsus*. Written in September 1957 by Pius XII, the encyclical focused on motion pictures, radio, and television. It asked Catholics to identify films not as "an instrument of the Devil," as previous documents of the church had insisted, but as a "child of God."[5] One of the main questions that Ziegler faced when interpreting this document was how to create a new cinematographic culture that would not only foster better films in the country but also adequately respond to the new youth images that became ever more frequent and widespread in the national industry.

The evolution of Ziegler is noteworthy because, even though her performance as a president of the JCFM did not radically differ from her peers during the 1940s, her role as a national representative of the OCIC was much more nuanced and influential. As one of the founding leaders of a national chapter of this international organization, she reinforced innovative relationships with cinematic groups in Louvain, Lima, and, particularly, prerevolutionary Havana, where the OCIC organized pioneer campaigns under the leadership of the Cuban activist América Penichet. With Penichet's support and advice, Ziegler extended the moralizing activities of the Mexican church beyond its traditional methods and campaigns of the past. She relied on the liberal discourse of *Miranda prorsus* to strengthen her networks with the headquarters of the OCIC in Belgium and pressured the more traditional ecclesiastical authorities in Mexico, including those affiliated with the

League of Mexican Decency in charge of censoring films from the 1930s to the 1950s. In her view, not only did this medium have the capacity to "form or deform the souls [of young people]," but it also had the power to "change the political and moral course" of their lives.[6]

The goal of "educating and orienting the consciousness of the people" that Ziegler assumed was not easy; she had to confront powerful individuals who competed for control of the art of making films.[7] She acknowledged the important role producers played in creating a robust national cinema but accused them of "film illiteracy" and labeled many of them "pornographic" because in their efforts to revive the industry and attract more people to the theaters they experimented with "vulgar" pictures, such as the *rumberas* (dance hall movies) that contained some of the first (partial) nudes of young women ever to be shown on the big screen.[8] At the same time, Ziegler criticized the old religious authorities for failing to appreciate the new leadership that secular women, like her and her friend Penichet in Cuba, held.[9] In particular, the two friends bemoaned the authoritarianism and ineptitude of the leader of the League of Mexican Decency, Jorge Núñez Prida, and openly criticized the directors who sought to film the youth of the time. Ziegler accused many of them of fostering licentiousness and Marxist propaganda and congratulated others on spreading a Catholic message in their films.

In this way, Ziegler positioned her movement between the two opposing worlds that marked the 1950s. On the one hand, her lifelong affiliation with the JCFM suggested that she had not dissociated herself from the conservative environment in which she had grown up. For example, she remained a cautious supporter of the League of Mexican Decency and its moralizing campaigns, despite her disapproval of its chauvinistic male leader. On the other hand, she echoed the new liberal discourse that characterized the publication of *Miranda prorsus*. Relying on this document and deepening her friendship with Penichet, she strengthened networks with the leaderships of the OCIC in Europe, Cuba, and South America. She fostered a dialogue with modernity and opened new cinematographic spaces at home that aspired to understand the new expressions of youth emerging in the national cinema.

In providing a partial biography of the fascinating but mostly unknown life of Emma Ziegler, this chapter examines the conservativism of the 1950s with an additional focus on cinematic representations of young women. The most influential films of the period presented these years as the peak of a new wave of modernization, which forced the lay organizations of Catholic

Action to redefine their role as social activists in a traditional country ever more distant from the militarism of its Cristero past (1926–29) and more in sync with the language of "national unity" simultaneously preached by church and state authorities in the aftermath of World War II. Moreover, this period was marked by a new wave of national films that created innovative representations of youth that, according to the directors, threatened the Catholic identity of the country not only with their liberal values but also with the moral corruption that many conservative authorities associated with the impulsive and drastically uneven urbanization that marked the presidential administration of Miguel Alemán (1946–52) and the years that followed. As others have noted, the 1950s were the moment in which the middle class gradually abandoned its folklore, North Americanized its culture, and denationalized its traditional taste.[10] The film portrayals of the so-called rebel girls reflected this alleged crisis. In the broader context of national unity, they coincided with the waning years of the golden age of cinema and served as the precursor of the more radical counterculture of the Sixties.[11]

The (male) directors of the films examined in this chapter agreed with religious authorities, and they too saw young Catholic women burdened with a double duty. Not unlike Ziegler, the less conservative voices in the church expected them, first, to interact with modernity, provided that they did not betray their moral values.[12] Second, by assuming the civic duties that the postwar context imposed on them, they were also obliged to guide their boyfriends. In the emerging context of the Cold War, they argued that young men felt pressured into participating in a type of student activism that led them away from Mexico, the church, and their faith. Both of these expectations were further evident in the pages of *Juventud*, where the defense of traditional femininity, chastity, and charity was often presented as an act of love.

THE YOUNG EMMA ZIEGLER

The exact year of Emma Ziegler's birth is unknown. Her leading role with the JCFM dates to 1931, when she served as the treasurer of its Puebla dioceses for two years. She was elected representative president in 1933, likely in her late teens, and added English and French to her native German and Spanish. In Puebla she led courses at the Feminine Social Institute and promoted charity services for "girls from humble origins." Emma remained active in similar projects with her sister Felícitas until 1939, the year their mother and a longtime supporter of Mexican Catholic Action, Felícitas Díaz-Barriga Guarneros, passed away. With their father, Julio Federico Ziegler-Weller, no longer in the picture and their younger brother, Carlos Guillermo, residing in Cuba, the Ziegler sisters moved to Mexico City and joined Sofía del Valle in the central directorate of the JCFM, composed at that time of Aurora de la Lama, Eugenia Olivera, and Isabel Gibbon. In 1940, Ziegler replaced them as the fourth president of the JCFM, while her sister worked as the treasurer. Between 1942 and 1944 Emma served as vice president of the organization and an active writer for *Juventud*. In October 1944 the JCFM reelected her president, and she held this position until 1946. As leader of the youth organization, Ziegler embodied the same modern Catholic woman and "model of piety and activism" that Sofía del Valle promoted with the establishment of the JCFM: "publicly confident and culturally up-to-date, intellectually driven, professionally trained and accomplished."[13] Like her peers, she "did not want to 'turn back the clock'" but rather to shape the world around her "in a way that reflected [her] moral values."[14]

Catholic Action asked Ziegler to preside over International Relief following World War II. Affiliated with the Red Cross, this charity organization was responsible for sending money, food supplies, and clothing to orphanages and Catholic schools in Europe, mostly to France, as a Mexican nun and former member of the JCFM resided in Paris and was doing similar work. These years were transformative for Ziegler, as she did exceedingly well at her work and got the opportunity to work with the director of the Mexican Social Secretariat, Fr. Pedro Velázquez. It was Velázquez, she later wrote, who provided her with the language and tools of social justice. She remembered him years later: "He made us vibrant and often repeated to us, 'we should not be satisfied with strengthening the membership of the Catholic Action; we should work, instead, to make sure that more and more Christians are represented in the factories, in schools, and in all spaces of entertainment.'"[15]

Ziegler also established a fruitful working relationship with Sofía del Valle. Under her recommendation, Catholic Action appointed Emma the foreign affairs liaison of the JCFM in 1950. She held this position for three years. During this time, she traveled across the nation and visited Cuba, where her brother lived and where she first collaborated with América Penichet, her lifelong friend who introduced her to the world of cinema and put her in contact with rising leaders in cinema in South America and

Europe. Her sister, Felícitas, also remained active with the JCFM, albeit not in leading roles. To complement her income, Felícitas worked as a travel agent, which allowed the Ziegler sisters to buy airplane tickets at a discount price. More importantly, with the emergence of commercial passenger jet travel, as advertised in the *Juventud* magazine, the sisters were provided with the opportunity to meet other single women doing similar work abroad.[16] Without male companions, they traveled together to South America, Canada, and Europe to attend several international conferences.

As a leader of the JCFM, Ziegler wrote several editorial columns and short articles in *Juventud*. These writings reflected the conservatism typical of the films produced during that period. As the historian Julia Tuñón has argued, these were the pivotal years of the golden age in which films celebrated the "selfless mother" and zealously kept watch over young women's social engagements and virginity. Tuñón's comprehensive analysis indicates that "women did not need to know much; just enough to be mothers, maintain order, and preserve the group's cohesion." Similarly, the films from these years typically portrayed the home as a "sacred but secular [and authoritarian] space" where any type of sexual relations or eroticism was "sinful."[17] This cinematic representation sharply contrasted with the image of streets, universities, and other, supposedly more masculine places. In a similar way, the writing of Ziegler and others in *Juventud* referred to the domestic chores of women and identified the internal and external enemies of the home.

Unlike most films, *Juventud* demanded a much more active role from women. It identified "the lack of religious training" and "the weakening of one's faith" as the nation's most imminent internal threats. These were further evident in "the lack of discipline [that] destroys family hierarchies," as well as in the "selfishness," "idleness," "luxury," and "excessive desire" for material and sexual pleasures alike. Furthermore, the magazine drew a distinction between four external threats: (1) ideas (individualism, communism); (2) customs (public immorality, harmful foreign influences, inconvenient fashions, luxury, sport abuses, pleasure); (3) legislative order (liberal laws that legitimated free love and divorce, as well as those that put limits on the size of a family, hindered the exercise of authority, and attacked the family's rights in education); and (4) economic concerns (injustices of employers, abuses of workers, upheavals in the artisan guilds and trade unions, and women's and children's labor).[18]

The writers, including Emma Ziegler and Sofía del Valle, attributed to young Catholic women a twofold duty in an effort to fight these alleged threats. According to them, the postwar environment demanded that women be "patriotic" by developing a "civic consciousness."[19] As documented in *Juventud*, "their participation in politics was no longer optional, but necessary[,] . . . with the concomitant right to vote and be elected in positions of authority."[20] Del Valle suggested that their civic obligation was no longer limited to gaining the right to vote, which they had worked toward for years, but also included holding professional positions of power, on the one hand, and participating in projects aiming to improve the condition of the marginalized, on the other.[21] Therefore, their second duty was to develop a kindhearted social consciousness without losing focus on the importance of professional training and higher education.[22] To do so, women were meant to actively participate in projects seeking to instill a spirit of charity by focusing on mercy as an act of love but without necessarily considering those economic and political structures that served to sharpen poverty and social inequality. According to Ziegler, the love associated with "charity is suffered, sweet and beneficial. . . . [I]t does not envy[,] . . . it is not ambitious, it does not seek to serve its interests, it does not irritate, it bears no bad thoughts, it does not delight in injustice, it seeks to please. . . . Charity is intimately linked to the spirit of . . . abnegation and without any self-interest."[23] Ziegler would remain loyal to these ideas, but her rising interest in the movies would force her to consider more liberal positions regarding modernity. These would also provide her with new opportunities to travel abroad and strengthen her relationship with América Penichet in Cuba.

AMÉRICA PENICHET, THE OCIC, AND THE HAVANA CONFERENCE

Unlike other writers for *Juventud*, Emma Ziegler frequently conceived her civic activism as a global project. Often disregarding the topic of patriotism, she preferred to talk about her mission in a broader, hemispheric context. For example, in one of her columns, she proposed to establish a "family day" across all countries in Latin America, and as a Catholic Action leader, she frequently called on her fellows to not forget their sisters across the continent.[24] Never married or with no children, she frequently traveled abroad and dedicated much of her life exclusively to the love she had for the projects of the church. Not only did she work for the "constant education of [the JFCM's] leaders," but she also participated in the exchange of ideas and collaboration with similar organizations affiliated with Catholic Action across the continent. In particular, she forged a close relationship with América Penichet in Cuba, who successfully expanded the presence of the OCIC across Latin America during this period.[25]

The origins of the OCIC date to 1928, when the International Union for the Catholic Women's League invited leading representatives from the film industry in fifteen countries in Europe and Latin America to coordinate their work for the benefit of the international Catholic family, including Edelmiro Traslosheros, the original founder of the League of Mexican Decency in 1933.[26] The European participants organized the first global congress on cinema in Munich in 1929, and it was there that the OCIC was officially founded as an international but mostly Western European organization. In 1933 the representatives created the General Secretariat in Brussels, which published the first OCIC documents that shaped the moralistic language that ecclesiastical authorities used across the world during this period, initially to warn viewers of the alleged dangers of cinema. Yet, with the Nazi occupation of Belgium, the OCIC was forced to shut its offices while its leaders fled into exile in the United States. With the defeat of the Germans in 1946, the organization returned to Brussels and continued its moralizing campaigns. Three years later the Vatican recognized the organization as the official representative of the Holy See and encouraged it to extend its operations in Latin America. Under the leadership of Abate J. Bernard (president), Yvonne Hemptine (general secretary), and André Ruszkowski (foreign relations representative), the OCIC rewarded films and published the *International Film Magazine*, initially in French and German and subsequently in Spanish and English. By the early 1950s, the OCIC had adopted more liberal language that insisted on the importance of engaging in dialogue with cinema as a rich instrument for evangelization and not simply as a negative medium that threatened Catholicism, as the League of Mexican Decency continued to insist in the United States and Mexico (see below).[27]

The Polish lawyer André Ruszkowski was the chief editor of the Spanish version of the magazine, *Revista Internacional de Cine*, during the 1950s, with the support of Penichet in Cuba, the main figure responsible for extending the presence of the OCIC in Latin America. Ruszkowski initiated this work with a visit to South America in 1948, where he promoted his magazine, presented several lectures on cinema, and warned of the dangers of Marxism. Between 1951 and 1952, he organized the Latin American Congress of the OCIC in Uruguay, opened an office in Peru, and supported the similar work that Penichet was doing in Cuba.[28] From Lima, Ruszkowski distributed, exchanged, and created new publications. From Havana, Penichet then organized international conferences and translated important documents from French, German, and English into Spanish. According to Ruszkowski, Latin America was in the clutches of rampant illiteracy as far as films were concerned. This illiteracy stood out with particular force in the Catholic spaces of the region. Creating institutions capable of producing and supporting a cinema of artistic quality and sound Christian criteria was a matter of urgency. Unlike the old generations of Catholics, Ruszkowski was "convinced that movies" were not an instrument of the devil or a purveyor of depravity, as religious authorities had previously insisted, but rather had the ability to "contribute to the audience's cultural and spiritual uplifting."[29]

In an effort to pursue this goal, Ruszkowski supported Penichet in establishing the Catholic Center of Cinematographic Orientation in 1950. Founded in Havana, the Center valued filmmaking. It institutionalized courses and workshops meant to educate specialists and movie lovers. Penichet went on to head it until 1959. Under her exceptional leadership, the Center created more than forty cine clubs and edited the influential magazine *Cine Guía*. Penichet also established workshops, film libraries, annual prizes, and continental "vanguards," where Emma Ziegler first discovered her passion for the movies. But the most important event that Penichet organized, relying on Ruszkowski's support, took place in Havana in February 1957, when the participants, a young Ziegler among them, were introduced to the liberal language that influenced the writing of *Miranda prorsus*. In particular, Ruszkowski—accompanied by a new generation of French and Belgian Jesuits—campaigned for the loosening of the criteria guiding the moral assessment of films. According to them, Latin America needed to support good motion pictures, reject the moralist language of previous years, and create a new culture of appreciation of cinema by establishing new film clubs, debates, study circles, and publications.

Representatives of more than thirty countries attended the 1957 congress in Havana, including Emma Ziegler.[30] By this time she had already been in communication for several years with Penichet, who had served as OCIC vice president for Latin America since 1954. Penichet advised and supported Ziegler from Cuba as the latter returned to Mexico and started her trajectory between two opposing poles: the small world of the liberal Jesuits who saw film as a positive instrument for evangelization and the broader and more influential world of her own country's conservative sector that continued to see cinema as a threat to the faith and morality of Catholics.

THE LEAGUE OF MEXICAN DECENCY AND ITS ROLE IN THE CLASSIFICATION OF FILMS

A young woman pleading for advice frantically wrote to *Juventud* in March 1934: "I went to the movies for the first time. The film had a disastrous effect on me. I was not able to sleep all night. I felt ashamed for having supported such a film." In response, the editors of the magazine lamented that Mexico lacked strict guidance on the topic and agreed that Catholics were in desperate need of having lists of recommended and prohibited films. *Juventud* asked its readers to become informed consumers and to use their purchasing power to boycott all films that threatened the Catholic sensibilities of the nation.[31] That same year a group from the JCFM traveled to Rome to attend the International Congress of Catholic Youth. The participants were encouraged to get involved in the film industry. By the late 1940s the JCFM paid greater attention to the importance of cinema, especially after Ziegler's return from Havana and Rome in 1947. This is when Ziegler first strengthened her relationship with América Penichet, the key figure responsible for negotiating the polarizing relationship between the OCIC and the more conservative League of Mexican Decency.

Founded by the Knights of Columbus in 1933, the League inaugurated its moralizing campaigns in 1934. Three years later it received the blessing of the Mexican episcopate, and under the leadership of Núñez Prida that same year, it was officially recognized as a national representative by the OCIC.[32] In 1941 the presidential administration of Ávila Camacho (1940–46) followed suit and officially recognized the League as the sole cinematic body responsible for classifying all national and foreign films featured in Mexico. Its most successful years in the censorship of films took place between 1948 and about 1955. As the historian Guillermo Zermeño Padilla has pointed out, these years marked the "peak of activity" of the League. Its moralizing campaigns managed to maintain "a great influence on the formation of the Catholic audience's opinion."[33] For example, different lay organizations, including the JFCM, participated in the weekly distribution across schools and parishes of thousands of leaflets with the "Assessments" that the League printed in an effort to identify the "bad" films banned by the Catholic

Church.[34] The model these assessments were based on was "borrowed by other bulletins already circulating in the United States which were banned by the Episcopal Conference."[35] At the very beginning, in the 1930s, the leaflets did not find much success in Mexico, but this changed over the next decade after the PRI officially recognized the League. "From then on, the [League] could openly claim to be a collaborator of the government." In this context, "the interests of the Church aligned with those of the State."[36] Not only did this turn of events facilitate the censoring of Mexican and foreign movies; it also opened up space for film directors to leave the topics of the rural revolution aside in favor of spreading (Catholic) moralist messages related to the modernization of the city. At the same time, the closer relationship with the United States generated a "Pan-American Catholicism" that strengthened the League and its moralizing campaigns,[37] the same ones that influenced Emma Ziegler.

During this period Ziegler collaborated with the League and encouraged Catholic Action to be attentive to cinema, which meant forming public opinion about the importance of film and boycotting all immoral pictures. She pressured producers to edit their movies and, when necessary, encouraged them to protest in front of theaters until the pictures were pulled from their screens. The classifications of films were published in *Apreciaciones*, for which the League drew inspiration from the Hays Code in the United States, ranking the pictures from A, unobjectionable for general audiences, to C-2, which condemned the films for everyone. But as Zermeño Padilla has argued, in adapting this rigid regulation, the League prioritized the specific needs of the nation. In this effort it engaged in heated discussions surrounding the cinematic representations of sixteen broad topics, ranging from depictions of government and religious authorities to gory and "amoral" scenes that, if not carefully censored, could threaten the Catholic sensibilities of Mexico (table 1).

Once the sixteen topics were discussed and the films classified, Catholic Action played a crucial role in distributing the ratings of the films across the nation. But with the end of the golden age of cinema in the 1950s and the passage of the Garduño Law in 1953, which gave government authorities greater control in the censoring of films, the influence of the League also diminished.[38] Nonetheless, Ziegler's work remained relevant.

In 1956 América Penichet and Emma Ziegler traveled to Europe to attend a conference in Rome, where they united with André Ruszkowski. Penichet encouraged Ziegler to meet Núñez Prida at the conference and

TABLE 1 Classification of films according to the League of Mexican Decency

Classification	Determining Themes
A = Unobjectionable for general audiences	1. Nudity
B-1 = For adults and adolescents only, 12 to 18 years old	2. Semi-nudity
	3. Dances
B-2 = For adults and young people only, 18 to 21 years old, with reservations	4. Passion
	5. Prostitution
B-3 = For adults only, 21 years and above, objectionable	6. Homosexuality
	7. Vengeance
C-1 = Condemned, not recommended for anyone	8. Crime
	9. Alcohol consumption
C-2 = Condemned, offensive to Christian morals	10. Drug consumption
	11. Social conflict
	12. Blood
	13. Brutality
	14. Religion (Catholicism and the church)
	15. Magic and folk religion
	16. Childhood and adolescence

initiate a better relationship with the League of Mexican Decency, which the Cuban activist found "out of touch" with the projects of the OCIC. In this effort, Ziegler sent an invitation to Ruszkowski to visit Mexico. He arrived in Mexico City a year later to attend the First Cultural Week of Cinema organized by the League with the support of Ziegler. The guests of honor included the film directors Emilio Gómez Muriel and Julián Soler, who sympathized with traditional Catholicism and were becoming increasingly concerned with the rebelliousness of youth. In 1957 the OCIC organized its most important congress in Havana whose central focus was the teachings of *Miranda prorsus*. Thereafter, Felícitas Ziegler was selected as the secretary of foreign affairs for the League and held the position for two years. With the support of her sister, Emma, she pressured Núñez Prida to adopt a less authoritarian approach to films, albeit with limited success. In addition, Ziegler organized student conferences at various Catholic high schools and successfully convinced other lay organizations, including the Christian Family Movement, to become more involved with her project and support the annual "Movie Weeklies," where Ziegler celebrated the best films of the year and preached the importance of cinema in parishes across the country.[39]

In this polarizing context, Ziegler took advantage of her relationship with Catholic Action and, making a name for herself in Mexican circles, became a pioneering activist of the new cinematic movement that emerged in the 1950s.[40] Frequently guided by Penichet's advice and bolstered by the new European publications, which she obtained with the help of Ruszkowski in Peru, Ziegler went on to publish various documents and open new spaces for national films.[41] In her leaflet "Estrellita [Little Spark]," she wrote film reviews and evoked *Miranda prorsus*.[42] In endorsing "ideal movies" capable of engaging in a dialogue with modernity and educating the movie audience, Ziegler also promoted study workshops and scientific investigations seeking to highlight the positive features of films. Together with the Jesuit priest and Ibero-American University professor, Jesús Romero Pérez, Ziegler pressured the League of Mexican Decency into "educating their new censors" in the language of the Havana conference.[43] This meant no longer scolding the audience with moralist campaigns and devoting more time to educating, cultivating, orienting, and elevating its consciousness. To do so successfully, Ziegler forged a stronger network with Penichet in Cuba. With her support, she demanded the education and training of specialized teams, opened up new spaces for cinema in the parishes, and introduced film education in Catholic schools.[44] At the same time, Ziegler relied on Penichet's advice in her growing criticism of the League of Mexican Decency's "lack of preparation" and its director Núñez Prida's "authoritarianism," "ineptitude," and "terrible routines." With her friend's guidance, she committed to establishing study circles and publishing *Cine-Temas*, another leaflet in which Ziegler educated her readers in the art and techniques of filmmaking and commented on foreign films.[45]

In sum, for Ziegler the 1950s marked a defining moment in her life, which coincided with the expansion of the OCIC in Latin America and the apex of Catholic Action in Mexico. Whereas the 1930s had represented a key moment of action for the JCFM to protest socialist education, the 1940s and 1950s welcomed a new wave of activism that promoted the civic responsibilities of all Catholics, which for the world traveler Ziegler translated into a call for a greater and more productive dialogue with modernity in general and with cinema in particular. This dialogue, which benefited from the relationship that Ziegler established with Penichet, would be tested at the end of the decade, when riskier films were produced in Mexico and abroad that not only introduced a new and more rebellious attitude regarding female youth culture but also questioned traditional notions of Catholicism.

Film historians describe the period from the 1930s to the mid-1950s as the "golden age" of Mexican cinema. They point to a unique era characterized by unprecedented success in the commercial production of national films and by the creation of new genres that drew from the aesthetics of world cinema (mainly Hollywood) but made a conscious attempt to depict national stories from a distinctly Mexican perspective. These films enjoyed substantial subsidies and protectionist policies from the state. They benefited from government-sponsored unions and received ample investment from the private sector. The most celebrated of these films transformed national artists and film directors into international stars, received praise from influential European and American film critics, and successfully introduced the aesthetics, sensibilities, and aspirations of Mexico to the rest of the world.[46]

Most of the films produced during these years mirrored the social conservatism of the era and viewed with apprehension the rapid urbanization that characterized the 1940s and 1950s. As they sought popular appeal, the vast majority of these films were family oriented and sensitive to the traditional Catholic identity of the country. They were reflective of national desires and attentive to the social changes of the postwar period in the transition to modernity. In their benign depictions of government bureaucrats, police officers, and religious authorities, they were redemptive and moralistic. The authorities representing political and religious institutions were frequently portrayed in a complimentary manner as responsible for protecting the buenas costumbres that presumably guaranteed national stability and progress. The films avoided nudity and kept the references to violent and sexual situations of an earlier era to a minimum.[47] They mirrored national aspirations of revolutionary (institutionalized but not radical) progress, as emblematic of the rhetoric of the government and saw the improvement of church-state relations as beneficial.[48] For the most part, they were overwhelmingly nostalgic about the countryside. The antimodernist critiques represented by the Indigenist films, for example, had little to say about the city and instead celebrated the beautiful landscapes of the countryside, which for many directors of this subgenre included the "natural" dignity, beauty, and resilience of the Indigenous (and largely homogeneous) people.[49] By contrast, the *cabaretera* (brothel) and *arrabal* (slum) antimodernist films centered on the social problems associated with the expansion of the city.[50] While the former relied on rich film noir techniques and sensual musicals to provide sharp and often condemnatory commentary on the social vices of modernity, the latter preferred the use of heartwarming tales and sentimental songs to bring attention to the presumed nobility of the marginalized and working-class urban poor.[51]

By the mid-1950s, the national film industry saw less success at the box office and the decline of the golden age seemed inevitable. Following the death of some of the nation's most beloved stars and an unwillingness to create new opportunities for a younger generation of directors, films experienced little aesthetic or thematic innovation. The crisis that brought an end to this period was further evident in an increasing middle-class preference for US pictures, as well as in a substantial rise in production costs, a more antagonistic relationship with Hollywood, a union of actors and directors that provided little space to new talent, and the emergence of technicolor and television. In response, film producers hoped to attract a new generation of viewers to movie theaters by shifting their attention to the creation of riskier B-movies.[52] These pictures, presumed to have less artistic integrity, have received less attention from film scholars and have been practically ignored by historians. They are rich in detail and insightful, nonetheless. In particular, the examples examined in this section provide a valuable look at the nation during the mid- to late 1950s, with special attention to the different ways in which influential directors turned to religion and their Catholic faith in response to the innovative expression of youth rebellion that epitomized the final years of the golden age. These films were primarily made to warn parents of the alleged dangers associated with youth rebellion, but they simultaneously provided young people with an opportunity to celebrate their identity, albeit still not on their own terms.

As the film critic Jorge Ayala Blanco has rightly indicated, it was around the mid-1950s when Mexican cinema "discovered" youth.[53] This is not to say that young people had not been represented in films before. It is worth remembering two successful pictures from the peak of the golden age in which the directors Juan Bustillo Oro and Alejandro Galindo dramatized intergenerational conflict against the backdrop of the country's transition, *Cuando los hijos se van* (1941) and *Una familia de tantas* (1948), respectively.[54] Both films provided lasting representations of Catholic parents who clashed culturally and ideologically with a new generation growing up in an ever more urbanized and modernized country. Nevertheless, though these and similar films from the period focused on intergenerational conflict, they saw little need to project young people as having their own identity. That is, aside from some rare exceptions, these pictures did not represent young people with their distinctive clothes, manners, music, language, or ideas.[55] This trend changed in the mid-1950s with the national screening of several influential Hollywood films, such as *The Wild One* (1953), *Blackboard Jungle* (1955), *East of Eden* (1955), and *Rebel without a Cause* (1956). These films presented youth as a threat to modern society. But as the historian Mary Kay Vaughan has argued, they also provided young men and women with new, more sensitive and tender expressions of gender that further influenced the changing identity of youth and the artistic expressions of the era.[56]

In Mexico this type of film saw significant box office success between 1956 and 1962.[57] While these films were almost exclusively made with conservative parents in mind, they also attracted young people and a new generation of Catholic cinema buffs (like Emma Ziegler), primarily on the basis of their focus on female youth rebellion. By the mid-1950s, the (male) directors of these films had already established influential careers as key figures of the golden age of Mexican cinema. And although some had identified as left-wing intellectuals on more than one occasion, it was clear that, not unlike the revolutionary state, their ideologies had abruptly swerved closer to the traditional values preferred by the church.[58] In the mid- to late 1950s, they all used authoritarian language to reproach Mexican youth. This moralistic tone was largely shared by ecclesiastical authorities.[59] According to these pictures, young people were experiencing "a state of crisis." With so many parents absent, liberal, divorced, and/or materialistic, this growing urban population had strayed from Catholic principles to end up victims of prostitution, vices, promiscuity, infidelity, murder, homosexuality, and abortion. What Mexico needed was a reaffirmation of its Catholic identity and a more prudent transition to modernity.[60] But as a young Catholic activist who came of age during this period explained, these films provided her with an opportunity to understand the distance she felt from the authoritarian thinking of her parents. She often sympathized with the youth rebellion portrayed in these films and the frustration many of the female characters expressed about the authoritarianism of the era.[61]

Radical Femininity

Perhaps the film that best captured the generational tension of the 1950s with a focus on female youth rebellion and the one that received great attention from Emma Ziegler is Alejandro Galindo's *Ellas también son rebeldes*

(1959). It tells the story of Graciela, a sixteen-year-old who wears trousers and a James Dean leather jacket. Misunderstood by her absent parents, the teenager is sent to a psychiatrist in the hope that he would cure her rebelliousness, which had intensified after the death of her older sister, who had presumably lost her life at the beginning of the film as a result of leading a life of vice and sexual adventures out of wedlock. During her first session with her psychiatrist, Graciela explains her attitude: "I want my parents to let me live my own life. I want to be famous. They refuse to understand that today we have our own morals." Galindo presents other characters to explain not only the rebelliousness of Graciela and the "new morals" of her generation and its fascination with commercialized images of artistic fame but also the supposed "family crisis" of a society that, in his view, had lost its civil values and Catholic roots.

The parents are depicted as materialistic, thinking Graciela's problems can be fixed by their wealth. This and similar films also focus on the vanity of youth, who, the directors believed, blindly adopted habits from the United States that only served to enrich commercial industries.[62] Other topics worthy of anxiety included the ghoulish fascination of the mainstream media with sensational crime and sex stories and the "out of control" divorce rate among urban families.[63] Galindo offered his opinion on the subject, using his psychiatrist character: "A new faith, without values, based on lies and wrong concepts about life ... and patterns of publicity ... has emerged. ... The rebel girls 'without a cause' who get married without spiritual resources, just to have a husband, fail in their roles of wives. The current rebelliousness is nothing more than a violent reproach of the bad examples set by the adults, the parents." The advice of the psychiatrist helps Graciela rectify her rebelliousness, and at the end of the film she repents and rejects "this new [and false] faith" of modernity that Galindo is so worried about.

Ellas también son rebeldes received positive reviews in the Catholic press, and the Jesuit Ibero-American University (UIA) recognized Alejandro Galindo with its annual Onix prize for best screenplay.[64] Though some reviews bemoaned the absence of religious characters in the film, many others appreciated its message. In a letter addressed to the Mexican archbishop Miguel Darío Miranda, Fr. Jesús Romero wrote in his position as a UIA professor:

> *Ellas también son rebeldes* ... portrays a leading problem affecting a sector of modern youth that, spoiled or abandoned by their parents, throw themselves into life without guidance or direction and end up committing excesses that distance them from society. ... It treats some necessarily harsh details

with delicacy. In general, it contains an instructive message for parents and youth alike that makes the movie remarkably positive for the viewers.... We warmly recommend it and have suggested to the producers that we hope they continue making such movies, since they constitute a significant social good.[65]

Emma Ziegler, who frequently appeared in Catholic publications, concurred with Father Romero: "We could single out the absence of God as ... the harmful element [in the film], but we understand that the director was trying not to explore this too much in an effort to avoid an unfavorable reaction from the public. He implicitly talks about God when he refers to spiritual values without creating the impression that he is delivering a sermon, which would have been unfortunate."[66]

The reviews written by Romero and Ziegler illustrate the incipient attitude of a new generation of Mexican Catholic cinema buffs during the 1950s. While they sympathized with the moralizing message of Galindo, they also saw the value of cinema as an opportunity for engagement. This openness to dialogue, however, was not shared by many in the most conservative Catholic circles. The screening of ¿Con quién andan nuestras hijas? (1955) sheds light on this tension. The conservative film company Alba was unhappy with the B-2 rating that the authorities gave the film and demanded that it be entirely censured with a C rating.[67] Ziegler voiced her disagreement, arguing that although many scenes were not particularly suitable for minors, the picture offered an excellent opportunity to discuss—"with care"—many of the problems that the youth of the 1950s were facing. For these purposes, she presented a list of questions to be discussed at the debate sessions that she organized at universities and parishes:

- Do you think that these stories are realistic?
- Which story impressed you the most?
- Do you think that the parents are the guilty parties?
- Are there any other factors of modern life that influence the youth's behavior?
- Do these cases bear on everyday life?
- What solutions would you propose?[68]

In ¿Con quién andan nuestras hijas? the conservative director Emilio Gómez Muriel presents the problems that many young people supposedly face in the midst of a growing Mexico City. As depicted in the poster advertising the film (fig. 1), these problems include "[sexual] desire, evil, love, seduction, vengeance, slander, and lust." Young Isabel represents a new generation of middle-class professionals. Despite the financial independence that her job as a secretary bestows, Isabel is obliged to come home early, ask her parents for their permission whenever she takes a walk with her fiancé, do the domestic chores, and, above all, preserve her virginity.

In contrast, Cristina, a fifteen-year-old high school student, whose presence in the film is more extensive, comes from a family with divorced parents. Though her father is wealthy and gives Cristina all the luxuries that she asks for, he is always absent on business trips. Cristina is clinically depressed and only yearns for the affection of her father, who, obsessed with material possessions, has abandoned his religion. Absorbed in her loneliness, she wanders the streets, and on leaving school one day, she is mercilessly deceived by an older woman and led to a house where she is almost prostituted (surprisingly, by her own mother, who does not know that Cristina is the daughter she abandoned in her youth). Lupita, a character who appears briefly at the beginning of the film, commits suicide by flinging herself from a balcony on realizing that her fiancé has cheated on her after she has had intimate relations with him.

¿Con quién andan nuestras hijas? was one of the first Mexican color motion pictures on this topic.[69] It documents the rapid growth of Mexico City and the social problems that allegedly emerged as a consequence.[70] Alicia, the younger sister of Isabel, has no fear of risking her honor and dreams of being able to kiss a boy on the street, dancing the mambo with her friends, gaining experience with more than one boyfriend, and going around in a convertible like the ones the young men from her social class boast (and where many girls presumably lost their virginity, according to other films of the period).[71] Nevertheless, in spite of identifying these and other "vices" as the new dangers of modernity, Gómez Muriel chooses to end his film on a positive note. Thanks in part to the great love of their mother, Isabel and Alicia embrace their Catholic values again and, accepting their religious identities, reject the temptations of modernity. In a similar vein, Cristina's father realizes his sins and saves his daughter from the dangers of the street, and her mother leaves the house of prostitution and reintegrates into society. She is forgiven for her sins, but the young girls who flirted with different— allegedly more immoral—expressions of sexuality in other films, or dared to have an abortion prohibited by the authorities, would have more difficulties with redemption.

FIGURE 1.   Advertisement for *¿Con quién andan nuestras hijas?* (dir. Emilio Gómez Muriel, 1955). From IMDb, https://www.imdb.com/title/tt0236114/

The More Delicate Topics of Abortion and Lesbianism

Unlike the two films discussed above, *Juventud desenfrenada* (1956), directed by José Díaz Morales, received a C-2 rating, meaning that it was unequivocally condemned for its alleged immorality and banned for all Catholics, regardless of age. The film touches on pregnancy, prostitution, abortion, drug use, and lesbianism. Like Galindo and Gómez Muriel, Díaz Morales adopts a moralizing tone to reproach young people, but unlike them, he is not interested in demonstrating the virtue of repentance. His films do not boast happy endings, and he presents the many dangers presumably threatening Mexican girls of the 1950s against a much darker backdrop. Similar to the US picture *Blackboard Jungle* (1955), rock music is portrayed as one of the roots of youth delinquency. Dancing "wildly," the girls show not only their legs but also their undergarments—something scandalous given the conservatism of the period. In an effort to make his characters realistic, moreover, the director bases his stories on documents that, according to the opening credits of the films, he gathered in the Archives of the Minors Tribunal.

Juventud desenfrenada dramatizes a number of juvenile crimes, such as drug trafficking, burglary, and the prostitution of minors. But the "illicit act" that stands apart is the presumed lesbianism of young Laura.[72] Unlike the great majority of "rebel girls" that other films present, Laura prefers to wear trousers, loose shirts, and men's blazers. At parties, she "behaves" like a man. She likes playing "strip poker" because she apparently likes seeing other girls take off their skirts. She does not dance and gets angry when anybody dares to call her "señorita." She drinks alcohol without hesitation and proclaims that "people need to live intensely and with no constraints." At the end of the film, Laura accompanies a friend to a poorer neighborhood to buy drugs. The police arrive, a shooting ensues, and Laura dies in the crossfire. In a somber tone, very typical of all Díaz Morales's films, the police officer explains, "This is a woman! If she had worn a skirt, I would not have shot at her."

Laura is not the only character in *Juventud desenfrenada* who dies to pay for her presumed sins. Graciela also comes to a tragic end. The drama starts when she goes on a trip to the Port of Acapulco without the consent of her family. There she is intimate with her boyfriend.[73] Once back at home, Graciela finds out that she is pregnant and decides to go to a clandestine clinic to have an abortion. Regretting her decision, she runs to a church and proclaims, as she stares at a somber image of Christ, "I am a murderer. My God, please forgive me!" After her confession, Graciela passes out and never regains consciousness, presumably due to an infection she contracted at the clandestine clinic. Díaz Morales presents her and Laura's deaths as "lessons" for an urban audience drifting ever further from its Catholic roots.[74]

El caso de una adolescente (1958) also touches on the topic of abortion, which was a criminal offense in the 1950s.[75] Nevertheless, unlike *Juventud desenfrenada*, the church did not censor this second film by Gómez Muriel.[76] The picture tells the story of Alicia, a romantic, beautiful, and dreamy seventeen-year-old. Unlike her brothers, who are busy with political and social activities at the university, Alicia is always alone and bored. Her parents are fascinated with the comforts of the modern city but are still held hostage to traditional mores that in her alienation Alicia simply does not understand. Her parents do not let her go to parties, attend university, or learn English abroad simply because she is a woman. Alicia's greatest worry —even fear—is that she will end up like her parents, that she will have to live like them: not tied to her husband by a bond of mutual love that any couple wed in a church owes one another but by virtue of the habit of a modern and liberal man who thinks that he can solve any problem with money and the economic convenience of a materialistic mother who prefers to go shopping and play cards with her friends to talking and engaging in a productive conversation with her daughter.

Alicia becomes pregnant by her fiancé, Rafael, a responsible and handsome (light-skinned) twenty-two-year-old, who promises her that he will obtain his university degree and marry her. However, in keeping with the tragic tone that characterized these melodramas, Rafael dies in a motorcycle race.[77] Alicia is newly alone and sadder than ever. Hopeless, the young woman approaches her parents for advice, but, entirely absorbed in their materialist world, they fail to register the pregnancy and depression of their daughter. Left without any support, Alicia asks a woman doctor to tell her how to proceed if she wants an abortion. The doctor refuses to help her and takes her to see the corpse of a man who had apparently committed suicide after his daughter died from a forced miscarriage. Afterward, the doctor refuses to discuss any plans involving abortion and instead assures the young girl, "The only thing that I could offer you is discretion. You could have the baby here and place him for adoption, but you would never see him again." Terrified, Alicia runs to a church and makes a confession to an old and out-of-touch priest who laments the traditional culture of the past. The priest employs the patriarchal tone typical of these films. He orders her to kneel and to "thank God for having considered her honorable enough to be a mother." The film ends with

Alicia accepting her baby and loudly reclaiming her happiness: "Today I realize that a woman needs a child to become a true woman."[78]

Another film of the era that more explicitly touched on the topics of lesbianism and teenage pregnancy is Alfredo B. Crevenna's *Muchachas de uniforme* (1951). A remake of the 1931 Leontine Saga classic German picture with the same title, *Maedchen in Uniform/Girls in Uniform*, the Mexican version tells the story of Manuela. She is a poor and illiterate sixteen-year-old who is sent to live in an authoritarian all-girls' Catholic boarding school after the death of her mother. The orphan falls in love with her liberal teacher, Lucila, who disapproves of the punishment and rigid discipline practiced by the mother superior, Concepción, who runs the school like a prison. The girls are locked behind bars and are prohibited from communicating with the outside world. When Concepción relaxes her authority in response to the suggestion by the liberal Lucila that the girls should be allowed to play on the patio, a young student named Claudia takes advantage of her freedom and ultimately gets pregnant with her boyfriend's baby. In response, Concepción reiterates the importance of running the school as a cloistered convent and orders the other nuns to be more rigid with the girls. Claudia is never seen inside the school, and Concepción gives orders not to mention her name ever again. Lucila disagrees and tells her mother superior that an open and healthier relationship with the students would have prevented Claudia's pregnancy. What the girls needed was genuine love in the form of dialogue and understanding.

The passionate love and physical desire Manuela and Lucila have for each other are never explicitly depicted onscreen, but when an inebriated Manuela admits her attraction to her teacher in front of her classmates after a school play, she is exposed as an irredeemable sinner. "Unlike Claudia," she is told, "her soul is beyond redemption." She will "burn for eternity in hell." The "sick" Manuela is ostracized and prohibited from getting in touch with Lucila. And her friends are given orders to break all ties with the sinful Manuela. But the young Manuela does not entirely understand why she has been punished and asks Lucila for forgiveness. The liberal teacher sympathizes with her "favorite student" but insists that it is better if they don't see each other again. A tormented Manuela climbs to the tower of the church, laments that no one ever loved her, and jumps. Only then, in Lucila's arms, is the dying Manuela told that "her death will not be in vain" and "God will forgive her sins." At the end of the film, Lucila is shown cutting her hair, getting rid of material wealth, and preparing to become a nun.

The love and attraction that Manuela and Lucila have for each other is irrefutable but never explicitly mentioned in the film. Men are completely absent. With the exception of a shadowed priest and the voice of Lucila's fiancé in the background, *Muchachas de uniforme* only includes female characters who are trapped in a claustrophobic patriarchal world behind bars.[79] It is precisely these cinematic decisions that made Crevenna's film so effective yet controversial. In an interview, the director commented that he received numerous complaints from angry religious authorities, petitioning against the release of his film. The magazine of the PAN, *La Nación*, classified the picture as "dismal" and "pornographic" and claimed that it introduced "vice" and "distorted faith" to the big screen that other directors had not dared to project.[80]

Muchachas de uniforme was widely discussed in Catholic cine clubs with similar disdain. América Penichet wrote to Emma Ziegler, requesting information on the film. The picture had "sparked contentious discussions" within various Catholic circles in Cuba, Penichet explained, but she did not understand why the League of Mexican Decency had not classified it in its publications in Mexico. She wrote, "While some [people in Havana] felt it should be classified with an A-2, others have demanded that it be prohibited at all cost with a C classification." Ziegler explained to her Cuban friend that the reason Crevenna's film had failed to appear in *Apreciaciones* was because of the "scandal" it created within League circles while the censors were consulting with members of Catholic Action for further input. She wrote, "The film has polarized the critics and has sparked an unprecedented wave of heated discussions. Initially the censors gave it a B-3 classification, but on the last day of the discussion, it was given a C-1." According to Ziegler, "The change took place after the censors consulted with the young women from the JCFM and its leading president [Concepción Labarthe]. [The League] invited them to watch the film and voice their opinion. All agreed that the script was morbid and raised concerns that the depiction of the religious boarding school was erroneous and unfavorable."[81]

Penichet agreed with the decision made in Mexico. In her response to Ziegler, she wrote that *Muchachas de uniforme* "was very interesting and beautifully filmed," but the ambiguity of its script could be easily misconstrued and thus it was capable of corrupting those who watched it, namely, young people.[82] Unfortunately, in their letters it is not clear what Penichet and Ziegler meant by "morbid." What was clear, however, was the commitment the two friends made to each other to continue sharing information on similar "immoral" Mexican films that had taken more interest in urban melodramas with attention to youth, as the Cuban activist emphasized.[83] The more radical of these melodramas, others insisted, threatened the "beauty" of Catholic Mexico.

The Beauty and Expected Behavior of Young Catholic Women

The dramatization of family crises and the moralist tone regarding Mexican youth were characteristic of nearly all Mexican motion pictures from the mid- to late 1950s.[84] But these concerns were not limited to the cinema. Catholic magazines of the period, including *Señal, Juventud,* and *Palestra,* shared similar concerns. These three magazines published numerous articles on the intergenerational conflicts of the era and extended practical advice on relationships and proper feminine (and masculine) behavior. In *Juventud,* for example, the writers Verónica, Maggy, María Alicia, and Cati reminded young women of their domestic duties. The authors described the prototype of Mexican beauty, preached against imitating Hollywood stars, explained what young men expected of their girlfriends, and suggested ways to win over good Catholic boyfriends and abstain from intimate relationships with them until marriage.[85]

The young actress Martha Mijares represented the prototype of Mexican beauty (fig. 2).[86] Her image coincided with those reproduced on multiple covers of *Juventud* and the national Catholic monthly *Señal.* Almost always, these representations of young Catholic beauty showed a mestizo young woman with a white phenotype. Her kindhearted, innocent, gentle, and melancholy gaze reflected her selflessness, her presumed submission, good soul, and virtue. Rejecting the frivolity and vulgarity that North American cinema allegedly inspired, the young Mexican beauty invited people to reflect about her simplicity, modesty, and decency.[87] In public she made sure to "avoid sleeveless dresses, low necklines, or dresses with provocative hems."[88]

The magazine *Palestra* was designed for young Catholic women entering college. It published frequent descriptions of the most appropriate ways for women to act in public and for them to navigate university life without actively participating in student politics and without sacrificing their femininity.[89] In a similar vein, *Juventud* and *Señal* included detailed articles by Drs. Jesús Gallardo and Aniceto Ortega who, like the psychiatrist in Galindo's film, frequently warned youth not to incur the vices (sins) of modernity and the alleged excesses of postrevolutionary liberalism. In their

No. 198 Martha Mijares

FIGURE 2. Martha Mijares, the prototype of Mexican beauty. From *Album de Oro del Cine Mundial* (Editor Almex Peru, 1959), #198.

columns and opinion pieces, the doctors offered Catholic solutions to the rebelliousness of youth and to communism. Not only did young women learn how to know and treat men and successfully navigate the art of transitioning from engagement to matrimony; they also became acquainted with the most relevant political problems and changes that affected their lives. As in many films of the period, the doctors advised young women to abstain from friendly relationships with boys who "wrongfully experimented" with communist ideas.[90]

The Catholic magazines and the films on Mexican youth of the 1950s identified young men as the constituency most vulnerable to the threat of communism because of their presumed immaturity. It was the task of their female classmates, girlfriends, and mothers to save them, as religious authorities worked toward the same. Films and magazines from the period assumed that many young people rebelled or flirted with communism precisely because they had strayed from Christ. Women, with their greater maturity, were to make sure that young men reconciled with their religion and with their civic duties.[91] One such young man who is imprisoned for his political activities is Julio in *¿A dónde van nuestros hijos?* (Alazraki, 1958).[92] His crime consists of having organized a rally of the University Student Federation. This action makes his father consider him a "*rojillo* [little red]," reminds him that Mexico already had a successful revolution and does not need to have another one, and accuses him of "betraying" his country.[93] Julio's mother does not reject her son completely but regrets that, absorbed in his "anti-Mexican" ideology, he has lost his Catholic roots. Embracing her motherly responsibility, she implores Julio to return to God's path. At the end of the film, Julio admits to regretting his behavior and confesses to his mother, "I should have been born a different man. I should have had your faith, and believed in God."

Juventud sin Dios (Miguel Morayta, 1961) portrays another young man, Raymundo, who strays from the values of the church. The film is loosely based on the true story of Lambert J. Dehner, a US Benedictine priest who moved to Mexico City in the 1940s to coach the American football team of the National Polytechnic Institute. Upon arriving in the nation's capital, Father Lambert is perplexed by the "Americanized" Mexican youth who are completely lost in the materialism of the period. The film portrays the young people in question as a new generation that, in its fast transition to modernity, grows up without "fearing God." The students are portrayed as overly wild. They do not respect their elders and are swept away by the vices of their city. They do not value camaraderie and lack discipline in sports and in spiritual matters. Raymundo is the team's quarterback. However, despite his talent, the young man is shaken by an identity crisis. Apart from straying from the church, his precarious financial situation (which is shared by many of his classmates) forces him to work to maintain an alcoholic father and condemns him to loneliness. In a streak of bad luck, he is unjustly accused of a theft he did not commit. Nevertheless, as in other moralistic pictures of the decade, Raymundo repents when he is arrested by a benevolent and compassionate police patrol. Thanks to the intervention of his pious girlfriend and the Benedictine priest, he reconciles with God. Like other contemporary films, the motion picture presents state authorities (police officers, judges, public attorneys, state psychiatrists, etc.) and religious authorities (priests and, to a lesser extent, nuns) as two complementary institutions that are capable of saving youth from their alleged errors by joining anti-patriotic forces, as they started doing in the 1940s. And, as the character of Father Lambert suggests, Mexico's northern neighbor is capable of playing an important role in the education of the nation's youth, if only the latter were premised on Catholic and not Protestant roots.[94]

In sum, though all of the films of the 1950s discussed here were directed by men and intended as precautionary tales for parents, they provide insight into a remarkably conservative society at a time when youth were viewed as a symbol of political, social, and moral decadence in a Mexico ever more modern and, ostensibly, less Catholic. Taken together, the dozens of films made at the end of the golden age portrayed the "errors" of Mexican girls but also provided an opportunity for young people to evaluate the tension that they felt toward their elders. These pictures reached their peak at the turn of the decade precisely at a time when Emma Ziegler (among others) embarked on her cinema movement calling for a better appreciation of films and a less rigid engagement with modernity.

CONCLUSION

The leadership of América Penichet ended in 1959 with the triumph of the Cuban Revolution. Initially, she shared her enthusiasm with Emma Ziegler regarding the arrival of "the rebel forces and their extraordinary commanders" to Havana. She wrote, "Only [with] tears of pain [and] . . . emotion, only with our hearts beating wildly and with the deepest respect, could one [understand] what happened." Penichet initially sympathized with the "humanism" and "brazen attitude" of Castro and wrote that she found it "impossible . . . to transcribe even briefly the atrocities, inhumanities, pain, suffering, anguish [and] sacrifice" that the Cuban people had lived through under Batista's authoritarianism. "For all intents and purposes," she added,

> our reviving revolution is an epic event. . . . But the true miracle took place because of the courage of all these men . . . *and women*! who fought in battle

with the invincible weapons of truth, reason, and the most noble and pure ideals, helped at great risk and sacrifice by a near majority of the Cuban population.... Our Fatherland is cleansed and more beautiful than ever. It has been Christened in blood and tears ... but the future shines green with hope, promising a new era of happiness.[95]

However, during her first visit to Mexico toward the end of the same year, Penichet was already expressing her doubts about the Cuban leaders.[96] Two years later, Castro declared that the revolution was Marxist-Leninist. In response, Penichet wrote to Ziegler from her exile in New York:

Fidel ... is practically a monster full of hate, deceit and everything bad in existence.... [H]e is an agent of international communism who is giving Cuba away to the Soviet bloc.... Fidel is a master of lies ..., the "fraud of the century." ... The Revolution that all of us sacrificed for and which we placed our best hopes was never even put in practice.[97]

By these years, the screening of Federico Fellini's neorealist film *La Dolce Vita* (1959–60) had scandalized various Catholic circles both in Mexico and in other parts of the world. It had a similar effect on Ziegler, who had watched the Italian film in Paris and was becoming ever more critical of the danger of communism in general and of socialist films in particular.[98] According to her, Fellini's picture, which tells the story of the ecstatic nights of a paparazzo in search of a photograph of the year for his show business magazine, occupied the very limit of the space that *Miranda prorsus* opened up in the most Catholic sectors. In agreement with Catholic Action, she sent "a call to readers [urging them to] abstain from watching [the film] when it is shown in Mexico." She saw the "pornographic" *La Dolce Vita* as "a slap in the face of the Church" and as completely disrespectful to its cinematic movement. It was "the epitome of a contemporary high society," an immoral society that celebrates "lovers of worldly pleasures" and one that is "possessed by an unstoppable sadness."[99] However, despite Ziegler's efforts, the film that she thought celebrated vices, sexuality, free love, homosexuality, and suicide was screened in Acapulco and Mexico City with "high commercialism[,] ... which fostered its box office success." Ziegler, who had welcomed the censorship of *Suddenly, Last Summer* (Makiewicz, 1959) and *The Subterraneans* (MacDougall, 1960) and applauded the unified protests that emerged across the nation to boycott *Les Amants* (Malle, 1958), could not understand why *La Dolce Vita* was not banned in Mexico.[100] Penichet, who was making plans to move to Peru with André Ruszkowski's help and harboring few hopes that Castro would lose power, wrote to Ziegler that although she had yet to see Fellini's controversial film, she disagreed with the attitude of her Mexican friend. "I dare remind you of the decision of the OCIC," Pinochet wrote to Ziegler, "to never wage a public campaign against bad films. . . . Negative campaigns should take place exclusively in private."[101]

Ziegler partially aligned with the advice given by Penichet but also saw it was necessary to navigate the conservative world of Mexican films that she moved in. With the director Gómez Muriel, for example, she organized a "National Campaign for the Movie Day," which asked Catholics to "abstain from seeing ill-advised and immoral shows."[102] It was clear, in sum, that although Ziegler had expressed her sympathy for the liberal movement of the OCIC, which grew into a worldwide phenomenon after the 1957 conference in Havana, she was not completely prepared to abandon the conservative world that remained firmly rooted in Mexico during this period.[103] Unlike the cinematic representations of young people by Crevenna, Gómez Muriel, Díaz Morales, and Galindo, *La Dolce Vita* lacked a positive message. It exploited sexuality without offering concrete advice and blatantly ridiculed the traditional femininity that the JCFM had championed since the 1930s.[104] Penichet eventually got to see the Italian film. Like Ziegler, she found it offensive, but she insisted that their movement could not afford to "fall into the traps of the past." Thus the focus should remain on promoting Catholic spaces for the creation of "good films" without giving unnecessary publicity to Fellini's and similar pictures of the era. Following a brief stay with her sister in New York, Penichet moved to Peru, where she worked tirelessly for the Latin American Secretariat of the OCIC.

Despite the disapproval of Penichet, Ziegler also led a negative campaign against *Viridiana* (1961), directed by Luis Buñuel. She reproached its attack on purity and its crude treatment of the delicate themes of suicide, murder, rape, and carnal love but also its "blasphemy." But what upset Ziegler most was the film's "gruesome psychological diversion" that "rejected the existence of grace in poverty" and its "unmerited" criticism of "charity."[105] In particular, she referred to a typical topic in the films of the Spanish director: the alleged failure, contradictions, and hypocrisy of the social projects organized by the church. In *Viridiana*, Buñuel addresses these topics through the failed and forgiven attempts by the protagonist to eradicate poverty, not in order to challenge the system, but, as a purely selfish act, in order to save her soul.

Leaving her convent, the sensual and young Viridiana devotes herself to the task of creating a refuge for the marginalized. She houses and feeds homeless people. However, they continue to be selfish, greedy, disorderly, and violent. Their characters never change, despite the supposedly well-meaning efforts of Viridiana and by extension the church.[106]

At the time Ziegler wrote her harsh reviews of *Viridiana*, Mexican Catholic Action had launched its effective "Christianity Yes; Communism No!" campaign, largely in reaction to the Cuban Revolution.[107] She expressed criticism of communism, but she never directly participated in the campaigns. Instead, she worked to help Cuban exiles, including friends of Penichet, but remained mostly committed to her cinema movement.[108] For her, the political context of the Cold War loomed in the background but did not shape her activism. In this sense, her story was a remarkable parallel to the history of the JCFM. Both peaked in importance during the 1950s, and both had difficulty adjusting to the changing notions of modernity that emerged at the end of the decade, namely, in the realm of culture that called for the liberalization of traditional gender norms and more open expressions of sexuality. Both Ziegler and the JCFM also respected the hierarchical structure that shaped the language and tone of their respective movements, but they were by no means under the complete control of the male leadership of the church. For Ziegler and Mexican Catholic Action, the competing notions of modernity that characterized the Cold War years of the 1940s, 1950s, and early 1960s represented a moment ripe for the professionalization of conservative women who saw the need to speak about the social and cultural movements that affected their lives, including, in Ziegler's case, love for cinema and charity. Her movement ultimately failed to create a Catholic national cinema, but, like the leaders of the JCFM and her friend América Penichet, she succeeded in educating and empowering her peers. The same would be true of their male counterparts who became involved in student politics, as described in the next chapter.

TWO

Student Activism during the Cold War

A group of Latin American students protested against the violent repression of their peers in Central America and the Caribbean during the seventh meeting of the International Student Conference in Ibadan, Nigeria, in September 1957. They asked their African and Asian counterparts to join them in defeating the economic and political forces of colonialism and argued against the region's economic subordination to imperialist nations.[1] Asian and African students had expressed similar sentiments two years earlier, during the Bandung Conference in Indonesia. With an emphasis on the economic development and decolonization of the Third World, the participants had pointed to peaceful coexistence and self-determination as their core goals. They called on their peers to protect human rights, end racial discrimination, and defend mutual respect for sovereignty. With Latin Americans notably absent, they demanded noninterference in internal affairs by the colonial powers, as they sought to build solidarity among the developing countries and reduce their reliance on Western Europe and the United States.[2]

The incipient language of the Cold War and the rising critiques of colonialism also influenced Catholic students across the world. Among them were many Latin Americans who traveled to Moscow during these years and appreciated the conservative Soviet state and the puritanism of its leaders. Despite their clear stance against communism, many Latin American Catholics shared with the Soviets a strong condemnation of US imperialism, and like them, they viewed the decadence of the West with apprehension, including the alleged immorality of its youth, their celebration of individualism, and their social acceptance of sexual deviancy and birth control. They praised the respect ordinary Soviet people had for the authorities and the strict policies implemented to champion collectivism, undermine the lure of materialism, and police the erotic in the arts.[3]

The Mexican Catholic students who were present at the Nigerian conference did not express admiration of the conservativism of the Soviets, but they were critical of US imperialism in the Third World. This chapter provides a comparative overview of the two most important lay organizations active in secular universities during the 1950s and 1960s, the Corporation of Mexican Students and the Movement of Professional Students (MEP).[4] The first section examines the nationalist goals of the Corporation during the postwar period, as evident in the stories of Jorge Bermeo and his spiritual leader, the Jesuit priest David Mayagoitia. The second section discusses the ecumenical and more radical politics of the MEP in the aftermath of Vatican II, with attention to the life of Luis Sereno and his international connections in South America. Both lay organizations were founded in 1945–47 to demand the "presence of Christ" inside the universities, but their unique histories and tactics point to a heterogeneous Catholic movement. Like the cinephile Emma Ziegler, the student activists Bermeo and Sereno traveled abroad, but they more assertively conceived of (male) youth as the vanguard of political activism. The third section examines the repression of this activism in the broader Latin American context.

"FOR CHRIST, THE UNIVERSITY"

The defense of the nation's youth became a central battle cry of the church and a priority for the students who joined the Corporation of Mexican Students during the 1950s. With the guidance of Jesuit priests, they promoted civic action and called for the professionalization of Catholic students. They cautioned against several evils, warning that, in the absence of moral support and direction, youth could be led astray by "foreign ideologies." These alleged threats were initially represented by Protestantism and by what these students saw as the "new faces" of liberalism, including secularization, existentialism, and the excesses of capitalism. Following the labor and student strikes that exploded during the late 1950s, these young men grew apprehensive about ultraconservative politics and especially communism. But in their condemnation of the institutions composing the Left, they did not create an "utterly reactionary" and "violent" movement, as often described in the government's espionage documents.[5] Rather, they often shared many of the same concerns that were articulated by their leftist adversaries. For example, in seeking an alternative position to capitalism, many of them contended that the Mexican Revolution was not only "dead" by the 1950s, as liberal intellectuals had proclaimed, but also that its institutions had been transformed into instruments of control and co-optation for the benefit of a few powerful leaders.

The activists affiliated with the Corporation became key players advocating for the professionalization of Catholic students. As a protagonist in the expansion of the Corporation in the National Autonomous University of Mexico (UNAM) during the 1950s, Jorge Bermeo found inspiration in the student activists of an earlier era. His peers cooperated with their female counterparts, but they overwhelmingly believed that political activism was "a man's job."[6] In the words of Bermeo, "As young men we saw ourselves responsible for protecting the Catholic nation and our *compañeras.*" To meet this goal, his movement set out to defend the autonomy of the university and transform the Corporation into a responsible organization invested in establishing the presence of Christ inside the schools.[7] Corporation leaders ultimately fell short in meeting this goal, but they succeeded in empowering their peers, including many who joined the PAN after graduating from the university.

Jorge Bermeo and David Mayagoitia

Jorge Bermeo received a conservative religious education in Tampico during the 1940s. As a teenager, his friends encouraged him to join the Vanguards of Catholic Action, but he found these groups too "pious and reticent."[8] Instead he spent his youth reading national history and learning about civics. In high school, he wrote his first columns in *Jaiba*, one of several mimeographed newspapers under the guidance of the Jesuits that introduced young readers to the history of the National Catholic Student Union (UNEC), precursor to the Corporation of Mexican Students.[9]

The Jesuit priests Ramón Martínez Silva, Jaime Castiello, and Julio Vértiz were responsible for creating UNEC in the early 1930s, primarily to counterbalance the university's leftist groups.[10] In 1933, they ousted the socialist rector, Roberto Medellín, and supported the rectorship of Manuel Gómez Morín (1933–34), who founded the PAN in 1939. Throughout the decade they engaged in ideological and physical battles against leftist students and successfully led campaigns denouncing Marxist teachers and intellectuals who publicly advocated for socialist education, labor militancy, the elimination of private property, collectivism, and anticlericalism.[11]

As the church called for a closer relationship with the state during the 1940s, the ecclesiastical authorities disapproved of the independent politics of UNEC and the violent methods of its members. They ordered the organization to be brought under the strict discipline of the church. But the students preferred to disband UNEC in 1945 rather than accept full incorporation into Catholic Action.[12] Two years later a group of them joined the Jesuit priest David Mayagoitia in creating the Corporation of Mexican Students.[13]

In his forties at the time, Mayagoitia traveled to various parts of the country to recruit young, talented students aspiring to leadership positions in the universities. In 1925, at the age of eighteen, he had enrolled at the Ysleta Jesuit College in El Paso, Texas, where he studied philosophy and English. After a few years of teaching in Puebla, he returned to the United States and studied theology at St. Mary's College in Kansas (1936–40). Once ordained as a priest, he taught at El Colegio Patria, a small private college in Mexico City, where Jesuits trained university students and provided education to the children of the elite. In 1944 Mayagoitia became a full-time professor of philosophy at UNAM, where he opened the Cultural Center, the same institution that established the Ibero-American University in the mid-1950s.[14] He served as university chaplain of a dying UNEC in 1945, and two years later, he received support from the episcopate to establish the Corporation.[15]

Jorge Bermeo "felt an immediate attraction" to the "generosity and intelligence" of Mayagoitia. "His encyclopedic knowledge of Mexican history was impressive," Bermeo recalled. He spoke to him like he had known him all his life, and he was particularly struck by his "soft-spoken, yet confident, overriding, and paternal voice." He first met Father Mayagoitia in 1947, and with his support, Bermeo served as president of the Corporation from 1955 to 1956.[16]

As the national director of the Corporation, Bermeo opened new chapters of the organization across Mexico, first eight and then thirty-three, each composed of one to a few dozen students. During this short but defining period, he also successfully placed young Catholics in secular organizations, transforming them into key spaces for conservative students at UNAM. Among these young Catholics was Diego Zavala (a rising leader of the PAN and the future father-in-law of Felipe Calderón, president of Mexico), who served as national leader of the Confederation of National Students from 1955 to 1957.

Bermeo and Zavala crossed paths with various influential figures of the era, including three intellectuals of the Mexican Revolution who shifted their politics to the Right during the 1950s and saw the Corporation as an important organization to reclaim the presence of Catholics in the universities: José Vasconcelos, Mariano Azuela, and Antonio Díaz Soto Gama. But it was their meeting with Fidel Castro that had "a profound impact" on them. The "intelligence and charismatic presence" of the leader of the Cuban Revolution, who had arrived in Mexico at the age of thirty to plan his armed rebellion against the repressive government of Batista, "impressed" Bermeo and Zavala. They sympathized with Castro when they first met him and "embraced his efforts to bring justice to his people." Like him, Bermeo and Zavala noted during an interview, "we were critical of the US policies in Latin America, but we never accepted his relationship with the Soviet Union." They explained, "In 1961, Fidel Castro identified himself as a Marxist-Leninist, and immediately he developed a hostile attitude toward the church." That is when they "drew the line." In their interpretation, "the world had experienced a drastic change" between 1956, when they met Castro, and 1961, when the Cuban Revolution aligned more closely with the Soviet Union and their "ideological position against Marxism had to be defined."[17]

In addition to their meeting with Castro, Bermeo and Zavala pointed to the 1957 conference in Nigeria as a particularly memorable moment in their lives. According to Bermeo, "[Zavala] gave one of the loudest and most memorable speeches" of the conference. He "paid homage to his Cuban friend José Antonio Echeverría," who had been assassinated by the Batista regime in March 1957, and "spoke against US imperialism" in the region.[18] While Zavala and Bermeo distrusted the Soviet Union, they sympathized with the student activists who had been tortured, "not only in Cuba, but also in Nicaragua and the Dominican Republic." They described the Batista, Somoza, and Trujillo regimes as "pawns of the American government" and detailed the long and complicated relationship that Mexico had with its "predatory neighbor of the North."[19]

From Tijuana to Campeche, Bermeo and Zavala called on their peers to embrace a new "university consciousness," which their mentor, Mayagoitia, understood in relation to sacrifice, morality, integrity, and love. "One cannot fight for Christ," the Jesuit priest argued, "unless one remains loyal to his message." As represented in the original banner of the Corporation, "For Christ, the University," the ultimate goal was to bring this "simple but powerful" message to the classrooms and in so doing transform the university from a political institution serving the needs of a few opportunistic leaders into a true representative body of the people.[20] In this effort, Bermeo and his peers inaugurated cultural, educational, and political events. They led athletic, oratory, and literary competitions, workshops, and conferences where young men advocated for unity and published new journals, including *Corporación*, which served as the foundational magazine for all Catholic students across the nation during the 1950s and early 1960s.

The Nationalist Project of the Corporation

David Mayagoitia launched the first issue of *Corporación* in March 1950. The purpose of the magazine was to provide "Christian solutions" to the nation's most pressing problems, and its slogan, "By Students for Students," emphasized the commitment of the Corporation to defending the autonomy of their schools, forging a productive relationship between students and teachers, exposing the university community to Christ, and fomenting a culture of civic action.

The pages of *Corporación* brought attention to the central documents that Catholic students distributed inside the schools, including, among others, Mayagoitia's "Let Us Define Ourselves! Catholics or Communists?" (1951) and "Our Civic Duties" (1952), which shut down the possibility for students to engage in a productive dialogue with the Left and called on young men to play a direct role in student politics.[21] The authors of the magazine lamented that Catholic youth lacked a basic understanding of the spiritual teachings of Christ. Youth had fallen through the cracks of a secular educational system that had disastrously supported a liberal concept of progress.[22] The term "progress" became an institutionalized catchphrase that had been monopolized by the state, they lamented, one that offered only vague and empty solutions to the social and economic problems of the nation.[23] Further, they contended that the government had corrupted the same principles of the Mexican Revolution that it claimed to defend, while, at the same time, it had deliberately erased the historical role that young Catholics had played at the vanguard of social justice, democracy, and liberty.[24] They celebrated the "heroic" role of Catholic students during the 1929 movement in guaranteeing the autonomy of the university. In addition to achieving freedom for the academy and gaining representational power at their schools, these earlier activists had mobilized an important voice that successfully exposed the "tyrannical" government of Plutarco Calles.[25] In a similar fashion, they made repeated celebratory references to the students affiliated with UNEC in the 1930s and their efforts to defend the hegemony of Catholics in the universities.[26]

The members of the Corporation were less kind in their interpretations of leftist students from the National Polytechnic Institute and the Universities of Michoacán and Guadalajara. With little recognition of the role these secular activists had played in effectively protesting state repression during the mid-1950s, the conservative leaders of the Corporation instead described their movements as "chaotic acts of sabotage."[27] In the interpretation given by a leader of the Corporation in the mid-1950s, Marxist elements, supported by Spanish professors who had arrived in Mexico in the 1930s, not only had infiltrated many schools in the 1950s, but they had also influenced dozens of leaders who competed for control of the student organizations. Their goal could not be more transparent. They had to organize and make sure not to lose any student elections to the Left or to the corrupt leaders of the government.[28] Occupied school buildings, street barricades, Molotov cocktails, and an unprecedented language of "hate" disguised with "Marxist catchphrases" had only brought "terror" to Mexico, other leaders of the Corporation insisted.[29] They stressed their concern about a new generation of "troublemakers" who "lacked Catholic values" and contended, "The chaos at our schools will only disappear when we reestablish our moral values . . . and eliminate, once and for all, the internal and external forces that have manipulated university students and have stimulated them to engage in violent uprisings and anarchy."[30]

"Internal forces" referred to the politics of *caciquismo* (local bossism) and paternalism. In indirect agreement with the Left, they accused government-sponsored intermediaries, pseudo-student leaders, and "thugs-for-hire" of taking advantage of the autonomous status of the university to infiltrate the most important student organizations.[31] But they differed in concluding that only a new movement that openly embraced the humanistic teachings of the church would put an end to the "politicking" that had proliferated inside UNAM. In particular, they called on their peers to exercise their voting rights, take over the presidencies of the different organizations, and, ultimately, replace government-sponsored and Marxist leaders with honest men committed to strengthening the autonomy of their schools and embodying the "justice, love and hope" of Christ.[32]

The young men who joined the Corporation identified first as Catholics and second as university students. As described by a former leader, the ideal student was proud of his national identity, impeccable in his clothing, studious in the classroom, virile in his politics, and ready to defend his Catholic faith.[33] He prioritized what the Corporation called "civic action." In the account given by a leader, this meant primarily calling for two tangible priorities. The first consisted of transforming passive Mexicans—so widely present in various sectors of society, including in their schools—into politically conscious and assertive citizens. The second involved infiltrating all spheres of power, including local positions of the university and higher offices within the political opposition and in the private sector.[34] In this dual effort, Bermeo remembered, it was crucial to transform the secular organizations into key spaces for recruitment where "the most basic constitutional laws and rights" were discussed with younger students and potential members of the Corporation.[35]

Under the strict guidance of Mayagoitia, Corporation leaders offered workshops on citizenship, labor rights, and the autonomy of the university.[36] They developed a comprehensive curriculum on civic rights and examined the idiosyncrasies of the Mexican political system.[37] In these spaces, they taught by example. They guided a younger generation of activists on how and why to organize, supervise, and delegate with prudence and virility. As young men, it was their obligation to protect their universities.[38] In this effort, they pressured their schools to replace "mediocre teachers" with humanists who understood the "values of Christianity" and reminded their peers of their goal to socialize the professions. Future doctors, lawyers, and engineers needed to care more about the collective needs of the nation and less about individual profit. They argued in their elitist voice, "As [privileged] students, we have inherited the most noble mission of leading our pueblo."[39] It was in the student organizations, Bermeo summarized, "where we formed activists, practiced academic freedom, Christianized our peers, and advocated for a vocation of service." "We were very effective," his friend added, as many of them remained politically engaged after graduating from the university. By and large, the overwhelming majority became involved with the PAN, which shared many of the positions that they defended as students. The "legacy of our movement," Bermeo noted, "can be seen in the "professionalization of our peers. While not all of us became prominent leaders of the conservative opposition, we remained devout Catholics, nonetheless, as doctors, lawyers, engineers, and university professors. The training that we received at the Corporation and the mentoring of our Jesuit leaders remained with us for the rest of our lives."[40]

By "external forces" that allegedly threatened the Catholic identity of the nation, the leaders of the Corporation were referring not only to Marxism but also to the wider influences of existentialism. A long history of liberalism, they contended, had created an unparalleled culture of "selfishness." Dominant during the nineteenth century and reappropriated by the revolutionary state from the 1920s to the 1950s, liberalism had given birth to a generation of young people who cared more about individual notions of prosperity, political ambition, and economic profit than the collective needs of the nation.[41] They contended that existentialist philosophy had made its way into liberal schools via the "idealist" theories of Immanuel Kant and the translated works of Martin Heidegger and Jean-Paul Sartre. These had further contributed to the unprecedented selfishness that "had sunk our students into a sterile state of anguish." This "egoism" was manifested in several ways. But, above all, it was demonstrated in the cult of personality that many young leaders had allegedly embraced as representative of the new organizations and in the consumerism of the era.[42] As leaders of the Corporation, they saw the existentialist philosophies, combined with the fascination with the materialist world, as a great threat to the *compañerismo* (comradery) that they championed within their group, one rooted in a Christian sense of solidarity and their mutual love for the university.[43]

Finally, the Corporation warned its members of the dangers of falling prey to the extreme ideologies of the Far Right. They lamented that ultraconservatives had brought an unparalleled level of violence to schools. In Guadalajara, for example, the Fascist Tecos "became concerned with the expansion of the Corporation in their schools," Bermeo said. "At first, they tried to co-opt us. When this didn't work, they too relied on violence and frequently threatened our members during elections."[44] What the school needed, they concluded, was a new generation of spiritual leaders who spoke against the violent elements of opportunistic intermediaries affiliated with the government, militant leaders of the radical Left, and the reactionary figures of the conservative Right. As conscious male Catholics, Bermeo, Zavala, and others insisted "it was our obligation" to reject the "extreme ideologies of the Left and the Right," expose "the false expressions of humanism" that questioned the existence of God, and counterbalance "the rising cult of materialism" of the era "with spiritual understanding of Christ."[45]

In sum, from the perspective of the Corporation, to be a young Catholic student in the 1950s meant to embody the principles of Christ in the university, with the ultimate goal of promoting civic and political action. In the emerging context of the Cold War, the leading figures of this movement encouraged their younger peers to be politically active in their schools. Many of them spoke against US imperialism and the abuses of capitalism, but the overwhelming majority saw communism as the greatest threat to the nation. Under the strict guidance of the Jesuit David Mayagoitia, they saw university students as defenders of Mexico's Catholic identity, and as privileged young men, they identified their missionary roles in the schools as the will of God. "We must unequivocally affirm," they noted as self-described apostles of the truth, "our commitment is with Christ. As leaders, it is Him whom we must follow. It is Him who has chosen and sent us here."[46]

THE MOVEMENT OF PROFESSIONAL STUDENTS IN THE BROADER LATIN AMERICAN CONTEXT

The Sixties brought an end to the most successful years of the Corporation of Mexican Students. A small number of its members moved further to the Right or to the militant Left. Others, constituting a larger majority, simply left the organization.[47] By contrast, the leaders of the MEP proved more receptive to the progressive changes that emerged across the continent in the aftermath of Vatican II, and for the same reason, their movement thrived thereafter. These students sympathized with the concerns raised at the Bandung (1955) and Nigerian (1957) conferences and also called for the urgent need for countries of the Third World to reduce their reliance on Western Europe and the United States. However, like their peers in Central and South America, they paradoxically reached out to the German organization Adveniat for financial support. With Adveniat's funds, the students attended international conferences and paid for the publication of their magazines, where they successfully advocated for Latin American unity.

Franz Hengbach founded Adveniat in the industrial city of Essen in 1961 in collaboration with a group of German bishops. These bishops were sympathetic to Christian Democracy and grew increasingly concerned with the radicalism of militant Catholics and the reactionary politics on those on the Far Right. By the late Sixties, Hengbach had transformed Adveniat into a key player in the Cold War in Latin America, sending an impressive average of $45 million annually to the region. Initially, the funds were used only to pay for the education of young priests in the form of scholarships to attend European seminars. By the mid-1960s nearly all lay projects, university events, and international conferences were fully or partially funded by Adveniat.[48]

This second section of the chapter situates the history of the MEP in this broader world context, with particular attention to the important role that South American leaders played in the radicalization of Luis Sereno, national leader of the MEP, in the mid-1960s.

The Latin American Secretariat and Catholic Students as the "Vanguard" of Radical Change

More than one hundred Catholic student federations met on July 20, 1964, at Georgetown University for the XXVI Inter-Federal Assembly of Pax Romana, the most important organization of international Catholic students, founded in Fribourg in 1921 and active in Latin America since the 1930s.[49] The central theme of the conference was "Christianity in an Age of Transition," and the keynote speaker was the then US attorney general, Robert F. Kennedy. In his remarks, Kennedy noted, "The ambitions, the sensitivity, and the responsibility of university students in every country today will soon shape the success or failure, war or peace, prosperity or misery of your countries and our world tomorrow."[50]

In response to the progressive turn after Vatican II and the alleged rise of communism across the continent in the aftermath of the Cuban Revolution, Kennedy argued that young Catholics could no longer afford to sit on the sidelines and wait patiently for change. They had to assume the role of the vanguard in facing the world's most pressing threats, including exploitation, extreme poverty, tyranny, hunger, nuclear armament, and communism. "These are not problems to be mulled over," he argued. "All of us are needed. The question is whether to be a critic or a participant. The question is whether to bring a candle to the barricade or to curse the darkness. At this assembly, devoted to social responsibility, I think the choice must be for light."[51]

Over seventy countries attended the congress in Washington, DC. With dozens of leaders representing numerous Catholic organizations, Latin America sent some of the largest delegations of students. Among them were the leaders of the MEP, Luis Sereno Coló and his friend María Vasquez. In July 1962, they had also been present at the XXV World Congress of Pax Romana in Montevideo, Uruguay. The central theme of that earlier event was "Social Responsibility of the University and the University Student." For the two friends, the Montevideo meeting came to represent a defining moment in the lives of a new generation of Latin American Catholic students who not only had assumed the social and political responsibility that Kennedy emphasized two years later but also had begun to see themselves as important agents of continental change. Initially concerned with the "rampant" communism across the continent but eventually more sympathetic with the Left, scores of young leaders grew critical of the nationalism, reformism, and Eurocentric language of an earlier era, including Sereno, Vasquez, and their friend Paco Merino. Over time, these students saw themselves as "Latin Americans" with shared problems, histories, and challenges.

The origins of the MEP date to 1947, when a group of students from the Catholic Association of Mexican Youth founded the organization. Not too different from the Corporation, the MEP expected its members to "take Christ" into schools. Initially, they shared the same tactics and conservative views of their counterparts, but they developed a different relationship with ecclesiastical authorities. Whereas the Corporation remained loyal to the Jesuits, the MEP instead swore alliance to the hierarchical authorities of Catholic Action. In the aftermath of Vatican II it became sympathetic to the Left, and under the leadership of Sereno in the mid-1960s, it adopted a Latin American identity that allowed its base to establish closer contact with various international organizations, including the Latin American Secretariat in South America (hereafter, the Secretariat).

In 1966 the Secretariat successfully brought together the two most important international organizations of Catholic students affiliated with Pax Romana, the Mouvement International des Etudiants Catholiques (MIEC; International Movement of Catholic Students), which was exclusively involved in the universities, and Juenesse Etudiante Catholique Internationale (JECI; International Young Catholic Students), which was more liberal and was also active in secondary schools. This alliance became possible with the financial support provided by Adveniat in Germany and the blessing given to lay students by the Latin American Episcopal Council (CELAM) under the progressive leadership of Manuel Larraín in Chile, Marcos McGrath in Panama, Hélder Câmara in Brazil, and Gustavo Gutiérrez in Peru.[52]

With offices in Montevideo, the Secretariat published *Víspera*, *SPES*, *Cuadernos de Comunicación*, and other documents and pamphlets that called for radical change across the continent. In the aftermath of the 1964 military coup in Brazil, this call included a new revolutionary consciousness that these students affiliated with the MIEC-JECI associated with

"Third Worldism," "youth power," and "martyrdom."[53] For inspiration they advocated the "See, Judge, Act" method, as originally articulated by the Belgian cardinal Joseph Cardjin in the 1930s and as reevaluated (Latin Americanized) in the aftermath of the Bandung Conference of 1955 and the Cuban Revolution of 1959. For these young Catholics, the humanist and anticolonialist goals of these two events coincided with the progressive turn that started with Vatican II, namely, the renewal of Catholicism, the redefinition of the church, the call for Christian unity, and the promotion of dialogue with the modern world.[54] In particular, the Revision of Life method asked university students to step outside their ivory tower and see the life conditions of the majority of the common people. They were then required to judge that situation by providing a critical analysis of that reality, not only through a close reading of the Bible, but also with the use of Marxism and dependency theory as theoretical instruments of social analysis. On reflection, they were then given the task to act, in the form of a dynamic response compatible with Christian ideals of justice, dignity, solidarity, and love.[55] Through this three-pronged method, the students learned the important role they could play to change the world around them.

The students who established the Secretariat in Montevideo in 1966 called on their peers to create a "committed Christianity" capable of providing "concrete solutions" to "Latin American problems." In the language of Third Worldism and in direct response to the encyclical *Mater et magistra* (Mother and Teacher, 1961), they demanded economic justice in the developing world. As they moved away from the historical condemnation of socialism and called for the modernization of the church, this new generation of students grew increasingly committed to religious ecumenism and domestic and international notions of social justice, dignity, and human rights. The state, they argued in reference to the most important document of Vatican II, *Gaudium et spes* (Joy and Hope, 1965), not only had the right to own the means of production but also had the moral obligation to intervene in matters of common welfare, including health care, education, and housing. With specific citations of the most radical encyclical of the Sixties, *Populorum progressio* (The Development of Peoples, 1967), they warned their peers against the new forces of colonialism and contended that wealthy nations had a historical obligation to distribute aid.

The establishment of the Secretariat had its roots in the 1962 XXV World Congress of Pax Romana in Montevideo.[56] While its central theme referred to the social responsibility of the university and the university student, its legacy pointed to one of the first moments when the MIEC, with conservative roots in Switzerland, Germany, and Spain, joined forces on the continent with the JECI, whose more liberal tendencies derived from Belgium, French Canada, and Brazil.[57]

The main presenters at the Montevideo conference ranged from fervent anticommunist leaders with a long history with Pax Romana, such as Frei Montalva, the intellectual of Chile's Christian Democratic movement and elected president of that country in 1964, to more progressive and younger intellectuals who sympathized with the action-driven approach of the Revision of Life, including the future leading figure in Latin America's liberation theology, Gustavo Gutiérrez, who had returned to Lima from Louvain in 1960.[58] Despite their ideological differences, however, the presenters were deeply concerned that little to no efforts had been made by previous generations of leaders to forge a Latin American unity that, from a Catholic perspective, would transform the university from an elitist to a popular institution. They drew on the writings of the Brazilian author Darcy Ribeiro, who encouraged Latin Americans to assume direct management of their schools.[59] They saw higher education as complacent with the status quo and completely disconnected from the social and economic realities that affected most people, including widespread poverty and political disempowerment. They were equally critical of the curricula and what many of these Catholic students saw as its anachronistic pedagogical methods that had little to no interest in solving the continent's most devastating social problems.[60] The goal, as it was further articulated during the CELAM conference of 1966 in Buga, Colombia (and during the JECI Congress in Montreal, Canada, a year later where Gutiérrez also gave a defining speech), was to transform the university into a politicized space that would give birth to a vanguard of responsible Third World leaders rooted in the shared principles of love and unity.[61] Present at all of these conferences was Luis Sereno, who played a crucial role in the creation of the Latin American Secretariat and assumed the leadership of the MEP in 1964.

Luis Sereno Coló and the Radicalization of the MEP

The participants in the Montevideo (1962), Washington, DC (1964), Buga (1966), and Montreal (1967) conferences pointed to the university student as the protagonist of the decade. However, they lamented that much work needed to be done to explain the importance of this idea throughout Latin

America. They realized that most students remained deeply divided by nationalism and weakened by competing factions of the Left. Because of their bourgeois upbringing, moreover, they were mostly unaware of the impoverished social reality that the majority of people confronted in their daily lives. In the hope of remedying this, the organizers of the Uruguayan conference asked their peers to conduct national polls to capture the central problems in their respective countries.

Luis Sereno was in charge of writing the polls for Mexico. Originally from Michoacán, he grew up in a devout and anticommunist middle-class family in the 1940s. As a teenager he sympathized with the Catholic Association of Mexican Youth. But it was in Colombia where his life took a drastic turn in the early 1960s and where he became involved with the MIEC of Pax Romana.

Sereno "arrived in Medellín on a hot afternoon in mid-December [1963]." He described this day as transformative and specifically pointed to "a young priest" who "opened" his eyes to a new "understanding of the world." He explained:

> A talk by a "young priest" recently returned from Louvain and Chaplain of the [Colombian] teams impressed me greatly.... [I spoke to him] at length [about] my life in Mexico, of my reasons for joining [Pax Romana].... But the most important aspect of that dialogue was the comments [he made about] his experiences in a parish in a poor section of Bogotá.... And there, among the cobwebs of my mind, concepts were forming on the "commitment of the university student," "service to one's neighbor," "how the university world does not end with the university," "what should be the road of [the MIEC] in Latin America[,]"... and many other things which are difficult to remember now.... This "young priest" whom I never saw again was *Camilo Torres*.[62]

People who met Sereno, including the Peruvian priest Gustavo Gutiérrez, remembered his "great sense of humor" and "tireless efforts to bring the Mexican church up to date and closer to the progressive Catholicism that he admired from his South American friends."[63] Also remarking on his "charisma and wit," the Jesuit priest Jesús García and Jorge Bermeo, leader of the Corporation of Mexican Students, commented, respectively, on his "skills of persuasion" and "remarkable abilities to bring people together, especially those whom he disagreed with."[64] His close friend María Vasquez similarly added, "The joyous personality of Luis, or Lucho, as he was widely known to all of his friends, was contagious." Everywhere he went, he found a way to be "the center of attention." People were drawn to his "edgy sense of humor" and deep determination to unite the Catholic student body. He had little patience for orthodox points of view and always found innovative and pragmatic solutions to promote dialogue and respect for one another. He "fell in love with the language of Vatican II," and as a firm advocate of nonviolence, he wanted others to see that a more progressive Catholicism was possible even in "a traditional country, like ours, still haunted by its colonial past and permanently suffocated by its ultra conservative ecclesiastical leadership." In the words of Camilo Torres, Lucho wanted his peers to adopt an "integrated approach" to their activism, defined above all by the love of others and for each other.[65] In pushing for a reformed church and a holistic form of political activism, Sereno reached out for financial help to Adveniat, explaining "the need to educate the university student body [in Mexico]," which he and other leaders of the MEP saw "as overwhelmingly detached" from the "exciting movements that had emerged from Central America and the Southern Cone."[66] "Though baptized for the most part," he argued, the majority of members of the MEP "lacked a true ethical and religious formation." Most had an "agnostic mentality" or were in need of "spiritual consciousness" attentive to the economic and political needs of the marginalized.[67] Other voices in the movement similarly insisted that university students needed to "shake off their lethargy" and usher it into "social action."[68] He had similar criticisms of Catholic students affiliated with the Corporation, whom he described as "privileged" and mostly "disconnected" from the needs of the people.[69]

The attitude, determination, and networks that Sereno developed abroad had positive results for the MEP. Before traveling to Colombia, he had received funds from Adveniat to strengthen the presence of the MIEC in Mexico. In 1962, he organized the national poll requested at the Montevideo congress and supported his peers in creating a "responsible" press in the schools, capable of "properly orienting the student body toward the noblest goals of human work... [and pressuring] the university toward fulfilling the responsibilities it has to society," first as president of the National Association of the Student Press in 1962–63 and then as regional secretary of Pax Romana in charge of Mexico, Central America, and the Caribbean in 1964–65.[70] In 1964, the leaders of Catholic Action named him national representative of the MEP.

In his new role, Sereno encouraged his peers to "tone down their divisive rhetoric" and entertain the possibility of "engaging in dialogue" with those who had historically opposed them.[71] This position grew out of his collaboration with the University Parish at UNAM, Vasquez explained, where the Dominican friars gave lectures on "the theology of the revolution" and where Sereno frequently visited in his efforts to "improve the spiritual education of his peers."[72] What mattered for the "pragmatic Lucho" was to raise the necessary funds to strengthen the numbers and value of their movement. Unlike the more nationalistic leaders of the Corporation, he was determined to bring the MEP closer to the "Latin American reality," namely, a "growing social inequality" that prevented the growth of democracy; a "passive university," unwilling to create real change and lacking visionary chaplains; and a "rampant militarism" that had swept the continent. He insisted that Mexico "was no exception as it too could fall into the abyss of *gorilismo* [a phrase frequently used in the Southern Cone in reference to the military juntas]." Other members of the MEP agreed and freely described the presidential administration of Díaz Ordaz as "dictatorial."[73]

Hoping to bring attention to this issue, Sereno introduced young Mexicans to the publications of Pax Romana, including the *Boletín Iberoamericano de Información* of the MIEC. What "he strongly believed," remembered Vasquez, was the idea that Mexicans were "too provincialized," even "xenophobic," and mostly "disconnected from the shared history of the broader Latin American continent." They knew more about their neighbor in the North and its involvement in Vietnam than the atrocities that were taking place across Latin America, or rather, in what "our South American friends often referred to as 'la Patria Grande' [the Great Fatherland]." If they were exposed to "the struggles of our Latin American comrades," Sereno believed, "they would unite and create more effective tools of combat at home."[74]

On his return to Mexico in 1964, Sereno promoted the Revision of Life method. He called for national unity of the MEP and demanded the greater integration of women activists in the movement. He rejected the idea that young women "jeopardized their femininity" if they got involved in student politics.[75] This was a progressive position in comparison to the emphasis that the leaders of the Corporation of Mexican Students placed on "virility." In addition, he expressed the need to create university parishes across the country, assisted in the creation of the *MEP Boletín* (based on the concept of the *Boletín Iberoamericano de Información*), and managed new student exchange programs that brought leaders from the United States, Canada, and South America to Mexico. With the help of a new generation of students, he successfully expanded the presence of the MEP in San Luis Potosí, Toluca, Campeche, Xalapa, and Monterrey.[76] By the end of the decade, Sereno had traveled to most Latin American countries; but more importantly, by the time he finished his work with the MEP in 1967, he had placed national leaders in influential positions in the MIEC and JECI in Central and South America, including his friend Francisco "Paco" Merino.

Paco and the Centro de Documentación

Francisco "Paco" Merino played an instrumental role in the publications of the MIEC-JECI. In the late 1950s he had graduated from the Carlos Septién García School of Journalism and served as the regional representative of the Catholic Association of Mexican Youth in Toluca. In the 1960s he studied philosophy and worked as the director of the Catholic newspaper *Saeta*. By the end of the decade, he had completed his studies, and in 1970, with the support of Sereno, he became the national representative of the MEP. Merino moved to Peru in 1971 where he studied theology and worked as director of the Centro de Documentación of the Latin American Secretariat until 1973. The Centro, founded in 1967, collected, archived, and classified all the information that arrived in Montevideo from Latin America, the United States, Canada, and Europe related to the different Catholic organizations in the universities (the MIEC) and the secondary schools (the JECI).

The correspondence that Luis Sereno and Paco Merino had with other Catholic leaders from Latin America and Europe shared language similar to that in the mimeographed pamphlets and news bulletins published by the MEP during the Sixties. The authors drew inspiration from an eclectic mix of ideas. These included references to the Spanish version of the *Dutch Catechism* and the encyclical *Populorum progressio* (1967), which demanded, respectively, an ecumenist dialogue with the modern world and denounced the legacy of colonialism in favor of social justice and human dignity. In addition, they cited a variety of figures who influenced the New Left in the Catholic world. Among others, these included Louis Althusser, who defended Algerian independence from France; Herbert Marcuse, who criticized the repressive tendencies of capitalist consumerism; Paulo Freire, who called for critical pedagogy; Iván Illich, who founded the educational center in Cuernavaca; Darcy Ribeiro, who called for university reform; and Pierre Teilhard de Chardin, who influenced the progressive reforms of Vatican II.[77]

Inspired by these intellectuals, Sereno and Merino expressed profound criticism of "charity" by insisting on transforming activism into a true "love that searches for the well-being of others."[78] In their letters, for example, they echoed their peers in Central and South America who called for greater understanding of the needs and problems shared across the "Patria Grande," ultimately blaming the United States for its underdevelopment, specifically, the "revolving [Democratic and Republican] governments of Washington" that sponsored military uprisings, coups d'états, authoritarian dictatorships, conditional or corrupt democracies, and the closures of universities and violations of their autonomy.[79] What was needed were "bridges of solidarity" across the continent, with the shared goal of "promoting peaceful love in the world."[80] Their mutual friend from El Salvador, Rosendo Manzano, agreed and further highlighted the support they received from Adveniat as crucial to building networks of solidarity across the continent.[81] He also pointed to his Colombian friend Carlos Urán as a central figure in the creation of the Latin American Secretariat and an influential voice in the radicalization of Sereno.

"Revolution through Peace"

In his letters to other Catholic leaders from Central and South America, Luis Sereno referred to Colombia as "his favorite" country.[82] In Medellín and Bogotá he met Camilo Torres, Gustavo Gutiérrez, and a new generation of leaders, including Carlos Urán, who brought together the MIEC and JECI in Montevideo in 1966.[83] Like Sereno, Urán had come of age in the 1950s as a leading figure in Catholic Action. In 1963 he traveled to Europe to attend workshops on "student leadership," and in Colombia he became critical of those who saw Pax Romana strictly as a "spiritual movement." What their movement needed, Urán argued in agreement with Sereno, was to adopt a "committed" approach in the name of "revolutionary love."[84] In this effort, he became increasingly involved in student politics in Bogotá, where a large group of students, workers, and campesinos protested the sharp price increases that accompanied the devaluation of the peso from 10 to 20 per dollar. A weakened government was forced to resign, only to be replaced by a more authoritarian regime. As civil uprisings spread throughout the country (mainly in response to nonpayment of salaries), the Colombian authorities declared the strikes illegal. Like many of their neighbors in South America, they relied on the use of "mano dura" (firm hand) to reestablish order and imprison those who participated in the protests, including Urán.[85]

On his release from prison in 1966, Urán was expelled from the university and prohibited from finishing his law degree at any national institution of higher education.[86] Like many of his peers, he left for Montevideo, and with the support from the University Department of CELAM, he established the Latin American Secretariat. In bringing together the MIEC and the JECI, as noted earlier, the Secretariat pointed to the "liberation of Latin America" as its central goal.[87] But unlike those who participated in the various "Camilo Torres movements" that spread across the continent following the killing of a Colombian priest in 1966, the Secretariat wholeheartedly rejected the use of violence. In its publications, it saw little relevance in the reformism of Christian Democracy and voiced a critical view of the ultraconservative Catholicism of those on the Far Right. But in promoting radical change, the Secretariat called on young Catholics to defend the peaceful path toward revolution.[88]

The most important publications of the Latin American Secretariat were *Víspera* and *SPES*. Urán played a leading editorial role in these publications from 1967 to 1972, and so did Paco Merino, who was director of the Cuadernos de Documentación from 1971 to 1973. These publications covered three central concerns of the Secretariat from its foundation in Montevideo in 1966 to its expulsion and move to Lima in 1971–76: the Latin American university as a space for dialogue and radical (yet peaceful) change, the threat of US imperialism, and the urgency of defeating poverty.[89]

In these publications the young men and women who were affiliated with the Latin American Secretariat examined the rich history of student activism on the continent. They celebrated youth as the vanguard of continental unity and radical change and called on their peers to increase the presence of "Catholic militants" in secondary schools and universities.[90] They responded to the key encyclicals of the era and followed the nonviolent methods of the Third World Priest Movement in Argentina, which emerged as an outspoken critic of military violence in the region. They celebrated the August 1968 takeover of the Cathedral in Santiago by the Young Church in Chile, demanding that ecclesiastical authorities "be on the side with the people," and followed the vanguard role a new generation of priests played in the antiwar movement in the United States. They pointed with enthusiasm to the spiritual and political retreats that welcomed a dialogue with Marxism and discussed the pedagogical, psychoanalytical, and philosophical movements of the era. Similarly, they celebrated the creative dialogue, social commentary, commitment to liberation, and revolutionary utopias of the "new song," the musical genre that combined folk-inspired styles and politically committed lyrics, and praised the Boom literature of the decade, which also imagined Latin America as a "Patria Grande," with shared problems of underdevelopment and legacies of colonialism.[91] Relatedly, they protested US involvement in Brazil, the Dominican Republic, and Vietnam. They condemned the Tlatelolco massacre in Mexico and pointed to the failures and contradictions of John F. Kennedy's Alliance for Progress, not as an economic assistance program to promote political democracy, economic growth, and population control, as Christian Democrats had insisted, but rather as an imperialist instrument of consumerism and anticommunism. In short, in its journals the Secretariat called for a critical consciousness among Christians and urged its members to promote the "de-Yankeefication" of Latin America.[92]

The journals of the Secretariat included discussions of *foquismo*, mostly in response to the theory of guerrilla warfare published by Régis Debray in Cuba and Uruguay. They simultaneously referred to Camilo Torres and Che Guevara as "Christian martyrs," whose "revolutionary love" appealed even to the most dedicated pacifists. But in leaning on the writings of the Brazilian bishop Hélder Câmara, they adamantly rejected the option of armed struggle.[93] Like Sereno, Vasquez, Merino, and Urán, they promoted political responsibility and demanded that others join them in defeating the widening gap between the rich and the poor.[94] They celebrated Salvador Allende's rise to power, protested Richard Nixon's doctrine of "law and order" and its dirty war against the New Left in the United States, and provided detailed accounts of those who felt the brunt of the military authorities, including political prisoners and the growing list of tortured and disappeared.[95] What Latin America needed in this time of despair was a complete rejection of all forms of violence. Concientización, participatory democracy, hemispheric unity, critical (Freirean) pedagogy, the Revision of Life method, and "revolution through peace"—in the name of love—were of foremost importance in conceptualizing a new way of engaging in politics, and so were the rising critiques of corruption within the church and its collaboration with military dictatorships.[96]

THE REPRESSION OF CATHOLIC STUDENTS

The Uruguayan authorities ransacked the offices of the Latin American Secretariat on October 20, 1971. They falsely accused Catholic university students of protecting the urban guerrilla movement of the Tupamaros and imprisoned some of them.[97] Andrés Campos, the nineteen-year-old leader of the JECI and a native of El Salvador, was apprehended at the Montevideo airport a few days after the government's attack on the Secretariat. Campos was traveling from a Pax Romana conference in Chile. Once arrested, Campos was put on a different plane and sent to a small cell in São Paulo, Brazil. According to his own testimony, he was beaten there and forced to endure psychological torture for a total of eleven days. Several times, the guard in charge of his cell pointed a gun at his head and pulled the trigger, but the gun was loaded with blanks. And as Campos witnessed the mutilation of other prisoners, he was asked to describe his alleged relationship, if not with the Tupamaros, then with Cuba. Campos identified himself to the authorities as a Christian militant but spoke of his disapproval of armed struggle. He insisted that he sympathized with socialism and Che Guevara but explained that his commitment was strictly to the church, which he understood not in relation to the institutional authorities that made up its hierarchy but as one embodied in the common people, including his own torturers.[98] For his part, Fr. Buenaventura Pelegrí, who had served as the chaplain of the Latin American Secretariat since its foundation in 1966, was forced to go into exile in his native Spain. Once in Europe, he visited ecclesiastical authorities in Rome and asked them to intervene in the repression of students in South America and demand the release from prison of all young Catholics who had been apprehended on the closing of the Montevideo Secretariat office, including Andrés Campos. Gustavo Gutiérrez and Marcos McGrath made similar demands from Peru and Panama.[99]

In his account, Andrés Campos alluded to a change of leadership within the church, which marked a more violent chapter in the history of the Latin American Catholic movement. By then, Gustavo Gutiérrez had already published his influential study on liberation theology.[100] But as Campos predicted, CELAM had elected a new general secretary, the anticommunist Alfonso López Trujillo (1972–84). A self-described enemy of "Marxist" theologians and native of Colombia, López Trujillo joined forces with conservative leaders of the global church, including the Belgian Jesuit Roger Vekemans.[101]

Vekemans had arrived in Chile in 1957 to support Frei's Christian Democratic Party. He collaborated with the Central Intelligence Agency, and with financial support from Kennedy's Alliance for Progress, he founded the Bellarmine Center for Research and Social Action. In charge of housing, educational and agrarian reform, and labor union projects, the Bellarmine Center's main goal was to dissuade young Catholics from joining leftist movements.

With the presidential election of Salvador Allende in 1970, Vekemans moved to Bogotá, where he founded the Research Center for the Development and Integration of Latin America and launched an ideological war against those who organized and attended the 1972 Christians for Socialism Conference in Chile, "whom he said were like a 'contagion' being multiplied around the world by the 'carriers of the bacillus.'"[102] More significantly, he founded the journal *Tierra Nueva*, in which conservative leaders of the church orchestrated a campaign against those who sympathized with the preferential option for the poor and the Revision of Life method, including many of the leading figures of the Latin American Secretariat who wrote in the pages of *Víspera* and *SPES*.

The closing of the Montevideo offices and the conservative movements against liberation theology "had a profound impact" on Luis Sereno and María Vasquez, as it coincided with the repression that the Mexican government "launched on the most radical elements of the left." Like their South American friends, they rejected armed struggle, but they also grew critical of what they interpreted as the "authoritarian and contradictory politics" of Luis Echeverría. As examined in chapter 5, the two friends would momentarily break ties with the MEP to dedicate their time to attend to their families, but in the mid-1970s, they would rejoin forces with their South American friends to create a new intellectual movement that called for the respect of human rights and the defense of liberation theology. Their friend Paco Merino would follow a similar path. In 1976, the bishop of Chiapas, Samuel Ruiz, ordained him a priest.

CONCLUSION

By 1964, *Corporación* had sold more than 80,000 copies over 64 issues. By then, new leadership at the Corporation of Mexican Students had taken the first steps to endorse a more progressive Christianity. The anticommunist language of the 1950s remained relevant, but so were key papal encyclicals that radicalized growing sectors of the church in the aftermath of Vatican II. This change in attitude became evident in the magazine's new name, *Rumbo*, meaning "direction" or "course." Contributors to the magazine responded favorably to the ecumenical path that a new generation of activists and journalists embraced at the end of the decade, ranging from ideas related to the preferential option of the poor to the rise of more liberating notions of

FIGURE 3. "Our teachers." From *Rumbo* (March–April, 1968).

gender and sexuality. The writers adopted a lenient attitude toward the Left and paid homage to the teachers who inspired them.

As depicted in figure 3, one of these teachers was Ramón Ertze Garamendi (second from the right).[103] He taught humanities at UNAM, provided political commentary in *Excélsior*, and was not afraid of openly identifying himself as a Catholic in his classrooms. In the cartoon, the more conservative Father Mayagoitia points his fingers and tells the students, "Forget what [these teachers] are saying," implying that these professors were too radical for the members of the Corporation. After all, some of them had provided an important forum at their schools for analyzing social problems and, in the case of Garamendi, promoted an open dialogue with non-Christians, including Marxists, who gained a significant presence at UNAM during the 1960s.[104]

Seated on a stool behind Mayagoitia is Fr. Jesús Hernández Chávez. He had played an instrumental role in establishing the presence of Jesuits in Monterrey during the 1950s. In 1963, he received financial support from the wealthy industrialist Eugenio Garza Sada to create the Cultural University Workshop. Their shared goal was to counter the influence of leftist activists and train young entrepreneurs in the social doctrine of the church. The Workshop expanded the presence of the Corporation inside the National University of Nuevo León throughout these years. But between 1964 and 1967, a new generation of Jesuits that included Herman von Bertrab,

Xavier de Obeso Orendain, and Salvador Rábago González took over the Workshop and transformed it into a key ally of radical Catholic students. Their relationship with Garza Sada experienced a drastic turn in 1968, when government and ecclesiastical authorities accused the Jesuits of supporting armed struggle, and they were consequently expelled from Monterrey in 1969 (see chap. 5).

The year 1968 marked a defining moment for the history of the Corporation. In addition to the student movement, that year witnessed the pain that many of its members felt upon the death of Father Mayagoitia on September 18. The Jesuit priest suffered a heart attack and died at the age of sixty-one. For Jorge Bermeo, "the coincidence could not be more tragic." Hours before his death, more than ten thousand soldiers had taken over the buildings of the university with tanks, violating the autonomy of the schools and setting the tone for state repression that culminated at the Plaza of Tlatelolco on October 2. The Jesuit order replaced Mayagoitia with Fr. Jesús Hernández Chávez, but a demoralized Corporation of Mexican Students ceased to be relevant at UNAM.[105] A former member of the Corporation recalled, "The student massacre [of 1968] had a profound impact on me and many of our peers. I could no longer see myself affiliated with an organization that failed to protest against the brutality of the state. I had to find new spaces that embraced a more committed Catholicism. I found it in the youth wing of Christian democracy, but a few of my compañeros saw greater relevance in the Christian base communities or joined various Marxist movements. Most of them simply left the world of politics."[106]

The history of the Corporation provides a glimpse of an elitist group of students that saw the 1950s as a crucial time in national history. In their interpretation, these years were "ripe" for the creation of an alternative movement that opposed the extremism of capitalism, socialism, and existentialism. The organization was fundamentally corporatist and overwhelmingly respected the hierarchical structure of the church, with particular loyalty to its Jesuit mentors.

Under the leadership of Fr. David Mayagoitia, a new generation of activists like Jorge Bermeo formulated an innovative concept of political activism and promoted unity among Catholic students. In the name of Christ, they conceived of themselves as active agents of political change and defenders of their faith. They argued for a holistic understanding of the social, political, and economic problems that the overwhelming majority of people faced during this period. This mission required aggressive but nonviolent participation by young Catholics in student politics, religious ceremonies, and social programs. In addition to defending the autonomy of the university, they advocated for the need to depoliticize their schools, humanize the professions, counterbalance the threat of existentialist philosophies, and ultimately transform Mexico into a more prosperous and independent nation. They were critical of US imperialism in Latin America and shared the sentiments of peaceful coexistence and self-determination of the Bandung and Nigeria conferences. But they never sympathized with the Left and saw little relevance in the conservativism of the Soviet Union.

Love for the university provided an important nexus and forum at UNAM for various Catholic student organizations during the 1950s. With charismatic leaders like Bermeo, the Corporation successfully infiltrated dozens of secular organizations. Independent from the Left, they exposed the corruption of those organizations that received support from the government, and they too saw political activism of these years as a "man's job." In the process, the Corporation created a new generation of leaders who continued their mission as members of the PAN after graduation and persuaded others to exercise their civic duties at the student and national polls. Following the death of Father Mayagoitia and witnessing the end to the most prolific years of their movement during the 1960s, some of them remained active in politics. Others lamented that the more radical environment of the Sixties had put an end to their movement. A small number remained active during this period, but similar to other Catholic movements of the era, they found themselves polarized in the aftermath of Vatican II and the Tlatelolco and Corpus Christi massacres.[107]

For María Vasquez, Luis Sereno, and their Latin American friends, the radicalism of the Sixties that Latin Americanized the MEP represented a unique moment that witnessed the emergence of a distinct spirit of love and despair. As a new generation of young Catholics called for hemispheric solidarity, an unprecedented push for religious pluralism, social action, political tolerance, and revolution defied the hierarchical structure of the church and brought a change in the way this new generation understood their religious "Latin American" identity. They understood this identity, not strictly in relation to the poor and the Third World, but also in accord with the anticolonial, humanist, reformist, and independence movements of the era. In embracing solidarity with the oppressed and emphasizing youth as the "vanguard" of the Sixties revolutions, they called for the "liberation" of the Latin American continent. This was a term that influenced the writings of progressive figures of the church, including Gustavo Gutiérrez, who returned to Peru from Louvain in 1960.

In Lima, the Dominican priest Gustavo Gutiérrez served as a chaplain for the National Union of Catholic Students, and in Montevideo, he spoke at the 1962 Pax Romana Congress, where he called on young people to reform their universities.[108] This event was instrumental in the identity that Catholic university students assumed as the vanguard of the era responsible for solidifying the "Patria Grande." This concept was further celebrated with the creation of the Latin American Secretariat that brought the MIEC and JECI together in Montevideo.

The leaders of the MEP and similar organizations active across the continent with ties to the Latin American Secretariat favorably responded to the radical Catholicism of the era. With the financial support of the German organization Adveniat and the blessing of progressive bishops from Latin America, they positioned themselves as key transnational players. Following the violent repression of the Secretariat in 1971, Catholic students continued their work. Like Sereno, Vasquez, and Merino, they remained critical of armed struggle, and following the attacks that conservatives launched against liberation theology, they increasingly adopted the language of human rights.

The progressive language of Vatican II had a profound impact on the students who joined the MEP. Under the leadership of Luis Sereno Coló, they distanced themselves from the nationalist and conservative approach preferred by the Corporation of Mexican Students, which had seen the apex of its movement in the 1950s. Similar to many of their peers, Luis Sereno and María Vasquez experienced a drastic transformation during the Sixties. They expressed little interest in Christian Democracy, and while they embraced the critical pedagogy of Paulo Freire, they primarily relied on the Revision of Life method of seeing, judging, and acting in their efforts to build continental solidarity. In alliance with Paco Merino, Carlos Urán, and other members of the Secretariat, their Catholicism also manifested in a new understanding of gender, which in the case of Luis Sereno meant a more inclusive notion of masculinity. He saw little need to champion the "virility" of his movement, as the activists of the Corporation had insisted, and instead framed it using a new language of ecumenism, continental solidarity, and love. In addition, he called for a pragmatic dialogue with Marxism, but similar to the leaders of the Corporation, he made little effort to collaborate with leftist students who, for their part, often mistakenly labeled all Catholic students as "reactionary." Instead, in collaboration with his Latin American peers, Sereno agreed with Robert Kennedy in assuming a vanguardist role in continental unity, but he grew critical of the imperialist role of the US government in the region. This critique was shared by María Vasquez, especially in the aftermath of the 1968 Medellín conference, when she adopted the language of human rights. This history is examined in chapter 5, but first it is crucial to see how Catholic journalists and priests responded differently to youth activism and state repression from the 1950s and early 1960s to the aftermath of the Tlatelolco and Corpus Christi massacres.

PART TWO

State Violence,
Progressive Catholicism,
and Radicalization

THREE

Combative Journalism and
Divisions within the Church

The conservative book publisher Jus published one of the earliest and most meticulous accounts of the Corpus Christi massacre, *Operación 10 de junio* (1972).[1] Many of its pages originally appeared in *La Nación: Órgano de Acción Nacional*, in which the author, Gerardo Medina Valdés, wrote his first militant column in 1955. He became director of the magazine in 1962.[2] He held this position as a loyal defender of the PAN until his retirement from the party in the late 1980s. Medina died in 1994 at the age of sixty-nine, with little recognition in the press.[3] The contributions that he made to journalism have also been absent in the scholarship.

This chapter provides an overview of the role Medina and other Catholic figures played in creating a combative journalism in response to student activism and state repression during the 1950s and 1960s. In addition to *La Nación*, it examines the Carlos Septién García School of Journalism and the monthly magazine *Señal*. These spaces have also received little attention from historians, but they were foundational for the expansion of the PAN and for the politicization of the nation's Catholic youth. The chapter touches on the shifting understandings of Christian Democracy that polarized *panistas* (members of the PAN), including a small but decisive group of young men who distanced themselves from their conservative peers, demanded a confrontational stance towards the government, and were critical of the traditional Catholicism of their elders.

With roots in Western Europe in the late nineteenth century, Christian Democracy combined modern democratic ideas with traditional Christian values of justice, order, and respect for hierarchy. In response to secularization, it demanded respect for family values and called for social welfare, recognizing the need for the state to intervene in the economy to defend human dignity from what its leaders saw as the extreme ideologies of the Left and the Right. In their critique of socialism, Christian Democrats defended private property and warned against excessive government intervention in education and social life. In Latin America, they gained significant ground in Chile and Venezuela in the 1930s, while in Mexico they founded the PAN in 1939 under the leadership of Manuel Gómez Morín.[4] Panistas expanded their presence across the nation during the postwar years when a new generation of lay activists and journalists called for more militant measures from their party leaders, making significant changes during the late 1950s and early 1960s.[5]

Among the latter were Gerardo Medina and his friend Horacio Guajardo, who were highly influential but remain largely unknown today. Both men contributed to the success of the Carlos Septién García School of Journalism and were key advocates of Christian Democracy. I contrast the cases of Medina and Guajardo with those of a group of younger writers who published in the monthly *Señal*, among them, Miguel Ángel Granados Chapa and his ultraconservative foe Felipe Coello Macias. These younger journalists, who came from conservative families, wrote extensively on state repression and student rebellion, but they differed from their counterparts in terms of their relationship with the PAN and the figures affiliated with the church. They framed their militant journalism according to their unique understandings of Catholicism, often as an act of love, and in defense of freedom of expression. But it was the younger Granados Chapa who welcomed the progressive reforms of Vatican II and became a vocal critic of ecclesiastical authorities, including those invested in financing ultraconservative student movements, such as Coello Macías's University Movement of Renovated Orientation (MURO). Originating in the state of Puebla in the 1950s, this violent organization was founded by a group of wealthy entrepreneurs at UNAM in 1961–62, largely in response to an increase in Marxist faculty in the nation's schools. But as further evident in the conclusion to this chapter, this group of activists was equally critical of all the manifestations of traditional Catholicism, including Christian Democracy. They described liberal Catholics as pawns of a subversive international attack against the nation.

The conservative movement of the 1950s reached its highest point of success in 1961.[6] In response to the radicalism of the Cuban Revolution and the adoption of the free and mandatory government texts in public and private schools, leaders in the church and the private sector came together under the banner, "Christianity Yes; Communism No!" Their message was delivered in local parishes across the nation and widely published in all conservative newspapers and magazines during the early 1960s. Centrist and ultraconservative ecclesiastical leaders were at the helm of the movement. Sergio Méndez Arceo, bishop of Cuernavaca, and Samuel Ruiz, bishop of San Cristóbal de las Casas, represented the centrist position, and so did the leading advocate of the social teachings of the church and director of the Mexican Social Secretariat, Fr. Pedro Velázquez. All three eventually welcomed the language of Vatican II, and with the exception of Velázquez (who died in 1968), they moved further to the Left in the 1970s. On the opposite and more influential side of the spectrum were the archbishops of Mexico City, Guadalajara, and Puebla—Dario Miranda, José Garibi, and Octavio Márquez Toriz, respectively. During the 1968 student movement these figures, as well as the overwhelming majority of the Mexican church's hierarchy, stood out as key allies of President Gustavo Díaz Ordaz.[7] Somewhere in the middle of these two groups was a new generation of leaders of the PAN and most of the lay journalists discussed in this chapter.

Historians of post-1940 Mexico have taken a new interest in journalism.[8] They have rejected earlier interpretations of a self-censored press under the complete control of the authoritarian government that only achieved some independence in the aftermath of the 1968 student movement.[9] Instead, they have provided telling examples of the role of reporters, photographers, editorialists, crime chroniclers, and cartoonists in criticizing the repression of the government, the shortcomings of its socioeconomic programs, and the corruption of its leaders. By and large, however, these revisionist studies have exclusively emphasized leftist venues and actors, including those who achieved notoriety in the centrist *Siempre!*, in the more radical *Política*, *¿Por Qué?*, and *Sucesos*; in the sensationalist pages of *Alarma*; or in provincial newspapers.[10] With a few exceptions, historians have overlooked conservative spaces where diverse Catholic writers simultaneously engaged in the combative journalism that emerged during the Cold War period.[11]

Surprisingly, this scholarship has expressed little interest in the history of the Carlos Septién García School of Journalism. One of the first of its kind in Latin America, the school quickly evolved into an instrumental space for training Catholic writers and key leaders of the PAN. Similar to other lay organizations, the school found itself polarized between its conservative leaders of the postwar era and those who welcomed a progressive Catholicism in the Sixties.[12]

Carlos Septién García served as the head of the editorial board of *Corporación*, one of the main journals for Catholic students during the 1950s.[13] He was a vocal supporter of the PAN and a central figure responsible for the creation of one of the first schools of journalism in Latin America. In 1953 the school adopted his name, and a year later it supported the creation of the magazine *Señal*. This was an instrumental Catholic platform with national reach that provided key interpretations of the Cold War in Mexico during the 1950s and a decade later gave young writers the opportunity to write on subjects of their choice.

The origins of the School of Journalism date to September 1948, when Catholic Action organized a conference at UNAM in collaboration with a group of intellectuals. The attendees included writers for *La Nación* and journalists from the national dailies *Novedades, Excélsior,* and *El Universal.* Their primary goal was to open a professional space for teaching where students could be introduced to the best theoretical tools necessary to forge a new generation of journalists invested in defending the religious sensibilities of the nation and reaching a broad middle-class audience.[14]

Active members of the PAN were the founding members of the school. They called for the professional practice of journalism as "an effective tool of action" and argued that journalists should be capable of "creating an informed and humane society" without having to fear state censorship.[15] Initially, these journalists included twenty-five students. Sofía del Valle, from the Superior Institute of Feminine Culture, provided the first classrooms in an old colonial house. Within a couple of years, the school moved to a bigger building in San Juan de Letrán, closer to downtown, as the total number of (mostly male) students doubled and continued to increase thereafter.[16]

Carlos Septién García was born in Querétaro in 1915. He wrote his first newspaper columns at the age of twelve. He founded several pamphlets in his teens that relied on humor to mock the liberalism of his teachers, including *El Tiliche, El Chinto,* and *El Escorpión.* As a university student in Mexico City, he directed the much more influential conservative *Proa,* which served as the main newspaper for Catholic students during the 1930s. In 1935 he completed his law degree. But without ever working at a firm, he remained committed to his passion for journalism. By the end of the decade Septién was recognized as one of the most influential Catholic journalists writing in *El Universal* and *Revista de la Semana.*[17] In 1941 he founded *La Nación* and worked as the director of this central magazine of the PAN until 1948; the same year he lent his support to Father Mayagoitia in establishing the Corporation of Mexican Students. Following his death in 1953, the number of students graduating from the School of Journalism continued to grow, and a larger building was again required. Its male authorities remained committed to strengthening their relationship with leading figures of the PAN, Catholic Action, and Jus. Responsible for publishing Medina's *Operación 10 de junio*, Jus was a conservative book publisher founded in 1930 by the leader of the PAN, Manuel Gómez Morín, and managed since the mid-1940s by the more reactionary figure and a sharp critic of Vatican II, Salvador Abascal.[18] During the 1950s Jus published dozens of history books on a broad range of topics that attempted to "rectify" the historical myths championed by the government in its textbooks surrounding, among other topics, the liberalism of Juárez, the radicalism of Cárdenas, and the legacies of the Cristero Rebellion.[19]

The new directors of the School of Journalism included three leading panistas: José N. Chávez González (1953–58); the historian Carlos Alvear Acevedo (1958–63); and the first director of *La Nación*, Alejandro Avilés (1963–84). The first two sympathized with the Center-Right politics of the founding generation of the PAN. Avilés, however, aligned himself with progressive Catholicism and emerged as the central advocate for Christian Democracy. He championed a pluralist approach in the classroom during his tenure and gave greater autonomy to the school by separating it in 1966 from its dependent relationship with Catholic Action. All three men emphasized "the social responsibility" of the journalist as a key ethical tool in building a democratic society. They asked students to avoid dogmatic and religious language and instead prioritize critical and precise reportage. In 1976 the secretary of public education officially recognized the bachelor degrees given by the school. By then only a few of its students pointed to Catholicism as a defining characteristic in their writings.[20]

"A Respectable Magazine for the Mexican Home"

The first students who graduated from the School of Journalism played a crucial role in creating *Señal*. Alejandro Avilés founded the magazine in July 1954, as a "respectable magazine for the Mexican home," meaning that it addressed the social concerns of the nation from the perspective of people of faith. Initially, most of its writers were invested in politicizing their readers in the urban context of modern Mexico, encouraging them to support the PAN, and providing them with practical advice for defending the nuclear family, mostly from the social and political threats that had emerged from rapid urbanization, divorce, juvenile delinquency, labor militancy, economic insecurity, capitalist exploitation, and communism.[21]

Following the Cuban Revolution, *Señal* promoted the social responsibility of Christians and encouraged its readers to embrace solidarity with peasants and the working class.[22] Yet it also adopted anticommunist rhetoric that at times minimized the significant role that its writers had played in highlighting those who had been left out of the economic growth of the 1950s and who had been disenfranchised by the governing elite. As the historian Laura Pérez Rosales has argued, *Señal* published hundreds of pages debating the consequences and particularities of the Cold War, ultimately concluding that capitalism represented the lesser of two evils.[23] Between 1960 and 1961 the magazine promoted the most important campaigns launched by conservative actors and the church, the "Christianity, Yes; Communism, No!" movement, and the protest that emerged in opposition to the National Commission of Free Textbooks. The commission established a unified system of free but required textbooks to all children enrolled in secular and private schools. While Catholics did not oppose the government investment in education and welcomed the institutions created during the López Mateos administration (1959–64), they adamantly opposed the adoption of the new books in private schools. As documented in numerous articles in *Señal*, these textbooks prioritized the official history of the Mexican Revolution and undermined the role of the individual. Moreover, they gave priority to a materialistic pedagogy that sympathized with communism while failing to include the values of "honesty, love, and veracity" in the education of "our children."[24] The greater threat of socialism and the attempt to homogenize education had the potential to undermine all forms of liberty at the expense of the individual and place all the resources and institutions of the nation in the hands of the state.

Gerardo Medina at *La Nación* and Horacio Guajardo at *Señal* highlighted the threat of socialism to individual liberties, albeit differently. Both encouraged workers to carry the flag of a "third" alternative path in the name of social justice, one that rejected the atheism of communism, on the one hand, and one that exposed the abuses of capitalism, on the other. They also placed great emphasis on political corruption and state repression.

Known to some of his friends as "the petard," Gerardo Medina built a reputation as one of the most combative journalists and sharpest critics of the government during the 1950s and early 1960s. His former classmate at the School of Journalism and future novelist Vicente Leñero once sneeringly described him as a talented poet and an "intelligent *cabrón* [hard-ass]" whose defiant prose and confrontational attitude were likely driven by the alleged inferiority complex he had from his working-class background and from his dark skin color. For its part, the intelligence services referred to Medina as a "meticulous" journalist with "irrefutable professional training." Others remembered him as a "hard-core supporter of the PAN" and a "relentless critic of the most egregious crimes committed by the state who refused to receive a single penny from the government." As an investigative reporter for *La Nación*, he was "feared and admired."[25]

La Nación published its first issue on October 18, 1941. Originally conceived as an "influential space of reflection," the weekly promptly developed into a recruiting tool for the PAN. Its intended audience was mostly middle-class and overwhelmingly Catholic readers. The goal was to provide them with a "weekly synthesis" of the most pressing problems affecting them and the nation.

Carlos Septién García served as the first director of *La Nación*, and its original contributors included conservative intellectuals and former writers for the *Boletín de Acción Nacional*, a pamphlet that was shut down by President Lázaro Cárdenas in 1940. Gómez Morín hoped that *La Nación* would play an important role in preventing such censorship from happening again while maintaining its commitment to being a service to the nation.[26] For this, it had to preserve a delicate balance between promoting the social doctrine of Catholicism and finding a space to criticize the corruption and violence of the state without jeopardizing its improved relationship with the church. In 1949 these goals materialized in the establishment of the Carlos Septién García School of Journalism. With the death of its first director that year, the new executives included Alejandro Avilés (1953–62) and Gerardo Medina (1962–89). Both recruited graduates from the school, and both welcomed the more militant reporting that emerged in the 1950s.

Medina was born in 1925 and grew up near a mining community in Hidalgo, Mexico. He had a reputation for being a quick learner and hot-tempered in his youth, and he was an avid reader of Mexican history and poetry. As a trained welder, he became sympathetic to the social doctrine of the church but expressed no interest in defending its moral teaching. Instead, he spoke openly about his political identity, his affiliation with the PAN, and his interest in labor activism. His life drastically changed in 1953 when he enrolled at the School of Journalism and was soon recognized as one of the most combative panistas of his generation.[27]

As a student, Medina routinely questioned his professors and sought his own writing style. *La Nación* gave him his first break in 1955, when Avilés hired him as a galley editor. A year later he published his first extensive report, in which he documented the student strikes at the National Polytechnic Institute and the Teacher's College. Akin to the anticommunist tone that characterized the magazine since its foundation in 1941, Medina described students as "naive" and lamented that old leaders of the Communist Party had used them as "cannon fodder."[28] Yet, as he continued to cover the most important social and political uprisings that erupted across Mexico during this period, his focus shifted, and he placed greater emphasis on state repression. This emphasis coincided with the 1956 election of Alfonso Ituarte Servín as national president of the PAN, a position he held until 1959. During Ituarte's tenure, the party adopted a combative stance toward the government, which became especially heated during the presidential elections of 1958, when a massive wave of labor uprisings swept the streets of Mexico City and a young generation of panistas demanded a more confrontational approach in defense of the conservative presidential candidate, Luis H. Álvarez.[29]

Unlike other Catholic journalists, Medina did not make the Cuban Revolution the central point of contention. Instead, he identified rural *caciques* (local bosses), *granaderos* (riot police), *charros* (union gangsters), greedy entrepreneurs, promoters of the law of social dissolution, shock brigades that infringed on the autonomy of the universities, and undemocratic *priístas* (members of the PRI) as the real enemies of the nation and as by-products of "presidentialism." His reports on state repression and official corruption were always combative and thorough. They vividly captured the language and disgruntlement of the popular classes and appealed to the social and political concerns of a growing Catholic middle class. Moreover, his investigative columns paid little attention to the unwritten rules of journalism by often pointing to the national figure of the president as ultimately responsible for the imprisonment and beatings of opposition leftist and conservative activists. Similarly, his tone criticizing state repression and electoral fraud was explosive, biting, sarcastic, ironic, and often

FIGURE 4. Police repression at the hands of the *granaderos*. From *La Nación* (September 14, 1958).

poetic, while the gripping images accompanying his reports taken by teams of photographers left no room for ambiguity.[30] Like Medina, the photographers for *La Nación* depicted the military and the police as mostly responsible for suppressing democracy in Mexico and especially took aim at the ill-trained granaderos (fig. 4).[31] Founded in 1950, the riot police violently repressed the students, teachers, and railroad workers' strikes that exploded between 1956 and 1961.[32]

For Medina it was the brutality of the government during the labor uprisings of 1958 and 1959 that largely shaped his career as a belligerent journalist and a sympathizer of Christian Democracy. Often invoking a broader look at state repression in Latin America, he refused to see Mexico as a democratic exception in the region and instead insisted that it all too often behaved like a military dictatorship. This argument was also made explicitly

FIGURE 5. "[Is this] Argentina or Mexico?" From *La Nación* (April 8, 1962).

in numerous cover pages of *La Nación*, including its 1962 issue in which Medina asked, "[Were these photographs taken] in Argentina [where President Arturo Frondizi bent to the military's wishes to break the relationship with socialist Cuba and crack down on Peronist leftists at home] or in Mexico [where President López Mateos pushed his government to the left—within the constitution]?" (Fig. 5.)

Between Liberty and Oppression

Gerardo Medina supported the political ambitions of other Catholic journalists who shared his concerns, including Horacio Guajardo Elizondo, a teacher at the School of Journalism and a regular contributor to the Catholic monthly *Señal.* The same age as Medina, Guajardo met two people who were instrumental in his first opportunities in journalism, Father Mayagoitia and Carlos Septién García, the columnist for *El Universal.* The former invited him to join the editorial team of *Corporación* and *Reforma Universitaria,* and the latter encouraged him to teach at the School of Journalism.[33]

The opinion pieces published by Guajardo in *Señal* beginning in 1957 were not as combative as those of Medina in *La Nación,* but they were equally critical of what he saw as the exploitation of capitalism and the abuses of communism. For both, the fight was between liberty and oppression. Yet, more than his friend, Guajardo remained invested in promoting Christian Democracy. In 1960, he hosted Emilio Máspero's visit to Mexico. Originally from Argentina, Máspero was general secretary of the Latin American Confederation of Christian Syndicates and a renowned educator who played an important role in strengthening the rise of trade unions as a social force across the region. With Máspero's support, Guajardo traveled to West Germany, where he enrolled in intensive courses on Christian Democracy.[34] On his return to Mexico, he served as first president of the Mexican Institute of Social Studies for one year and provided guidance to a youth wing of the PAN, which demanded greater action from the party and rejected its efforts to collaborate with the central government.[35] These young panistas were radicalized during the 1958 presidential election and remained politically active throughout the 1960s. They published key studies on a wide range of issues related to social justice, reproductive politics, and economic development.[36]

Medina and Guajardo championed the creation of the Authentic Workers' Front in 1960 in their respective publications. Within two years, the Front had transformed into the nation's only truly independent labor union.[37] By then, the PAN had named Medina director of *La Nación* (a title he held until 1989). He toned down his sympathetic views on Christian Democracy, but he remained committed to his combative journalism. From 1961 to 1967, he provided names of the victims killed, beaten, and harassed in the student uprisings at the hands of the government in Chilpancingo (1961, 1962), Puebla (1961, 1964, 1966), Veracruz (1963), Mexico City (1964, 1966), Morelia (1966), and Sinaloa (1967). All of these atrocities were key antecedents to the Tlatelolco massacre and involved the use of the military.

But as Medina remained a thorn in the side of the PRI (and a harsh critic of both the radical Left and the ultraconservative Right), he was also forced to support his superior, Adolfo Christlieb Ibarrola.[38] As director of the PAN from 1962 to 1968, Christlieb Ibarrola marginalized the younger generation of panistas who had demanded greater action from their elders. But more tellingly, he adopted a collaborative relationship with the presidential administration of Díaz Ordaz.[39] Guajardo independently disapproved of this relationship but published very little to publicly condemn it. Instead, he remained involved in strengthening Christian Democracy. In his columns, he reported on the local abuses of power in schools, factories, and campesino leagues.[40] A younger generation of journalists writing for *Señal* would take a more radical approach and, instead of Christian Democracy, would find greater relevance in the language of Vatican II.

"YOUTH SPEAKS"

Señal created a new editorial section titled "Youth Speaks" in 1960. Its goals were to attract young readers to the magazine, provide them with a space for expressing their views, and engage in dialogue with them. These aspirations evolved as a response to the internal divisions that polarized panistas. The authors, ranging from progressives to moderates and ultraconservatives, grew critical of the complacent politics of the party and called for "greater action" from their leaders.[41]

The themes addressed in their columns varied in content and style, but they were all meant to provide the perspective of youth. In common, they presented a notion of masculinity that paralleled the one championed by the Corporation of Mexican Students.[42] According to the writers, Mexico was experiencing a transitional moment of crisis defined by social turmoil and political instability, coupled with the lack of spiritual leadership that required young men to be at the vanguard of change. Each argued similarly that "youth could not afford to remain indifferent." For some, the commitment had to be rooted in "love" and "dignity." For others, it was overt "political action" that should be given the highest priority. While some opposed the tacit relationship of the PAN with the government, others demanded a concrete affiliation with the Christian Democratic movements in Europe and South America. For nearly all of them, it was necessary to bring greater democracy to Mexico and transform the universities into hubs of significant change. In this fight, young women played an important but secondary role, mostly in relation to moral and social campaigns.

Above all, it was the "virile power" of youth that determined the success of their respective movements, they all argued. "We don't want" a "frivolous," "coward[ly]," or "indolent Catholicism," they wrote. "The time had arrived" to decide whether "we stand with or against Christ." "We must fight against all forms of injustices," some explained, "whether these originate from a communist or a capitalist [system]." "Today we stand up in solidarity with the oppressed, the politically disenfranchised, and the exploited," many of them similarly noted. "In the face of fear mongering and the politics of hate," others insisted, "we must embrace progress and the spirit of faith and love." In agreement, nearly all of them implied that "we can no longer allow [our leaders] to provide us with charity in the name of justice." "We are far from having a government [that is truly] responsive to the needs and aspirations of the people," they all argued. "The time has come to realize that Heaven is conquered here on earth," one writer noted. Others insisted, "We must achieve a true sense of justice," making sure that "the worker is provided with a dignified salary," "the entrepreneur sees his profit in relation to the well-being of his employees," "the teacher does not use the space of the classroom to indoctrinate our peers with foreign ideas," and the "Imperialist nation no longer plunders the colonized world." But to achieve success, they all agreed, "we must develop a profound understanding of our religion," making sure that "our collective fight is always rooted in our faith [and in] the [particularities] of our nation." "We are ready for the challenge," they concluded. "After all, equality, respect for the other, and the fights for liberty and against oppression are already embedded in our faith." "We have no option but to join the fray in defense of the nation."[43]

Collectively, the writers pointed to four central problems they saw facing the nation at the beginning of the 1960s: (1) the lack of freedom of expression that made the opening of Catholic spaces a priority; (2) the absence of religious liberty specifically evident in schools and textbooks; (3) the authoritarianism of the PRI; and (4) the timid attitude of religious leaders, invested more in defending the hierarchical structure of the church and less in the socioeconomic needs of its people. In overcoming these challenges, they concluded, "the fire of Christ cannot be reduced to diminutive bonfires."[44]

Despite their shared sense of urgency, the young writers for *Señal* did not follow a unilateral path. Some embraced the progressive Catholicism of Vatican II and eventually welcomed the liberalization of women at the end of the decade.[45] Others remained committed to Catholic Action, welcomed Christian Democracy in Mexico, or eventually sided with the progressive wing of the governing party.[46] Yet others moved to the Far Right. This was the case of Felipe Coello Macías, whose ultraconservative movement emerged as a violent response not only to less conservative Catholic journalists who expressed sympathetic views with various social movements, like Medina, but also to those on the Far Right who became critical of the pope and accused him of leading a "Jewish conspiracy" against Mexico after Vatican II.[47] In this sense, *Señal* embodied the multiple expressions of Catholicism that polarized activists of faith throughout the Sixties in Mexico and abroad. The most extreme interpretations of Catholicism were those championed by Felipe Coello Macias's violent MURO.

Fists and the Truth

Born in Tuxtla Gutiérrez, Chiapas, in 1942, Felipe Coello completed his education in Catholic schools in the conservative city of Puebla. In 1955 he stood out as one of the mythical "twelve apostles" responsible for creating the University Anticommunist Front. This was a violent Catholic movement responsible for strengthening the presence of ultraconservative professors and students at the University of Puebla throughout the 1950s and 1960s. In 1958 Coello moved to Mexico City and enrolled at UNAM's National School of Economics, where he excelled as an extraordinarily gifted student. He befriended other anticommunist students who shared similar views. Like them, he grew critical of the "passive" attitudes of Catholic students, and with some of them, he joined the massive demonstration that took place at the Basilica of Guadalupe on May 15, 1961, in favor of the "Christianity Yes; Communism No!" campaign. With others he published op-eds in small university tabloids, where Coello accused Spanish professors who had arrived in Mexico in the 1930s of indoctrinating students with Marxist texts.[48]

His columns caught the attention of *Señal*, and Coello was invited to publish a small piece in it in February 1962. He encouraged his readers to rise in defense of Cuba, "our sister country" that had been "terrorized" and "drowned with the blood" of its people. Like others of his generation, he saw Cuba in the broader context of Latin America, writing, "We must defend our Western tradition" across the continent and "stand together" in the name of our shared "Catholic faith." He further wrote, "Those who fail to join this struggle will be considered deserters [and traitors to] our love for liberty." A month later, Coello emerged as one of the "illuminating founders" and first president of MURO, the most influential and violent right-wing student organization of the 1960s, which attracted some members of the Corporation of Mexican Students who became critical of Father Mayagoitia and his less combative approach.[49]

Muristas (MURO members) were largely responsible for harassing students and professors who did not share their values. Specifically, they "adopted a dual strategy for accomplishing their goals: the battle was to be waged not only '*a puños*' [with fists] in the schools but also through the new journalistic and cultural spaces of contestation." In this two-pronged effort, the tabloid *Puño* played a particularly important role from 1962 to 1969.[50]

Muristas achieved their greatest victory in 1966 when they successfully forced the rector of UNAM and vocal critic of President Díaz Ordaz, Ignacio Chávez, to resign. But in their broad understanding of the Left, they also included moderate Catholics, reformist members of the Corporation of Mexican Students, and young panistas who sympathized with Christian Democracy. In its September–October 1964 issue, for example, *Puño* identified the Catholic magazine *Crucero* as one of their enemies and encouraged readers to take their battle to its journalists, namely, its "vaudeville" and "pothead" writers who made up "sensationalist lies" about their movement. The reference to marihuana alluded to the war MURO simultaneously launched against the counterculture.[51] In particular, the conservative writers accused the journalist Miguel Ángel Granados Chapa of writing a "fictitious account" of MURO, without revealing his identity as the author. In the chauvinistic language of the Sixties, muristas concluded that he was a "feminine coward" who needed to be taught a lesson.

In May 1965, a group of muristas kidnapped Granados Chapa. They beat him and threatened him not to publish any more columns denouncing their activities. On his release, however, Granados Chapa wrote additional and more revealing articles exposing in greater detail the violent nature not only of MURO but also of various paramilitary groups composed of pseudo-students sponsored by the government who terrorized the schools, first in *Crucero* and then in *Señal.* By the early 1970s Granados Chapa had been recognized as one of the most trusted investigative reporters of his generation. For his part, Felipe Coello broke ties with MURO in the aftermath of the 1968 student movement. In the early 1970s he reemerged as a director of the daily *Heraldo* in Monterrey, in which he launched new campaigns against the "socialist" Luis Echeverría (1970–76).

GRANADOS CHAPA AND DEMOCRATIC SOCIALISM

Señal witnessed significant changes during the mid-Sixties. While most of its writers remained committed to the anticommunism of an earlier era, others, like Miguel Ángel Granados Chapa, instead aligned themselves with "the signs of the times." Coined by Vatican II, the phrase called on the church and its followers to listen to and learn from the world around them. In the numerous obituaries written after his death in 2011, Granados Chapa was remembered by friends and scholars "as the nation's most influential teacher of investigative journalism." They stressed his important role in the creation of the three most influential publications of the nonmilitant Left: *Proceso* (1976), *Unomásuno* (1977), and *La Jornada* (1984). Yet few remembered the columns he wrote for *Señal* between 1968 and 1972 in the midst of the Tlatelolco and Corpus Christi massacres. These were two events that changed his views on state repression. His columns point to an attitude shared by a rising generation of Catholics who expressed no interest in the ideas of the PAN or in Mayagoitia's Corporation of Mexican Students and instead opted for an independent path of political engagement.

Like Medina, Granados Chapa was born in Hidalgo, in the small town of Mineral del Monte, in 1941. Yet unlike the director of *La Nación*, the younger journalist broke ties with the PAN right away. He became critical of all political parties and rejected the ultraconservative Catholic movements that sparked in direct response to the "Christianity Yes; Communism No!" national campaign. He saw journalism as the most reliable space to create the substantial political change that the nation needed to be truly democratic. In this effort, he first looked for inspiration to Christian Democracy. But over time, he found greater relevance in his own version of democratic socialism, which rejected the orthodoxy of Marxism and selectively borrowed from the progressive Catholicism of the era to demand collective control of the economy alongside an inclusive political system of government.

At a young age, Granados Chapa expressed interest in journalism and politics. In his teens he joined the Catholic Association of Mexican Youth. This was a loyal institution of Catholic Action that in the 1930s and 1940s had played a crucial role rejecting the policies of Lázaro Cárdenas but lost many of its members to more progressive organizations in the Sixties, such as the Movement of Professional Students.[52] After graduating from high school, he was admitted to the Carlos Septién School of Journalism, but instead he enrolled in the National School of Political Science at UNAM. There he broke ties with Catholic Action, received a dual degree in journalism and history, and rubbed shoulders with the ultraconservative Felipe Coello Macías. Of the same age, they both wrote for the conservative *Brecha Universitaria*. As many contributors to this student newspaper wrote for

Puño, however, Granados Chapa evolved into a rising critic of student violence and a vocal sympathizer of Christian Democracy, first, and democratic socialism, later. In this transition, he joined the Authentic University Party. This was one of the dozens of small groups that competed for control of the university and introduced students to the writings of Christian Democrats from Chile, Venezuela, Germany, and Italy.[53] At UNAM, he also met two figures who played a profound role in his changing view of the world: the Dominican friar Tomás Alláz and his professor of political science, Horacio Guajardo. Father Alláz introduced him to the radical tradition of labor priests in France, where he had studied in the late 1950s; and on his return to Mexico in the Sixties, he participated in founding the University Cultural Center at UNAM.[54] Guajardo invited him to collaborate with *Señal* and put him in touch with a journalist at *Excélsior* and *La Prensa*, Manuel Buendía.

Once interested in becoming a priest, Manuel Buendía had begun his career in journalism in the 1940s as a supporter of the PAN in *La Nación*. But like his mentee Granados Chapa and their mutual friend Guajardo, he grew disillusioned with the conservative opposition. Like other Catholics of his generation, he also taught at the Carlos Septién School of Journalism, and in 1964, he founded *Crucero*. It was in this magazine where Granados Chapa first collaborated with the Catholic novelist Vicente Leñero and where the young Miguel Ángel quickly emerged as an influential writer.[55]

Within a few years, Granados Chapa had adopted many of the same traits that had made the journalism of Buendía so widely respected, even by his harshest critics: succinct and clear prose backed up by extensive and meticulous research. With the support of Buendía, Granados Chapa also wrote for the national newspaper *Excélsior*. A year later, he reconnected with Horacio Guajardo as he started publishing regular columns in *Señal*, where he remained a strong critic of MURO and a scrupulous investigative reporter on a variety of themes related to student activism. In his columns he exposed the government and ecclesiastical authorities who undermined the autonomy of the National University in Mexico City, where he taught political science for more than twenty years, starting in 1965.

Granados Chapa published several articles in *Señal* between 1968 and 1972. Meant to attract a young readership to the magazine, these articles did not share the explosive prose that characterized Medina's columns. But like Medina, Granados Chapa made it a priority to expose the authoritarianism of the government, its role in undermining democracy, and its failure to provide economic justice to the masses. Moreover, instead of relying on sensationalist and sarcastic language that made the more popular columns of Medina so effective, Granados Chapa adopted an academic yet clear tone, free of unnecessary jargon and rich in detail. Many of his investigative columns included citations ranging from political speeches, newspaper reports, and literary texts to encyclicals, political manifestos, and historical documents.[56]

But it was the infringement of the autonomous status of the university and the repression of students that mostly concerned Granados Chapa. His first column published on these topics appeared in February 1968, "Tensions in the University." He lamented that the university had done little to resolve the political fractures that had resulted in the violent overthrow of the rector Ignacio Chávez in 1966. The coup involved members of MURO, as well as shock brigades financed by the governor of Sinaloa, Leopoldo Sánchez Celis (1963–68). A key supporter of Díaz Ordaz, Sánchez had also brutally crushed student activists in northern Mexico. Granados Chapa warned his readers that unless the authorities provided an inclusive space for unity and debate that welcomed divergent points of view, the year 1968 was destined to bring greater and more violent tensions inside the universities and a repressive response on the part of the government.[57] What institutions of higher education needed was the implementation of a truly democratic process that valued the autonomous principles of the university. This included shared power among students, researchers, professors, and staff in all of the most important financial and political decisions of the schools and a university that favored a truly humanistic pedagogy that attended to the historical needs of the nation without ignoring its modern ambitions. Similarly, he lamented that working-class students from the National Polytechnic Institute did not receive a well-rounded education that examined the structural and historical problems of poverty and underdevelopment and instead prioritized "foreign solutions" that paid little attention to the particularities of the nation.[58]

The forging of a new consciousness attentive to the most prominent social problems of the country and dialectical pedagogy in the classrooms were crucial to achieving democracy, and so was attention to love in the forms of dialogue, unity, social justice, and human dignity. These aspirations were present during the 1968 student movement, Granados Chapa argued, but so was the re-creation of the same hierarchical structures of power that activists were rejecting, namely, the priority that the loudest voices of the movement unfortunately gave to a handful of leaders. For him, it was the autonomous and nonviolent brigades that instead epitomized the most promising structures of the movement, not a handful of leaders representing the National

Strike Council. In the broader context of the Sixties, he also lamented that students had been strictly trained in aspiring to personal profit and individual political ambitions without understanding their mutual relationship with society. It was precisely this detachment from the popular sectors of society and unwillingness to reject the reestablishing of vertical structures of power, he concluded, that prevented some of the students from seeing revolutionary potential of their movement.[59]

Granados Chapa saw the undemocratic nature of the university as a microcosm of a nation in despair that lacked accountability of its corrupt leaders and that all too readily relied on violence and intimidation to govern its people. In providing one of the earliest and most thorough historical accounts of the phenomenon of *porrismo* (the use of agents provocateurs, *porros*, in schools), for example, he lamented that competing politicians had always taken advantage of educational institutions for their personal ambitions, but he argued that significant changes had taken place in the late Sixties that transformed the university into a particularly violent environment. He pointed to the administration of Echeverría as mostly responsible for these changes and detailed the role that new paramilitary groups composed of thugs for hire and agents provocateurs played in harassing student activists, intimidating school authorities, and introducing drug trafficking in schools, not only in Mexico City, but across the nation. Yet students were not entirely innocent, he lamented, as they too often readily saw violence as a viable strategy. He saw this as counterproductive, but noted that their violence paled in comparison to that employed by the government.[60]

What Mexico needed, Granados Chapa concluded in *Señal*, was what he called "democratic socialism." He saw the progressive Catholicism of the Sixties as compatible with his vision of the future. In making this argument, he expressed no interest in the traditional language employed by many of his peers. Instead, he pointed to the conclusions of progressive bishops in Medellín during the Second Episcopal Conference of Latin America, including the urgent need to focus on the most oppressed sectors of society and their collective empowerment from below. He encouraged his readers to endorse the preferential option for the poor by rejecting individual notions of progress and property in favor of what he called "public, communitarian, and collective" alternatives, based on horizontal notions of collaboration and democratic political engagement. The priority, he explained, should be the creation of grassroots movements and base communities and not state monopolies, large bureaucratic institutions, or Catholic corporations that welcomed excessive power in the hands of a hierarchical structure, as Marxists, populists, and traditional Catholics preferred.[61]

Granados Chapa ended his professional relationship with *Señal* in 1972. That same year, the magazine ceased to be a relevant source for progressive Catholics as conservative leaders of the church removed defiant priests from other publications that similarly condemned state repression, including Fr. Enrique Maza at the Jesuit magazine, *Christus.* Along with Buendía, Granados Chapa turned to the daily *Excélsior,* the most influential national newspaper, which was under the leadership of Father Maza's cousin Julio Scherer García, where nearly all leftist intellectuals, progressive leaders of the church, and journalists claimed their alliance or disaffiliation with the state. President Echeverría initially welcomed the defiant journalism published in *Excélsior.* But as has been well documented in the scholarship, his democratic opening reached a limit in 1976. The president ousted Scherer García and put a less talented director in charge. An influential group of Catholics, composed of Miguel Ángel Granados Chapa, Vicente Leñero, and Fr. Enrique Maza, joined Scherer García. Together they founded *Proceso,* which proved to be much more radical than *Excélsior* and in whose pages they continued to be critical of the government and state repression.

CONCLUSION

The publisher Ser released *La cruz: ¿Un ariete subversivo?* in 1970. This was the same ephemeral printing house that launched the ultraconservative Red Books series during the Sixties. A few months later, it released *La secta socialista,* in which the author, Salvador Abascal, pointed to many of the journalists for *Señal* and the founders of the Carlos Septién School of Journalism as the central enemies of the Mexican church, primarily because of the public presence they established in their journalism.

Like Felipe Coello, the author of *La cruz,* Federico Mügemburg Rodríguez, was a key supporter of MURO who similarly described the 1968 student movement as a seditious event that terrorized the streets of Mexico City. According to him, the students had disrespected the Catholic sensibilities of the nation and insulted the revered figure of the president with the ultimate goal of destroying the social and political institutions of the country. But in his description of the "belligerent" events that characterized the student movement, the year 1968 also marked the zenith of Christian Democracy in

Mexico. He argued that Christian Democrats had failed in Mexico because they lacked original thinkers. Instead, they had "plagiarized" the ideas of "brighter intellectuals" from Europe, especially those of the Belgian Jesuit Roger Vekemans, as evident in the repeated references in their writing to "marginality," "integration," "popular promotion," "structural changes," and "revolutionary praxis."[62] Specifically, Mügemburg described the national representatives as "counterfeit dupes" and pointed to their involvement in the 1968 student movement as the ultimate proof that Christian Democrats were ultimately invested in destroying the nation.

Mügemburg provided an ultraconservative, yet largely accurate account of the rise, failure, and limitations of Christian Democracy in Mexico.[63] He traced the origins of the movement to the late 1950s, when a young generation of panistas broke ties with their elders by more aggressively combating election fraud, corruption, censorship, and government repression in the local municipalities of the northern states of Chihuahua, Durango, and Coahuila. Similarly, he also pointed to the aftermath of the Tlatelolco massacre as the moment that brought an end to the little that remained of the Christian Democratic "experiment," when many of his contemporaries joined diverse political parties and became critical of the leaders of the church. Others questioned their Catholicism, became sympathetic to armed struggle, or looked for alternative paths in innovative grassroots movements. Overall, Mügemburg portrayed the history of Christian Democracy as one mostly composed of failures, which fell short in establishing lasting political institutions due to the robust relationship between government and religious authorities but which experienced significant victories in the field of journalism, especially in the lasting spaces created by the Carlos Septién School of Journalism and in the widely read pages of *La Nación* and *Señal*.

In *La Nación*, Gerardo Medina devoted little space to condemning the violence of the Far Right and instead saw the demagoguery and populist policies of the PRI as particularly detrimental to Mexico. He described the PAN as the only political authority with the moral license to criticize the corruption, brutality, fraud, and contradictions of the state. Granados Chapa differed from Medina in *Señal*. The younger writer expressed a sympathetic view of the Left and said little in favor of the conservative opposition. Nonetheless, for both writers, a resilient and uncensored form of journalism was crucial to transforming Mexico into a democratic nation. In making their respective arguments, Medina and Granados Chapa capitalized on the success of the School of Journalism. It emerged as a seminal space in the early

1950s precisely as an effort to provide a new generation of Catholics with the necessary tools to contest what its founders from Catholic Action and the PAN saw as the monopolistic power of the PRI government. While their elders grew equally apprehensive about the orthodoxy of Marxism and the abuses of capitalism, younger journalists like Granados Chapa found inspiration in the more progressive Catholicism of the Sixties.

But the "updating to the signs of the times" also marked the beginning of the end of an era. For *Señal*, the reformist language of Vatican II undermined the influence it had enjoyed during the 1950s. The decade pointed to a new anticommunist era that simultaneously saw the need to defend the nation from the "social ills" that allegedly came with modernity. The new and heterogeneous generation of writers rejected older notions of charity. They called for greater political action from conservative institutions and criticized the older leaders of the PAN. *La Nación* also experienced substantial changes during this period. From 1956 to 1959, the magazine published its most combative columns highlighting with photographic detail the repression of workers, campesinos, and students at the hands of the government and its ill-trained and corrupt police forces. This defiant journalism continued in the 1960s and was particularly evident during the 1968 student movement. For the most part, however, the writers for *La Nación* followed the more centrist position of the leader of the PAN, Adolfo Christlieb Ibarrola. They found it necessary to tone down the militancy of the conservative party. Instead, they favored a constructive opposition capable of strengthening lasting relationships with key institutions, including those in the government willing to cooperate with the goals of the PAN. Partly influenced by the progressive Catholicism of the Sixties but restrained by the legacy of the "Christianity Yes; Communism No!" movement, Christlieb Ibarrola called for greater "dialogue" and political flexibility with the PRI.[64] This reformism brought new internal disputes within the rank and file of the PAN and pushed many of its members to return to their militant rhetoric, including Medina, who published some of the most compelling columns condemning the 1968 and 1971 student massacres, as described in the next chapter.

The internal disputes that divided members of the PAN during the 1960s also polarized the new generation of writers who published in *Señal*. From a youthful perspective, they interpreted the Cold War primarily as a fight between the aspiring love for liberty and the frustrating consequences of oppression and despair. In this tension, some expressed a willingness to embrace the Left or saw relevance in the language of Christian Democracy. Others, like Felipe Coello and Federico Mügemburg, instead took an ultraconservative path, transforming MURO into a key and violent player of the Sixties. Many supported Díaz Ordaz and described the Tlatelolco massacre as a tragic but consequential event that ultimately saved the country from the external threat of communism.[65] But those who welcomed the progressive Catholicism of the time were also profoundly influenced by state repression, including a group of radical priests and Catholic intellectuals who strongly condemned the government of the PRI in the aftermath of the Tlatelolco and Corpus Christi massacres.

FOUR

Responses to the Tlatelolco
and Corpus Christi Massacres

A young boy stood patiently inside the Franciscan Church of Santiago Tlatelolco in Mexico City on October 2, 1968. He was waiting for the celebration of a wedding, scheduled for that gloomy evening. His family had arrived early to welcome those attending the ceremony. But as his parents greeted the guests, a group of young men dressed in civilian clothes and wearing white gloves on their left hands swarmed into the church while a growing number of people gathered outside in the Plaza of Tlatelolco to listen to the leaders of the student movement. Physically fit and sporting military haircuts, the infiltrators violently interrupted the wedding. A group of them stood at the main entrance, preventing more people from entering the church. A second group made its way to the upper floor, where members of the choir had started to rehearse for the ceremony. Both groups, composed of no more than three dozen young men, took over the rest of the church, guarding the remaining doors and making sure that no one entered or exited.

Shouts, helicopters, and multiple rounds of gunfire were heard through the windows minutes later. Panic followed outside the church as heavy rain flooded sections of the Plaza. Students ran for their lives as the gunfire intensified. It came from snipers located on the roofs of the church and surrounding buildings. Inside the church, the young men gave orders to all of those present to lay on the floor and stay quiet. In terror, the priest called for calm. Fearing that people would get hurt, he encouraged everyone to remain composed and obey their captors' orders.

A different, smaller group of men also wearing civilian clothes entered the church. They were carrying rifles and cameras as they made their way to the roof of the building, where they filmed and opened fire on the crowd of students attempting to escape the Plaza. An imposing man dressed in a military uniform entered the church and told everyone that if they listened to his words carefully, no one would get hurt. The people complied, while wounded students were brought inside the church to be interrogated by unidentified officers. Once the shooting ceased and mayhem turned to chilling silence after midnight, the groom, his bride, and the guests were ordered to get on a military bus, which eventually dropped everyone off in Naucalpan, in the state of Mexico. As all the captive passengers got off the bus, the anonymous military officer allegedly advised everyone who had been present in the church, "We know who each of you are," and "Do not tell anyone what you have witnessed tonight."[1]

In the scholarship written on the 1968 student movement it is not clear if the Franciscan priest scheduled to officiate the wedding ceremony on that violent day was one of the people forced to get on the bus and also threatened by the military officer to remain quiet. It is also unknown who he was or what his position was in relation to the new voices that emerged in that Mexican church in the aftermath of Vatican II and especially in the context of the Second Episcopal Conference of Latin America held in 1968 in Medellín, Colombia. This is where progressive priests embraced the preferential option for the poor and concluded that the developmentalist projects of the imperialist North had only intensified dependency and exploitation in the Global South.

For many leading voices of the 1968 movement, "the damn priest," as a student activist once called him, simply represented the worst and most conservative face of the Catholic Church and its failure to condemn the Tlatelolco massacre. A young man who witnessed a group of students knocking on the door of the church claimed years later, "The unwillingness on the part of the priest to provide shelter to students escaping the violence marked the moment when I lost faith in my religion. I never went back to church after that day." According to this widespread interpretation, the anonymous Franciscan priest not only "refused" to open the doors of the church to give shelter to those running for their lives on October 2, but, worse yet, he also collaborated with the government of Gustavo Díaz Ordaz by providing the necessary space where a number of students were interrogated and some were subsequently disappeared.[2] Similar interpretations were shared by two of the most important intellectuals of the Sixties, Elena Poniatowska and Carlos Fuentes. While Poniatowska accused the priest of failing to "even spare half an hour to pray for the dead" in the years following the massacre, Fuentes specifically accused the archbishop of Mexico, Miguel Darío Miranda, of siding with the government. He noted, "Bodies piled up by the church door that did not open because the Archbishop of Mexico followed the official order not to give refuge to the victims."[3]

Criticism of the ecclesiastical and government authorities grew louder in the aftermath of a second student massacre, this time at the hands of President Luis Echeverría, whose populist policies indirectly benefited a select group of progressive Catholics but limited those who welcomed more radical expressions of Christianity. Also known as the Corpus Christi massacre, this tragic event took place on June 10, 1971, when more than five thousand young people marched in the streets of Mexico City in solidarity with students from Monterrey who had been repressed by the governor of Nuevo León a few weeks earlier. A group of plainclothes paramilitaries known as Halcones (Hawks) ambushed, shot, and brutally beat the students in Mexico City, killing an undetermined number of them and marking the intensification of the dirty war at the hands of the government that executed, illegally detained, tortured, and disappeared thousands of people during the 1970s and 1980s.[4] More than the violence at Tlatelolco, this second massacre made a profound impact on the lives of progressive Catholics, and while many of them reconfirmed their preferential option for the poor by building Christian base communities, others moved further to the Left or abandoned their faith.[5]

This chapter examines the responses to the Tlatelolco and Corpus Christi massacres as differently expressed by various figures of the church, lay activists, and Catholic intellectuals. Following a brief description of the competing ecclesiastical positions taken in response to the 1968 student movement, the second section prioritizes the story of Enrique Maza, a Jesuit priest and the director of the theological journal *Christus*.[6] The third section of the chapter returns to the panista journalist Gerardo Medina, with attention to his pioneering book on the 1971 student massacre, *Operación 10 de junio*. The chapter concludes with a brief section on the Catholic intellectual Gabriel Zaid. Like Medina and Maza, he voiced strong condemnation of the administration of Luis Echeverría, describing him as more cynical and Machiavellian than his predecessor, Díaz Ordaz. Overall, the cases described here place the tragic events of 1968 and 1971 in the broader history of state repression described in the previous chapter and point to the two massacres as crucial in the radicalization during the Sixties in Catholic Mexico.

ECCLESIASTICAL RESPONSES TO
THE 1968 STUDENT MOVEMENT

In March 1968 a group of priests that included Samuel Ruiz and Pedro Velázquez published one of the earliest and most progressive ecclesiastical documents of the Sixties, "Development and Integration of the Country." Written to commemorate the first anniversary of the anticolonial encyclical *Populorum progressio*, the document called for greater consciousness of the national reality. It argued that the government had improved the lives of many people, but the country was still marked by drastic economic inequalities. It saw the social uprisings of workers, campesinos, and young people as direct responses to these injustices and the infringement of constitutional rights. The document radically rejected the views prevalent in most government, media, and religious circles at that time that instead saw social movements as irrational and the result of foreign manipulation.[7]

A second ecclesiastical document touched more directly on the subject of student activism. Directed as a letter to "The People of Mexico," the untitled document was widely distributed in the national press on September 10, 1968, nine days after Díaz Ordaz promised the return of law and order to the streets of Mexico City in his fourth presidential address to the nation and eight days before he sent thousands of military troops to occupy the central campus of UNAM and the National Polytechnic Institute. By then what started as an ordinary protest against police brutality in late July had evolved into a massive student movement that in August articulated six central demands: (1) freedom for all political prisoners; (2) removal of the chiefs of police; (3) dissolution of the riot police and a commitment to not reinstate them; (4) repeal of articles 145 and 146 of the Federal Criminal Code and incorporation of the "law of social dissolution," which served as a legal recourse for the aggression inflicted on the students; (5) compensation to the families of those injured and killed since July 26; and (6) an outline of responsibility and sanctions for those functionaries found responsible for the repression of students.[8]

Thirty-seven priests signed the letter. They called for "a respectful dialogue" between state authorities and the nation's youth and rejected the widely published narrative that international communist forces were leading the student uprising. Instead, they referred to the movement as a generational conflict that demanded freedom and justice. The priests pointed to a psychological campaign of moral panic composed of a combination of lies widely circulated in the media and the illegal use of agents provocateurs as evidence that the government of Díaz Ordaz had launched a dirty war against the students.

The signatures of Sergio Méndez Arceo and Pedro Velázquez were notably absent from the letter.[9] But as the Jesuit priest Jesús García explained in an interview, "The Bishop of Cuernavaca was the central figure responsible for the drafting and the publication of the document." He explained:

> In collaboration with the director of the Mexican Social Secretariat [Pedro Velázquez], Don Sergio put together a group of priests during the month of August. For more than a month this group met twice a week behind doors with representative students and professors from the universities and secondary schools to discuss the outcome and significance of the movement. In these conversations, it became clear that the students were on the right side of history and had organized a legitimate protest that demanded a more democratic nation.[10]

With the exception of Manuel Velázquez, the majority of priests who signed the letter were unknown leaders of the church whose importance to progressive Catholicism mostly rested in their local parishes. Velázquez assumed leadership of the Mexican Social Secretariat in December 1968 after his younger brother and early leader of the organization died of a heart attack. Throughout the 1970s the Secretariat distanced itself from the moderate and diplomatic approach favored in the past by Pedro Velázquez and instead emerged as one of the most progressive institutions of the church.[11]

With the exception of a homily given by Sergio Méndez Arceo, no additional letters from ecclesiastical leaders were published in the aftermath of the military occupation of the university campuses on September 18–25. In his homily, the bishop of Cuernavaca confessed to his flock, "It terrifies me to remain silent and behave like a muted dog. . . . I will make it my duty to identify those who side with the antichrist . . . , including those who claim alliance with the Church and the Revolution."[12]

The silence from the Episcopate was overwhelming in the aftermath of the Tlatelolco massacre. According to Jesús García, the ecclesiastical authorities "were censored," meaning that each bishop received a phone call from the executive office of Díaz Ordaz immediately after the massacre "demanding their absolute silence." A seminarian with the Marist order who had organized meetings with representatives of the student movement in August and September gave similar testimony. He recalled, "Our leader received a call from the archbishop of Mexico, Darío Miranda, prohibiting each and every one of us from expressing a public statement related to the October 2 events."[13] This accord was broken on October 9 when the conservative archbishop of Oaxaca, Ernesto Corripio, published a pastoral letter on behalf of the Episcopate Committee. "Unfortunately," Father García explained, "[Corripio] failed to capture the sentiments we had championed in [the] September [letter]." Specifically, his document condemned all forms of violence, including the alleged acts of vandalism committed by the students. Without making reference to the government, the military, or political prisoners, Corripio inconceivably noted that "we were all responsible" for the massacre in the Plaza of Tlatelolco, García added. Similar statements emphasizing the culpability of society were made by other influential figures in the church, including the president of the Episcopate, Octaviano Márquez, and the bishops of Mexico City, Guadalajara, and Zamora, Miguel Darío Miranda, José Garibi Rivera, and José Salazar, respectively. According to García, the vast majority of the central figures in the church opted for "a diplomatic position," meaning that they preferred to stay silent, fearing that a public statement would jeopardize the relationship of conciliation between state and ecclesiastical authorities.[14]

In sum, the diplomatic support that the majority of priests gave to the administration of Díaz Ordaz was resolute. However, there were some isolated but powerful voices who took a more critical view of state repression. In addition to the bishop of Cuernavaca, these figures included Enrique Maza.[15]

CHRISTUS AND THE "SUBVERSIVE CHURCH" OF ENRIQUE MAZA

For the Society of Jesus, the preferential option for the poor coincided with the naming of Pedro Arrupe as superior general of the Jesuit order in 1965, the same year as the closing events of Vatican II.[16] Shortly after, he sent a letter to all Latin American Jesuits to assume the role of "contemplatives in action" by making the struggle for social justice a high priority.[17] This message was reiterated in his "Rio Letter." Written during Arrupe's visit to Latin America in 1968, this (and similar) documents of the era asked all Jesuits to "trust love." In the interpretation given by the Mexican Jesuit Enrique Maza in *Christus*, this meant living a simple life, rejecting the materialism of the privileged past, and demanding peace on earth. Maza and those who sympathized with Arrupe were given the tall tasks of challenging the paternalism of hierarchical structures of power, resuming a horizontal relationship with the underprivileged, and dismantling unjust social structures.[18]

The Society of Jesus named Enrique Maza director of *Christus* in 1968. He held this position until 1973, when his superiors asked him to resign from the theological journal and replaced him with the conservative priest Javier Cuenca. Three years later, President Echeverría ousted Julio Scherer García from his executive role at *Excélsior*. In collaboration with his cousin Julio Scherer García and friend Vicente Leñero, Maza founded the leftist magazine *Proceso* in 1976. Its pages provided an important space for other Catholic writers who protested the authoritarianism of the government and advocated for freedom of the press and respect for human rights across Latin America.[19]

Christus experienced a radical change under Maza's leadership. It published articles by some of Latin America's most influential figures and sympathizers of liberation theology, including Marcos McGrath, Segundo Galilea, Hélder Câmara, Gustavo Gutiérrez, and the Mexican leaders Sergio Méndez Arceo and Samuel Ruiz. The themes covered in their articles and pastoral letters varied. Many touched on the topic of student activism and specifically emphasized the role youth should assume in providing a better future for the continent. Representative examples are the short pieces on the counterculture as liberation by the Claretian priest Enrique Marroquín, the celebration of youth power articulated by Hélder Câmara and Hernán Larraín, the call for young priests to embrace their role as organic intellectuals by Luis del Valle, and the socioeconomic critiques of the "establishment" written by Martín de la Rosa.[20]

Enrique Maza was born in the United States in the border city of El Paso in 1929. His parents came from an upper-middle-class family of bankers from Mexico City and moved to Texas during the Cristero Rebellion. His family returned to Mexico City in 1931. There Enrique benefited from a private Catholic education. In his youth, he developed an interest in journalism and became closer to his cousin (and Jesuit-educated) Julio Scherer García, who was three years older. During the 1950s, Maza attended the Montezuma Seminary in New Mexico and was ordained a Jesuit priest. Soon after, he enrolled as a graduate student at the University of Missouri, where he pursued a degree in journalism and joined a group of like-minded priests who welcomed the progressive turn in the church. With them, he discussed the documents of Vatican II, volunteered his services in the prisons of Saint Louis, and protested the death penalty. Once back at home, he published his first columns with the national daily *Excélsior* in 1964 and two years later with *Christus*.[21] His columns in the latter focused on the particularities of the progressive Catholic movements in Mexico and voiced clear condemnation of the authoritarianism of the government and those who ignored state repression within the church.

As director of *Christus*, Maza called on young priests to reform the church, which he understood as the "body of Christ" (in reference to the 1964 encyclical on the Feast of Transfiguration, *Ecclesiam suam*, or His Church) and not as a hierarchical space or divine institution claiming a monopoly on the truth. Maza gave priority to dialogue, which he consistently described as "a concrete expression of love."[22] He lamented that the "deaf ears" and "superficial hearts" of the majority of ecclesiastical authorities had prevented the possibility of having a genuine engagement with the people, namely, the politically disgruntled and the oppressed. "We are not prophets," he explained, but servants of the less fortunate, the silenced. "We cannot afford to dismiss the diversity of opinions" that had polarized so many during the Sixties. In agreement with Superior General Arrupe, he specifically called on the church to welcome criticism and "free itself" from its "historical relationship with the oppressor." For Maza, in short, this period pointed to a "defining moment" that forced everyone, including representatives of the church, to assume a clear political position on the side of the poor. "Silence" and "failing to get involved in improving the lives of the oppressed" constituted direct and unambiguous positions of complicity that had contributed to the institutionalized violence and rampant economic disparities that characterized the era. To ignore this was disingenuous to those claiming to be on the side of the poor and detrimental to the future of a reformed church, by and on the side of the people.

Using the authority of the pulpit to demand greater justice was not enough, however. What was needed to "heal a nation" in this time of despair, "rampant with injustices and corruption," was "unselfish love." But he regretted that Mexico "had yet to receive notice of *Gaudium et spes*," the Vatican II document that had demanded dialogue and cooperation with the entire human family. Young priests needed to assume a "committed position." This meant leaving behind the moralistic language of the past, putting an end to paternalistic works of charity, asking people to no longer rely on prayers, and breaking the relationship with the powerful. He lamented that Jesuits had historically sided with the elite, but the time had come to create a "subversive church," one capable of "radically transforming" the "existing social order."[23]

Enrique Maza transformed the Jesuit journal into a subversive space, the reason for his expulsion from the directorship in 1973. The tensions with the church hierarchy were first noticed in January 1971 when *Christus* announced "a new era" that tested its relationship with the Episcopate. The content changed dramatically as Maza gave the magazine greater space to discuss social and political issues that addressed state repression, demanded freedom of expression, and, as noted earlier, called on young priests to assume a resolute position in solidarity with the oppressed. One of the earliest and most contentious articles penned by Maza as director appeared in reference to the student movement in December 1968, the same month the activists dissolved the National Strike Council and the movement officially ended. An earlier version of the article appeared in the Jesuit journal *Pulgas* and was subsequently distributed with the support of the Intercultural Center of Documentation (CIDOC) for the consumption of a broader Latin American audience in *Cuadernos del Miec*.[24]

In his coverage of the 1968 movement, Maza strongly condemned state violence and sharply criticized those who supported the government, including the Mexican church, which refused to listen to the students. In his detailed chronology of the events, he mentioned the students who were killed in July and September and suggested that at least one hundred people had died during the October 2 massacre but admitted that it was difficult to determine the exact figures because the government held tight control of information. Maza called for an immediate investigation but lamented that the media had only created greater confusion by failing to make a responsible distinction between apocryphal news sponsored by the state and the truth. He provided a list of government-sponsored lies associated with the movement in which students were overwhelmingly described as dupes of political forces and foreign institutions on both the militant Left and the reactionary Right. Instead, he described the movement as a genuine protest that successfully exposed the limits of the economic growth of the era and the nation's lack of genuine democracy. He admitted that some students had made mistakes but argued that their movement had successfully challenged the "dictatorial" powers of the government. In agreement with them, he argued that the nation lacked a just judicial system and a responsible and democratic press. The corrupt governing elite had relied too often on illegal and repressive mechanisms of control and was the first to violate the constitution. He concluded without ambiguity, "The PRI had suffocated the movement." But in the optimistic tone of his article, Maza simultaneously argued that students "have awakened our consciousness." They have "opened a space for reflection and [have demanded that we adopt] a politicized mentality." According to Maza, the movement represented a "social-political-cultural revolution" that was violently repressed, smeared by government-sponsored lies, and therefore poorly understood. For its part, the church was also to be blamed, and so were all Catholics in positions of power. Their silence had made them complicit. In ignoring the teachings of Vatican II, they had failed to see the democratic nature of the movement and its commitment to social justice. Students were imprisoned and many lost their lives, he stated indignantly, but church leaders had remained absent and thus culpable for the repression.[25]

Sergio Méndez Arceo, bishop of Cuernavaca, was one of the few church leaders who escaped Maza's condemnation. After all, the bishop had expressed early support of the movement and harshly criticized the ecclesiastical and government authorities.[26] In the aftermath of the massacre, Méndez Arceo argued that the nation had turned its back on its people. "A true believer," he said in agreement with Maza, "is one who is a rebel [and] rejects all forms of injustices . . . ; one who is committed to a *permanent* and not an *institutionalized* revolution," an unambiguous critique of the governing party.[27] Years later, Maza and Méndez Arceo concluded that the political situation had failed to improve during the 1970s, and while President Echeverría capitalized on the legacy of the revolution, the repression had only intensified, as further dramatized by the 1971 Corpus Christi massacre. The *panista* journalist and director of *La Nación* Gerardo Medina provided a more damning description of Echeverría.

OPERACIÓN 10 DE JUNIO AND THE CONTRADICTIONS OF DEMOCRACY

On October 4, 1968, Gerardo Medina took over the office of the legislature to voice one of the clearest and most damning condemnations of the Tlatelolco massacre. Similar to the militant Left, he emphasized his criticism of the government with a gruesome photograph on the front page of *La Nación*; and like Enrique Maza, he saw the movement as a legitimate democratic response to the authoritarianism of the PRI. As depicted in figure 6, on the cover of the magazine was an unambiguous image of those who were brutally killed in Tlatelolco, mirroring the equally disturbing images published in magazines of the militant Left such as *¿Por qué?* Both demanded an immediate investigation of the massacre and called on the leaders of the PRI to take swift responsibility with clear explanations of the crimes.[28]

FIGURE 6. The Tlatelolco massacre, shown on the cover of *La Nación*. From *La Nación* (October 15, 1968).

Three years later Gerardo Medina also wrote one of the first and most thorough book-length accounts of the Corpus Christi massacre, *Operación 10 de junio* (1972), in which he identified the presidential administration of Echeverría as primarily responsible for the killing of dozens of students. He interpreted the 1971 massacre as more atrocious, if less conspicuous, than the massacre that had taken place in 1968. Whereas the Tlatelolco massacre had happened in part as a result of poor judgment and miscommunication on the part of the government, he argued, the Corpus Christi massacre was perversely and painstakingly orchestrated. According to him, Echeverría had made every effort to crush the 1971 uprising at its roots. He had relied on extensive use of agents provocateurs and ultimately put the blame on what he called the "emissaries of the past," an intentionally vague phrase that included radical leftist and ultraconservative forces alike. In Echeverría's view, the goal of the activists was to undermine his anti-imperialist and democratic politics.

Gustavo Díaz Ordaz had made terrible mistakes, Medina contended, but he ultimately took blame for the 1968 massacre. In making this argument, Medina cited the 1969 presidential address to the nation where Díaz Ordaz defended his decision to use the army to put an end to the student movement. "With integrity," the president had said, "I assume all the personal, ethical, social, political, and historical responsibilities related to the events that took place [at the Plaza of Tlatelolco]."[29]

By contrast, Echeverría went to great lengths to sow confusion and institutionalize illegal and more perverse mechanisms of state repression during and after the Corpus Christi massacre. Specifically, in interviewing a group of thugs for hire and citing extensively from a police manual that documented the events that took place on that violent day in 1971, Medina detailed the use, training, and protection of the Halcones. He provided a detail account of the role these shock brigades played in attacking the peaceful protest that killed an undetermined number of students during the bloody day of Corpus Christi and in selectively terrorizing journalists who were present during the massacre. Díaz Ordaz had a conflicted relationship with journalists. He had pushed for censorship when the stories went too far, Medina contended, "but we were never beaten while doing our work." By contrast, following his presidential campaign to move the country "Upward and Forward," Echeverría went to unprecedented lengths to portray himself as a democratic leader. But it was the selective and brutal force of his power that ultimately characterized his politics.[30]

The second central argument that Medina made in his book was one of continuity. For him, there was not a single Mexico before 1968 and a new and more democratic Mexico after.[31] According to Medina, 1968 and 1971 witnessed the latest and most egregious examples of a long history of state repression that dated to the late 1920s with the establishment of the postrevolutionary government and was further evident during the postwar period with the consolidation of the PRI in 1946. As examples, he drew attention to the León and Villahermosa massacres of 1946 and 1968, when the army killed activists and students protesting electoral fraud and state corruption. But abuse by government forces was also evident in the violent crackdown of social and political activists during the 1952 presidential elections, during the 1958–59 labor uprisings, and during the medical student strikes of 1964.

The difference between the 1968 and 1971 massacres was largely discursive and stylistic, Medina argued. Echeverría had made every effort to correct the four central mistakes that Díaz Ordaz had made during the student movement of 1968: (1) failing to crush the movement at its roots during the month of July, when students organized the first protests against police brutality; (2) making publicly visible all the forces of repression, including the riot police and the military; (3) unwillingness to identify scapegoats and thus refusing to selectively punish individual figures in the government; and (4) admitting full or partial responsibility for the Tlatelolco massacre.

According to Medina, the ubiquitous but covert nature of the Halcones served as the preferred mechanism of repression for Echeverría during the Corpus Christi massacre and thereafter. Composed of young men from poor neighborhoods between the ages of eighteen and twenty-three and dressed in civilian clothes as "students," he explained, they were specifically trained in martial arts and lethal weapons to crush the urban uprisings that continued to erupt in the aftermath of the Tlatelolco massacre, especially outside the nation's capital. The use of shock brigades to intimidate, beat, and kill students was not new in the 1970s, Medina further argued. But it was Echeverría who modernized and institutionalized the use of these clandestine actors as the preferred tool of repression in the form of paramilitary units at a moment in which he made a conscious attempt to co-opt leftist activists and intellectuals who turned a blind eye to state repression.

The covert nature of the Halcones produced positive results for the president, Medina lamented. Not only did they crush the incipient student movement of 1971 and continue to terrorize those who dared to remain politically active afterward (including journalists, as the author insisted in his book), but they also provided a useful narrative for a complicit press that repeatedly blurred the lines between bona fide activists who demanded a democratic Mexico and "terrorists" who were presented as foreign elements threatening the presumed stability of the nation. This language resonated because it was employed precisely at a moment in which a small but growing number of young people erroneously saw no other option but to engage in armed struggle. For their part, Medina argued, the ill-trained granaderos and the more powerful forces of the army were given strict orders not to intervene during the Corpus Christi massacre, unless these interventions were designed to "protect" the students. According to Medina, the goals were to publicly present the government forces as on the side of the students and simultaneously highlight the violent nature of competing youth groups composed not only of the Halcones but also of several shock brigades that received regular salaries from rival politicians.

As documented in *Operación 10 de junio*, the subdirector of General Services of the Federal District, Colonel Manuel Díaz Escobar, created the Halcones in 1968. The group was part of the same paramilitary forces that had participated in the student massacre in the Plaza of Tlatelolco. Yet the Echeverría administration never publicly admitted to their existence, nor were the politicians who supported them ever convicted of the crime, despite the evidence that journalists like Medina presented to the authorities in their newspapers and magazines.[32]

The third central argument that Medina made in *Operación 10 de junio* was one of complicity. In the preface, he identified himself as a "militant journalist" with a "moral obligation" to side with the truth. For him, postrevolutionary Mexico had emerged as an authoritarian, corrupt, violent, and undemocratic nation that had failed to overcome its historical dependency on the United States and, for the same reason, its economic underdevelopment. The PRI had capitalized on the rhetoric of the Revolution, but it had failed to bring social justice to the masses and create a truly inclusive system that welcomed dialogue and political debate. Its longevity had relied on terror and innovation that allowed each administration to place a personal stamp on the revolving executive powers that ruled the country with an authoritarian hand. To remain silent and not denounce the many examples of state terror, Medina argued (in indirect agreement with Enrique Maza), was to be part of the problem. It was to be complicit with the government. The local police forces and the powerful forces of the army were natural allies of the president, despite rumors of a possible coup d'état spread by Echeverría at the time. But intellectuals and journalists had the "moral obligation" to document the authoritarianism of the state. Unfortunately, Medina feared, leftist intellectuals had a long history of siding with the PRI and championing the false narrative of exceptionalism that portrayed Mexico as less authoritarian and violent than its Latin American counterparts.

Medina pointed specifically to the director of the center-leftist magazine *Siempre!*, Fernando Benítez, as a key ally of the president. He was one of the authors of the "Declaration of 14 Intellectuals"—the document that defended the right of students to protest in the streets, condemned the 1971 massacre, demanded an investigation on the origins of the Halcones, and called on Echeverría to identify the individuals who financed them. Yet in March 1972, Benítez published an article in *Excélsior* in which he asked his readers to select between the rise of fascism that had swept many countries in South America and the preferred *echeverrismo* that had left a door open to leftist intellectuals and activists.

But for Medina it was the novelist Carlos Fuentes who did the most damage in legitimizing the administration of Echeverría. Like Benítez, Fuentes had signed the "Declaration of 14 Intellectuals," but he had more assertively sided with the president. Fuentes had also failed to use his influence to demand a serious investigation of the Corpus Christi massacre. Specifically, Medina pointed to the widely circulated book published by Fuentes in 1971, *Tiempo mexicano*, as an example of the treacherous narrative that had legitimized Echeverría and ultimately justified his government's remaining in power. In *Tiempo mexicano*, Fuentes encouraged his readers to side with the president, whose democratic policies were allegedly under attack by a wide range of conservatives (including writers like Medina) and competing figures of the PRI, the church, and the entrepreneurial class.

For Fuentes, according to Medina, there was a clear distinction between the provincial and anticommunist Díaz Ordaz and the populist and internationalist Echeverría. The former had personified the most atrocious aspects of the PRI. The Tlatelolco massacre had largely taken place as a result of the schizophrenic provincialism, vulgar anticommunism, and inferiority complex of the president, Fuentes argued, not as a by-product of the long history of state repression and the lack of genuine democracy, as Medina insisted in his book. Fuentes claimed that activists and intellectuals would be foolish if they failed to take advantage of the democratic opening and the spirit of transformation that Echeverría championed so as to put a final end to the "disastrous" legacy of the previous administration. According to Fuentes, echeverrismo pointed to the "renovated *Tiempo mexicano* that followed the 'tragic obscurantism' of Díaz Ordaz." Medina presented a completely different picture and instead described the populist politics of Echeverría as much more detrimental but reminiscent of a longer history of state repression. He was not alone. The poet and Catholic writer Gabriel Zaid made a similar argument.

GABRIEL ZAID AND THE "HISTORICAL CRIME" OF ECHEVERRISMO

The renowned poet and member of the "14 Intellectuals" Gabriel Zaid expressed a radically different position from that of Fuentes. In response to

Fuentes, he sent a short document to *Siempre!* that read, "The only historical criminal is Echeverría"; the editor in chief refused to publish it.[33]

Zaid shared Medina's concern regarding the radicalism that followed the 1968 and 1971 student massacres. He saw the question of armed struggle as suicidal madness and detrimental to building a truly democratic nation, one free of demagogy and corruption, as he saw it, but also free of revolutionary nationalism and gigantic bureaucratism. But in his condemnation of the Echeverría administration, Zaid was equally critical of leftist intellectuals who benefited from an alliance with it. His criticisms of the Left dated to his columns in *Excélsior* in the mid-1960s, and his sympathetic view of progressive Catholicism can be traced to a few years earlier.

Gabriel Zaid had moved to Mexico City as a teenager in 1958 from Monterrey. He pursued his career in poetry and met Gaspar Elizondo, the intellectual and manager of the bookstore Bible, Art, and Liturgy. The store sold crafts made at the Benedictine monastery of Cuernavaca and contained the most comprehensive collection of books on Catholicism published in Europe. But perhaps more significantly, it also served as an informal gathering place for a group of Catholics who collaborated with Elizondo to found the journal *Informaciones Católicas Internacionales* (*ICI*). With origins in Paris, the journal translated key religious texts from the original French into Spanish, commented on foundational documents of the church, and provided an informative section called "Latin American News" from 1963 to 1972.[34] *ICI* was a liberal publication that welcomed the progressive Catholicism of the era but cautioned against what many of its writers saw as a reckless opening with Marxism. It also played a key role in condemning all forms of violence, which its writers saw as the antithesis of love. According to Zaid, the publication was financed by the "socially responsible capitalist Lorenzo Servitje" and had 3,500 regular subscribers, many of whom became critical of the conservatism of the past but simultaneously expressed concern about "separating faith and culture."[35]

The writer Octavio Paz, who had resigned as Mexico's ambassador to India in 1968 to protest the Tlatelolco massacre, escaped Zaid's criticism. Paz discontinued his columns in *Excélsior* in 1971 and created *Plural*, where Zaid responded to Fuentes with the following words: "If you are indeed a friend of Echeverría, why don't you help him, and in private convince him that the Corpus [Christi massacre] was not a mere exception in his Opening but rather an opportunity to publicly demonstrate how democratic we could be; or is it, like don Porfirio [Diaz] once said, that [the nation] is not ready [for democracy]?" A similar position was adopted in *Plural* by the historian and cofounder of El Colegio de México, Daniel Cosío Villegas, in his 1974 book, *El estilo personal de gobernar.* Written two years before his death as a political essay, in witty and sharp prose, Cosío Villegas presented a biting account of the contradictions, limitations, and shortcomings of Echeverría. He initially welcomed the possibility of change that the president promised with his democratic opening, but, like Zaid, he grew critical of Echeverría's personalistic style and ultimately found him incapable of effectively governing the nation and engaging in a genuine dialogue with his critics. Both described Echeverría as flamboyant and a demagogue with little knowledge of the needs of the nation. He was more interested in listening to his own voice than actually hearing what people had to say, including those who accepted the president's invitation to criticize the system.[36]

The presidential administration of Echeverría, in sum, polarized not only the Left but also outspoken Catholics who shared a distrust of the government but did not constitute a monolithic group. While the majority followed the position taken by Carlos Fuentes or simply stayed silent, a small but authoritative minority saw Echeverría's populism with apprehension. In their eyes, the Corpus Christi massacre and the unprecedented wave of state repression only delegitimized his aspirations to democracy.

CONCLUSION

Luis Echeverría traveled to Rome in 1974 to visit the pope, making him the first Mexican president to set foot inside the Vatican since 1857. He presented Paul VI with an official letter "From the Third World," explaining the leading role Mexico had assumed under his presidency in defending human rights and the economic and political rights of the developing nations. This was an argument that Echeverría had also made during his 1971 visit to the United Nations and during his 1972 meeting with President Salvador Allende in Chile. His personal secretary, Fausto Zapata, explained that the visit was a reaffirmation of Echeverría's willingness to improve his relationship with the head of the Catholic Church, who he saw as "a moral leader of the first magnitude, a man always searching for justice and who, in moments of great convulsion in the world, has been present in negotiations to restore peace." The general secretary of the PAN, Bernardo Bátiz, agreed and saw the visit as the "first step [to amend] relations," but he seemed less enthusiastic about the president's visits to China, the Soviet Union, and Cuba (which were a first for a Mexican president).[37]

On his return to Mexico, Echeverría approved large government funds to complement the extraordinarily high costs required for the new modern building of the Basilica of Guadalupe.[38] Significantly, he also provided the hierarchy with sensitive political information during his tenure and welcomed individual members of the clergy into his cabinet meetings to deliberate policy. In building reliable allies capable of counterbalancing the critiques and pressures he received from the powerful business elite, he also maintained cordial relationships with progressive members of the church who favored liberation theology. Among others, these included the radical priest of Cuernavaca, Sergio Méndez Arceo, who became the first bishop to regularly visit Los Pinos, the presidential residence, since the outbreak of the Revolution, despite (or because of) his harsh criticisms of state repression.

In his efforts to create a contrast with his predecessor, Diaz Ordaz, Echeverría passed a series of laws aimed at dealing with a variety of social and cultural issues concerning conservative and progressive ecclesiastical authorities. Historically a pro-natalist, for example, he became a vocal supporter of "responsible" family planning, on the one hand, and a key advocate for the continued criminalization of abortion, on the other. In this context of contradictions, moreover, he welcomed criticism from the church and allowed the hierarchy greater access to mass media and private education.

More sinister than previous presidents, Echeverría simultaneously launched a series of aggressive measures aimed at eliminating the extreme and "irrational" wings of the reactionary Right and especially the militant Left, including those that welcomed armed struggle and more radical expressions of liberation theology. For example, as Echeverría claimed to champion the language of human rights in his travels abroad, his administration launched an aggressive media campaign designed to obscure his role in the 1971 massacre, including the publication of the apocryphal *Jueves de Corpus Sangriento* in 1972. Allegedly penned by the Halcón Antonio Solis Mimendi, the book was a fictitious testimony of the massacre and listed the actors who were presumably responsible for the deaths and beatings of students and journalists, including, among others, an unnamed "group of Jesuits" who had "radicalized" the nation's youth in the aftermath of the 1968 movement.[39]

The illegal and obscured nature of the Corpus Christi massacre captured the contradictory elements of the presidential administration of Echeverría and ultimately outweighed his democratic agenda. But for some leftist intellectuals and key members of the church, too much seemed to be at stake to more assertively criticize his administration. Criticisms were instead pushed to the margins and into the hands of a few actors. While some innovative spaces only reached a small number of sympathizers, like *Christus*, which published one of the best accounts of the student movement and Tlatelolco massacre at the time, others enjoyed a larger but mostly conservative readership, like *La Nación*. At the end of the spectrum of the Left were those who saw no other option but to engage in armed struggle, as examined in the next chapter, and while many like Medina saw this as suicidal madness, others joined Zaid and interpreted the guerrilla uprising as a by-product of the repressive politics of Echeverría. Enrique Maza agreed. In *Proceso* he continued his criticism of state repression that had forced him out of the directorship of *Christus*, and like many on the Left, he eventually described the administration of Echeverría as a dark chapter in Mexico's dirty war, as a moment of despair that brought an end to the most utopian aspirations of the Sixties that the student movement had embodied.[40]

FIVE

The Thorny Questions of Armed Struggle and Socialism

The Catholic novelist Vicente Leñero celebrated the theatrical release of his controversial play *Compañero* in March 1970. The central plot featured a heated debate between the two opposing personalities that the author saw in Ernesto Che Guevara, the utopian thinker and the practical man of action. Leñero's goals were to demystify the idea of the "heroic guerrillero," so widely celebrated across Latin America during the late Sixties, and invite audiences to reflect on the importance of Guevara's cause without ignoring the contradictions that made up his myth. The heated conversation between "Comandante 1" and "Comandante 2" hours before his execution in Bolivia in October 1967, placed the question of armed struggle at the center of discussion, suggesting—in the eyes of Leñero—that violence ultimately undermined the humanist aspirations of Guevara.[1]

Compañero polarized its audiences and critics. Bishop Sergio Méndez Arceo and the Marxist artist David Alfaro Siqueiros enthusiastically cheered at the debut of the play, but presumably less exuberant was Iván Illich, who a few months earlier had been given orders to secularize his educational center in Cuernavaca and leave the priesthood. Known for his criticism of armed struggle, Illich allegedly stormed out of the theater without voicing an opinion.[2] Cuban embassy officials were similarly upset and angrily dismissed *Compañero* as "defamation." Not only was it an aberration to suggest that Guevara was an individual split between two conflicting personalities, they argued, but it was also a scandal to exclude the importance of Fidel Castro in the Argentinian's life, even after the latter's departure from Havana in 1965. For accuracy, Leñero relied on the *Bolivian Diaries* of Guevara; the more critical accounts given of his death in La Paz by the journalists Luis González and Gustavo Sánchez Salazar; and the widely read book

Revolution dans la revolution?, in which the French writer Régis Debray defended armed struggle.[3]

According to a young man who attended the play, *Compañero* made many people uncomfortable, largely because of the indirect allusion that Leñero made between Christ and Guevara, complete with an imposing crown featured in the background of the stage. He explained, "The crown of thorns was an unambiguous reminder of the painful crucifixion of Christ," and while he did not see Guevara in those terms, he understood the nearly religious admiration many people had for El Che. The famous photograph of Guevara taken after he was killed in Bolivia and widely circulated across the world had a striking resemblance to Jesucristo (fig. 7).[4]

This was an observation that likely got under Leñero's skin as he later became an outspoken critic of the authoritarianism of the Cuban Revolution.[5] The journalist Miguel Ángel Granados Chapa agreed with this interpretation, and according to Leñero, he too praised *Compañero* in *Excélsior* as a welcome opportunity to bring competing, even antagonistic voices of the Sixties into fruitful conversation.[6]

Some of the earliest debates surrounding the need for a productive dialogue between Marxism and Catholicism took place in 1962. These were published in the centrist magazine *Siempre!* and involved the participation of the founder of the Dominican parish at UNAM, the friar Alberto de Ezcurdia.[7] Following the killings of Camilo Torres in 1966 and Che Guevara in 1967, these debates took on somber overtones and placed the questions of armed struggle and engagement with Marxism as central points of contention. Many, for example, referred to a passage from the Medellín documents that said that popular armed insurrection was justified in the case of prologued tyranny.[8] These debates resonated more strongly after the 1971 Corpus Christi massacre.[9] According to a government surveillance document, the first "Camilo Torres Group" in Mexico was founded in November 1966, eight months after the death of the Colombian priest.[10] Unlike those in South America, these groups merely attracted a handful of sympathizers and quickly dissipated, mostly as a result of a conservative church that continued to align itself with the authoritarian apparatus of the government.[11] Within a few years, however, a growing number of lay activists left their respective organizations to join the various guerrilla uprisings that proliferated across the nation. This was the widely published case of Ignacio Salas Obregón. Also known by his biblical nom de guerre "Oseas," he became a key figure in the Movement of Professional Students

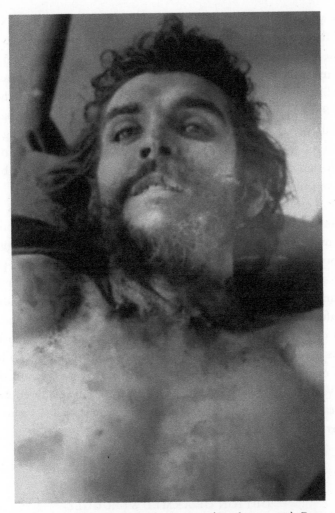

FIGURE 7. The Martyred Che Guevara (October 9, 1967). From Gustavo Villoldo, CIA operative, CIA, National Security Archive, Public Domain, https://commons.wikimedia.org/w/index.php?curid =3835880

and a central intellectual of the September 23 Communist League, the largest guerrilla movement in Mexico, founded in 1972.[12] Other young radical Catholics who joined the League and the more than thirty armed groups that proliferated across the nation during this period similarly originated from the more conservative Corporation of Mexican Students and the youth wings of Christian Democracy.[13]

The young priests who served as chaplains of these militant students found themselves polarized. While some, like the Jesuit Martín de la Rosa and the Claretian priest Kiko Hernández, abandoned the church, others found relevance in the pedagogical teachings of Paulo Freire or were caught in the line of fire and fell victims of state repression, like the Marist priest Rafael Reygadas. These are the protagonists of this chapter. They engaged in heated debates that directly responded to the radicalization of young Catholics, and following the pioneering work of the French Dominican friar Alex Morelli (among others), they demanded a productive dialogue between Marxism and Christianity.

Like the play *Compañero*, the diverse stories examined in this chapter shed further light on the radical Catholicism of the Sixties and provide a better understanding of the New Left in Mexico. The chapter begins with the story of José Luis Sierra, a young journalist for the Catholic publications *Contacto* and *Liberación* and former member of the Corporation of Mexican Students. Like many of his peers, he joined the guerrilla movement in the aftermath of the Corpus Christi massacre. The chapter concludes with a short discussion on the language of human rights, which a number of lay activists used in opposition to armed struggle, including the two historic leaders of the MEP introduced earlier in the book, Luis Sereno Coló and María Vasquez. The final pages tell the love story of Eufemia Belén Almanza Villarreal and Héctor Torres González, two Catholic students who joined the guerrilla movement in the late Sixties.

JOSÉ LUIS SIERRA AND THE OPTION OF ARMED STRUGGLE

The once-conservative student activist José Luis Sierra Villarreal wrote a strong condemnation of the presidential administration of Luis Echeverría in the September 1971 issue of *Contacto*, the central magazine of the Mexican Social Secretariat. He provided an important account of the Corpus Christi massacre and called on readers to join him in a socialist revolution. He was twenty-three years old and a leader of the Critical University Center (CECRUN). This was the same organization of Jesuits who published the radical *Liberación* and played an instrumental role in creating the socialist group Priests for the People (SpP) in 1972. Following the publication of his article in *Contacto*, Sierra broke ties with his Jesuit mentors, Luis del Valle and Martín de la Rosa, and joined a small group of Catholic and Marxist students who called for armed revolution. In February 1972 the police apprehended and tortured him. Sierra remained behind bars until 1978, when President López Portillo (1976–82) gave amnesty to some political prisoners. While Sierra was in jail, various newspapers falsely pointed to the Jesuit priests of Mexico City and Monterrey as the intellectual authors of the guerrilla uprisings that proliferated after the Corpus Christi massacre.[14]

José Luis Sierra grew up in Guadalajara during the 1950s and received a Jesuit education. At the age of seventeen he enrolled at the Technological Institute of Higher Education in Monterrey and joined the conservative Corporation of Mexican Students in 1965. Two years later his peers elected him president of the Student Federation, the central organization representing competing leftist movements in Monterrey. This period coincided with the arrival of two Jesuit priests from Guadalajara who transformed the universities of Monterrey into key spaces for progressive Catholic students, Javier De Obeso Orendáin and Manuel Salvador Rábago González. Under their leadership, the Corporation of Mexican Students lost ground, and the MEP became the most important organization for Catholic students in the northern state of Nuevo León, among them, Ignacio Salas Obregón, who was elected national leader of the organization in 1968. With the Marxist student leader Raúl Ramos Zavala and Salas Obregón, Sierra led several student protests demanding freedom for political prisoners, alliance with transportation workers, and greater democratic participation in the universities. In the aftermath of the Tlatelolco massacre, the three men led the only mass protest organized in the nation.[15] Three months later Sierra participated in the school play that finally got him expelled from the university, despite the support he continued to receive from the Jesuits in Monterrey. In the play, Sierra allegedly represented the industrial magnate Eugenio Garza Sada as a corrupt politician.[16]

Once expelled from the university of Monterrey, Sierra reconnected with Salas Obregón in Mexico City, where they shared a house near the Ibero-American University with the Jesuits Luis del Valle and Martín de la Rosa. The priests taught Latin and introduced students to the writings and pedagogical methods of Paulo Freire, which they applied to organize poor communities in the popular neighborhood of Nezahualcóyotl. De Obeso joined them after returning from a trip to Colombia, where he allegedly met with the socialist group Golconda. Sierra also traveled to South America during this period, including Chile with De la Rosa, where they met with other radical figures in the church. While residing with the Jesuits, Sierra and Salas Obregón pressured ecclesiastical authorities to support a hunger strike in the Lecumberri prison demanding freedom for the political prisoners of 1968. But the only leading church figure who visited the prisoners and pressured the government to release them was the bishop of Cuernavaca, Sergio Méndez Arceo.[17]

With the Jesuits, Sierra and Salas Obregón provided logistical assistance to the CECRUN. The goal of the Center, as its central publication *Liberación* explicitly noted in its December 1972 issue, was to raise the political consciousness of all Catholics. According to Del Valle, the CECRUN originated at the Ibero-American University, where he taught courses in theology and first encouraged students to adopt the preferential option for the poor. Martín de la Rosa instead said it originated at the Freirean communities in Nezahualcóyotl. Both referenced the mimeographed journal *Liberación* as the foundational space that gave rise to the SpP.[18]

In its July 1971 issue, *Liberación* compiled a list of the most decisive responses to the Corpus Christi massacre published in the major newspapers by leaders of the church and lay Catholics. For the chief editor and key founder of the Jesuit magazine, De la Rosa, the massacre could only be explained in relation to the long history of state repression. He placed Echeverría's administration in the company of other "pseudo-revolutionaries" and saw his populist policies as particularly detrimental to the nation, as they were largely designed to obscure the repressive nature of the government while giving the misleading idea that Mexico was democratic and genuinely interested in engaging in a productive dialogue with the nation's youth.[19]

Sierra made a similar argument. In his article published in *Contacto*, he described Mexico as far from democratic and equally as repressive as its South American counterparts. In making this contention, he placed the role of the Halcones (responsible for the Corpus Christi massacre) in relation to other paramilitary groups operating across the nation, including the Student Federation of Guadalajara in Jalisco and the porros in Mexico City, Michoacán, and Puebla. "What use is it to find an individual responsible for the creation or training of the Halcones?" he asked. Political violence was rooted in the capitalist system that had emerged after the Mexican Revolution and further manipulated by Echeverría in his attempt to adopt a populist and developmentalist approach. The ambiguous and illegal character of the Halcones served his administration well, as it blurred the lines between political activists and pseudo-student leaders. Worse yet, bona fide activists were no longer described as subversives but as "terrorists." The manipulation of this rhetoric, he argued, provided the government with a justification to violate the autonomy of the universities, call on others to demand law and order, and place the blame on the nation's youth. But, above all, Sierra concluded, the covert use of paramilitary agents provocateurs was used strategically by Echeverría to undermine the political legitimacy of armed struggle that had taken root in the state of Guerrero throughout the 1960s and was further noticeable in the aftermath of the Tlatelolco and Corpus Christi massacres.[20] In this sense he in part agreed with his mentor, De la Rosa, but unlike the Jesuit priest, he called on others to take up arms.

Sierra founded Los Procesos in Mexico City with Salas Obregón and Ramos. Initially, the group was responsible for providing a counterweight to the government-sponsored gangs, but after the Corpus Christi massacre, it went underground. It moved to Monterrey and served as one of the bases for the creation of the September 23 Communist League. The Jesuit Luis del Valle tried to dissuade the young men. He emphasized the importance of nonviolence, albeit with little success.[21] By 1973, the League had emerged as the largest guerrilla movement in Mexico and the main target of state repression.[22]

In addition to *Contacto*, Sierra published his interpretation of the Corpus Christi massacre in *El 10 de junio y la izquierda radical,* a 1971 book coauthored with Manlio Tirado and Gerardo Davila.[23] In "The Revolution Is Not Made in the Cafeteria," De la Rosa wrote a sharp review of the book. While the authors did an excellent job of providing a detailed chronology of the student movement that ended with the massacre, De la Rosa wrote, they were less successful defining an "alternative revolutionary path." In his view, the book had demanded a radical alternative. The authors accused their liberal counterparts of failing to assimilate the lessons of the 1968 student movement, identifying the internal causes that prevented the movement to reemerge in the aftermath of the Tlatelolco massacre, and buying into the rhetoric of the government that the nation had become democratic during the Echeverría administration. The liberal Left, in short, was complacent while the institutionalized Left was lost in its bureaucratic and dogmatic Marxism. The arguments were valid, De la Rosa concluded, but the book had failed to define a concrete and pragmatic alternative solution. How could they "expect the masses to follow a militant path" if they had failed to define it themselves? Or worse yet, why would the masses follow the call to armed struggle if this radical decision placed them in greater danger?

This was a reckless proposition considering how violent and reactionary the government had already proven to be.[24] The young Jesuit Martín de la Rosa was not alone in his criticism of armed struggle. His elder Alex Morelli made a similar argument in the pages of *Contacto*. Morelli was a French Dominican friar who called for the "efficacy of love" in the path to a nonviolent socialist revolution.

THE EFFICACY OF LOVE AND NONVIOLENCE

Alex Morelli officiated his first masses in Dusseldorf, Germany, in 1942. During the war he was apprehended by the Nazis and sent to the Dachau concentration camp in Bavaria, where countless foreign political prisoners were detained and many of them executed.[25] Once liberated in 1945, after three years in the camp, Morelli returned to his native France, where he had been ordained a Dominican priest at the age of twenty-three and where he served at the Toulouse convent in the capital city, Haute-Garonne. He served for fourteen years as a university chaplain there and as a leading champion of the Catholic Worker Movement.[26] In 1959 Morelli was among the dozens of European priests who traveled to Latin America in response to the pope's efforts to send 10 percent of European and North American priests to the continent. First he moved to Montevideo and then to Mexico City.

In Uruguay, Morelli solidified the presence of worker-priests and pointed to Louis-Joseph Lebret as the most influential figure in his shifting understanding of Catholicism.[27] Like the French Dominican philosopher and pioneer of development ethics, Morelli called on others to place the economy at the service of the people. In labor and university circles, he successfully promoted dialogue with leftist militants, including sociologists, anarchists, and Marxists who published some of the early work on dependency theory. He welcomed the visits to Montevideo by Fidel Castro (1959) and Che Guevara (1961) and publicly declared his sympathy for the Cuban Revolution. By the mid-Sixties he had been recognized as an outspoken critic of authoritarianism and a thorn in the side of conservatives, who ultimately convinced church authorities to expel him from South America.[28]

After several months of reconnecting with his friends in Paris, Morelli arrived in Mexico City in October 1967. Initially, he resided with a group of Dominican friars at UNAM, where Agustín Desobry and Alberto de Ezcurdia had transformed their University Parish into an influential institution for young Catholics interested in the arts.[29] He gave lectures on the "theology of the revolution" at UNAM. But he saw little relevance in what Morelli described as the "bourgeois" character of its Dominican Center and its "chic" artistic projects.[30] He was equally critical of bohemians in Europe who looked to "yoga, gurus, and transcendental meditation" in search of liberation, as well as those who looked to the counterculture in "response to the questions of a consumer society." He wrote to his friends, "I am very sensitive to the danger of evasion and depoliticization represented by these various responses."[31] Instead he found greater importance in the social work of the Mexican Social Secretariat and immediately joined the organization. With the support of Fr. Pedro Velázquez, he moved to Ahuizotla, a poor neighborhood in the northern part of the city located in Azcapotzalco. However, the daily commute to the offices of the Secretariat in downtown prevented Morelli from truly interacting with the locals, as he had hoped. He continued his lectures at UNAM, and once elected continental representative of the Catholic Worker Movement in March 1968, he traveled to nearly all Latin American countries until the mid-1970s. During this period, Morelli wrote numerous columns in *Contacto*. He emerged as a key advocate of nonviolence in its pages and concluded that meaningful change could not take place in a capitalist system, which exclusively benefited a privileged minority.[32]

Founded as the main journal of the Mexican Social Secretariat in January 1967, *Contacto* welcomed a radical expression of Catholicism. This was evident after the death of Fr. Pedro Velázquez in December 1968 and especially noticeable under the direction of Alex Morelli from 1970 to 1974.[33] Its pages provided a defining space for progressive Catholics who enthusiastically embraced the preferential option for the poor.[34] But in his writings Morelli also drew attention to various political events that shaped the radicalism of the times. He provided short reviews of the books that he argued "all Catholics" should read, including, *If They Come in the Morning* (1970) by Angela Davis and *La noche de Tlatelolco* (1971) by Elena Poniatowska, which provided powerful testimonies of the experiences of Black Panther Party members in prison and those who were jailed and brutally repressed during the Tlatelolco massacre, respectively.[35]

But perhaps the book that most influenced Morelli during these years was *Spiral of Violence* (1971), in which the Brazilian bishop Hélder Câmara called for radical, nonviolent transformation based on the hopeful principle of love.[36] In reflecting on the atrocities that Morelli witnessed as a young man in Europe, he called on others to protest the US Vietnam War. He condemned the Tlatelolco and Corpus Christi massacres in Mexico and explained the role that international forces played in overthrowing the socialist administration of Allende in Chile in 1973. He highlighted the imperialist tendencies of John F. Kennedy's Alliance for Progress, celebrated the militancy of the Chicano movement in the United States, detailed the tortures of political activists and religious figures in the Southern Cone, and exposed what he called the "Colombianization of CELAM," that is, the international attempts by Roger Vekemans and Alfonso López Trujillo to undermine liberation theology in Latin America.[37] But it was the attention to revolutionary nonviolence that characterized Morelli's columns in *Contacto*.

A few weeks after the Tlatelolco massacre, Alex Morelli had organized a conference in Cuernavaca on the topic of nonviolence. He invited the attendees to reflect on the attributes, legacies, accomplishments, and key thinkers of what he called "pacifism as a form of action." Specifically, he defined nonviolence as the "ultimate act of revolutionary love" and "the exact opposite of passivity." In this sense, it was more radical than violence. But it was also more demanding, as it required practicing love, even with those who were on the side of economic exploitation, political repression, and multiple forms of discrimination. "He who embraces non-violence is one who possesses love," Morelli argued in relation to the writing of Mahatma Gandhi, Hélder Câmara, and Martin Luther King Jr. (who had similarly spoken about the Greek concept of agape as brotherly love, as compassion, creativity, and redemptive will to overcome racial violence, hatred, and despair). Hatred cannot be an element in the struggle of liberation, Morelli specifically contended in response to Che Guevara's 1967 message to the Tricontinental in which Guevara concluded (like Fanon in *The Wretched of the Earth* [1963]) that "a people without hatred cannot triumph over a brutal enemy."[38] Rather, Morelli insisted that liberation is rooted in what Camilo Torres called "efficacious love," that is, love as an act of solidarity and empowerment.

For love to triumph over hatred in the struggle for liberation, it was crucial to follow what Morelli saw as the four central tenets that were necessary to the success of nonviolence: (1) the collective formation of leaders invested in the education of the masses, which he understood, in agreement with Freire, not as blind victims of oppression or inferior subjects but rather as active agents of their lives; (2) collaboration with people in key positions of power who were willing to embrace a new consciousness of solidarity and use their positions of privilege to side with the oppressed in grassroots movements; (3) the formation of intermediary groups willing to break the chains of social, political, economic, ideological, and racial segregation; and (4) the building of a heathy democratic society rooted in the principles of human dignity, social justice, mutual respect, and solidarity.

Nonviolence, in short, was exclusively rooted in the principles of love. By contrast, violence was "sterile and unnatural," even if organized in the name of revolution or social justice. It primarily thrived under a capitalist system with historical roots in the enduring legacies of colonialism. By contrast, nonviolence could purify hatred in the name of love and thus effectively embark on the creation of a socialist alternative willing to share its power with what some of his peers called a new "Proletarian Church," one that created its own praxis, liturgy, and theology of love.[39]

Martín de la Rosa's Nonviolent Revolution

The Jesuit priest Martín de la Rosa agreed with Alex Morelli, as he dedicated the February 1972 issue of *Liberación* to the memory and significance of Camilo Torres on the sixth anniversary of his death. De la Rosa lamented that Torres had evolved into a mythical martyr whose contributions to Catholicism and socialism were largely misunderstood and exclusively described in relation to violence. Instead, he described Torres as an advocate of "the efficacy of love" who demanded the creation of an inclusive, anticapitalist world. According to De la Rosa, the Colombian priest had advocated for a socialist revolution but one exclusively made in the name of *amor eficaz*, which Torres understood as a "praxis of concrete action" invested in uniting people around the aspirations of social justice, grassroots empowerment, and mutual respect. Only the creation of a new "integrated man," rooted in "effectual love," Torres advocated (and Morelli and De la Rosa similarly concluded), could bring people together in solidarity and build a dignified future where the hungry could be fed, the poor clothed, the unschooled educated, the homeless sheltered, and the disenfranchised empowered.[40]

Eighteen years younger than Morelli, Martín de la Rosa was born in 1937 in the small town of Matehuala in San Luis Potosí. In his late teens, he joined the Society of Jesus and moved to Mexico City to study at the Institute of Philosophy (1958–62). For the next four years he taught history and philosophy at the Science Institute in Guadalajara, where he also developed a specialty in psychology. In 1966 he traveled to Europe and studied theology for three years at the Sarriá Institute in Barcelona and the Catholic Institute in Paris. In

France, he strengthened his friendship with Javier de Obeso, the Jesuit priest who mentored Catholic students in Monterrey, and Porfirio Miranda, who had returned to Europe in 1967 (after being expelled from Chihuahua) to complete his doctoral dissertation, "Marx and the Bible: A Critique of the Philosophy of Oppression."[41] In the mid- to late Sixties De la Rosa witnessed the French student protests, and so did Miranda and De Obeso.[42]

De la Rosa returned to Mexico in 1969, dressed in jeans and sandals and sporting long hair and a full beard.[43] His new countercultural look represented what the Jesuit Enrique Maza described as the "new integrated priest" (citing Camilo Torres), one who eagerly responded to Pedro Arrupe's call to become "contemplative in action."[44] In 1972 De la Rosa described himself as a "Christian revolutionary," the "fruit of multiple interactions and conversations that I have had over the last two years with [a group of] committed Christians . . . [that included] men and women who have worked effortlessly for the salvation of our people."[45] In particular, De la Rosa referred to the university students and fellow Jesuit and Dominican priests who collaborated with him on various projects, including the organization of the First National Congress of Theology and the creation of the Critical University Center in 1969–70. Among them were Enrique Maza, who invited De la Rosa to write in *Christus*; Ignacio Salas Obregón, who helped with *Liberación*; José Luis Sierra, who took classes with him in Guadalajara in the mid-Sixties and traveled with him to Colombia in 1971 to meet the group Golconda; and Alex Morelli, Esther Alicia Urraza, and Patricia Safa, who joined him in building a base community in Nezahualcóyotl, which in 1973 took the name Popular Educational Services. With Del Valle and Morelli, he also put together the national team that traveled to Chile in 1972 for the Christians for Socialism Congress. Disillusioned with the internal divisions among progressive priests who followed Arrupe's critiques of socialism, De la Rosa delved further into community work in Nezahualcóyotl, which remained affiliated with the Jesuits but broke all ties with the church in 1974. A year later De la Rosa left the priesthood and got married. He continued his pedagogical work of "self-determination" with Popular Educational Services for the rest of the decade. With the support of younger priests and lay activists who sympathized with socialism, he founded a similar project in Tijuana during the 1980s.

The year 1974 also marked a defining moment in the life of Alex Morelli. This is when he published his last columns with *Contacto* and when his health began to deteriorate while residing in Nezahualcóyotl. From 1974 to

1979 he gradually moved away from his utopian language of love and found greater relevance in the Marxist interpretation of class struggle.

The "Hungry Coyote" in "Dictatorial Mexico"

Alex Morelli was crucial in the radicalization of younger socialist priests in Mexico, including Martín de la Rosa.[46] In his writings he pointed to three factors that transformed his life and contributed to his endorsement of socialism: the government response to the student movement of 1968, the "brutal poverty" of the people of Nezahualcóyotl, and the CIA-sponsored overthrow of Salvador Allende in 1973.

When Morelli arrived in Mexico in October 1967, he wrote numerous letters to his friends in France. His impressions of the country were shocking and often in contradiction to those expressed by many of his friends, who insisted that Mexico was democratic in comparison to other countries in Latin America. Rather, he saw the nation as "dictatorial," replete with contradictions, including policies in the name of the revolution that had created the "largest shantytowns in the continent." The students who were massacred in the plaza of Tlatelolco were not the only ones who felt the brunt of state repression, he wrote to his friends; there were also young Catholics affiliated with the Catholic Worker Movement who demanded independent labor unions, campesinos who were expelled from their lands, and radical priests who sided with the oppressed.[47]

For Morelli, Mexico was a country of violent paradoxes. While anticlerical in theory, he wrote, it was also a pagan place that allows priests to govern in an authoritarian fashion, with "an almost magical halo." He explained, "[The priest's] hand is kissed, he is the abode or the manifestation of the divinity. He is asked to bless all kinds of objects, to read prayers." But worse yet, he profits from the sacraments and overwhelmingly sides with the government. In his view, state and ecclesiastical authorities were two sides of the same coin. But the "advantage of such dictatorship is that it lasts and allows for a facade of political stability." Despite rampant corruption and a mythical sense of freedom of the press, "the government has an effective bureaucratic network." In alignment with the church, "it controls everything and thus has effectively avoided civil war."[48]

It was this repressive context that explained the importance of the 1968 movement, which Morelli supported not only in his writings but also in his meetings with and advice to students. "The youth of '68," he said, "have protested against a society than enslaves man, a society dominated by the appetite of power." The movement "is a rejection of a rotten political system," where "everything is exploitation of the weak by the strong, where the elections are rigged, where the opposition is nonexistent, where the economy is entirely dominated by the capitalist elite, [and where] there is no independent radio or television." He added, "I try to make students understand that changing the regime is not enough. We must change society and the change in society will only happen through the change of man, which is more difficult" but possible through revolutionary nonviolence. This "does not mean selfishness, resignation or fears." Rather, it "requires rigorous investigation of the [national and international] situation." The "study groups [formed during the movement]," he explained, "are currently analyzing the situation of violence imposed on the Third World by the international money of imperialism." Unfortunately, he concluded, "the carnage of October 2" at the Plaza of Tlatelolco put an end to the movement and his engagement with students. "Besides the many dead, all of my students are in prison, some with heavy sentences (twenty years), clubbed, tortured," he explained.[49]

For Morelli, state repression was also evident in Mexico's extreme poverty.[50] "In Paris, students threw stones at a society of abundance," he explained to his friends, citing a Mexican student, "while in Mexico City they threw stones at a society of misery."[51] Nowhere was this misery more blatant than in Nezahualcóyotl—"hungry coyote," as Morelli often translated the Nahuatl term in his letters—where he lived from 1972 to 1979. He wrote to his friends:

> Nezahualcóyotl is an agglomeration of eight kilometers long and five kilometers wide, without a flower, without a plant, without birdsong, without drinking water, without garbage collection. The soil is saturated with saltpeter. It is practically impermeable [and] refuses plant growth. In the dry period, we live and bathe in dust. . . . Imagine the hotbeds of infection provided by dust, a dust mixed with detritus and organic waste, where the water is stagnant under a tropical sun; imagine the smell too.[52]

Although some people referred to Nezahualcóyotl as a proletarian city, he said, "nothing could be further from the truth." He wrote in 1972:

> Two hundred thousand adults go to work every day or look for work at the center. About two hundred fifty thousand kids are hanging around in the mud. There are only classes and teachers for a tiny minority. A Mexican magazine recently reported on children who do not get the calories, protein

or iodine needed for normal brain cell formation; the democratization of education is a challenge in such conditions. Our closest neighbors have fifteen children. I became friends with Lalo, the second to last, a little cripple. One hospital in the whole area: only the privileged people who are entitled to social insurance are admitted.... We see a lot of funeral homes where they sell coffins of all sizes. It is not uncommon to come across a group of people carrying a tiny white coffin in the cemetery. We are overwhelmed by the immensity of misery, the multiplicity of needs.... Misfortune, [daily] violence, [and] assassinations are endemic.... [It is] impossible to count the deaths of hunger or cold.... The police are rotten—[the force] is made up of delinquents who exploit and brutalize instead of protecting.[53]

For Morelli, the "mushroom city" of Nezahualcóyotl, which had grown from 800,000 inhabitants in 1972 to more than 2.5 million by 1978, was a place of "despair, cynicism, and fatalism," inhabited by a people subject to an authoritarian pastoral care who had yet to reach their human potential. They were not only poor, but marginalized, silenced, oppressed, and deprived of love. To have them appreciate the importance of love often feels like an impossible task, Morelli explained to his friends, where "injustices are so cruel" and the local "clergy takes part in this exploitation." He added, "The local priests earn money by charging for masses, baptisms, weddings, first communions. One priest owns buildings, another has a pharmacy, another a restaurant." They were the caciques who saw his methods of concientización as a direct threat to their local power. They disapproved of his unwillingness to charge for his services and his interactions with the poor as active agents of their fate, as opposed to empty recipients of charity. "Without explanation," the local bishop has withdrawn my "power to confess [and] to officiate masses," he wrote. He added in a 1973 letter to his friends, "I feel that my days in Mexico are numbered.... I do not know what sauce I will be eaten in.... The Provincial of the Dominicans in Mexico no longer wants to defend me and would like to see me leave. Many bishops here see me as a source of all evil; for the [director] of CELAM, a Colombian man [Alfonso López Trujillo], I am the man to tear down. It makes my work [at Nezahualcóyotl] a permanent roller coaster." But Morelli remained defiant. "This [is] an open struggle," he added. "I am not afraid of the future; in any case, nothing can change my loyalty to the poor."[54]

In his letters to his friends Morelli nearly always placed the repression in Mexico in the broader context of Latin America, where "fascism had taken hold," partly in reaction to the radicalism of liberation theology, culminating in the 1973 military coup in Chile that put an end to the so-cialist administration of Salvador Allende. "How can we remain quiet?" he angrily asked his friends in France, who had welcomed the progressive lan-guage of Vatican II but who had grown critical of the radical Catholicism that emerged in Latin America after the Medellín conference, adding that his commitment to nonviolence had perhaps encountered a dead end. Fol-lowing the 1973 military coup in Chile, Morelli referred to Marxism as his "preferred method of analysis." He wrote, "Class struggle seems to me to perfectly explain the situation we are experiencing here [in Latin America]. Two social classes with competing interest clash in a fight to the death. With the difference that the repressed class simply wants to survive and get out of its growing misery, while the class with the economic, political, and military power, in the hands of a small minority, does not want to give up its privileges, and often uses religion as an additional weapon." He con-cluded without ambiguity, and in a more radical tone than he had used in the past, "I am a priest and a revolutionary. Because there is a division of classes, we must be with those whom God preferred: the exploited, the op-pressed. I want with Don Sergio [Mendez Arceo] to form a socialist society that would be fraternal, [egalitarian, and] transparent." In short: "Political engagement was not a luxury, or even a political choice. . . . [W]hether I like it or not it is a dimension of my life."[55]

Despite the opposition from ecclesiastical authorities in Mexico and CELAM, Morelli's political life remained relevant to the people of Ne-zahualcóyotl until 1979, when he died of bone cancer. During the last two years of his life, he often found himself resting from the chemotherapy treatments or traveling to France and South America as a retired regional director of the Catholic Worker Movement. He welcomed a new genera-tion of nuns and priests to Nezahualcóyotl. Among them was a small group of Jesuits from Central America; his Dominican brother Miguel Concha, who became a leading figure in Mexico's human rights movement; and the Spanish friar Ángel Torrellas, who encouraged the use of music and theater as tools of concientización.

Before departing to France, for one last trip, he called his Jesuit friend Enrique Maza to come to his home for confession. Maza explained, "He wanted to make a general confession of his whole life. It was a situation in which he couldn't contain his tears, simply because of the density of his pain." According to his friends, this pain was one of the heart, as Morelli feared that he had failed to do more for the people of Nezahualcóyotl, to build an equitable society with them, without class struggle and based on the principle of love.[56]

THE SOCIALIST PATH AND STATE REPRESSION

Rafael Reygadas was one of the few priests who joined Morelli and welcomed a socialist path. Like Martín de la Rosa, he found great relevance in the work of Paulo Freire, but unlike most of his peers, he was illegally detained and tortured at the hands of the Echeverría administration in 1972. Born in Mexico City in 1944, Reygadas received a private education at the Melchor Ocampo School, where he met Fr. Manuel Jiménez. The Marist priest encouraged the young Rafael to pursue a career in philosophy and introduced him to the Jornada Seminary in the Tapasco municipality in the state of Mexico. The priests led various grassroots programs at the school that had an immediate impact on Reygadas. He later remembered in an interview "the effective work they did to improve the living conditions of the poor." In 1961, he completed his high school education at the Colegio Franco-Inglés. A year later, he enrolled at the Marist Seminary and studied philosophy. As an aspiring priest, he organized a series of Youth Campaigns. These were composed of middle-class students from Mexico City with the two-pronged goal of "bringing young people back to the church" and "encouraging them to get involved with the organization and empowerment of popular movements." One of the most successful of these grassroots projects was established in a poor neighborhood located in the Indigenous zone of the Mazahua people in the state of Mexico, where the powerful Atlacomulco group of Hank González controlled most of the land and where similar groups of Jesuit and Dominican priests created their own base communities. "It was pragmatism that distinguished us," explained Reygadas, "whereas the Jesuits and the Dominicans were respectively more spiritual and theoretical in their approach." He added, "We did not prioritize the use of religious language but instead emphasized the need to engage in what we called 'promoción social y popular' [grassroots empowerment], that is, in making sure that our programs directly benefited the poor."[57]

As a leader of the Youth Campaigns, Reygadas strengthened his relationship with students from Mexico City to create a cooperative that raised and sold poultry. For financial support, they approached a government program that received funds from the Alliance for Progress, which Reygadas saw as "paternalistic" and "not too different from the charity projects of the church." Both had "little interest in improving the lives of the people," explained Reygadas. Overall, they were primarily interested in defeating the leftist opposition and co-opting social activists, "but, the economic opportunities that came with the program were real and we did not hesitate to use them." "We received cargo for two or three years loaded with yellow corn, powdered milk, animal cookies, flour, and liquid butter. We then sold this merchandise at a store that was owned and managed by the cooperative." The goals were to improve the dietary conditions of the local people, make them financially independent of the caciques, and teach the young members under his supervision the importance of grassroots empowerment. With the students, Reygadas read and discussed the work of Teilhard de Chardin, whose liberal views influenced the reforms of Vatican II.[58] "The readings of liberation theology had yet to be published," he explained. Instead, "from European theologians, we learned the importance of combining historical analysis with reflection of contemporary problems as the best and most practical way of creating an ecumenist church that advocated for a horizontal relationship with the common people."[59] The friars Alberto de Ezcurdia and Alex Morelli, who established a parish at UNAM, were also crucial in this regard.[60] "From the Dominicans," he added, "we learned of the importance of engaging in dialogue with the Left."[61]

After completing his studies at the seminary in 1967, Reygadas was sent to Our Lady of Peace Parish in the southern neighborhood of Tlalpan in Mexico City. His work with students remained a priority. After receiving an invitation from Fr. Carlos Talavera, he accepted a leadership role in the training of Communitarian Vanguards. Similar to the Youth Campaigns, these grassroots movements were composed of middle-class students whose main task was to promote the social work of the church. Talavera recruited and educated the students. Once accepted to the program, the volunteers underwent preliminary training that the Marist priests organized in the form of spiritual retreats. "These were secluded spaces that lasted for three to four days discussing the reality of the country," Reygadas explained. They spoke of "the needs of the people, and the importance of engaging in social transformation." After the retreats, Vanguard members were housed with a local family with ties to other lay organizations.[62] "We needed to understand how people lived," he said, "eat what they ate and sleep like they slept. Only then did we earn their respect and develop a better understanding of their needs." Once part of the community, the Vanguards established cooperatives, led literacy campaigns, opened health clinics, and organized public workshops that encouraged people to voice their understanding of the world in their own words. For theoretical inspiration, they turned to Freire.[63]

CRITICAL PEDAGOGY

The Brazilian educator Paulo Freire first visited Mexico in 1968 when Iván Illich invited him to lead a series of workshops in Cuernavaca.[64] By the end of the decade, a group of priests that included Reygadas came to the conclusion that the best and most effective way to work toward social justice and ameliorate the living conditions of the oppressed was to engage in critical pedagogy.[65] "Only through the process of concientización, by achieving an in-depth understanding of the world," Reygadas explained, "the oppressors, like the oppressed, were able to understand their respective positions of power." As an example of how the Vanguards relied on the Freirean method, he pointed to a screening of *Los olvidados*, the 1950 film by Luis Buñuel that told the story of a group of children in Mexico City in the 1940s whose violent poverty prevented them from having a future based on love. After watching the film, the priests presented the members with statistics on the rampant poverty of the various neighborhoods surrounding Mexico City. This information was then discussed in relation to a series of questions that encouraged participants to evaluate their own economic conditions. "These discussions were not intended to make anyone guilty of their privilege but rather to examine the role each of us played in normalizing the same socio-economic structures that allowed for poverty and exploitation to exist," Reygadas explained. The second and related goal "was to expose the participants to the reality of the nation and invite them to commit themselves to a practical solution." For many, this meant creating cooperatives, leading literacy campaigns, opening health clinics, forming self-defense brigades, establishing trade schools, attending political workshops, or collaborating with Maoist groups that were involved in similar projects.[66]

In 1968, Reygadas moved to a new house in Tlalpan, which he shared with other seminarians and young priests. "What differentiated our community," he said, "was the fact that we did not depend on the church for financial support." The residents did not charge for the sacraments and held jobs in the local community, where they had direct contact with the everyday struggles of the people. By August, the uprisings turned into a massive movement, and their "community came in complete support of the students." The seminarians held meetings with student leaders and protested in the streets with them. According to the Jesuit priest Jesús García, the first of these communities was organized in 1967, primarily with the goal of taking the university out of the ivory tower and transforming it into a genuine space of promoción social.[67]

After the Tlatelolco massacre, the Marist order sent Reygadas to work with a group of high school students at the Colegio Franco-Inglés, the same private institution where he was first introduced to the social teachings of the church in his youth. In 1970 he was ordained a priest, and in his role as chaplain of the school, he organized "youth groups of action and reflection." He introduced students to the Freirean method and encouraged them "to discuss the reality of their school, including their sense of privilege, as a microcosm of society." In June 1971 the ecclesiastical authorities could no longer ignore the radicalism of Reygadas. Following the Corpus Christi massacre, they sent him to the Polytechnic Center of Development. A small group of Marist priests had founded the Center at the National Polytechnic Institute in 1964, three years after the Dominicans established their University Parish at UNAM and the Jesuits founded their University Cultural Workshop in Monterrey. While the parish at UNAM prioritized dialogue with the arts and the counterculture, those in the National Polytechnic Institute and Monterrey placed greater emphasis on student politics and provided spaces for the radicalization of Catholic students.[68]

Reygadas worked with the Polytechnic Center of Development for just a few months, but it was this short period that drastically changed his life. Pedro Herrasi and Oscar Núñez were the two central figures responsible for the Marist Center. While both had signed the September 10, 1968, letter defending the students (see chap. 4), it was Herrasi who had grown concerned with the "militancy at the Politécnico." He saw the Center as a spiritual space of evangelization, responsible exclusively for introducing students to the teachings of the church. Reygadas's superiors hoped he would follow the same path. By contrast, Núñez welcomed the preferential option for the poor, and in collaboration with Reygadas, he used the Center to introduce students to the Freirean method of concientización. With students, Núñez and Reygadas led various community projects near the campus. They opened cooperatives and organized grassroots movements in collaboration with Jesuit and Claretian priests. Together a group of them joined Alex Morelli in forming Priests for the People in 1972. Similar to its counterparts in

Central and South America, it envisioned a new socialist society based on the historical life of Christ.

Priests for the People

The founding members of SpP were twenty priests. They first announced their "anticapitalist movement" in a letter published in *Excélsior* on April 14, 1972. Also in 1972, the more moderate Episcopal Union of Mutual Aid saw the end of its ten-year project to unite progressive parishes and bishops across Mexico. Alex Morelli was the central figure responsible for the creation of the SpP. The Jesuit priests Luis del Valle and Martín de la Rosa soon joined him. Both were trained in Europe and returned to Mexico in the late 1960s when they participated in the base communities that welcomed the same group of students who called for armed struggle in the aftermath of the Corpus Christi massacre. Other signers of the April 1972 letter, supporters of the SpP, and key players in the radicalization of youth included Manuel Velázquez from the Mexican Social Secretariat; the Claretian Javier Kiko Hernández; the Marists Núñez and Reygadas; and the Jesuits Maza, Rábago González, and De Obeso. As noted earlier, De Obeso had been present in Paris in the mid- to late Sixties with De la Rosa and Porfirio Miranda, author of the polarizing book *Marx y la Biblia* (1971) whose "merit," according to *Contacto*, was evident in its "courage" and "earnestness."[69] On their return to Mexico, Obeso and De la Rosa worked, respectively, with students at the University Cultural Workshop in Monterrey and the CECRUN in Nezahualcóyotl.[70] These and similar grassroots movements that proliferated across the country during the late Sixties were the roots of the SpP, and so was the ephemeral journal *Liberación*.

Founded with the support of Del Valle and De la Rosa, *Liberación* was published in a total of twenty-six issues between 1969 and 1972. In its pages, the editors translated articles by André Gunder Frank and Immanuel Wallerstein on dependency theory. They wrote columns on Freire and Illich and their critical pedagogy. There were also features on Méndez Arceo, including his conversion to socialism in 1970 and his solidarity movement to bring liberty to the political prisoners of 1968; on the US Jesuit Daniel Berrigan, who burned draft files in protest of the Vietnam War; on the French biblical scholar Xavier León-Dufour, who discussed the question of violence as depicted in the Bible; on the US theologian Harvey Cox, who defined the church as a people of faith and action; and on the dozens of radical priests who called for the creation of a socialist society in Chile, Peru, Argentina, and Colombia. Special reports were included on Camilo Torres and the question of armed struggle; on Miranda's controversial book, *Marx and the Bible*; on the worker-priests in Europe; on the killing and torture of political activists in South America; and on the impact of the Tlatelolco and Corpus Christi massacres in Mexico.[71]

In addition to the April 1972 letter in *Excélsior*, the founding documents of the SpP (written primarily by Alex Morelli) simultaneously appeared in *Christus* and *Contacto*. These sources mentioned hundreds of sympathetic members, but those included in these printed sources never exceeded more than two dozen priests. In separate interviews, both Reygadas and Jesús García attested to the importance of the movement, nonetheless. According to Reygadas, most of its members "preferred to keep their names out of the documents." And García explained that "the year 1972 marked the peak of state repression." In this time of despair, "many priests welcomed the radical positions championed by Priests for the People, but out of fear of retaliation from our superiors, they preferred to keep their names out of the documents."[72] Specifically, the movement called for the "creation of a new society," defined by the principles "self-determination" and "mutual love." Regarding the latter, they wrote largely in reference to the ideas of Che Guevara and Camilo Torres: "Only in a socialist society is it possible to create a New Man," capable of "making a reality *the precept of the Love of God.*" The italicized phrase originated from an idea formulated in the Gospel according to Luke: "One cannot love one, without loving the other." By "the other," they stressed their new loving relation to "the oppressed" and called on their fellow priests to use their hearts, souls, and strength to transform "selfishness into solidarity," "competition into collaboration," and "the society of classes into a struggle for justice." In this sense, members of the SpP radically argued that they opposed capitalism, as well as all ideological propositions pushing for a third alternative to socialism, including what they saw as the failed "mixed developmentalist economy" of Luis Echeverría.[73]

SpP did not shy away from criticizing the state and saw the populist policies and demagogic language of Echeverría as detrimental to the nation. His "democratic opening" gave the illusion that it was possible to challenge the same status quo that explained the existence of the oppressed. His government differed little from previous administrations. They all prioritized the continuous expansion of private enterprise, developed a cult of material progress under the banner of revolutionary nationalism, and maintained the historical dependency of Mexico on the United States. Only in a socialist society, the priests concluded with the words of Camilo Torres, would the "integrated man" be capable of replacing promises with action. The integrated man would give equal voice to the marginalized, break the chains of imperialism, place the church at the vanguard of liberation, and form a collective consciousness of love.[74]

The socialist goals of the SpP came to an end in 1975. For three years, the group refused to create a hierarchical structure, and perhaps for the same reason, it failed to attract progressive bishops. But what was more damaging was a short letter written by Pedro Arrupe in 1972 giving Jesuit priests strict orders to break ties with the movement "without any real explanation." While some of them did, noted Del Valle, others instead "became disillusioned with the church."[75] According to Morelli, this year coincided with the beginning of Alfonso López Trujillo's war against liberation theology at CELAM. Similarly, in Mexico the authorities began to crack down on progressive publications of the church, including *Christus* under Maza and *Contacto* under Morelli.[76] Pressure from the majority of ecclesiastical authorities further limited the national expansion of the group, and so did the choice its members made to refuse to sustain themselves by charging for the sacraments. The overwhelming majority of the priests composing the group instead worked for a living. For additional support, in 1975 they changed their name to Solidarity Church and welcomed lay activists to the movement.[77] In their popular work with the poor, many of the leaders saw little need to hold on to their fragile relationship with ecclesiastical authorities and left the priesthood altogether, including Martín de la Rosa in 1974 and De Obeso and Hirata in 1976.[78] Similarly, the Claretian priest Javier "Kiko" Hernández, who inherited the leadership of the MEP in 1966, left Mexico and its church in the aftermath of the Corpus Christi massacre.

JAVIER "KIKO" HERNÁNDEZ AND THE RADICALIZATION OF THE MEP

Javier "Kiko" Hernández was born in Michoacán in the late 1930s. In his teens he enrolled at the Claretian Seminary in Toluca, where he completed his studies in philosophy in 1960. While De la Rosa moved to Paris to study theology, Hernández traveled to Rome to be ordained a Claretian priest. He also lived in Zurich, Switzerland, where he took an internship with the Young Christian Workers movement and learned the Revision of Life method of seeing, judging, and acting.[79]

Hernández returned to Mexico in 1966 and became university chaplain of the MEP. This year coincided with the concluding years of Luis Sereno Coló as leader of the movement and the emergence of Ignacio Salas Obregón as its leader in Monterrey. For the next three years, Salas Obregón and his spiritual leader Hernández wrote letters to each other and to their friends in South America. They discussed the importance of the MEP and their plans to extend its presence to Central America. Sympathetic to the 1968 student movement, they grew angry at the government and ecclesiastical authorities in the aftermath of the Tlatelolco massacre. However, they disagreed with each other on tactics. Whereas Salas Obregón had initially agreed with the Claretian priest in prioritizing seeing, judging, and acting as a valuable tool of concientización, he became disillusioned with the method and argued that "more radical solutions were needed."[80] Initially, Salas Obregón found this radicalism in Nezahualcóyotl and Monterrey while collaborating with the Jesuits De la Rosa, Del Valle, and De Obeso. Over time, he sought concrete answers in armed struggle with the September 23 Communist League.

While residing in Mexico City in 1970, Salas Obregón found spiritual guidance from Luis del Valle and Martín de la Rosa. There he was introduced to the Freirean method of critical pedagogy and met other young university students who instead found greater appeal in Camilo Torres. Among others, they included two former leaders of the Corporation of Mexican Students who joined the guerrilla movement after the Corpus Christi massacre, José Luis Sierra and Ignacio Olivares Torres. It is in this context that Salas Obregón wrote "The Problem of Man." Exclusively written for members of the MEP, it highlighted the "problems of humanity" and posed Salas Obregón's first doubts about nonviolence, although he reaffirmed his commitment to Catholicism. To Hernández, he expressed his disillusionment in student politics and growing interest in becoming a Jesuit priest, "just like his older cousin," Pepe Toño Orozco Obregón.[81]

In May 1968 Salas Obregón abandoned his academic career in Monterrey and became the central leader of the MEP. It is also during this time when the Jesuits from Guadalajara, De Obeso, Rábago, and Von Bertand, transformed the University Cultural Workshop into an important place for dialogue between Christianity and Marxism.[82] In its academic roundtables, young Catholics came together with Marxist students to discuss the authoritarianism of the PRI and the lack of political representation of youth in Mexican universities. While Alex Morelli and Kiko Hernández emerged as clear advocates of nonviolence during this period, the Jesuits at Monterrey appeared more flexible, and some have argued that "De Obeso openly sympathized with armed struggle."[83]

Salas Obregón stayed in close contact with the Jesuits in Mexico City. With their support, he learned Latin, led literacy brigades, and organized a series of workshops on Marxism at UNAM and the Ibero-American University.[84] His relationship with Hernández remained strong. For his part, the Claretian priest continued to serve as the chaplain of the MEP, which suffered significant problems during this period, especially in the aftermath of the 1968 student movement, when the group publicly sympathized with the students and lost the support it had enjoyed from ecclesiastical authorities. In a January 1969 letter to the director of the Latin American Secretariat in Montevideo, Hernández wrote:

> Salas [Obregón] is the national director of the MEP. My hope is that he serves under this position for at least one more year. He is currently residing in Mexico City and working for the movement full time. But he is no longer receiving a penny from the Church. Msgr. [Rafael] Vázquez Corona [an advocate of the hierarchical structure of Catholic Action who had been a cautious ally of the MEP before 1968] claims to support us, but these are only empty promises.[85]

Without national resources, Hernández and Salas Obregón wrote several letters to the secretary of Adveniat, Pregadier Schmidt, hoping that the German organization would provide financial support to their movement. The Germans did not give them financial support as they had grown increasingly concerned about Catholic students in Latin America. Similar requests were sent to the central offices of the Latin American Secretariat in South America.[86] But in a letter sent to his peers in Montevideo in March 1969, Hernández said that, in addition to financial problems, the MEP was experiencing an ideological crisis that was bringing a slow end to the movement. Some members of the group remained loyal to the Revision of Life method. Others questioned its effectiveness. He wrote, "The consciousness of revolution has overtaken the mentality of many of our leaders with anguish." In Monterrey, "where the MEP has its greatest presence, the members prefer to talk about educational reform." In Morelia, "the leaders instead speak of a campesino consciousness, and in Toluca, where the activists are much younger," the see, judge, act method was "strictly understood by its political characteristics with little attention to its religious dimensions." This new generation of Catholic leaders, in short, "is quite radical." Some of the "members in the North have already joined the guerrilla movement."[87] What the MEP needed, Hernández noted in a memorandum to all members of the movement, was "patience and dialogue."[88] In a September 1969 letter to the head of the Latin American Secretariat in Montevideo, he wrote, "I am now in touch with Fr. Porfirio Miranda [author of *Marx and the Bible*] and other Jesuits," but the future of the movement had never been more uncertain. "We are hoping that the first anniversary of the Tlatelolco massacre gives us new momentum. Unfortunately, the ecclesiastical authorities are now more intolerant than ever." He explained, "Vázquez Corona has ordered Salas [to present his resignation] and leave the offices [of the MEP]. Salas Obregón is now resting in Aguascalientes, where he told me that he is no longer interested in becoming a Jesuit priest. It is uncertain what he will do next."[89]

In November 1969 Hernández and Salas Obregón came together one last time at the First National Congress of Theology, the event that officially marked the beginning of liberation theology in Mexico. In attendance at this transformative event was also Alex Morelli, who used the opportunity to stress the importance of nonviolence as a direct act of revolution. But Hernández discussed the first anniversary of the Tlatelolco massacre and its significance for the future of the MEP. He agreed with its radical members that the future of their movement rested in the implementation of subversive tactics, but he strongly disagreed with them on the question of armed struggle. He worried that the Jesuits of Monterrey, Rábago and especially De Obeso, were playing with fire. His commitment to the see, judge, act method seemed more important than ever, and so did the pacifist teachings of Morelli. This was Salas Obregón's last appearance as a representative of the MEP. A month later he moved to Mexico City, to a house owned by Del Valle near the Ibero-American University, where he taught courses on Marxism and joined the projects of the CECRUN.

The 1970s brought an end to Hernández's relationship with the MEP. After the first anniversary of the Tlatelolco massacre, he expressed concern that others would corrupt and capitalize on the memory of 1968. He wrote in a "reflection of the church" to his friends, "We must be careful and not let people transform the legacy of the [student] movement into a myth. This is precisely what the state did with the Mexican Revolution. Once emptied of its transformative meaning, the myth of '68 will be used to co-opt leaders who are genuinely interested in fomenting 'a new consciousness.'"[90] Months later, his name was included in the list of participants scheduled to attend the Christians for Socialism Conference in Chile. But instead he traveled to India, where he waited to hear from the leaders of Pax Romana in Fribourg. Weeks earlier Hernández had submitted an application hoping to be elected general chaplain of Pax Romana. In March and April 1972, he wrote his last letters as a leader of the MEP to his friend Paco Merino who was residing in Lima as the director of *Cuadernos de Documentación*. The letters expressed a profound sense of sadness and frustration, placing the crisis of the MEP and the "rising authoritarianism in Mexico" in the broader Latin American context. While the Uruguayan government of Pacheco Areco (1967–72) had forced the closing of the Latin American Secretariat, Hernández implied, the administration of Echeverría had cracked down on the Left and progressive Catholic movements. From his perspective, it was the "repressive character of the president" that ultimately pushed gifted activists of the MEP, like Salas Obregón, to the brink of radicalism. Hernández remained critical of armed struggle and lamented that his efforts to generate greater support for nonviolent forms of political activism had failed. He wrote, "Thank you for sending me Gustavo [Gutiérrez]'s book. I am almost finished with it. . . . In the meantime, it is clear that I will not be invited to travel to Fribourg. My life has come across a brick wall and I frankly do not know what awaits me behind it."[91]

Those who loved Kiko Hernández lost track of him. While some of his friends believed that he left the priesthood and moved to a popular neighborhood near the city of Toluca to practice the preferential option for the poor, others feared that he might have been killed or disappeared by the government. All remembered him with great joy as a passionate and caring person who was deeply committed to helping the nation's youth.[92] In her last interaction with Hernández "in 1972 or 1973," the leader of the MEP, María Vasquez, remembered that her friend was "heartbroken" as he feared that Salas Obregón, who had a "brilliant but impulsive mind," had "made a terrible mistake" in going underground, joining the guerrilla movement, and putting his life and that of his comrades at risk.[93] "A few months later," in April 1974, the once-aspiring Jesuit Ignacio Salas Obregón was detained following a violent confrontation with the police in Tlalnepantla, in the state of Mexico. He was sent to the infamous Military Camp #1, where countless activists were tortured and disappeared.[94] By then "everyone who knew Kiko had lost track of him," Vasquez said. "I prayed for my friend, hoping that nothing happened to him."[95]

The Pax Romana leader in Central America, Rosendo Manzano, provided further information on the fate of Hernández. According to him, Kiko was an extraordinary leader with a profound sense of justice, solidarity, and love. Unfortunately, he lived in Mexico, a country with a violent anticlerical past and with one of the most conservative churches of the Sixties in Latin America. When Manzano first visited Mexico in 1967 from El Salvador, he could not believe how marginalized and even impotent the progressive priests were. They could not wear their cassocks in public. Their public statements were always under close scrutiny by the church. But Hernández was different. He was a Lone Ranger in the world of student activism, according to Manzano. His only reliable ally was Father Villaseñor, the priest in charge of the Morelia region, but his movement's influence only extended to Michoacán. A few years after leaving the church, he married a political activist in El Salvador, where he continued his work with the poor, no longer in pursuit of a utopian society but more practically in solidarity with the oppressed. With the new language of human rights, he remained a strong critic of armed struggle.[96]

THE DEFENSE OF HUMAN RIGHTS

The language of human rights had roots in the postwar period with the signing of the Universal Declaration of Human Rights in 1948. But according to the historian Ariana Quezada, it was thirty years later that it was widely and more regularly employed in Mexico, primarily as a result of four significant factors that took place during the 1970s: (1) the rise of a nonviolent and noninstitutionalized democratic Left; (2) the emergence of an independent press that transformed the National Center of Social Communications (CENCOS) and *Proceso* into crucial spaces for championing freedom of the press; (3) the arrival of South American exiles, including Chileans, Argentineans, and Uruguayans, who assumed leading positions in the universities and in the publishing industry; and (4) the politicization of priests and feminist activists in the aftermath of Vatican II and the Tlatelolco and Corpus Christi massacres.

Progressive journalists, lay activists, and radical priests were crucial in disseminating the language of human rights and in taking advantage of President Jimmy Carter's implicit use of the term in foreign policy on Latin America, particularly the Southern Cone. At the forefront of this change were José

Álvarez Icaza from CENCOS and Enrique Maza from *Proceso*, Quezada concluded.[97] Surprisingly overlooked in her excellent analysis of the administration of Echeverría, however, is the important role these two figures played in articulating a clear condemnation of the brutal repression of religious figures. Among those who were tortured at the hands of the government in 1972 were the Marist priests Oscar Núñez and Rafael Reygadas.[98] "Oscar took the brunt" of the beatings, Reygadas noted in an interview. But they both remained terrorized. As his friend left for Paris, he also considered going into exile, but after consulting with one of his superiors, he decided to take refuge at a Dominican convent in Tolantongo, Hidalgo. Reygadas stayed there for thirty days with the help of the friar and key advocate of human rights, Miguel Concha Malo. Five years later the radical priests Rodolfo Escamilla and Rodolfo Aguilar were assassinated, and months later Reygadas left the priesthood.[99]

By this time, a younger generation of Catholics saw little relevance in their religious faith and left what remained of the MEP. Others made an attempt to keep the movement relevant, including two of its leaders, Luis Sereno Coló and María Vasquez. In 1973, the two friends turned their energy to building a new Catholic movement, "capable of bringing together prominent professionals invested in expanding the work of the MEP to an older generation of lay activists."[100] In this effort, they reconnected with their friends from the Latin American Secretariat (then stationed in Lima) who had been politically active in university Catholic circles during the Sixties.[101]

With financial support from Adveniat, Sereno and Vasquez traveled to Rome in April 1975 to attend the World Congress of the International Movement for Intellectuals and Cultural Affairs. Their central goal was to "revive the importance" of its Latin American affiliate, the International Movement of Catholic Intellectuals, which had lost relevance in the region. A year later, Sereno was selected to be the Latin American director of the organization. His friends succeeded him in the 1980s. Encouraging their members to "put their faith into action" and organizing three important conferences in Rio de Janeiro (1975) and Mexico City (1976 and 1979), with further support from the Germans, Sereno, Vasquez, and their friends brought together lawyers, doctors, jurists, scientists, engineers, architects, psychologists, university professors, and sociologists from all over the continent into a single organization that in the 1980s effectively fought for the creation of human rights organizations and the return to democracy in the region.[102] But as they wrote in their 1979–82 letters to their peers in South America and

Germany, "Our task [seemed] impossible [at first]."[103] Vasquez explained in an interview, "We only saw more significant results during the 1980s, when [more Catholics] finally embraced the language of human rights."[104]

Luis Sereno and María Vasquez referred to three central challenges that initially undermined their work during this period: (1) "the false premise" that Mexico was democratic in comparison to their Latin American neighbors, as championed by the populist administrations of Echeverría and López Portillo; (2) the "strengthening of the conservative wing of the church" that successfully aligned itself with the anticommunist policies of the PRI government and López Trujillo's CELAM; and (3) the "misguided idea" embraced by a small but vocal minority of young people that "irresponsibly" called for a violent revolution. They adamantly rejected armed struggle and instead insisted in their letters to their European and Latin American friends that real structural change could only be initiated from a place of peaceful love and within the institutional path toward democracy and the universal respect for human rights.[105]

CONCLUSION

The centrality of Ignacio Salas Obregón and José Luis Sierra in the history of armed struggle in Mexico is exceptional. But their stories are emblematic of dozens of young Catholics whose biographies have received less attention from historians, including Héctor Torres González and Eufemia Belén Almanza Villarreal. With conservative roots in the mid-1960s, both were radicalized in the aftermath of the Tlatelolco and Corpus Christi massacres. When asked why they had left their families, adopted pseudonyms, and lived underground to join the September 23 Communist League, Héctor and Eufemia simply answered, "For the love of Christ and for each other."[106]

The young couple first met as members of the MEP in Monterrey during the 1960s. Héctor came from a family of railroad workers with a long history of labor activism. As a child he was an altar boy, and in his youth he expressed interest in becoming a priest. In high school he met a Marxist professor and engaged in his first political protests. At the university, he fell in love with Eufemia, who introduced Héctor to the Jesuit priests Javier de Obeso and Salvador Rábago. Together the new couple were introduced to the Revision of Life method of seeing, judging, and acting at the university.

A native of Monterrey, Eufemia grew up in Ciudad Reynosa, Tamaulipas, where she enrolled at the Salesian Institute of Columbus. In Monterrey, her parents then transferred her to the Mexican College, a boarding school run by the Sisters of Charity of the Incarnate Word. While the congregation was overwhelmingly conservative, "a small group of radical nuns" introduced Eufemia to the social teachings of the church and to the Jesuit priest Rábago. "I thought of becoming a nun," she said. "But instead I enrolled in the chemistry school of the Autonomous University of Nuevo León, where I met Héctor and strengthened my relationship with the priests. With them, I organized a series of literacy campaigns. . . . When my parents found out that I was politically active, they tried to convince me to return home to Tamaulipas, where they both worked. But ultimately they trusted my judgment and believed that my interaction with the Jesuits would keep me safe."[107]

In 1971 and 1972, the young couple participated in various student protests, and with Ignacio Olivares Torres (a member of the Corporation of Mexican Students), they organized what the students at Monterrey called "contra-cursos." These informal "counterhegemony workshops" provided crash courses on a variety of topics that students found relevant but were missing in the university curriculum. These ranged from introductory teachings on Marxism and roundtable discussions on the French student movement and the Vietnam War to Freire's critical pedagogy and "more specific themes related to our religious interests." The latter included detailed discussions with the Jesuits on the Revision of Life method, the life of Camilo Torres, the teachings of Pierre Teilhard de Chardin, and liberation theology, explained Héctor. He pointed also to the spiritual retreats with the Claretian priest Kiko Hernández in Toluca, Torreón, and Guatemala as central events that politicized his view of the world during this period and put him in touch with other Latin American leaders, including a group of Uruguayans who introduced him to their publications and told him of the torture and disappearances of their comrades. With Paco Merino in Peru, the *Cuadernos de Documentación* of Pax Romana found greater distribution in Mexico.[108] "The book by Gustavo Gutiérrez had just been published," remembered Eufemia, and with the priests they discussed it in relation to the anticolonialist encyclical *Populorum progressio*. When the Jesuits were expelled from Monterrey in the late Sixties, many of their compañeros lost faith in nonviolence. Then, in the aftermath of the Corpus Christi massacre and the violent repression of railroad workers in Monterrey in 1972, they "found the radicalism of the militant Left more attractive." This "radicalism, of which we were part," added Eufemia, only intensified after the brutal repression of their peers that followed "the expropriation of 1972" (the bank robbery in Monterrey that led to the creation of the September 23 Communist League).[109] That same year, a group of government agents illegally detained and tortured the Marist priests Rafael Reygadas and Oscar Núñez.[110]

In February 1973, Héctor and Eufemia were picked up by the police. Along with other young people, they were interrogated about the bank robbery. Their names were added to the thick surveillance files of the Directorate of Federal Security, which intensified its repression of the militant Left following the 1973 assassination of Garza Sada.[111] Momentarily released from prison and ordered to present themselves in court, the young couple instead went home. They said goodbye to their respective families and saw some of them for the last time before they went underground. From 1973 to 1988, they lived clandestine lives as "Mario" and "Dolores," but for their comrades at the Communist League, they were part of a larger group of "Christians" that included former members of the Corporation of Mexican Students, the MEP, and the Christian Democratic movement. They got married during this period and had four children. In 1976 they "underwent a process of rectification," meaning that they abandoned armed struggle but continued to support the militant Left as social activists in underground networks in Mexico City.

Throughout this period the young couple organized an independent union of garbage collectors and led literacy campaigns with them. In 1988 they were no longer included on the list of "wanted terrorists," and they reclaimed their birth names. They remained politically active in oppositional parties, including the Socialist Mexican Party and the Democratic Revolutionary Party. To this day, many of their peers with similar backgrounds find it difficult to step inside a church, but like them, Eufemia and Héctor have remained committed to their progressive Catholic faith and reflect on their clandestine lives with a mixed sense of nostalgia and profound sadness. But when asked about their relationships and interactions with the Jesuits at the University Cultural Workshop, they both expressed a great sense of joy and pride. Eufemia remarked, "The Jesuits introduced us to a meaningful faith, based on the principles of love, that resonated with the [utopian] language of the times." Héctor nodded his head in agreement during the interview and added that he learned to speak the more orthodox language of the Left at the university, but what got him through those difficult years were the lessons that he learned with the priests and Catholic activists they met at the Monterrey workshops, including Kiko Hernández and especially the Jesuits De Obeso and Rábago. In the context of the Sixties, the priests reinterpreted the historical life of Jesus as a conscious person who rose up against a tyrannical system, and it was because of this that many of them were falsely accused of instigating violence. "There is nothing further from the truth," added Héctor. The priests always spoke to them of the importance of love. It was De Obeso and Rábago, Eufemia explained, "who taught us, by action, that the [the possibility of creating] the Kingdom of God [was] here, not after death." All they needed to do was express a "committed sense of love for each other," not in the abstract, but as a "concrete gesture of dignity and mutual respect."[112]

As noted in chapter 2, it was the wealthy entrepreneur Garza Sada who had paid for the establishment of the University Cultural Workshop in 1962. His goal was to create a conservative space capable of counterbalancing the rise of leftist activism in the schools. For support, he initially reached out to the leader of the Corporation of Mexican Students, Father Mayagoitia.[113] But with the arrival of the younger De Obeso and Rábago in 1964 and 1966, the Workshop soon extended its relationship with the MEP. Monterrey newspapers did not welcome the Jesuits and often accused them of instigating violence. By 1970, these criticisms had reached a larger audience, a "silent majority," in the words of the Argentinian historian Sebastián Carassai, that tacitly sided with the repressive government authorities.[114] The archbishop of Monterrey, Alfonso Espino, prohibited them from officiating university masses. Rábago fell ill and eventually left the priesthood to join the leftist Democratic Revolutionary Party. De Obeso was expelled from Monterrey. Porfirio Miranda had suffered a similar fate, and he too was expelled from Chihuahua, before his trip to Europe. After a short internship with worker-priests in Colombia, he joined De la Rosa in Mexico City. Like him, De Obeso grew disillusioned with Pedro Arrupe and left the priesthood in 1976. Miranda, who had been influential to young Catholics in Chihuahua, continued his social work with De la Rosa and Morelli in Nezahualcóyotl. He became one of the central founders of Metropolitan Autonomous University in 1975 and remained politically active in televised debates and in his columns in *Proceso* for the rest of the decade.[115]

Héctor and Eufemia learned the Revision of Life method with the Jesuits at the University Cultural Workshop. They participated with them in "debate masses," where the priests broke with tradition by inviting the attendees to discuss the documents of Medellín and other foundational texts that shaped the Catholic radicalism of the era, including *Populorum progressio* and the pedagogical teachings of Paulo Freire. They carried these lessons with them, and so did many of the Christians who ultimately joined the September 23 Communist League, remembered Héctor. He added, "Do I regret joining the League? The answer is no." They believed in the possibility of creating a better world, and while the League gave them that opportunity, it was their Catholicism that strengthened their cause.[116]

The accounts given by Héctor and Eufemia are emblematic of the radicalism shared among hundreds of Latin American university students during the Global and Catholic Sixties, a period with utopian roots in the Revision of Life method in the mid-1950s that ended with a greater sense of despair following the state repression of the early 1970s.[117] "Colonialism," "the system," "self-determination," "Third Worldism," "revolutionary love," and "youth power" formed part of their vocabulary, as further evident in the letters written by other members of the MEP and in the Pax Romana publications from South America. According to young Catholic activists of the era, they were "going through a decisive moment for the future life of our [continent]." The student body "represented an essential factor" that was "capable of creating the situations that determine necessary or irremediable change."[118] It was fundamental, then, to adopt social responsibility for the people, analyze their problems, transform the egoist vision of previous generations into a communitarian sentiment, and, in the words of Che Guevara and Camilo Torres, call for the creation of a new and more integrated person.[119] In addition, they had to eliminate hatred within the student sector of the Left and of the extreme Right and replace it with a much more critical attitude of self-reflection.[120] For these activists, it was no longer sufficient to criticize immediate surroundings without also "being aware of our own attitudes regarding God's plan for salvation, which are still very poor."[121] Finally, it was necessary to break down the anachronistic nationalism that kept people in an economic and religious state of misery. The religious life of the student should not be circumscribed to a privileged sector or nationalist rhetoric. Catholic students, they insisted, had to open the borders to the universal fraternity of humanity.[122] For many of them, the nation ceased to exist as a point of reference. Instead, with the guidance of extraordinary chaplains like Hernández, Reygadas, Del Valle, De la Rosa, and Morelli, they conceived of their movement in the broader continental context of la

Patria Grande, which they came to understand in relation to their changing Catholic faith.[123] Luis Sereno Coló and María Vasquez shared this sentiment, but like many of their peers, they found greater relevance in the language of human rights. Others, as examined in the following chapters, would find liberation in the counterculture and the arts.

PART THREE

The Counterculture, Liberation, and the Arts

SIX

La Onda as Liberation and the Making of *La contracultura como protesta*

More than seven hundred participants attended the First National Congress of Theology in November 1969. The goal of the congress was to discuss the future of the liberationist movement in Mexico. But "liberation" proved to be a contentious term. In evaluating its significance and national particularities, the participants were encouraged to present their ideas in the form of roundtable discussions. The young Claretian priests Javier "Kiko" Hernández and Enrique Marroquín took advantage of this opportunity to present their different understandings of liberation in relation to the needs of the nation's youth. For Hernández, the term was overwhelmingly political and largely revolved around the question of student militancy, as examined in the previous chapter. What options were students left with in the aftermath of the Tlatelolco massacre? he and the others who attended the roundtable discussion asked.[1] His friend Marroquín expressed no interest in politics and instead spoke about the counterculture, not as a by-product of imperialism, a cheap imitation from the United States, or a reflection of the moral decay of the Sixties, as many leftist and conservative intellectuals argued at the time, but rather as a genuine form of liberation. The consumption of natural drugs had played a defining role in this process. But he simultaneously warned that its abuse had become a serious problem across the world, as many young people had become enslaved to it. What the church needed was not to blindly condemn drug use but to understand why young people saw a need for it. In one of the several roundtable discussions organized by the Dominican priest Alex Morelli, Marroquín asked what was the goal of the counterculture, how did it shape the nation's youth, and what did it reveal about the changing attitudes of the times? What role, if any, should young Catholics and religious leaders play in shaping the movement?[2]

This chapter provides partial answers to these questions by examining figures in the church, lay Catholics, and filmmakers who demonstrated an interest in promoting a dialogue with "la onda," as the counterculture came to be understood in Mexico from the mid-Sixties to the early 1970s. It places the biography of the hippie priest Enrique Marroquín at the center of this story and in contrast to the ambivalent interpretations of the counterculture in the films made from 1962 to 1968 and in the more conservative pages of the Catholic magazines *Juventud* and *Señal*. Marroquín wrote one of the most detailed books on the subject of la onda, *La contracultura como protesta* (1975), but his contributions to the counterculture are also examined here in relation to his bohemian years in Europe and in the columns that he wrote for Mexico's *Rolling Stone* magazine, *Piedra Rodante*. For Marroquín, the most valuable lessons of la onda were the awareness it brought to the rising environmentalist movement and its celebration of youth culture.

ENRIQUE MARROQUÍN: FROM ALIENATION TO THE EXCITING WORLD OF THE COUNTERCULTURE

The eldest of three brothers, Enrique Marroquín grew up in a middle-class household in Colonia Roma. He was diagnosed with dysthymia in the 1940s. His parents hoped that an athletic life would help him with his episodic lapses into depression and boredom. Instead, he found excitement in "adventure and mystical" books. He also loved doing magic tricks, listening to music, and attending Sunday Mass. At school, he earned the nickname "el mago." He practiced card tricks and illusions at school. But it was listening to music that allowed him to cope with the mounting alienation that often left him lying on bed at home. While enrolled at the British elementary Windsor School he learned English and became familiar with French, which his parents often spoke at home.

Marroquín enrolled at the prestigious Mexican College at the age of twelve. The Marist priests managed this secondary school and introduced him to the teachings of the church. He studied philosophy and hoped one day to be a professor. At fifteen, he entered the Claretian Seminary in Toluca where he first met Javier "Kiko" Hernández. Together they participated in various clubs, often free of ecclesiastical authorities, where they discussed religious texts and tried to make sense of the modern world. This is when Kiko first became interested in student politics, but Enrique remained fascinated with philosophy and the arts. He was captivated by the exciting world of music. US jazz and its English-language lyrics spoke to his heart like no other music in Spanish did at the time. Learning lyrics and delving into philosophical questions, in short, gave Marroquín an opportunity to envision his life outside the constraints of his bedroom and helped him cope with his childhood depression and boredom.[3]

In 1960 Hernández and Marroquín finished their studies in philosophy at the Seminary of Toluca, where the Claretians had established their first order in Mexico in 1884. The two friends had decided that they wanted to become priests, but there was nowhere to study theology in Mexico at that time. Their superiors sent Hernández to Rome and Marroquín to Salamanca. The authoritarianism of Franco was stronger than ever, recalled Marroquín, as he reflected on his arrival in Spain. The ultraconservative attitude of the Spanish church was "suffocating." He remembered learning about the outbreak of the Cuban Revolution, as discreetly discussed by some of the Latin Americans enrolled in the seminary. But the anticommunist environment of the place made it impossible to openly talk about this and similar topics that politicized his generation.[4]

In July 1964, at the age of twenty-five, Marroquín was ordained a Claretian priest. As the reforms of Vatican II challenged the most conservative sectors of the church, the Spanish authorities could not entirely silence the progressive voices that emerged in the seminary. Marroquín met a group of Latin American students who held heated discussions based on their reading of the journal FERES (Federación Internacional de Investigaciones Sociales y Socioreligiosas), where the aspiring priests were encouraged to discuss the reality of the colonized world using the tools of sociology. Collectively, they advocated for a return to the sources of the Christian faith and a more systematic openness to dialogue, as progressive figures of the church had insisted in Western Europe since the 1940s.[5] It was in these discussions, Marroquín remembered, where he first discovered that he was Latin American and where he became familiar with the concepts of colonization, underdevelopment, the Third World, and liberation. He sympathized with the idea of establishing a productive dialogue with modernity and encouraging a proactive role of the church in documenting the socioeconomic conditions of the Latin American continent, as championed by his friends. However, unlike most of his peers, he was disinterested in politics and expressed little excitement about the social work of the church. Rather, it was the innovative expressions of music from the United States and Great Britain that fascinated Marroquín, and so did the rebellious attitude of young people that swept most of the Western world in the early Sixties.

Once ordained, Marroquín received permission to continue his studies in Europe. He enrolled in a graduate program in philosophy at the Università San Tommaso in Rome, where he hoped to reconnect with Kiko Hernández, unaware that his friend had returned to Mexico as the spiritual leader of student activists, as discussed in the previous chapter.

Marroquín joined a small group of bohemian intellectuals who met regularly in Rome to discuss philosophy, religion, music, and poetry. With a group of them, he traveled by train or hitchhiked to various cities in Europe. He learned what and how much to carry in his backpack and where to find cheap places to sleep. He was often the only priest in the group. Together they visited museums and art galleries. But they also frequently ended up in the "shadiest of bars" and at the "strangest house parties," where they often drank red wine until the early hours of the following day. It was in these places and specifically in the basement of a Lutheran church in London where Marroquín saw "the first young people consuming heavy drugs" and where he was introduced to the latest and most exciting music he had ever heard. This is the time he first heard "Satisfaction," released by the Rolling Stones in the United Kingdom in 1965 and performed by a local rock band in Rome. "Its anticonsumerist message" not only resonated with the bohemian life he was living in Europe, he recalled, but this and similar songs spoke to what he saw as some of the contradictions in his life, including questions related to his faith, his God, his sexuality, his nationalism, and his bourgeois upbringing.[6]

At the University of Louvain, Marroquín enrolled in a philosophy class (with Robert Guelluy) and imagined the possibility of bringing together the two worlds that shaped his identity but continued to pull him apart: the traditional religious faith that he learned in Mexico and Salamanca, on the one hand, and the new and exciting bohemian world of the Sixties that fascinated him, on the other. This demanded a direct dialogue with the sexuality, music, attitude, and aesthetics of a new generation of thinkers and artists. With beatniks, he drank absinthe and discussed *Howl* (Ginsburg, 1956), *On the Road* (Kerouac, 1957), *Naked Lunch* (Burroughs, 1959), and *Island* (Huxley, 1962). With "long hairs," he listened to rock music and learned about the anarchist movements from Europe that organized happenings in the streets, gave free meals in public parks, and provoked the police authorities with nonviolent acts of defiance. With university students, he read Sartre, de Beauvoir, Camus, and Marcuse, and with other young Catholics, he attended one of the first "Beat Masses" held in Rome. This is when he first listened to the rock band Barritas (the Little Berets), and he could not have been "more thrilled." Held at the San Filippo Neri Oratorium in Rome and with the goal of bringing young people back to the church, the Mass took place on April 27, 1966. Using electric guitars, keyboards, bass, and percussion, Barritas performed with the Bumpers and Angel & the Brains. They employed beat music that "encouraged young people to think of peace and brotherhood" as they reconnected with God and celebrated what many saw as the spirituality of the Sixties, namely, innovative notions of liberation, social justice, solidarity, and love.[7]

In Rome, Marroquín also became interested in existentialism. For his thesis project, he proposed a comparative study of existence as differently understood by Aquinas and Heidegger. But he lamented not having completed his graduate studies. His superiors were frustrated with his free spirit and ordered him back to Mexico, where he arrived in the summer of 1967 wearing jeans and thick eyeglasses. Marroquín was furious with the uncompromising attitudes of the ecclesiastical hierarchy and depressed, as he was close to defending his thesis and only getting increasingly consumed in the bohemianism of Western Europe.

But to his surprise Marroquín realized that Mexico City had changed significantly. It was not as asphyxiating as he remembered it in 1960, when he left for Europe. He was delighted to reconnect with his younger brother, by then a university student at UNAM, who introduced Enrique to the countercultural scene of the Zona Rosa and to the urban communes that Mexican hippies had built on the rooftops of buildings in the Colonias del Valle and Roma. This is where Marroquín first learned of the psychedelic work of José Agustín, Parménides García Saldaña, and Alejandro Jodorowsky.[8] Like them, Marroquín emerged as a key, though more reserved, player in la onda.

LA ONDA IN CATHOLIC MEXICO

The roots of Mexico's counterculture can be traced to the mid-1950s.[9] This is when Jack Kerouac and other American beat poets first traveled to Mexico, when rock music and the "rebels without a cause" first debuted on national television and films, and when the American mycologist R. Gordon Wasson first published the findings of his visits to Huautla de Jiménez in the southern state of Oaxaca. There Gordon met María Sabina, the Mazatec traditional healer who shared the hallucinogenic powers of the *santitos* (little saints, or sacred mushrooms) with him.[10] Soon after, the Mexican historian and journalist Fernando Benítez published similar studies in the national daily *Excélsior* on the peyote of the Huichol culture from the desert regions in the northern states of the nation.[11] By 1962 scores of beatniks and bohemians from the United States had arrived in the mountains of Oaxaca in search of María Sabina and other shamans in the region and their magic mushrooms. Others hitchhiked to Real de Catorce (in San Luis Potosi), Acapulco (in Guerrero), and Puerto Escondido (in Oaxaca) in pursuit of peyote and similar drugs.[12]

The irreverent young writers Parménides García Saldaña and José Agustín also published their experimental literature in the daily *Ovaciones* in 1962 and soon after in the magazines *Pop* and *Claudia*.[13] Within four years, these and other authors had written some of the most influential books of the counterculture, including *La Tumba* (1964), *Gazapo* (1965), *Pasto Verde* (1968), and *Larga Sinfonía en D* (1968).[14] What distinguished this literature was its aggressive and erotic ethos. In irreverent and violent prose, the authors celebrated the values and language of the marginalized sectors of society and were critical of all forms of authoritarianism. They poked fun at political and religious authorities, violated grammatical rules, and rejected the nationalistic tendencies, so valued by earlier writers. They provided their readers with vivid descriptions of getting intoxicated and spoke openly about experimental sex outside marriage, homosexuality, alcohol, and rock music.[15]

The bold discussion of these themes was also evident in the multiple artistic movements that emerged during the early Sixties, particularly in the realms of theater, poetry, and painting. Led by José Luis Cuevas, Mathias Goeritz, Felipe Ehrenberg, Sergio Mondragón, Margaret Randall, Alejandro Jodorowsky, and others, this new generation of artists aggressively mocked the nationalistic language of the muralist movement and rejected the convenient relationship that older artists had developed with the state (mainly through government commissions). They translated foundational texts of the era, opened new independent spaces for artistic expression, spoke against the commercialization of art, and challenged the boundaries of censorship.[16]

"Free Love" in the Conservative Press

By the mid-Sixties, la onda had developed into a full-blown movement that grabbed the attention of politicians, intellectuals, filmmakers, and an array of religious figures and lay Catholics who expressed diverse positions on the subjects of sex, drugs, alcohol, and rock music. In November 1966, for example, leaders of Mexican Female Catholic Youth (JCFM) organized their Second Cultural Forum of Mexican Youth in San Luis Potosí; there the women affirmed that it was "time for us, and for the church, to talk about sex."[17] A year later the Dominicans at UNAM led similar discussions and also organized a conference where they concluded that the time had come to break old taboos related to sexuality and start a productive conversation about the new notions of femininity and masculinity.[18] It was agreed in both of these meetings that religious authorities could no longer afford to turn their backs on young people but had to find tangible ways to make them return to the church. However, these discussions contrasted with the conservative overtones of *Humanae vitae*. First published in July 1968, the encyclical was a theological reflection on sexuality and heterosexual Christian marriage and reaffirmed the ban on all forms of artificial contraception, including the pill, which was first available for purchase in Mexico in the early Sixties.[19]

Leaders of JCFM, who had radically called for an open dialogue about sex, quickly retracted their 1966 comments, and after the publication of *Humanae vitae* they cautioned young women about the dangers of "free love" outside marriage.[20] The young Catholic women who published in *Señal* made similar claims, suggesting that although it was true that young women could no longer afford to be as pious as they had been in the past, they had to make every effort to defend their virginity until marriage. According to the young university student Diana, free love was something men had "invented." It was for "cowards" who were afraid of assuming the responsibilities of marriage. For her peer Beatriz, it was "simply silly," but for their friends Cristina, Eva, and Yolanda, free love was no laughing matter and seemed rather "unnatural." Like Diana, they believed that it reduced women to sex objects. It was "harmful" to their health and "detrimental to love."[21] In *Juventud*, writers continued to condemn flirting, which they described as a dangerous game that blurred the lines between lust and love. As they had maintained since the 1940s and 1950s, a healthy relationship was based on trust and respect and could only be guaranteed if women were "pure."[22]

In November 1968 and August 1970, the JCFM organized its Third and Fifth National Encounters of Youth in the conservative cities of Guanajuato and Puebla under the central theme, "The Female Student in the World of Today." During the encounters, the organizers presented theatrical performances representing the "world of today" from the perspective of youth. In Guanajuato, the play included two contrasting floating boats. In the first of these allegorical plays the audience could read the words "rebelliousness, tensions with parents, vices, immorality, laziness, and sexual licentiousness" as some of the central problems students faced while enrolled in school. In a second allegorical boat, the organizers included the words "joy, strength, fiery, initiative, hope, and tenacity" as the tools necessary to overcome their problems. They also portrayed contrasting groups found in their schools. While the first group was made up of male and female hippies, exaggeratedly depicted as dirty, smelly, intoxicated, and sexually licentious, the second celebrated what members of JCFM saw as the ideal female student: a well-kept and virtuous young girl, attentive to her beauty but primarily committed to her studies, family, and work. She is shown sewing, cooking, studying, working at the office, volunteering in hospitals, and engaging in charity projects in poor neighborhoods.

In Puebla the organizers opted for a staged happening. It included rock music and a series of heated conversations between students, hippies, doctors, and a priest, each providing their own ideas of youth rebellion. The concerns varied little from the tone of the Guanajuato encounter, but this time the organizers were more explicit about the specific dangers associated with "dropping out" of society, namely, getting lost in the world of drugs, joining militant movements, living in communes, and relying on contraception to have experimental sex outside marriage.[23]

By 1970, leaders of the JCFM and some writers for *Juventud* and *Señal* had concluded that the pill was detrimental to the health of young women and antithetical to their faith.[24] Similarly, many (male) doctors who published in these Catholic magazines not only argued that pharmaceutical contraceptives likely caused cancer, depression, psychosis, hemorrhages, and infertility but also associated it with the "de-feminization" of the nation's young women.[25]

Numerous articles were also published in Catholic magazines regarding the use of drugs and the emergence of hippies in Mexico. These publications presented the polarizing voices that existed within the national church. In *Señal*, for example, the philosopher and advocate of Vatican II, Gaspar Elizondo, published a sympathetic and emblematic 1968 article. Compellingly, he condemned the state repression of hippies. He defined la onda as a "stammering" yet "natural" response to a materialistic world that had abandoned the spiritual well-being of society.[26]

By comparison, the priest, poet, and weekly contributor to the more conservative daily *El Sol*, Joaquín Antonio Peñalosa, made an attempt to introduce the readers of *Señal* to the phenomenon of la onda by suggesting that both the "negative" and the "positive" characteristics of the hippies needed to be understood before making a final judgment. He published interviews he conducted with twenty-five students from the United States enrolled in his journalism class at the University of San Luis Potosí in 1968. In his interpretation, the American students described hippies as dirty, lazy, ill-advised, and shallow, yet idealistic and genuinely invested in imagining a better future for society, free of violence and materialism. Like Elizondo, Peñalosa suggested that perhaps the phenomenon of la onda had something important to say. It should not be ignored, much less repressed. Yet his ambivalent attitude to hippies did not extend to the topic of drugs. In agreement with other contributors to *Señal*, he called for strict regulation of the trafficking and consumption of all drugs. He lamented that little reliable knowledge was available on the subject in Mexico. Concretely, how much of a problem was it, he asked, and who was to be blamed for its popularity among the nation's youth?[27]

These questions were at the center of the discussion in the pages of *Señal* and directly addressed during the Second International Youth Forum held in Mexico City in February 1970. Specifically, the forum identified "violence, drugs, and eroticism" as the three most detrimental problems facing Mexican youth.[28] In agreement, *Señal* demanded that its readers come to the defense of the nation, suggesting that the rise in youth criminality, alienation, and suicides, allegedly associated with the consumption of drugs, was due to the breakdown of the Mexican family and the commercialization of la onda by films and the music and fashion industries. Not too different from the filmmakers of the 1950s, its writers placed most of the blame on liberal parents and entrepreneurs in the cultural industry. While the former had abandoned their faith and embraced a cult of leisure, money, and consumerism, they argued, the latter had jumped at the opportunity to profit from the commercialization of the "hippie trend."[29]

Alberto Barranco Chavarría was a regular contributor to *Señal* and a teacher at the Carlos Septién García School of Journalism. In his articles on the counterculture, he described la onda as a cheap imitation imported from the United States, not much different from the description often given by leftist intellectuals of the era, arguing that it lacked authenticity and political legitimacy. But in adopting a Catholic perspective, he also described the counterculture as the antithesis of love. He and others in *Señal* argued that the hippie slogan "peace and love" had only brought "degeneration" and the "eroticization" of the nation's youth. In questioning traditional marriage, he concluded, using anecdotal quotes from young people allegedly affected by the radicalism of la onda, the imitating hippies had "de-feminized the national woman." It had normalized the consumption of drugs and corrupted the notion of true love. [30]

However, what the hippies needed was not an authoritarian hand but instead greater understanding from parents, who should engage in sincere dialogue with their children, and a stronger presence of Catholicism in their lives. From the perspective of *Señal*, rock music and psychedelic clothes were not a problem as long as these were complemented with the love of Christ. In short, true Catholic love needed to be brought back to the rebellious Mexico of the times, based on the principles of charity, faith, hope, respect, and modesty.

The Threat of Aggiornamento and the Psychedelic Liberation of Young Women at the Movies

Filmmakers of the early Sixties also commented on the rise of la onda, and similar to the conservative magazines, they provided rich descriptions of its intersections with Catholicism.[31] Unlike those examined in chapter 1, their films made a more conscious effort to examine countercultural rebellion from the perspective of young people and offered intriguing commentary on the liberation of women. They also documented the difficulties priests and nuns had in adapting to aggiornamento, the Vatican II efforts to bring the church "up to date" in a productive dialogue with modernity.

Los perversos (a-go-go) (Gilberto Martínez Solares, 1965) is an emblematic film of the early Sixties. It tells the story of Miguel Antonio, a priest caught between the reforms of Vatican II and a traditional Mexican society that is unwilling to accept the youth rebelliousness of the decade.[32] In his effort to engage in dialogue with youth, he welcomes rock music and organizes "a-go-go" dances with university students.[33] The conflict begins when the young Julieta claims to have fallen in love with him. Initially, the priest appears flattered and acknowledges her beauty. Yet he is ultimately loyal to his faith and rejects the seduction of the young girl whose broken family (divorced parents, the drunk mother abandoned and the father a cheater and materialistic) is depicted as an explanation for her rebelliousness. Father

Miguel remains close to Julieta, nonetheless. He hopes that he can help with her misguided emotions.

Tony and Loreni are also in need of guidance from the priest. A leader of a criminal gang, Tony represents the most undesirable of his generation. Raised as an orphan by a greedy uncle, Tony has no moral upbringing. He is a petty thief and regularly cheats on his pious girlfriend, Loreni. The young man resents the paternal image of the priest as he repeatedly retaliates against him throughout the film. He crashes the dance parties organized by the church and accuses Father Miguel of hiding behind his cassock to seduce young girls. Tony is audacious and unpredictable. After having been publicly humiliated by the priest, he steals the priest's car and in his attempt to escape from the cops runs over his pregnant girlfriend. The drama only intensifies after this tragic incident. In public, Tony accuses Father Miguel of getting his girlfriend pregnant. Worse yet, after tearing her own dress, Julieta also publicly denounces the priest and falsely accuses him of sexually assaulting her in his office. A traditional family, already suspicious of the modern methods of the priest, witnesses Julieta's public accusations and makes a formal complaint to the bishop of Mexico City. Humiliated, Father Miguel confesses to his superior that he is experiencing a crisis of faith. He expresses doubt about the modern approach he has implemented with youth but assures the bishop that all accusations made against him are false. The bishop sides with the priest, and so does Julieta's mother, who discovers the truth in her daughter's journal.

The film concludes with the same moralistic overtones that characterized the pictures of an earlier era.[34] Loreni dies in the hospital after confessing to the priest that she had a sexual encounter with Tony outside wedlock and is now carrying his child. The boyfriend also dies after crashing his motorcycle as he attempts to run away from the police, who are depicted favorably throughout the film. Clearly, both of these young sinners are beyond redemption in the conservative and lawful Mexico of the early Sixties. Yet Julieta's parents realize that their daughter's salvation depends on their getting back together and renewing their Catholic vows. With the blessing of the priest, the parents send Julieta to a psychiatric hospital where she will be treated for her rebelliousness. The film concludes with a scene depicting a rejoicing Father Miguel officiating Mass in a full church as he presumably learned from his mistakes and perhaps will now move away from the modern and apparently misguided methods demanded with aggiornamento.

Los perversos was released in 1967. That same year Carlos Velo and Juan Ibáñez filmed *Cinco de chocolate y uno de fresa* and *Los caifanes*, respectively.

Influenced by *Los jóvenes* (Alcoriza, 1961), both films successfully touched on the topic of the counterculture from the perspective of young people.[35] They effectively mocked the authoritarianism of the era, celebrated the liberation of young women, and in the case of *Cinco de chocolate y uno de fresa,* alluded to the shifting perceptions of Catholicism in post–Vatican II Mexico.

Cinco de chocolate y uno de fresa is a raucous fantasy comedy that pays particular attention to the counterculture, state repression, the liberation of female sexuality, and Catholicism. It tells the coming-of-age story of Esperanza, a young novice raised in a cloistered convent that refuses to adhere to the orders of the church following Vatican II, which demanded that nuns modernize their traditional practices of solitude, solemnity, and sacrifice, including putting an end to self-flagellation, getting rid of their flowing robes, and abandoning the idea that they are closer to God than anyone else.[36] As Esperanza's childhood comes to an end, she has to decide whether she wants to follow the example of the seven women who raised her and take the solemn vows to become a nun or instead experience life outside the convent for the first time and enroll in a secular school.

In her late teens, Esperanza is a beautiful and charming blue-eyed blonde with a sweet tooth and an "angelic" face. Her only sin is to eat chocolates and other treats without the knowledge of her superiors. Her biggest regret is not knowing what life is like outside the walls of the convent. One day she learns that one of the nuns has received a gift from an Indigenous village in Oaxaca containing a box of mushrooms. The aspiring nun, who cannot seem to control her desire for sweets, swallows the hallucinogenic santitos and suddenly transforms into Brenda. As portrayed in the poster of the film, Brenda is a beautiful brunet who wears a miniskirt and go-go boots.[37] She embraces her sexuality, sings and dances to rock music, and speaks the language of la onda.

The clash with the outside world is portrayed every time Esperanza consumes the magic mushrooms. Her psychedelic trip to the countercultural Sixties begins when Brenda breaks into the house party of a wealthy conservative family. After performing a "subversive" song celebrating her feminist liberation, she gets kicked out of the house and convinces a group of five young men to follow her for a night of adventures. They steal the luxurious gray car of the bishop. He is a special guest at the party who eventually labels the group of teenagers a "band of red subversives."

The six new friends drive to the nocturnal city. They stop at a Sanborns restaurant, and with plastic guns, they stage a robbery. They steal six scoops of ice cream, five chocolate for the male members of the new gang and one strawberry "with marmalade" for the female (and now *fresa*, or hip/self-centered) leader, Brenda. The outrageous robbery captures the attention of the director of the International Intelligence Agency, whose headquarters in Mexico has multiple ringing telephones conveying the latest information from the most influential authorities in the nation, including the bishop of Mexico City, who demands "law and order" be imposed on the "communists," as well as a high-pitched and incomprehensible voice from Washington that the director receives on the largest telephone on his desk.

What follows is a long list of frivolous adventures depicting key concerns shared by the nation's youth during the Sixties. These include the public humiliation of a powerful and corrupt labor leader (or *charro*, a symbol of the government in labor unions) who is forced to dance "zapateado" after having been stripped to his underwear in the streets and a break-in at the Animal Protection Society to liberate all the "imprisoned creatures," a clear reference to the political prisoners of President Díaz Ordaz. Other outrageous scenes include the sabotage of a commercial radio station playing "sanitized" rock music; the kidnapping of a wealthy entrepreneur in exchange for ransom money, a topic that would be of great concern to the authorities in the early 1970s; and a series of hilarious clashes with Mexico's top-secret agents, known as Green Carnations. These specialized agents are extraordinarily well informed about all the alleged crimes taking place in the city, but they are incapable of capturing the gang of young psychedelic "terrorists." The rebels are presented roaming wildly in the streets. They are armed with chocolate-filled bazooka missiles, which they fire at their adversaries during a parade commemorating the anniversary of the Mexican Revolution. The riotous film concludes as Esperanza comes to terms with her wild inner self, Brenda. Her appearance blends the best of these conflicting personalities, as the now red-haired protagonist takes off with her boyfriend Miguel on an intoxicated horse, who transforms into a motorcycle after having consumed magic mushrooms.

Cinco de chocolate refuses to reprimand the behavior of young people or provide them with an outrageous lesson to overcome their rebellion. This is a drastic and welcome contrast to the 1950s films that touched on these topics.[38] Through a blend of outrageous humor and fantasy, the film succeeds in capturing the sensibility and irony of la onda and the contradictions of a middle class fixated on defending good Catholic values but equally obsessed with indulging in modernity. In the broader context of the Cold War period, moreover, the film also succeeds in poking fun at a sensationalist media invested in exaggerating fictitious moral panic, an embellished reaction of a paranoid and largely inept state that becomes obsessed with its otherwise squandered power of surveillance (the Directorate of Federal Security), and then anachronistic attitude of an anticommunist church that refuses to engage with the outside world and the progressive reforms of Vatican II. For authenticity, the director, Carlos Velo, relied on a script written by José Agustín, the leading novelist of la onda. It includes performances by the rock band the Dug Dugs, which had achieved fame during this period by writing original songs in English and celebrating a distinctive countercultural sound.

But more importantly, unlike most of the films made during this time, *Cinco de chocolate* effectively depicted the female protagonist in charge of her own body and sexuality. This is also embodied by the lead actress, Angélica María, the beautiful "girlfriend of Mexico," as she came to be known soon after the film.[39] The actress has no interest in expressing the Catholic virtues that made Martha Mijares the prototype of Mexican beauty during the 1950s (see chap. 1) and instead celebrates her independent spirit and flaunts her sexuality. In her interpretation of Brenda, she is the one who selects her boyfriend, Miguel, who is not depicted as a central character of the story. Instead, she is represented as a superhero who succeeds in humiliating all the male authorities of the film.

Cinco de chocolate was released to theaters in December 1968, two months after the Tlatelolco massacre and a year after Enrique Marroquín returned to Mexico. While it is difficult to determine the reception of the film, it is evident that additional and more experimental films were made after the student movement. As examined in the following chapters, these films depicted a more somber and at times aggressive interpretation of la onda with a continued interest in Catholicism. Marroquín welcomed this radicalism of the counterculture and lamented its demise at the end of the Sixties.

THE "GROOVY PRIEST" AND HIS "HIP MESSAGE OF GOD"

Enrique Marroquín returned to Mexico in June 1967, the same time the United States witnessed its "Summer of Love," when the culmination, excess, and most utopian aspects of the counterculture were celebrated in a massive gathering in San Francisco. A few months earlier, Bob Dylan had transitioned to the electric guitar, John Lennon and George Harrison experienced LSD for the first time, a group of hippies founded the commune Drop City in Colorado, and Timothy Leary was arrested for drug possession at the US-Mexico border. Once released on bail, he initiated his "Turn on, tune in, drop out" crusade in New York and created the League for Spiritual Discovery. Also in 1967, the Beatles released their *Sgt. Pepper's Lonely Hearts Club Band* album, *Time* and *Look* magazines featured the pill and hippies on their covers, Jimi Hendrix returned home from London, Jim Morrison's The Doors performed "Light My Fire" on the Ed Sullivan show, the Yippies nominated a pig for president, and *Hair* featured the first frontal nudity onstage.[40] In short, by 1967, the most radical elements of the counterculture were in full swing in the United States, and as the historian Eric Zolov has argued, Mexico played a crucial role in this radicalization.[41]

Once in Mexico, Marroquín was asked by the Claretian order to lead a series of philosophy workshops at the hacienda of Santa Cruz de los Patos in Zinacantepec, in the state of Mexico. But conflicts quickly developed with the order. It disapproved of his lectures on existentialism and warned him that if he wanted to pursue his goal of establishing a career in teaching, he needed to stop speaking openly about his fascination with modern music and his experiences with the bohemian culture in Europe. Limited interaction with the outside world also made this a difficult time for him. Most of the priests teaching at the workshops were persuaded to limit their interactions with visitors, unless these were close family members or religious figures affiliated with the church. Nonetheless, Marroquín reconnected with his younger brother and with his friend Kiko Hernández. Both informed him of the 1968 student movement and provided him with details on the Tlatelolco massacre. Hernández expressed particular anger at what he described to his friend as a complicit Mexican church.[42]

By 1969, Marroquín had grown increasingly impatient with his superiors. They remained dissatisfied with his lifestyle and relocated him to the Sacred Heart of Mary Parish in the middle-class neighborhood of Colonia del Valle. By then, the most progressive religious authorities had made small but important steps to bridge the widening gap between the church and the nation's youth. As in Rome, a small number of local parishes had introduced poetry in their spiritual retreats and welcomed emerging rock bands that sported la onda style at their masses, including a group composed of long-haired musicians affiliated with the Jesuit order who called themselves La Fauna (fig. 8).[43]

FIGURE 8. The Jesuit rock band La Fauna. From *Señal* (October 23, 1971).

La Fauna visited the University Parish at UNAM on more than one occasion. Besides rock instruments, the band was influenced by the Nicaraguan poet and priest Enrique Cardenal and the Uruguayan singer Daniel Viglietti, whose poetic lyrics on love and justice influenced protest music in Central and South America. In an interview, a Dominican friar said that La Fauna represented the "ecumenical happenings of the era," which in Mexico had important antecedents in the 1950s in Cuernavaca with Sergio Méndez Arceo's Pan American masses, where the bishop got rid of the Gregorian chants, well before Vatican II, and to the dismay of many instead complemented his Spanish liturgy with mariachi music.[44]

Marroquín welcomed this gradual but radical opening within small sectors of the church that angered the majority of ecclesiastical authorities and conservative intellectuals.[45] In his new parish, he organized what he and others called *misas de juventud* (youth masses). During his homilies, he introduced his flock to the lyrics of the Beatles and responded to the critical take on Christianity often expressed by the famous British band. He made references to Native spirituality and preached on the importance of indiscriminate love. He also spoke openly about his passion for the blues and called on other priests to welcome electronic instruments and sounds into church choirs. For Marroquín, the Beatles epitomized the best of the counterculture. Their music not only brought together the atheism of John Lennon and the mysticism of George Harrison but also their shared discovery of transcendental meditation in the pacifist teachings of the Indian guru Maharishi Mahesh Yogi.[46] According to Marroquín, "The love celebrated by the [British] band spoke of harmony and a communal sense of well-being."[47]

While some churchgoers welcomed Marroquín, many attending his masses grew increasingly frustrated with the hippie priest and demanded his removal. Once again, his superiors transferred him to a different church. They sent him to the Parish of San Hipólito, near the Paseo de la Reforma (where, he remembered, "one could easily find marihuana plants cultivated in plain sight on the sidewalks of the central avenue"). This time, Marroquín was explicitly prohibited from using the pulpit to touch on the subject of the counterculture, and it became clear that his goal of becoming a philosophy teacher had started to dissipate. He abided by the orders given to him by his superiors, but he remained active in la onda outside the confines of the church, in rural and urban communes.[48]

Following an invitation from the Dominican friar Alex Morelli, Marroquín participated in the National Congress of Theology in 1969.[49] He spoke against the "alarmist tone" employed by the media in its coverage of la onda and accused it of creating unnecessary moral panic. Journalists had exaggerated the threat of drug consumption and oversimplified the reasons a minority of young people felt compelled to experiment with drugs. He also recognized and expressed dissatisfaction with the conservative church authorities for their unwillingness to listen to the needs of youth and criticized the government for censoring and indiscriminately repressing those who welcomed the style, language, attitude, and philosophy of la onda. He concluded that drugs could be detrimental to the nation's youth, as many people could become enslaved to it, but he defined the broader countercultural movement as an act of liberation. In making a distinction between the United States and Mexico, he argued that xipitecas had made a more conscious attempt to connect with the Native roots of the nation and its natural environment. Specifically, he drew a contrast between the consumption of the more dangerous LSD in the United States, which had been criminalized since 1966, and the more natural drugs found in Mexico, including mushrooms, peyote, and especially marihuana. In addition, he saw the smoking of marihuana as less harmful than the much more popular and commercialized consumption of alcohol.[50]

In his experimental interaction with drugs, Marroquín was equally critical of the moralistic language preferred by the ecclesiastical authorities. He expressed his dissatisfaction with the government-sponsored media and conservative filmmakers alike. The consumption of drugs "had nothing to do with sin," he said in a 1974 interview. Rather, "it [was] a sign of the times." Unfortunately, "the church had failed to demonstrate the sensibility" that was needed at the time. In its moralistic campaigns "it had lumped together" all drugs without making a distinction between those who consumed it respectfully in search of genuine liberation and those who became enslaved to it or abused it as a product of consumption. In their most liberating form, drugs were used by xipitecas in search of a new consciousness that, similar to the *Island* in Huxley's 1963 novel, effectively exposed "the decadence of the Western culture." La onda—including its psychedelic elements—allowed for the "possibility of imagining a less industrialized, alienated, artificial, materialistic, selfish, and contaminated world." The goal was to create a true "cosmic culture," not as the philosopher of the Mexican Revolution José Vasconcelos had once imagined it in his celebration of racial *mestizaje*, but as "a universal, more catholic culture, in the Hegelian sense," that is, as a criterion of moral responsibility and authority of individual conscience. Marroquín added that the most radical and utopian elements of the counterculture provided an opportunity to make the church "truly catholic," as Christ had envisioned it: universal, ecumenical, and based on the concepts of peace and love.[51]

The utopian interaction Marroquín had with the nation's youth in the early 1970s initially took place in private homes where he was free from ecclesiastical authorities and where the first urban communes in Mexico were created. He also frequently traveled to rural communes in Oaxaca, Veracruz, and Puebla where xipitecas interacted with US hippies.[52]

Marroquín often found himself talking about his spiritual journey in Europe with xipitecas and, when welcomed, he provided his religious opinion on the rising counterculture in Mexico. With them, he also became acquainted with other figures of la onda, including a small group of young people from the Colonia del Valle who called themselves El Quinqué Mágico (The Magic Five).[53] Together, they smoked marihuana, spoke of the health benefits of vegetarianism, experimented with yoga, and discussed a wide range of esoteric and theological readings. He introduced them to the *Sacrosanctum concilium*, the 1963 Constitution of Sacred Liturgy, which encouraged greater lay participation in the liturgy of the Catholic Church. He discussed their shared interest in astrology and commented on the readings his new friends found instrumental in the countercultural movement, namely, those of Dowling (*Aquarian Gospel of Jesus the Christ*), De la Ferriere (*Yug, yoga, yoguismo*), and Castañeda (*The Teachings of Don Juan*). They discussed Huxley's *Island*, where rationalism and environmentalism came together to form a utopia and the hostilities between capitalism and communism did not exist. Instead, people relied on Eastern spiritual practices (the "yoga of love") and hallucinogenic drugs. They valued the ordinary and did not see the need for armies, armaments, or exploitation.[54] In the company of xipi-tecas, Marroquín also discussed existentialism and blessed nonconventional weddings in open outdoor spaces (which blended romantic references to In-digenous traditions and esoteric rituals with the burning of sage and Native instrumental music in the background and the use of Masonic crucifixes and astrology cards). He favored simplicity, as the newlyweds often celebrated their love barefoot in the middle of an open field in plain white clothes, Native jewelry, and jeans. Finally, with his friends, Marroquín attended a theatrical performance by Jodorowsky on one occasion, which he found "hi-larious and silly," yet refreshingly "liberating." According to him and others of his generation, the outrageous and even violent approach preferred by the artist not only successfully exposed the hypocrisy and outdated language of a very conservative and nationalistic society but also tested the boundaries and limits of freedom of expression.[55]

At the communes, Marroquín befriended a small group of Christian xipi-tecas and discussed the hippie movement with them as "a sign of the times." He sympathized with their growing dissatisfaction with organized religion and welcomed their ecumenical efforts to engage in a fruitful dialogue, not only with other religions, but also with nonreligious points of view. He recalled experiencing an immense sense of despair during this period, and like some of his friends, he was interested in further experimenting with the psychedelic aspects of the counterculture as an effort to "liberate his mind." With Marroquín, many of them discussed sex in all of its expressions as a beautiful and natural celebration of love and interpreted *Humana vitae* as an anachronistic document that was "out of touch with the progressive language of the times." Marroquín welcomed the rise of the feminist move-ment as an empowering expression of love, and when asked for advice on the use of contraceptives, he told young people to rely on their conscience. Sex was only sinful if it was abused and used to hurt others.[56] Similarly, many of the young people who welcomed Marroquín saw in the experimen-tation with organic drugs an opportunity to get in touch with their most intimate feelings and fears, while others expressed to him a loss of faith in traditional Christianity. Overall, they shared their different understanding of God with Marroquín and came to understand the Sixties as a moment of fragmentation "ripe for realigning and eventually decolonizing the church," by rediscovering the liberating, pluralistic, and peaceful message of Christ. In this effort, they discussed the history of the early Christian church, as primarily described in Luke–Acts of the Apostle. With the same purpose, they revisited the biographies and writings of colonial missionaries and paid particular attention to the ascetic friars Louis of Granada (1504–88) and especially St. John of the Cross (1542–91), who had inspired *The Holy Mountain* (Jodorowsky, 1973).[57]

On one occasion, Marroquín hitchhiked to Huautla de Jiménez in search of María Sabina with a group of friends. But like most of the young people who embarked on the same pilgrimage to southern Mexico during this period, he lamented "never finding her." On another day, he took a bus to Zipolite (a nudist beach, also in Oaxaca) where he met with a group of hippies. Together they consumed hallucinogenic mushrooms. He remembered these experiences years later as a defining moment in which his life was pulled in two conflicting directions. On the one hand, in delving deeper into what he once called "lost Mexico," he reflected on these years with great joy as the time when he rediscovered the historical Christ. He was one who was at odds with the establishment of his day, lived among the poor and the wretched, and believed that, through true love for each other, ordinary people could form a society free of exploitation and discrimination. On the other hand, he described these experiences with an enormous sense of guilt as a moment of great confusion, contradiction, and despair. Consuming drugs provided him with clarity, which coincided with an intimate relationship with rural Mexico and a better appreciation of the sensibility of la onda. Like many xipitecas during this time, his direct interaction with Indigenous people and the extreme poverty many of them faced on a daily basis left Marroquín with a profound sense of sorrow. In particular, he felt guilty about his bourgeois upbringing and appalled by what he saw as the "disrespectful attitude" most foreign hippies and their Mexican counterparts all too frequently expressed regarding the local people and their customs. While some outsiders treated the locals solely as intermediaries to purchase drugs, others viewed them simply as part of the folkloric and homogeneous background of the nation or as a romantic symbol of the commercialization of la onda. As he later recalled, with a few exceptions—those who really understood the value of xipismo—there was "little reflection" about or interest in the broader countercultural movement. By and large, most hippies "did not care to learn about the local people," their customs, their understanding of their history, or their socioeconomic realities. For Marroquín, it was this lack of commitment that largely brought an end to la onda.[58]

By the early 1970s, it was evident that the dream of the counterculture had come to an end. According to Marroquín, this was further evident in the government's repression of xipitecas, which first intensified in the late 1960s and increased during the Echeverría administration. He saw this first-hand on his way back to Mexico City from a 1969 trip to Huautla when the federal army pulled over his bus and dragged "anyone resembling the look of a hippie," including Marroquín. He was arrested and held in a local jail in Teotitlán, near the foothills of the Sierra Juárez of Oaxaca. Released after a few hours (thanks to his affiliation with the church), Marroquín understood that if he wanted to remain a priest he needed to reconsider his relationship with xipismo.

Marroquín pointed to the day of a solar eclipse, March 7, 1970, as one of the last times he experimented with hallucinogens. He remembered buying a bag of peyote at the Sonora market, near the historic center of Mexico City, where, he said, "it was openly sold." He then hiked with a group of his friends to La Marquesa, a mountain in the state of Mexico. There he left the group, removed all of his clothes, and put on a serape. He set up a bonfire, burned some sage, and consumed the peyote. Marroquín found himself loving Christ "like never before" and reconnected with his historical message of peace, solidarity, and justice. He reaffirmed his view of nature as a beautiful and holistic creation of God with greater clarity and understood that it needed to be protected, in harmony with the people.

The next day, still feeling "a bit out of his body," Marroquín got on the plane and traveled to New Orleans. This was a trip that he had planned for months. He hoped for a long visit, but with a limited budget and mounting pressures from his superiors, his travels were cut short and limited to a shorter stay in neighboring cities in the US South.[59] He delved further into his appreciation of the blues there and went to a theater to see the rock musical *Hair*, which had been banned in Mexico after its 1969 debut in Acapulco.[60]

Marroquín returned to Mexico after having visited the United States for only a few days. He hoped to improve his conflictual relationship with the church but without entirely sacrificing his interaction with la onda. He left behind his experimental days with psychedelic drugs and taught his first classes to high school students. Soon after, he started writing in the magazine *Piedra Rodante*, where he collaborated with two key figures who provided him with additional opportunities to continue engaging with la onda, José Agustín and Alfredo Elías Calles. Alfredo was the grandson of the former president of the country, owner of the famous Acapulco discotheque Tibeiro, and leading producer of the musical *Hair* in Mexico. While Agustín presented Marroquín with the support he needed to publish *La contracultura como protesta*, Calles put him in touch with the twenty-three-year-old English composer Andrew Lloyd Webber with the understanding that Marroquín would be responsible for writing the Spanish translation of *Jesus Christ Superstar*, the successful rock musical that had debuted on Broadway in the summer of 1971.

According to Marroquín, Webber was excited that a figure of the church would work on the project and would understand the importance of depicting the gospel accounts of the last week of the life of Jesus. He immediately provided Marroquín with an advance for the translation, with the agreement that the Claretian priest would use the language of la onda but without making any changes to the script. Marroquín worked eagerly on the project and quickly gave the Spanish version to the English producer, "replete with the slang of la onda," he recalled. Webber simultaneously requested a translation from Juan José Calatayud, a pianist and leader of the jazz band 3.1416, but both translations were ultimately rejected. Four years later, in 1975, *Jesus Christ Superstar* debuted in Mexico. Julissa, the youthful actress of the 1960s, once leader of the rock band Spitfires and stepdaughter of Carlos Fuentes, played Mary Magdalene and worked as the main translator of the musical. A year later, she produced and translated into Spanish Richard O'Brien's iconic cult musical *The Rocky Horror Show* (1976).[61]

Teaching at the Preparatoria Popular

Marroquín lamented not having participated in the musical *Jesus Christ Superstar*. But he recalled his experiences at the Preparatoria Popular (Popular High School) with great joy, as they provided him with the opportunity to teach philosophy. Officially founded as a grassroots project in February 1968, these schools emerged as a collective and grassroots effort to provide education to those who had not been formally accepted to the National Preparatory School, the public secondary school system affiliated with UNAM.

The teachers did not get paid, nor were they recognized as employees of the Ministry of Education. Instead, they volunteered and led official, experimental, and often counterhegemonic courses. The teachers ranged from university students and new teachers to independent writers and intellectuals who generally sympathized with the Marxist-Leninist ideology that shaped the foundational pedagogical goals of the schools. They promoted a "critical, scientific, and popular" education and aimed to raise the political consciousness of students. For this, the founders turned to the Marxist writings of the political activist José Revueltas and endorsed the concept of self-determination. Independence from the state and an education that promoted mutual respect between students, teachers, and the popular sectors of society, they argued, were crucial for the process of liberation that they saw themselves participating in.[62] Yet these aspirational goals not only attracted leftist teachers to these schools but also independent thinkers like Marroquín who cared little about the Marxist overtones but welcomed the broader commitment to liberation. On paper, many of the courses varied little from those offered in the public schools. But they placed greater emphasis on Marxism and touched on a variety of themes that ranged from neocolonialism to dependency theory, Latin American literature, and revolutionary art.[63]

At the Tacuba Popular School (founded in 1970), Marroquín led a series of workshops that touched on the question of nonviolence as the most viable response to state repression and as a genuine expression of love.[64] He also organized lectures on philosophy and logic, in which he examined xipismo as a liberationist movement capable of creating a harmonious and balanced relationship between humans and nature.[65] He did not tell anyone at the schools that he was a priest, but he soon discovered that all the students were well aware of his affiliation with the church, especially after they saw him on Jorge Saldaña's TV talk show, *Anatomías*. The host invited Marroquín to engage in a dialogue with a group of young Pentecostals on the topic of the counterculture as celebrated by the so-called Jesus Freaks in the United States. According to Marroquín, the students appreciated his knowledge of rock music, and despite the overwhelming emphasis on Marxism preferred by the other teachers, they welcomed the progressive references he made to spirituality. During the talk show, Marroquín sympathized with the Jesus Movement. Like its Pentecostal followers, he called for the church to go back to a closer biblical picture of Christianity. Yet he did not share their charismatic beliefs in "the gifts of the spirit," namely, the attention they gave to miracles, speaking in tongues, and praying as a form of healing. Rather, in language similar to that employed by some of his peers who welcomed liberation theology, Marroquín called for Catholics to embrace a pragmatic Christian faith not only committed to improving the everyday life of ordinary people but also attentive to the structural forces responsible for the increasing deterioration of the environment.[66] He made similar arguments as a contributor to the countercultural magazine *Piedra Rodante*.

Piedra Rodante: Mexico's *Rolling Stone*

Marroquín depicted la onda as a liberation movement in five articles for *Piedra Rodante* without failing to highlight what he saw as the myriad contradictions that ultimately brought an end to the most utopian aspects of the counterculture. The magazine published its first issue on May 15, 1971, under the editorial direction of Manuel Aceves, a philosopher and publicist who had enjoyed a successful career in advertising. Containing original reporting on la onda and Spanish translations from *Rolling Stone*, the Mexican version claimed a distribution of fifty thousand copies.[67] It featured pieces on drug consumption, rock music, sex, art, national politics, and state repression by leading figures of the counterculture, including, among others, José Agustín, Parménides García Saldaña, Benítez ("el Booker"), and Enrique Marroquín.[68]

In the first of his articles in *Piedra Rodante* Marroquín criticized the repression of xipismo and pointed to the best qualities of the counterculture as depicted in the rock musical *Hair* (1968; film version 1979): the celebration of the hippie philosophy of "peace and love," which heralded the dawning of the astrological Age of Aquarius. He wrote, "If the adult generation and the church truly desired to understand the profound significance and intimate aspirations of the [nation's] youth, they should see the musical." He then noted in the language of la onda, "no nos azotemos" (let us not act like squares) by getting caught up in the moralistic language of the past. "We are supposed to be breathing more liberal air by now." Marroquín then asked, how could it be that in Mexico the musical had been censored but in the supposedly more repressive countries of Brazil and Argentina, *Hair* had been welcomed? "Let's leave behind the sterile clashes of generations," he concluded. "Let's open ourselves up, and embrace the spirit of dialogue, peace, and love."[69]

In a second article Marroquín provided a detailed review of Lennon's debut album after his breakup with the Beatles in April 1970, *Plastic Ono*

Band (December 1970). It included a photograph of the priest, described by *Piedra Rodante* as a "groovy leader of the Church ... interested in preaching the hip message of God." In his review Marroquín described the album as a turning point in the life and philosophy of John Lennon. The British singer had departed from the most radical elements of the counterculture, Marroquín explained, indisputably declaring that "the dream was over" and suggesting in his song "God" that he believed in nothing or nobody, except his wife, Yoko Ono, and himself. In his songs Lennon touched on multiple personal issues, including his conflictual relationship with his parents and religion. He rejected Jesus and the Bible and lumped them together with Tarot, Hitler, Elvis Presley, Buddha, the Gita, yoga, Robert F. Kennedy, and the Beatles. The singer stated that he was no longer the "Dreamweaver" or "The Walrus" but "just John," declaring the end of an era, including the utopian dreams of the counterculture. "The album," wrote Marroquín, "is impregnated with suffering." It is a critique of the abuses and commercialization of a dream. According to him, the album touches on Lennon's disillusionment with psychedelic drugs, the pain associated with the death of his mother, and his rejection of an abstract notion of Christ, whose true meaning he never fully understood. According to Marroquín, in this time of despair John rejected a false image of God, as one frozen in an anachronistic description of an earlier era whose main purpose was simply to bless the suffering of people. What Lennon failed to see, he claimed, was a God exclusively composed of love; not one who demanded charity, passivity, penitence, and condolence, but one who instead called for direct action in the form of a concrete commitment to those living on this earth and who called on others to engage in a search for respect, solidarity, and justice.[70]

In his third and fourth articles Marroquín delved further into the topic of rock music with attention to state repression at the September 1971 Avándaro festival, which event took place near the town of Valle de Bravo in the state of Mexico. The nation's most popular rock bands performed in front of a crowd of more than 250,000 young people. But unlike other countercultural events of the era, it enjoyed the support of the local administration of Hank González and advertising from Telesistema Mexicano. For these reasons, Marroquín described the event as the apex of la onda, meaning that Avándaro represented the best and worst aspects of the counterculture.

The best aspects were evident in the youthful expression of the crowd, in their collective search for self-discovery, and in the rock music calling for a new understanding of the world and celebrating an emerging consciousness of cooperation. In the words of Marroquín, the participants witnessed "an incipient Socialism of Love." In his interpretation, a better world seemed possible as countercultural defiance provided an opportunity to "reinvent national identity." It allowed for the possibility for young people to celebrate more liberating expressions of sexuality. The latter was captured in a photograph taken at the festival by Jesús Pavlo Tenorio (fig. 9).

A contemporary of Marroquín, Pavlo Tenorio was a Catholic journalist who had rubbed shoulders at the Carlos Septién García School of Journalism in the late 1950s with two leading figures of Mexico's beat poetry movement, Sergio Mondragón, husband of Margaret Randall and cofounder of the countercultural magazine *El Corno Emplumado*, and Homero Aridjis, author of the 1965 erotic novel *Mirándola dormir*.[71] Like Maroquín, Father Tenorio celebrated la onda as liberation, and in *Christus* and *Señal*, he commented on the urgent need to engage in dialogue with the nation's youth.[72]

The most negative aspects of the counterculture that were in evidence at the festival, according to Marroquín, were the commercialization of la onda, the senseless overuse of drugs without attention to its liberating qualities, and the antagonistic coverage in the press. He lamented that the national press had described those at Avándaro as "criminals" and "depraved degenerates" who "flaunted their sexuality" and, in so doing, simultaneously created an official narrative shared across leftist and conservative sectors of society that ultimately justified the state repression that followed.[73]

Finally, in his fifth article, Marroquín examined "drugs and their transcendental consciousness" in relation to his rising awareness of environmental politics. In citing some of the same authors he engaged with in his book *La contracultura como protesta* (Heidegger, Nietzsche, McLuhan, Marcuse, Lennon, García Saldaña, Randall, Huxley), he pointed to the consumption of natural drugs as an inherent if potentially dangerous response to the "alienating" structure of the "establishment." Modernity, as he also argued in his book, had failed to bring real progress to the world in the form of justice, harmony, and love and had instead pushed people away from the beauty and healing sensibilities of nature, including its clean waters, unpolluted air, and precious crops. Ideas associated with Marxism, he concluded, had pointed to the myriad contradictions and multiple forms of exploitation associated with modernity. Yet these and other Western ideologies had failed to explain how and why capitalism was also detrimental to the environment. Xipismo, in short, could provide some answers and should not be ignored, much less commercialized and repressed.[74]

FIGURE 9. Sexual liberation at Avándaro. From Jesús Pavlo Tenorio, "Escenas del festival Avándaro," Museo del Estanquillo digital archive, Colección "Carlos Monsiváis," http://museodelestanquillo.com/Sexualidad/obra/escenas-del-festival-de-avandaro/

Piedra Rodante published its eighth and last issue on January 15, 1972. Its critics had grown frustrated with the content of the magazine. Those on the Right labeled Manuel Aceves a "pornographer" and "corruptor" of the nation's youth and called on the government to arrest him.[75] Those on the Left saw the magazine as a cheap imitation of the one published in the United States.[76] "Facing threats of physical harm," as the historian Zolov has written, "the editor simply ceased publication."[77]

For Enrique Marroquín, the censorship of *Piedra Rodante* and the state repression that intensified in the aftermath of the Avándaro festival of 1971 marked the end of la onda. This was further evident in the suspension of all government permits to organize *tardeadas* (evening rock gatherings), the boycott of rock bands, the commercialization of the counterculture, and the widespread consumption and distribution of drugs. By the time all four thousand copies of *La contracultura como protesta* were published in 1975, Marroquín had distanced himself from the xipitecas. He delved further into the social teachings of liberation theology but remained committed to the central arguments of his book.[78]

In *La contracultura como protesta* Marroquín pleaded for the creation of a "new culture" in which he hoped society would assume a holistic relationship with the natural environment and the Indigenous peoples. Specifically, in drawing from encyclicals and countercultural novels of the era, he argued that all of God's creations have value and that all will be redeemed in God's eyes if the world's resources are universally shared.[79] Marroquín hoped to bring awareness to what he foresaw as some of the main causes for the increasing depletion of nature and the contamination of the environment. These included overpopulation; the massive consumption of highly processed foods; the overmanufacturing of plastics and cheap disposable products; the deforestation of the Third World to meet the demands of the imperialist powers; the urban obsession with and increasing dependence on combustible energy, technology, and synthetic medicine; and the massive consumption of cattle and forests. He concluded his book with the following words:

> Christ will not come from the clouds to resolve our problems. But, as the most pessimistic have insisted, [environmental] disaster might indeed be upon us. It is not too late, however. We could still take control of our own destiny and live in a balanced world by making more efficient use of our

[natural] resources. Earth has the capacity to feed us all for thousands of years to come. But this requires change to our cultural habits of consumption, labor, and sociability. It requires massive socioeconomic changes of our system, [in favor] of justice, thrift, and simplicity. Perhaps a better world is possible, as the hippies once imagined. It is up to us to create the new Age of Aquarius.[80]

For Marroquín, in short, the most important aspect of la onda was the attention xipitecas gave to environmental justice, a utopian ecosystem based on humanism, rationality, and spirituality. The rampant abuse of nature, he insisted throughout his writings, was particularly detrimental to the poor and to the developing world.

The story of Enrique Marroquín is exceptional, but it did not take place in a vacuum. A broad range of Catholics, including lay activists who wrote for *Juventud* and *Señal*, also expressed an interest in the counterculture. While most of them did not embrace the radicalism of Marroquín, they did make an effort to engage in dialogue with the multifaceted aspects of la onda, including the celebration of rock music, the liberation of sexuality, the shifting expressions of youth rebellion, and the consumption of drugs. The same was true of the commercial films made between 1962 and 1968. These differed from the films made during the 1950s by making an effort to depict youth rebellion and the liberation of sexuality from the perspective of young people. More radical interpretations of the counterculture emerged in the aftermath of the Tlatelolco massacre. As examined in the following chapter, a group of Dominican friars played a crucial role in creating a new space at UNAM, and like Marroquín, they welcomed a dialogue with the arts, youth, and the counterculture as a gesture of love.

SEVEN

Dialogue as Love and Countercultural Cinema at UNAM

Hasta el viento tiene miedo (1968) was a box office success and a favorite among youth.[1] The first of Carlos Enrique Taboada's "gothic trilogy," it is a horror film that places the "irrational authoritarianism" of the era at the center of the story. The plot takes place in an all-female boarding school where the presence of men is notably absent but a rigid patriarchal system alienates the young girls to the point of despair.[2]

Miss Bernarda rules the private school with an iron hand. She is a rigid principal of traditional Catholic faith who prohibits the young girls from reading Freud, sharing graphic novels, keeping photographs of boyfriends, wearing flirtatious clothing, listening to rock music, and dancing to the twist. For surveillance, she relies on Josefina, the teacher's pet, who spies on her peers and provides the principal with information on their presumed immoral behavior. The interns refer to Bernarda as the "witch," the "gestapo," and the "poisonous snake." For comfort, they lean on Lucía, a liberal teacher who is kind and generous to her students. Unlike her superior, Lucía is not afraid of holding her students in her arms and often saves them from the harsh punishments and strict rules of Bernarda. At the end of the academic year a group of interns breaks into an off-limits building and climbs the stairs to the tower. It is the exact place that haunted the young protagonist Claudia in her nightmares. As punishment, the girls are prohibited from returning home and forced to spend their winter vacation taking classes.

During the climax of the film, the viewer learns that the tower is the same building where a student named Andrea committed suicide years earlier. Her lost soul haunts the students during their stay. In a conversation with the girls, Lucía explains that Andrea had killed herself after the death of her mother, but it becomes evident that her suicide was actually caused by the harsh rules implemented by Bernarda. The restless Claudia is tormented by Andrea during her sleep, until the latter lures her to the tower in the middle of the night. Once at the top of the building, Claudia falls to the ground and is declared dead. A remorseful Bernarda at last realizes that her rigid rules had contributed to the deaths of Andrea and Claudia. She prays over the dead body and asks for forgiveness. But in a "miraculous way," the young girl wakes up from the dead. Lucía and the students soon discover that Claudia is not herself but has adopted the personality of the more mature, intelligent, and reserved Andrea. Once in possession of the resurrected body, Claudia lures Bernarda to the tower, where the school principal uses a rope to hang herself, the same way Andrea had committed suicide years earlier.

At the end of the film, a joyous Lucía is presented as the new principal of the school. She is congratulated for having finally reformed the boarding school into a modern educational institution free of the traditionalism of the past. The ghost of Andrea rests in peace, and the girls are no longer wearing their conservative uniforms, which had covered their shoulders and extended well below their knees. Instead, they are shown swimming in a pool, sporting skimpy clothes, and having fun: an optimistic view of a new and less repressive future.[3]

The boarding school depicted in the film and the eerie scenes that made Taboada a talented director of the horror genre effectively captured the irrational authoritarianism that many young people felt during the 1950s and 1960s. Like Bernarda, government and ecclesiastical authorities saw the nation's youth with distrust and in need of surveillance and strict authority. By contrast, a small but influential group of Dominican friars responsible for establishing the University Cultural Center at UNAM saw the youthful rebellion of the era as "a sign of the times." Like Lucía, they insisted on the importance of establishing a dialogue with young people. They celebrated the arts and imagined the possibility of creating a more liberated nation. When these utopian aspirations were not met, many grew alienated and instead expressed sentiments of despair. In making this argument, the last section of this chapter examines the countercultural film *Crates* (Joskowicz, 1970). But first attention is given to a group of Catholic students at the Dominican Center at UNAM who called themselves "Cerf." The second section examines the role of the Dominican friars in establishing the University Cultural Center as a foundational space for the exhibition and discussion of European films that further shaped the Catholic Sixties in Mexico.

The Cerf was a small intellectual group active at UNAM during the Sixties. Its name originated from the French, meaning "male deer," which the students understood as an irreverent and apolitical symbol at a time when most of their leftist counterparts used ideological names for their organizations. Its members were primarily progressive Catholic students enrolled in the school of philosophy who welcomed the academic discussions, workshops, and film screenings of the University Cultural Center (CUC), a de facto university parish founded by French and Mexican Dominican friars in 1961. Not much different from the countercultural figures of the era, Cerf members saw "love" as crucial to the construction of a better and more egalitarian society.[4] Like their religious mentors at the CUC, they prioritized a dialogue with the arts and welcomed the counterculture as a liberating response to the authoritarianism of the era.[5]

In their celebration of the utopian aspirations of the Sixties, the students composing the Cerf found inspiration in the writings of Pierre Teilhard de Chardin, a French theologian whose publications influenced the language of *Gaudium et spes*, the 1965 document of Vatican II that demanded a dialogue with the entire human family, including with those who held nonreligious points of view, engaged in scientific explanations of the cosmos, and explored the artistic expressions of humanity.[6] Specifically, the members of the Cerf were drawn to Teilhard's description of "love," which he defined as "an energy" that if collectively embraced had the power to forge greater harmony, goodwill, and solidarity. Not too different from the values of the counterculture in the United States, the positive energy of love was capable of moving humanity and, by extension, the universe away from alienation and closer to Christ. In direct reference to Teilhard, they described "reciprocal love" as the ultimate force of life in relation to God. Teilhard wrote, "Christ was to be loved not just for him, but as the heart of the universe." In this sense, "the only subject ultimately capable of mystical transformation is the whole group of mankind forming a single body." Only "seeing God in this way," Teilhard wrote, would Catholics "truly love God, and only through loving God," would the world become a better, more harmonious and equitable place. Members of the Cerf found inspiration in these ideas and saw the qualities of love as a unifying force in celebration of a historical Christ who had challenged the establishment in his own life and who had envisioned a better future.[7]

The Cerf members also found inspiration in the German philosopher Herbert Marcuse, specifically, his *One-Dimensional Man* (1964) as a foundational text in the creation of their group.[8] According to Marcuse, capitalism was "enslaving" the generation of the Sixties "softly," that is, not exclusively by overt violent repression but also through "comfortable temptation" in the form of consumerism. The irrationality of production and consumption had become so dominant during this period, the Cerf argued in agreement with Marcuse, that people had forgotten about the importance of alternative, more humane values based on love. Consumption had deprived them of resisting the status quo, and in the words of Marcuse, they had become "alienated," pacified, and transformed into cheerful robots of the capitalist system. The utopian values of the counterculture and a dialogue with the arts provided members of the Cerf with "an opportunity to imagine a different, more sensible, and less chauvinistic society based on the humanist principals of peace and love."[9]

The existentialist writings of the feminist Simone de Beauvoir and the European films of the era played a crucial role in the critique that students of the Cerf made of the patriarchal system. "I came to understand that society had normalized masculinity," Edith Sánchez explained, "and that my feminine identity and the points of view that I expressed as a university student were seen as marginal, outside of the system." Francisco Aguirre, who was mostly responsible for officially creating the Cerf in 1963, agreed. He explained in an interview, "It was the anti-bourgeois cinema of Paolo Pier Pasolini, Federico Fellini, [and] Luis Buñuel" that had a "profound impact in our lives." The students of the Cerf often saw these films in the company of the Dominican friars of the CUC, and according to Aguirre, they were "instrumental in our changing interpretation of the world." In conversation with their philosophy texts and the Dominican friars, they came to understand the eroticism, irreverence, and artistic expressions of these films as a "genuine rejection of the dominant culture," Sánchez added. Similarly, María Eugenia Hernández noted in an interview, "I fell in love with the European films of the era. The CUC was the only place we could see many of these films." She was personally touched by the religiosity, sarcasm, and humanism of Paolo Pasolini and Luis Buñuel. Their films "opened [her] eyes" to the changing awareness of her sexuality and to the new and more exciting relationship that she developed with her Catholic faith, "one free of the moralism and materialism of my parents, and more in tune with the ecumenism, dignity, and utopian love of the times."[10]

The Cerf remained active for most of the decade and grew modestly to include a few dozen students from the philosophy school at UNAM. Its main goals were to promote a dialogue with the pluralist world of the Sixties based on the principles of love and in so doing open "creative spaces" of collaboration with students interested in understanding the most pressing problems of the times, ranging from the "direct exploitation of the most vulnerable" to the more ambiguous alienation that emerged with technological production and "rampant consumerism."[11] In describing love as a unifying force, they criticized the authoritarianism and bigotry of the older generation of Catholics and university professors alike. They were equally critical of "conservatives, moralists, and liberal leftists" and accused them of indirectly collaborating with the state in censoring opinion and limiting freedom of expression inside the university. For these progressive Catholic students, the "liberating" future of the nation and that of their ecumenical Catholic faith depended on unconditional respect for diversity, loving commitment to one another, and fruitful dialogue with the competing opinions of others, not exclusively framed in political terms, but more commonly in conversation with sexuality, existentialism, and the arts.[12]

Rather than an ideological movement, the Cerf was conceived as a space for cultural engagement and productive dialogue. In consultation with the Dominican friars, they organized conversations with Jewish and Protestant students.[13] On Saturdays, they led a series of workshops and informal meetings that touched on a variety of topics that they felt were otherwise excluded from the university curriculum or were organized by academic authorities but did not speak to their countercultural interests in poetry, philosophy, the contradictions of consumerism, and "the burgeoning feminist movement."[14] In roundtables and multidisciplinary seminars, they led discussion sessions on the history of jazz, religion, and psychoanalysis; Latin American poetry, cinema, and colonialism; and sexuality.[15]

According to Edith Sánchez, the "most exciting events" organized by the Cerf were the overnight musical gatherings (*veladas*), poetry readings, and informal workshops. There the students discussed the 1967 encyclical *Populorum progressio* in conversation with Marxism, existentialism, and selected books that they "shared with each other."[16] Among the latter were Rampa's theological autobiography of a Tibetan lama, *The Third Eye* (1956), and Vicente Leñero's most influential novel, which placed Catholicism in contemporary Mexico, *Los albañiles* (1963). But the book that had a profound impact on these students was the *Dutch Catechism* (1966), which included sections on Buddhism, Hinduism, Islam, Humanism, and Marxism. Radically, it also provided progressive commentary on the erotic and marriage as well as sympathetic but still condescending references to homosexuality.[17]

The students affiliated with the Cerf saw the liberation of women and homosexuality as genuine expressions of love, at a time when the Left had dismissed all topics related to gender equality as bourgeois.[18] Despite its sympathetic views of the New Left, the Cerf saw UNAM as an "authoritarian space" with little tolerance for religious students. Its members were critical of the orthodoxy of Marxist students, who they described as "authoritarian" and "closed-minded." Specifically, they pointed to the "machista" attitude and the "cult-like personalities" of many leftist leaders as contradictory to the central demands of the times, mainly to the growing call for a democratic and less chauvinistic nation.[19]

These students were equally apprehensive of the "traditionalists" affiliated with Catholic Action and their conservative publications, *Juventud* and *Señal*. They pointed to their "charity projects" and "defense of the hierarchy of the church" as detrimental to the future of Catholicism, responsible not only for the widening gap between the rich and the poor but also for censoring the diverse opinions of others who disagreed with their faith.[20]

In sum, the students who participated in the Cerf argued that leftists and conservatives had hijacked the university during the Sixties and accused them of dismissing the burgeoning sexual revolution as either "insignificant" or as a "by-product of US imperialism." By contrast, they welcomed the radicalism of the counterculture, the writings of Teilhard, and the philosophers of the era. They sympathized with their defense of individual freedom of expression, and like them, they questioned the consumerist values of the times and brought attention to reciprocal love.[21] Only mutual love as a "genuine act of dialogue," they argued, "gave us the possibility to envision a better, less alienated and authoritarian world."[22] The Dominican friars were of foremost importance in the education that they received outside the classrooms. They introduced hundreds of university students to the most exciting European cinema of the era.[23]

The European films shown at the CUC provided a stark contrast to the countercultural movies made in Mexico before 1968. As examined in chapter 6, these national films touched on the interconnected topics of youth rebellion and Catholicism, albeit in a less effective and more commercialized way. A new cinema emerged in the aftermath of the Tlatelolco massacre that addressed these issues in a more radical fashion, as represented in this chapter by *Crates*. This was an existentialist picture that touched on the concerns raised by the members of the Cerf and one of the first countercultural films made by the graduates of the University Center for Cinematographic Studies (CUEC) at UNAM. Established in 1963, the CUEC found inspiration in the international films shown at the University Cultural Center and in the Dominicans' emphasis on dialogue with the arts.

THE DOMINICAN UNIVERSITY PARISH AT UNAM AND ITS IMPORTANCE IN THE ARTS

The CUC, located off the main campus of UNAM in the neighborhood of Copilco, was dedicated to promoting a dialogue between representatives of the church and the secular student body. Since the outbreak of the Mexican Revolution, the separation between church and state had made it impossible for Catholics to establish a space of faith inside the university.[24]

When the Dominican friars planned for the creation of the CUC, they understood that the installation of a formal university parish would never be possible in Mexico, even though these had expanded across Latin America, mostly as a result of the greater emphasis that the leaders of the Latin American Episcopal Conference gave to higher education in the Sixties.[25] Instead, the Dominicans opened their parish strictly as a cultural center. In theory, this meant that it was involved solely in celebrating the arts and cultural events. Yet in practice the CUC also performed the same activities that other university parishes organized in Latin America. These included spiritual retreats, daily masses, and roundtables to discuss religious texts that attempted to bring young people back to the church, precisely at a moment when an increasing number of students across the Western world found Catholicism irrelevant to their lives.[26]

Alberto de Ezcurdia and Agustín Desobry were mostly responsible for creating the CUC. They championed ecumenism and called for productive engagement with modernity. By the late 1960s, other Dominicans from France, Spain, and Mexico joined their project. While some students affiliated with the CUC engaged in politics and encouraged their peers to form Christian base communities in the surrounding areas of the campus, the overwhelming majority used the center to learn about psychoanalysis, engage in conversation with the counterculture, discuss avant-garde films, share poetry, and listen to music, including US rock and the new song music from South America.

This section focuses on the stories of Alberto de Ezcurdia and Agustín Desobry in relation to the arts and the importance of plurality, including religious ecumenism and diversity in political opinion. Trained in France during the 1940s, the two Dominicans welcomed the teachings of the *nouvelle théologie*, which arose when a new generation of French and German theologians residing in Paris and Louvain demanded a return to the sources of the Christian faith and a productive engagement with the contemporary world. Their biographies shed light on the importance of the CUC and the role they played as protagonists of the Catholic Sixties in Mexico.

Alberto de Ezcurdia and the Founding of the CUC

Born and raised in a Basque family in Guadalajara, Alberto de Ezcurdia received his religious and philosophical training in the 1940s, first at the San Esteban convent in Salamanca and then at the Sorbonne in Paris. In France he was introduced to the teachings of the Dominican friar Marie-Dominique Chenu, an advocate of the reappropriation of historical theological sources that led to the emergence of the nouvelle théologie and whom Fr. Gustavo Gutiérrez cited as a key influence in his *Teología de la liberación* (1971). Specifically, Ezcurdia was drawn to the new Christian humanism that rejected the scholastic theology of the past, which had favored an absolute view of the world, and instead called for the need to return to the writings of the thirteenth-century theologian Thomas Aquinas as a source, meaning that the Catholic faith was in harmony with historical reason and dialogue with all other branches of knowledge, including science and the arts.[27]

In 1951, at the age of thirty-four, Ezcurdia returned to Mexico. He pursued a law degree, and two years later, he was ordained a priest. He continued to study theology and officiated masses at the Rosario Parish in Mexico City for four years. He taught philosophy at the Ibero-American University and published his first columns in *Siempre!* in the mid-1950s. This Left-centrist magazine dedicated significant space to the reforms of Vatican II and included short pieces by Ezcurdia on the value of political plurality and religious ecumenism in creating a democratic society.[28]

Ezcurdia first conceived of the idea of creating a university parish at UNAM in 1957. His plans became a reality when his superiors transferred him to the Santo Domingo Convent in January 1960, the same time the Cuban Revolution revived the enthusiasm of the New Left and the ecclesiastical authorities in Mexico initiated their "Christianity Yes; Communism

No!" campaign.[29] Located in the southern part of Mexico City, the convent was within walking distance of the central campus of UNAM, where a new generation of leftist students sympathized with the radicalism of Fidel Castro's revolution and founded new leftist organizations. There he bought a house near Copilco Avenue, which served as a de facto university parish, initially attracting no more than a handful of students. His goals were to privilege debate, create a productive space to celebrate the gospel in a way that resonated with the nation's youth, and confront the agnostic and anti-Catholic mentality that, he believed, characterized the Marxist environment of the university. For support, he reached out to his superiors, and in collaboration with the Dominican friar Mariano Monter, he officiated the first university masses. He organized weekly discussion groups with students, including leftist leaders at the university who welcomed the first series of conversations between Catholicism and Marxism.[30]

By 1962, Ezcurdia had left the work of the CUC to other Dominicans. He joined the Faculty of Philosophy and Letters and translated a number of texts from Greek, Latin, and French. He published his own books on philosophy and served as a regular participant in Radio UNAM. This was an influential space of poetry and debate, created in the mid-1950s, which reached massive audiences during the 1960s under the leadership of the cultural chronicler Carlos Monsiváis and the feminist writer Nancy Cárdenas. Ezcurdia engaged in multiple conversations with leftist intellectuals on their program and addressed the main topics of the day.[31] But as he became more involved with his publications at UNAM, the friar Agustín Desobry emerged as the most influential leader of the CUC and the person responsible for its growth during the Sixties.

Agustín Desobry and the Growth of the University Parish

Agustín Desobry directed the University Cultural Center from 1961 to September 1969. He had worked for twenty years as a university chaplain in his native Paris during the 1940s and 1950s, where the nouvelle théologie had brought prominent theologians into productive dialogue with secular philosophers and where Desobry advocated for unity between the Catholic Church and the secular student body.[32] In 1959 he joined hundreds of priests who favorably responded to John XIII's goal of renewing life in the church by having one-tenth of European, Canadian, and US priests work in Latin America.[33] Initially, he moved to Brazil, but after a short period of visiting various Latin American cities, he arrived in Mexico City in March 1960.[34]

Ezcurdia convinced Desobry to take charge of the CUC in 1961. José Luis Argüelles soon joined him. Argüelles was a Spanish friar who had also immigrated to Mexico in March 1960 and who advocated for the use of poetry and modern music in the liturgy of the university parish. By the mid-Sixties, Desobry had expanded his group of progressive friars to include Mariano Monter, Tomás Aláz, Laudelino Cuetos, Benito Marín, and Justo María Fernández.[35] With their support, Desobry moved the CUC to a larger (and its current) location closer to the university campus that included a new parish. Similar to the Convent of Our Lady of Resurrection in Cuernavaca, the building favored simplicity and austerity.[36] It lacked the imposing images of saints and bloody references to Christ found in most churches across Mexico and included a modern space for musical performances and poetry reading. In addition, the new center had an auditorium for showing films and hosting academic conferences. It opened a cafeteria, a patio featuring the work of artists who became regular guests of the center, and classrooms to host smaller gatherings, including workshops intended to promote a dialogue between the Dominicans, people from other orders and creeds, and students representing different disciplines.

The students affiliated with the CUC grew from a handful of regular participants in 1961 to more than eleven thousand in 1965. This was a remarkable achievement, as noted by the friar and future director of the CUC, Miguel Concha Malo, years later, considering the number of young people who had abandoned their faith in those years.[37] But the originality and effectiveness of the parish did not rest on its aesthetics and numbers but instead on what some students called its "effervescence." The masses were "empowering," remembered a student affiliated with the CUC. She recalled, "The Dominicans knew all of our names, and during the liturgy, they frequently called on us, not to give us a moralistic sermon, as we were so accustomed to in other churches, but to truly interact with us, placing our concerns at the center of their words, and demanding unity and comprehension with those who had different points of view."[38]

For support, Desobry reached out to the archbishop of Mexico City, Miguel Darío Miranda, and to Adveniat. The leaders of Adveniat expressed enthusiasm for the artistic and cultural projects organized at the CUC and, like Miranda, saw it as a safer alternative to the more radical university projects that emerged in other Latin American countries during these years.

In France, Desobry kept his friends informed of the activities of the parish with the publication of *Copilco* between 1964 and 1965, and he received sympathetic letters and guidance from the bishop of Panama and director of CELAM, Marcos McGrath, and from the university chaplains who founded the Latin American Secretariat of Pax Romana in Uruguay in 1967.[39] In addition, a number of intellectuals welcomed the CUC's emphasis on culture and the arts.[40]

By the mid- to late Sixties, the CUC had developed into an influential space that attracted a wide range of artists, intellectuals, and politicians from across Mexico, Europe, and Latin America. Among its most regular visitors were the film director Luis Buñuel, two of the country's most influential writers, Carlos Fuentes and Octavio Paz, and the abstract painter José Luis Cuevas (whose drawings were often included in their publications and pamphlets). But signatures registered in the guest log also included those of various figures who shaped Mexico's New Left, including the chronicler Carlos Monsiváis and Jorge Portilla, humanist philosopher and author of the *Fenomenología del relajo* (1965). Among the others were the expressionist painter who rejected the didactic goals of the muralist painters, Rufino Tamayo; the leftist essayist Víctor Flores Olea; the Brazilian educator Paulo Freire; the liberation theologian Gustavo Gutiérrez; the bishop of Cuernavaca, Sergio Méndez Arceo; and the American writer Carlos Castañeda, who was invited to the CUC to present *The Teachings of Don Juan* (1968). The latter was an anthropology work that increased scholarly and countercultural awareness of shamanism and the consumption of peyote in Mexico.[41] Notably, the list of guests did not include the names of Elena Poniatowska, Nancy Cárdenas, Marta Acevedo, or other important feminist intellectuals who also shaped the New Left.

The guests led workshops and presented their work. They engaged in private conversations with the friars and often participated in roundtable discussions with students that addressed philosophical questions, political events, and ideas related to the counterculture. A list of the most successful workshops organized by the friars included those on psychoanalysis and its relationship with religion, on the theological thinking of Teilhard, and on the social responsibility of the university community.[42] By the end of the decade, large numbers of students also enrolled in a series of workshops on European cinema and student activism, organized, respectively, by the friars Benito Marín and Tomás Aláz. The latter often published in the magazine *Siempre!* to condemn the violence of ultraconservative students who made the CUC one of their preferred targets throughout the decade.[43]

The Dominicans left a good impression on their guests. The Peruvian theologian Gustavo Gutiérrez remembered his visit to the CUC as "extraordinary," explaining that in addition to the workshops, roundtable discussions, and conferences organized by Iván Illich in Cuernavaca, the Dominican parish at UNAM quickly earned the respect of foreign priests and intellectuals interested in having a productive and open dialogue with the secular world. The Claretian priest Enrique Marroquín provided a similar description, explaining that the CUC evolved into a pedagogical space for the arts and the cultural movements of the Sixties. The Jesuit priest and historian of the Mexican church, Jesús García, simply described the CUC as "splendid" and argued that it was "profoundly influential for the growth and sophistication of the cultural and artistic movements of the era."[44]

Luis Buñuel, famous for his anticlerical films of the 1950s and 1960s, was one of the most regular visitors and a chief supporter of the CUC.[45] Besides leading discussions on cinema, he donated personal copies of his most celebrated films to the friars. He gave them financial support to build a robust film library and organize weekly cine clubs. The Spaniard Laudelino Cuetos, who arrived at the CUC in 1964, remarked on Buñuel's regular presence there:

Many mistakenly believe that Buñuel was a vulgar atheist who had no interest in Catholicism, except as a topic of ridicule. This could not be further from the truth. He had a profound thirst to comment on the most important questions that concerned all of us. We watched and discussed his films and used these opportunities to talk to students about religion and the existence of God in the context of the Sixties. During his visits, Buñuel welcomed long conversations with the Dominicans. As someone who was also born in Spain, I was always delighted to see him when he visited our center.[46]

By the late Sixties, the cine clubs and the film festivals organized at the CUC had emerged as "the most exciting and thought-provoking of the times," remembered Francisco Aguirre, founding member of the Cerf. He described some of the Dominican friars as "experts on European films" whose "love for the movies was truly contagious." With their support, "we watched some of the best cinema coming from France, Poland, Italy, Sweden, and Germany," he said. The friars were always open and ready to "engage in productive conversations with us," even to "discuss the sexual revolution of the times." Many of the films that the students discussed with the Dominicans "were not shown anywhere else." They "allowed us to feel connected to the political and cultural movements that were taking place all over the world."[47]

According to Aguirre, one of the most controversial films that the Dominicans screened was *Teorema* (1968). Directed by the atheist and openly homosexual Italian director Pier Paolo Pasolini, the "blasphemous film" tells the outrageous story of a God who descends on a bourgeois family and seduces the father, mother, and two children, only to leave them behind in agony and despair. "After watching the film," Aguirre remembered, "many people in the audience were outraged and walked out in disgust." But a small and more progressive group of students led several discussions after watching this and similar films. These discussions ranged from the sexual oppression of the times to their changing understanding of their Catholic faith.[48] But the allegorical film *Teorema* also touched on the topic of the corruption of the bourgeoisie, and similar to the writings of Herbert Marcuse, it pointed to an affluent family caught up in the alienation of consumerism. These were topics that concerned many students at the time.[49] "At first, *Teorema* shocked me," said Marcela Eugenia. "You have to understand, I was raised in a traditional Mexican home." Her parents disapproved of her watching this and similar films of the era. But it was one of the "most impressive films" that she watched at the CUC. It "resonated" with the readings that she did on the sexual revolution and those of Marcuse. Like the philosophers of the era, these films provided them with an "opportunity to shatter" their "traditional and provincial understanding of the world."[50]

By 1971, the University Cultural Center had successfully exhibited dozens of foreign films and had built a large film collection that allowed it to organize annual exhibitions of international cinema, starting with Russian cinema, followed by an Italian festival the next year, and concluding with a festival of the best international directors in 1973. A year later these festivals were institutionalized under the name "Cine Arte CUC," which continued to thrive for the rest of the decade, attracting larger audiences from outside the university community.[51]

The Forming of New Leaders

Cinema was crucial to the success of the University Cultural Center. But it was not the only medium that allowed the Dominican friars to effectively reach out to university students during the Sixties. These spaces also included the innovative *cuquitos* (small centers of the CUC) under the guidance of

Didier Leurent, and the School of Leaders, under the direction of Desobry. The Dominican friar Leurent had arrived in Mexico from France in 1964 and quickly opened the cuquitos in each of the nine Preparatory Schools affiliated with UNAM.[52] Their three central goals were to assist high school students with their academic work, provide them with spiritual guidance, and introduce them to a youthful Catholicism that resonated with them.[53] In a 1967 letter to his superiors, Desobry enthusiastically noted, "Leurent had made significant contributions in the Preparatory Schools. Many students are now familiar with the CUC, and we have reasons to believe that they will join us once they are admitted to the university."[54]

Once enrolled at UNAM, students were invited to submit applications to the School of Leaders. These were designed to "form the leaders of tomorrow" and "provide them with a humanistic education" that they otherwise failed to receive in secular classrooms.[55] Desobry argued that great technological and scientific changes had taken place during the Sixties that demanded that the tools of the humanities be placed in the hands of a new generation of Catholic leaders. To be admitted, the applicants were asked to fill out a short questionnaire in which they explained their reasons for wanting to become leaders rooted in the Catholic faith. Once enrolled at the school, the students were provided with a religious formation that included multidisciplinary training in the humanities. For this training, Desobry invited professionals and teachers who organized workshops on civics, oratory, sociology, ethics, economic development, psychology, the arts, and theology. Luis Leñero Otero was one of these guests. He was the brother of the Catholic novelist Vicente Leñero and the husband of the feminist anthropologist María del Carmen Elu. In consultation with the Dominicans, he led a series of "journeys of development" workshops that introduced students to the latest tools of sociology and to the politics of reproduction rights.[56]

Similarly, in his workshops on the community practices of liberation, the Spanish Dominican friar Laudelino Cuetos encouraged his students to join the Center of Social Action. This was a cooperative founded in 1966 that organized literacy, hygiene, drainage, and sports campaigns in the popular neighborhoods of Copilco. But, as noted earlier, the workshops and roundtable discussions that drew the largest number of students from the School of Leaders were those that touched on humanism and the university, psychoanalysis, existentialism, consumerism, and European film.[57]

Students interested in joining the School of Leaders were asked to sign a contract in which they committed to participate in the courses, workshops, and roundtable discussions. They promised to pay the required fee of 150 pesos, attend the Sunday dinners with their mates, and not get involved with political groups that were antagonistic to the university parish, including those on the Far Right. When the ultraconservative University Movement of Renovated Orientation, or MURO, was officially expelled from the university in 1968, this last requirement was removed from the application. Instead, it was noted that the Dominicans had the right to expel any student who failed to assume the responsibilities of a leader and instead used the CUC for "politicking."[58]

By 1969, more than three hundred male and female students had been admitted to the program. Among them was José Raul Vera López, who submitted an application to the CUC in 1967 and several years later emerged as a key ecclesiastical leader of liberation theology. In his description of the CUC, he wrote, "I first encountered the Dominicans as a Chemistry student in 1963. I was immediately impressed with them . . . [and their] modern version of the Gospel." They taught him to see the world in a less materialistic and selfish way. He pointed to the influence of the friars as one of the reasons he decided to become a priest. The social world around him "suddenly mattered."[59]

Olivia Jiménez Valdés, who was accepted to the School of Leaders as a conservative student in 1966, similarly noted, "From timid and prudish, I became a rebel and a leader." Her compañeras Yolanda Estrada García and Rebeca Arrieta Soto were also raised in traditional homes where their parents demanded prudence and submissiveness. They similarly noted, "The Dominicans taught [us]" how to "effectively work with others in a team," present ourselves "with authority" in front of "[our male] *compañeros*," and "see the benefits" of the commitment of the CUC." Elvia Díaz de León D'Hers, who was raised in "a profoundly pious family" that warned her of the dangers of "Marxism" and "other philosophical tendencies" promoting "atheism" at the university, described the CUC as the space that radically shaped her view of the world. She specifically listed Agustín Desobry, José Luis Argüelles, and Laudelino Cuetos as the authorities who introduced her to a "more mature faith," one that was ecumenical, reflective, and willing to engage in dialogue. The friars "made me realize," she said, that orthodox and inflexible points of view not only "threatened liberty" but also often led "to totalitarian behavior." Carolina Álvarez de la Cadena Rivero expressed similar appreciation of the friars and pointed to the *Dutch Catechism* as the reading that introduced her to a tolerant understanding of her faith.[60] Edith Sánchez described her interactions with her peers from the Cerf similarly and, as noted earlier, further referred to Teilhard, Marcuse, and de Beauvoir as foundational in the education that she received at the CUC. María Eugenia Hernández also highlighted the importance of these authors and emphasized the role that European films played "in her liberation, from a prudish to a more exciting view of the world." Francisco Aguirre agreed and mentioned the magazine *Diálogo* as instrumental in his intellectual formation.[61]

Diálogo *as an Expression of "Love"*

Diálogo played an instrumental role in the spiritual, intellectual, and professional education of university students affiliated with the CUC. The magazine appeared in a total of eleven issues between 1964 and 1967, with financial support from Adveniat. It defined the concept of its title as a "process of enrichment," with the "urgent goal" of bridging the gaps between generations, social classes, educational disciplines, and hierarchical relationships within the university.

In meeting these goals, the Dominicans further referred to "dialogue" as a concrete gesture of humanity, urgent in a world of alienation that "required love," which the friars presented to the students as a mutual action of respect. To guarantee "liberty" and effectively transform the university into an inclusive space of acceptance, moreover, this praxis of engagement could not afford to be "forced, hurtful, proud, or offensive."[62] It had to be generous, peaceful, and attentive, and—as shown in figure 10—it had to be openly discussed in public, as a collective "promise of love."[63]

Agustín Desobry served as director of *Diálogo*, but it was the space given to the students that gave the magazine its unique character. Unlike other Catholic publications of the era, many of the columns were written by students representing a variety of disciplines and various points of interest. But male and female students were also included in the management, decision making, and editorial process of the magazine. Many of them went on to become influential in their respective disciplines, including, among many others, the future professors at UNAM Jaime González Graf and Elizabeth Luna Traill. With this editorial position of power, the authors did not see the need to include questions related to morality or the alleged threat of communism, ubiquitous in *Corporación*, *Palestra*, and *Juventud*.[64]

Instead, the students took advantage of *Diálogo* to explore questions that presumably concerned the readers the most. For example, writing from the

FIGURE 10. Anonymous student calling for a collective promise of love. From *Diálogo* (February–March, 1967).

perspective of "female students," several authors expressed dissatisfaction with the discriminatory practices they often found at the university, especially in liberal spaces that protested the status quo but often re-created the same misogynistic structures of power. From their respective disciplines, other students expressed dissatisfaction with the university curriculum, lamenting that little attention was given to the importance of the humanities in favor of material and individual success. The authors appreciated the role that the CUC played in filling this gap by providing workshops that prioritized a holistic education outside the classroom. For example, a veterinary student discussed the relationship between caring for animals and its benefits for humanity; a law student expressed the importance of learning about economic justice; and a medical student appreciated the need to learn about social healing. Similar columns were published by students majoring in economics, business, and political science praising "the religious formation" and "exciting liturgy" championed at the CUC that allowed for a productive conversation with the arts, including pop art and experimental theater.[65]

The magazine presented its readers with succinct and relatable summaries of the central concepts and documents from Vatican II, as well as the ideas promulgated in what students at the CUC referred to as "the most revolutionary encyclical" of the era, *Populorum progressio*.[66] Written in 1967 by Pope Paul VI on the topic of "development of peoples," the encyclical not only demanded respect for the socioeconomic rights, a just wage, job security, freedom to join labor unions, and safe conditions at work but also addressed the legacies of colonialism and the ethics of globalization. In this sense the encyclical went beyond earlier Vatican documents addressing social justice by condemning poverty, injustice, and oppression in the context of what the pope called a Christian "dynamism of love."[67] There was no room for violence, and as interpreted by the members of the CUC, the dynamism of love largely depended on a genuine dialogue with culture and the arts.[68] In making this argument, the magazine made references to the authors and artists who shaped the intellectual education of the students, including filmmakers.

Diálogo and the pamphlets of the CUC took particular interest in the European directors Federico Fellini, Michelangelo Antonioni, Paolo Pasolini, and Ingmar Bergman, pointing to the attention these artists gave to Catholicism in relation to desire, despair, death, and alienation. The Swedish filmmaker Bergman, for example, often alluded to God in his films as a protagonist with human flaws. The Italians Fellini, Antonioni, and Pasolini were more explicit in their message. In *8½* (1963) by Fellini, the Catholic Church is portrayed as an institution that is completely disconnected from the needs of the people.[69] Of interest to the students were also Pasolini's *The Gospel according to St. Matthew* (1964), a biblical film made in the neorealist style about the life and repression of Christ; and Antonioni's *Blow-Up* (1966), a philosophical thriller set in a postreligious world that explored questions of murder without the guilt of sin and the passion of love free of spiritual meaning.[70] These and other European films shown at the CUC, in sum, provided the Dominican friars with an opportunity to engage in dialogue with students at UNAM. Like their publications, these films effectively captured the sentiments, aspirations, and hopes of the Sixties with an emphasis on progressive Catholicism.

The CUC at the End of the Sixties

In its final, October 1967 issue, *Diálogo* included a somber column documenting the Vietnam War. That same month, Alberto de Ezcurdia published one of his last articles in *Siempre!* demanding a dialogue between Christianity and Marxism.[71] He became ill, disappeared from public life, and died three years later. For his part, Desobry used his authority to denounce the multiple attacks the University Cultural Center had endured at the hands of ultraconservative students. In late August 1968, the government followed suit, as it too found a need to describe the CUC as a "subversive threat" to the nation, falsely accusing Desobry and his group of Dominican friars of encouraging students to break into the cathedral and ring its bells as a signal to attack the government.

In reality, the students had obtained permission from the church authorities to ring the bells of the Metropolitan Cathedral with the intention of celebrating the popular nature of the movement, no longer strictly composed of students but also made up of intellectuals, professors, and artists. A different group of students, likely led by agents provocateurs, lowered the Mexican flag from the center of the Zócalo that same night of August 27 and replaced it with a red and black banner. Other students occupying the plaza insulted President Díaz Ordaz and demanded that he come out of his presidential palace to engage in a public dialogue with them. As well documented in the scholarship, these events marked a pivotal moment for the 1968 movement. For the media outlets, they provided "evidence" that the students were not only "communists" who had been manipulated by external forces but also "anticlerical."

From the perspective of the government, the events justified state repression. That next day, the commanding officers of the military mobilized their tanks, snipers, and tear gas and forced all students to leave the Zócalo. Paramilitary groups composed of agents provocateurs used machine guns to fire at various schools an hour later. These attacks intensified for several weeks, until the army took over UNAM and the National Polytechnic Institute in late September and the movement came to an abrupt end in the aftermath of the Tlatelolco massacre.[72] That violent night of October 2, the Dominicans turned their center into a "refuge." A group of armed agents knocked on the doors of their building, but the friars refused to give access to the police, keeping dozens of students safe.[73]

Agustín Desobry denied the accusations made against him in the press, insisting that the university parish was a peaceful space of dialogue and ecumenism that since its creation in 1961 had remained at the margins of political activism and mostly invested in religion and the arts.[74] Criticism against him continued, nonetheless. Under continuous pressure, Desobry presented his resignation from the CUC in 1969. The new directors, Justo María Fernández (1969–72) and Laudelino Cuetos (1972–79), continued to defend the CUC as a humanist center of debate. Under their management, the parish remained an important space for film, the arts, and religious formation that gradually abandoned the Eurocentric vision of the early Sixties in favor of an increasingly Latin Americanist approach.[75] For Catholic students, the CUC had successfully provided the university with a space that valued the importance of dialogue as a gesture of love, and for those who fell in love with the movies, the CUC gave them a space to enjoy an international cinema that had a profound impact on the new and more exciting films that were made in Mexico in the aftermath of the Tlatelolco massacre.

ALIENATION IN *CRATES*

By the end of the 1960s the national film industry was in decline. It reached an unprecedented economic and structural crisis primarily because of the minimal support it received from the presidential administrations of López Mateos and Díaz Ordaz. But as the film scholar Tomás Pérez Turrent has argued, "Things could not remain the same after the events of 1968." Following the student massacre in Tlatelolco, it became "necessary to renovate, reform and revitalize certain structures [not only] to avoid the collapse of the entire edifice" but also to reconnect the middle class to Mexican cinema and to provide important spaces of expression for political dissidents and innovative artistic expression. In these efforts, censorship relaxed while the state "sided with the post-1965 directors and other newcomers."[76]

These directors were trained at the University Center for Cinematographic Studies, first established at UNAM in 1963 and most influential in the aftermath of the 1968 movement. As the film scholar Alvaro Vázquez Mantecón has documented, a new generation of Mexican filmmakers trained at the CUEC took advantage of the technological innovations offered by the Super 8 mm format to produce more than two hundred experimental low-budget films between 1970 and 1974. These films formed a heterogeneous movement that addressed the most pressing concerns of the nation, including what many saw as the trauma of the Tlatelolco massacre.[77]

This period of extraordinary film production coincided with the presidential administration of Echeverría and his democratic opening. In drawing a contrast with the authoritarian administration of Díaz Ordaz (infamous for creating a hostile relationship with artists and intellectuals), Echeverría relaxed the government censorship that had pushed artists to go underground. His administration built new distribution spaces for the production of a new national cinema and welcomed a process of creativity that coincided with the expansion of the Dominican University Cultural Center at UNAM as a central space for the exhibition of European films. This process called for the rejection of conventional (golden age) genres, the opening of new cine clubs in the universities, the undertaking of socio-political commentary, the importance of initiating self-criticism, and the rise of a new generation of filmmakers.[78] Partly influenced by the political radicalism of the Third Cinematic Movement of South America, these filmmakers preferred the use of nonprofessional actors. With aesthetic inspiration from Italian neorealism and the French New Wave, they rejected the Hollywood models of film production and the moralistic language of Mexican cinema. Reminiscent of the most radical elements of militant art, many of these filmmakers saw cinema (and specifically the camera) as a political and/or countercultural weapon that called for collective action and individual transformation.[79] *Crates* (1970), the first fictional feature made by CUEC students, is an example of these films. With an emphasis on the topic of alienation, its director, Alfredo Joskowicz, framed the counterculture according to his interpretation of the nation's Catholicism.

Joskowicz enrolled at the CUEC in 1966, and within three years, he completed his first two short documentaries: *La Manda* (1968) and *La Pasión* (1969). The first provided a sociological view of a group of people doing penance to the Virgin of Guadalupe, and the second documented the Passion of Christ performed during Holy Week at the popular city of Iztapalapa. During this period, he also became a close friend of Leobardo López Arretche. Arguably, López Arretche was the most talented filmmaker of his generation. In 1968, he produced *El Grito*, the powerful film about the student movement and the Tlatelolco massacre.[80] With Joskowicz, he served as cowriter of *Crates*, but on July 24, 1970, he committed suicide. This was a tragic allegory of the Tlatelolco massacre and a point of reference to the despairing end of the Sixties.

Crates is based on the life of the Cynic philosopher of ancient Greece, Crates of Thebes (ca. 360–280 BCE). Born to a wealthy family, he gave away his inheritance after realizing "the futility of material possessions and the shallow values espoused by society." Once removed from all his personal wealth, Crates moved to Athens, where he studied philosophy, lived on the streets, and loudly professed his beliefs to the public.[81]

The film opens with a chaotic scene depicting a television crew storming into Crates's house. Played by Leobardo López Arretche, Crates is a young man in his late twenties who gives away all of his possessions to a random group of people, including his records, clothes, paintings, furniture, money, and books. Some of his friends (including Joskowicz, who makes a brief cameo appearance) try to reason with him and plead with him to recant what they see as his irrational decision, claiming he will regret it soon. But Crates appears determined and threatens to burn everything to the ground unless his bourgeois friends take possession of the remaining materials in his home. Once free of all his belongings, Crates follows the same path as St. Francis of Assisi, whom hippies in the United States had discovered in their aspirations to austerity and environmental awareness.[82]

Crates is depicted roaming the outskirts of the city. He wears torn clothes, broken sandals, and a long and dirty beard. He removes his clothes, and with Andean music in the background, he swims naked in a dirty lake. In harmony with his environment, he eats plants that he finds by the shore, and in the city, he sleeps with the homeless who are portrayed in the film with agonizing and voyeuristic detail. Crates is attentive to their pain, and when the city gets crowded in the middle of the day, he shares bread with strangers. Similar to Pasolini's *The Gospel according to St. Matthew* (1964), *Crates* plays the Creole Mass in the background, reminding viewers of the importance of thanking Christ for the sacrifice he made for humanity. Crates talks with those who are willing to listen to him and invites them to follow his path. A cunning young man follows him but only to steal what Crates carries in his bag. After realizing that the aspiring Messiah has no money or anything of value in his bag, the thief leaves quietly as Crates pretends to be asleep.

The film then introduces a young girl who is rushed to the hospital by her brother after a suicide attempt. On regaining consciousness from the drug overdose, she tells her brother to take her to see their friend Crates, who welcomes her but tells her he has nothing to offer her other than his humanity and love, which, like St. Francis, he understands in relation to his devotion to Christ.[83] Crates finds a pair of shoes in a dumpster and gives them to his new girlfriend. Her brother joins them, and together the three roam the streets searching for food in city dumpsters. Crates and his girlfriend make love in a public park. Their physical appearance deteriorates, but they remain loyal to their lifestyle and appear genuinely happy. But the brother, whose hunger is causing him physical pain, begins doubting his decision. He ultimately abandons the couple to return to the comforts of his wealthy house, where he burns the letters he had once written to Crates. As the film comes to an end, Crates and his pregnant girlfriend bathe in a lake and turn a cave into their new home. She gives birth there with the help of Crates. The new father cuts the umbilical cord with his teeth. The liturgical song "Agnus Dei," typically recited at Sunday Mass during the fraction of the host, plays in the background to remind the viewers once again of the crucifixion of Christ. The couple walks away taking the sins of the world with them, observed afar from the top of the mountain by the doleful brother.

Joskowicz never released his film commercially and only showed it at university cine clubs. *Crates* is dreadful at times and frequently romantic in its depiction of the poor. Yet it provides a faithful view of the concerns that many young people expressed in the aftermath of the Tlatelolco massacre. It also serves as a drastic contrast to the countercultural films produced by the commercial film industry before the 1968 student movement. With a persistent dialogue with the Christian faith, Joskowicz draws specific attention to a world of filth and extreme poverty while simultaneously demonstrating his commitment by depicting scenes that were otherwise considered offensive and even sacrilegious in the state-sponsored cinema. Besides the breaking of the bread and the brash delivery of his child, he films Crates defecating in the same dumpsters where he frequently searched for food. Radically, Joskowicz also depicts Crates publicly urinating on the feet of a uniformed policeman, swimming naked in the lake, and making love with his girlfriend, not in paradise, but in a world whose natural environment is deteriorating, a concern, as examined in chapter 6, that also shaped the hippie priest Enrique Marroquín. Unlike most countercultural films produced during this period, which frequently used rock music in the background, Joskowicz opts to incorporate religious music in key moments of the film. For him, the spiritual search for liberation was not too different from the noninstitutional version of the Catholic faith, as represented in the historic life and sacrifice of Christ. In this sense, *Crates* had a remarkable resemblance to many of the films shown at the CUC that expressed divergent views of Catholicism in relation to the Sixties. Like many of their films, *Crates* is also a film that places the alienation of youth at the center of the story, and similar to other cinematic representations of Mexico's "New Cinema" of the 1970s, it successfully blurs the lines between the political and the countercultural.

CONCLUSION

Film scholars often describe the University Center for Cinematographic Studies as the first film school in Mexico and the most important player in the emergence of the "New Cinema" of the 1970s. While the latter is true, the first national film school was in fact the Institute and School of Cultural Cinema at the Ibero-American University. The Jesuit priest Jesús Romero Pérez founded the school in 1957, five years before UNAM opened the CUEC and weeks after he returned to Mexico from the 1957 Havana conference. As examined in chapter 1, this conference marked a watershed in the lives of lay activists and religious figures, like Emma Ziegler and Fr. Romero Pérez, who favorably responded to the liberal language of *Miranda prorsus*, the 1957 encyclical that asked Catholics to identify films not as a tool of perversion, as previously described by the church, but instead as a "child of God."[84]

The Institute and School of Cultural Cinema trained students in script writing and directing until 1962, when it was incorporated into the School of Science, Technology and Information. Romero Pérez remained active as a film professor there and as the central organizer of the Ibero-American cine club. He also institutionalized the Onix Prizes, which were given annually to the best actors, directors, and films from 1958 to 1968. Finally, during this period, he oversaw the monthly magazine *Séptimo Arte*, and he received support from other lay organizations to bring greater awareness of Catholics in Mexican cinema.[85]

A year before the foundation of the Institute, Romero Pérez had published *El cine: Arma de dos filos* (1956). It was in this book that he explained the importance of his movement and where he laid out the central tenets and goals of the school. As the title of the book states, cinema was a "double-edge sword." If left in the hands of materialistic entrepreneurs solely interested in making a profit or in control of leftist propagandists invested in popularizing Marxist ideas, he argued, it had the potential to destroy society and diminish national culture. By contrast, if carefully studied, produced, and managed by humanists, it had the pedagogical potential to exalt joy, fight ignorance, and transform passive viewers into active agents responsible for building a harmonious world, based on the principle of love (for the arts and for one another). Like other Catholics who became interested in film during this period, he reproached those who understood the Catholic film movement strictly as a censoring project, and instead he called for greater appreciation of all the different aspects related to filmmaking, ranging from the theoretical, pedagogical, and philosophical tools of cinema to its technical, aesthetic, and artistic elements.[86] In this effort, *Arma de dos filos* provided extensive details aimed at introducing readers to the exciting world of cinema. These included a basic glossary of the technical language and tools of film, as well as useful references from key texts on the subject, namely, passages of the encyclicals and Vatican documents that influenced the author and translations of French texts that inspired his work.[87]

By 1968 the Institute and School of Cultural Cinema at the Ibero-American University had ceased to be an important reference in Mexican cinema. By contrast, the University Cultural Center at UNAM remained an important space for university students. As Alberto de Ezcurdia and Agustín Desobry had insisted during the 1960s, the university parish effectively kept a low political profile and remained committed to championing the arts throughout the 1970s and 1980s. The importance of dialogue as an effort to engage with the nation's youth also remained a priority for the Dominicans, and so did the exhibition of avant-garde and controversial films, including those that escaped the scrutiny of government censors.

Many of the friars in charge of the CUC had arrived from or were trained in Europe, where young people grew increasingly disillusioned with Catholicism. At UNAM, they played a crucial role in championing the importance of ecumenism as an expression of love. In so doing, university groups like the Cerf contributed to the emergence of the counterculture and the formation of a new generation of progressive Catholic thinkers. They looked to Pierre Teilhard de Chardin, Herbert Marcuse, Simone de Beauvoir, Pier Paolo Pasolini, Luis Buñuel, and other European philosophers and filmmakers for inspiration. Like many of these intellectuals and artists, these progressive Catholic students grew critical of the consumerism of the times. They spoke against the authoritarianism in their schools and welcomed the rising feminist movement.

Commercial films made in Mexico before the 1968 student movement also addressed these topics. In comparison to the more conservative pictures of an earlier era, these films made a conscious attempt to examine youth rebellion from the perspective of youth, including a more welcoming view of the sexual liberation of young women (as exemplified in Taboada's *Hasta el viento tiene miedo*). But it was the films made with the support of the CUEC in the aftermath of the Tlatelolco massacre that took a radical approach to these topics and more effectively addressed the countercultural sensibilities of the era, with attention to Catholicism and youth alienation.

"Diálogo" became a contentious term during the 1968 movement when the students demanded that Díaz Ordaz come out of his presidential palace and engage in public negotiation with students. As well documented in the scholarship, the president refused to meet with representatives of the movement and ultimately took responsibility for the Tlatelolco massacre. In 1969 he made the unapologetic argument that he had "saved the nation from foreign elements" who had allegedly taken advantage of the movement to jeopardize the Olympics and bring anarchy and communism to Mexico.[88] Among this long list of enemies were Agustín Desobry and his team of Dominican friars at UNAM. Largely inspired by the reforms of Vatican II, they saw the arts, in general, and European cinema, in particular, as an opportunity to strengthen the relationship between the church and the nation's youth. The following chapter similarly looks at the case of Vicente Leñero, the catholic novelist, journalist, and film writer who saw value in the importance of engaging in dialogue with the counterculture. Like the students of the Cerf, he interpreted the liberation of the sexual revolution of the Sixties as necessary for building a more democratic nation.

EIGHT

Sexual Liberation and the Redemption of Homosexuality

Vicente Leñero wrote *El monasterio de los buitres* in 1973. This was a controversial cinematic drama that drew inspiration from the radical elements of la onda. It centered the story on the reactionary columns published in the press during the 1960s on the Belgium Benedictine monk Gregorio Lemercier, who shocked ecclesiastical authorities in Rome after opening the doors of his monastery of Cuernavaca to psychoanalysis in 1961. Played in the film as Father Prior, Lemercier is depicted as a gentle and caring yet unyielding priest who encourages the monks living with him to openly confront their "depravity" without guilt or prejudice. Ranging from lust and alcoholism to homosexuality, vanity, and greed, these "sins" are embodied by the individual monks "seeking refuge" in the monastery. Only honesty with each other and "true love" for Christ rather than blind devotion to the church—Father Prior insists throughout the film—will lead his followers to the healing path of redemption. Yet his ambitious project of liberation is a futile one. At the turning point of the film, the beloved priest is condemned by the patron who has financed his monastery since the 1950s. Following a trial in Rome, he is excommunicated by the ecclesiastical authorities and abandoned by his flock. Surprisingly, the only person who remains by his side is Father Pablo, an old Spanish priest who had adamantly disapproved of the experimental methods of his superior and who had warned the younger priest of the potential dangers of following the radicalism of Vatican II. In the last scene of the film, they both walk out of the monastery wearing civilian clothes as they get ready to create Emaús, the secular institution that emerged as one of the most important centers of psychoanalysis in Mexico.[1]

Leñero originally captured the story of Lemercier in the first of many of his plays, *El pueblo rechazado* (1968). Years later, he described the film as "shameful," not because of its homoerotic and sacrilegious stories, but because of what Leñero saw as its distorted representation of the Resurrection of St. Mary Monastery in Cuernavaca.[2] In 1962, he had spent several weeks there drafting what many consider his masterpiece, *Los albañiles* (1963). Presented as an allegory of Christianity, this detective novel documented a marginalized community in the outskirts of Mexico City condemned by its own selfishness and involved in the brutal murder of the epileptic Don Jesús.[3] This protagonist was a nightwatchman killed at a house under construction whose murder was never solved by the corrupt police and whose filth, alcoholism, drug addiction, suppressed homosexuality, and sexual depravity were meant to symbolize the sins of humanity that Christ had hoped to redeem with his death.[4] A few years later, Leñero returned to Cuernavaca and bought a house with his wife, Estela Franco, a modern Catholic and future author of the psychoanalytical biography of the feminist writer Rosario Castellanos.[5] It was also in this city in Morelos where Leñero met the Austrian priest and founder of the Intercultural Center of Documentation (CIDOC), Iván Illich, and where he befriended the radical bishop Sergio Méndez Arceo and the Belgian abbot Gregorio Lemercier.

El pueblo rechazado premiered at the Xola Theater in Mexico City to unanimous praise on October 15, 1968, thirteen days after the Tlatelolco massacre and days after the inauguration of the Olympic Games. By then, Lemercier had been excommunicated by the Vatican for over a year; but he continued providing therapy at the secular Psychoanalytic Center Emaús. Similarly, the authorities in Rome prohibited all Catholics from visiting CIDOC and demanded that Illich abandon the priesthood. The recalcitrant attitude of Illich and Lemercier provided fodder to the most reactionary voices of the church and left no doubt of their disapproval of the liberationist tendencies of Méndez Arceo. Following a brief stay in Europe with a Guggenheim Fellowship during the student movement, Leñero quickly emerged as a vocal supporter of Vatican II. He became one of the sharpest critics of the conservative wing of the church, of the authoritarianism of the government, and of the violent militancy of the radical Left.[6]

Leñero addressed his concerns for the poor in his prolific writings, which included novels, short stories, theatrical plays, interviews, television scripts, and journalistic chronicles. He made an effort in these publications to point to the corrupt political institutions and recalcitrant religious figures responsible for their exploitation. He confessed the sins of the generation of the Sixties and documented the possibility of creating a humane church, receptive to the progressivism of the times, and provided sharp critiques of Mexico's conservative society, with specific attention to the concept of the family, in general, and to the topics of machismo, homosexuality, and female liberation, in particular.[7]

As Leñero moved closer to the progressive teachings of the church in the late Sixties, he also delved further into the world of cinema. Yet in his memoirs and interviews, he expressed little interest in talking about the scandalous but emblematic cinematic collaborations with the director Francisco del Villar, including *El monasterio de los buitres*.[8] Instead, he emphasized his pride in the production of *Cadena Perpetua* (1978). This was an award-winning film noir and one of the most celebrated cinematic projects of the 1970s. Directed by Arturo Ripstein, this political thriller examined the fatalistic story of Javier Lira, an ordinary man who failed to free himself from his flamboyant criminal past.[9] The film pointed to the impossibility of redemption and stressed the institutionalized corruption that the novelist saw in post-1968 Mexico. This was a concern he further condemned as one of the key writers for and Catholic founders of *Proceso*, along with Miguel Ángel Granados Chapa and the Jesuit priest Enrique Maza.[10]

Like Leñero, film scholars have paid little attention to the low-budget and less prestigious films of Francisco del Villar. Instead, they have emphasized the instrumental role a new generation of filmmakers played in creating the artistic cinema of social conscience that took advantage of the democratic opening of Echeverría to revive the moribund national film industry.[11] As censorship relaxed during this period, new spaces flourished in the arts. Moreover, as unprecedented government funds poured into the film industry, Arturo Ripstein, Paul Leduc, Jaime Humberto Hermosillo, and Felipe Cazals (among others) emerged as the exciting faces of the new national cinema. They embarked on multiple projects that debunked the old cinematic tropes of *mexicanidad* from the golden age era. Responsive to the sexual revolution, they specifically condemned patriarchy, and similar to the film projects by Del Villar and Leñero, they brought cinematic representations of homosexuality out of the film closet. They responded favorably to the liberation of women, pushed the historical restrictions of censorship with riskier nudity and foul language, questioned the sanctity of marriage, and depicted the church as an anachronistic institution out of touch with the nation's youth.[12]

This chapter examines the artistic expressions of the Sixties with emphasis on the interconnected themes of sexual liberation and redemption. The first section traces the intellectual transformation of Leñero from his early (and mostly overlooked) writings in the conservative magazine *Señal* during the 1950s to the attention that he gave to the sexual liberation of women and progressive Catholicism in *Claudia de México* during the 1960s and 1970s. I also discuss his humorous "Zona Rosa" gazette, on which Leñero collaborated with the irreverent novelist José Agustín and other key players of the counterculture. The second section examines the erotic cinematic projects that Vicente Leñero made with Francisco del Villar. These pictures centered on male homosexuality and lesbianism. Although quite risky and even progressive at times, their films did not completely break from the moralistic language of the past.

THE LIBERATION OF WOMEN AND THE MOCKING OF THE COUNTERCULTURE

The Leñero family moved from Guadalajara to Mexico City in the early 1930s. Like his siblings, Vicente enrolled in the conservative schools of Columbus, from his elementary to his high school years. As a teenager, he grew fascinated with theater, and with his brothers, he organized popular puppet shows in his middle-class neighborhood, San Pedro de los Pinos. At school, he wrote in student newspapers, and after graduating from high school, he enrolled at UNAM to study engineering, just as his father had hoped. But Vicente never followed this path. He remained interested in writing and made minor contributions to *Impulso*, *Horizontes*, and *Reforma Universitaria*. According to Cuauhtémoc Cárdenas, the son of the former president Lázaro Cárdenas (1934–40), who shared the classrooms with Leñero during this period, these "were sharp political newspapers that often relied on irony to poke fun at the government and its anticlerical politics." Leñero, who was a year older than Cárdenas, used these columns "to mock" the government. In the interpretation offered by Cárdenas, "Catholics had lost important spaces at the university since the 1940s," but these ephemeral papers proliferated across campus, mostly with "the support of former Cristeros and rising panistas who remained influential in some of the schools."[13]

As a writer for these student newspapers, Leñero joined the youth wing of Catholic Action. He attended several of their meetings, including one in 1958 in which he met Estela Franco, his future wife and mother of their three daughters. He later described these meetings as "dull and out of touch with reality." Over time, he found the Catholicism preached there excessively pious and irrelevant to his understanding of Christ. It was in these meetings, nonetheless, where Leñero came across key Catholic leaders who provided him with his first opportunities to start earning money with his writing and where he met rising intellectuals from other countries.[14] In April 1955, he collaborated with other young Catholic leaders from Mexico, Central America, and the Caribbean to organize a conference in Havana to discuss the "presence of Catholic students in the university." The organizers hoped to strengthen the role of Pax Romana in the region, create more "effective propaganda" in secular schools, and shed light on the "neo-Malthusian experiments." This experiment had led to the sterilization of women in Puerto Rico and provided the first scientific studies of contraceptives.[15]

Still enrolled at the School of Engineering, Leñero took classes at the Carlos Septién García School of Journalism in 1955 and soon published short columns with *Señal*. He did not have aspirations to become a journalist, but he wanted to improve his writing, which he considered mediocre and conventional. His first teachers of journalism were key intellectuals involved in modernizing and strengthening the channels of communication of the church, including Jorge Mendoza Carrasco, a former militant of Catholic Action who had an entertainment column in the national daily *Excélsior*.[16] With his support but no background in cinema, Leñero published film reviews in two small sections of the newspaper called "Magic Lantern" and "Who Is Who in Cinema?" Yet it was his writings in *Señal* that put a more reliable income in the newlywed's pocket and provided him with a greater opportunity to express his faith in Catholicism.[17]

Señal published its first issue in July 1954. Designed as a modern magazine, its goal was to address the social concerns of the nation from a Catholic perspective. But its writers were also invested in politicizing their readers, encouraging them to support the conservative PAN, and providing them with practical advice for defending the family.[18] Leñero continue his work with the Catholic magazine upon his return from Spain in 1958, where he had lived for a year with the financial support of a grant and where he took further classes in journalism.[19] He wrote a series of articles addressing his concerns over what he and others at *Señal* saw as the rapid deterioration of family values. In describing divorce as a "social sickness," for example, he cited the relevance of *Casti connubii* (Of Chaste Wedlock), the 1930 encyclical, which also condemned adultery, contraception, abortion, and eugenics. Leñero provided his readers with "alarming" statistical data comparing Mexico to France, Cuba, and the United States. He lamented that in his native country the number of divorces had increased significantly faster than in these other countries, by 56 percent in four years, from 21 registered cases each day in 1951 to 35 in 1955. He pointed to two factors as the cause. The first was the relaxation of the Civil Marriage Law, which, according to him, had expanded its definition of "irreconcilable differences," mostly to attract US citizens to Mexico where the laws were more flexible. The second and related factor had to do with the increasing acceptance of divorce as widely depicted in the entertainment industry and as often "celebrated" in a sensationalist press interested in providing the names and stories of all the Hollywood stars who traveled to Mexico to file for divorce.[20]

Relatedly, in an article published in September 1959, Leñero described the newly founded Christian Family Movement as "the most reliable hope" of defending the Mexican family from "the threats of modernity."[21] In different articles, he identified one of these "solemn" threats as the increasing problem of youth delinquency as embodied in the image of the "rebel without a cause." Similar to the conservative language employed by the film directors of the 1950s, he claimed to provide a space for young people to explain this phenomenon "in their own words." Yet, in these early writings, he mostly understood youth rebellion as a by-product of the Americanization and secularization of the country.[22] Also of great concern to him were the societal abandonment of the nation's poor and the increasing threat of communism. To reach out to a young readership and encourage them to acknowledge the external threats that put the nation at risk, Leñero addressed the young readers of *Señal* in its new editorial section, "Youth Speaks." He encouraged them to "create a social consciousness," attentive to the needs of the nation's poor, and asked them to embrace a "more dynamic" understanding of their Catholic faith.[23]

Leñero's career took a drastic turn in 1962, when he met the television producer largely responsible for the successful debut of the modern *telenovela*, Ernesto Alonso. With his support, he scripted radio and television soap operas. He later described the scripts as "corny" but important experiences that gave him the courage to take a more critical view of his conservative past. In "The Blood under the River," "Silver Wedding," "The Three Faces of Women" and other scripts with similarly catchy titles, Leñero explored the romantic relationships between young responsible couples composed of hardworking men, like himself, and modern young women caught between the conservatism of the past and the changing environment of the modern city, like his wife, Estela.

By 1965, Leñero had been married for five years. He had stopped collaborating with Ernesto Alonso and writing for *Señal*. Instead, two years after the publication of *Los albañiles*, he gave greater priority to his novels, and following an invitation from the editor Ernesto Spota, he got a steady job working with *Claudia*, first as a regular contributor from 1965 to 1970 and then as director of the women's magazine from 1970 to 1972. By then, Leñero had traveled frequently to Cuernavaca, where he embraced the progressive Catholicism of Vatican II and where he spent some of his time strengthening his profile as the nation's most important Catholic novelist.[24]

The Feminism of Claudia

The founding director of *Claudia de México*, Ernesto Spota, presented the monthly magazine as an embodiment of the modern Mexican woman of the Sixties.[25] First published in September 1965, "she" was described as a "sympathetic friend" to her cosmopolitan and middle-to-upper-class readers. *Claudia* was "optimistic" about the cultural changes that were taking place in Western Europe and in the United States but "proud" of her national identity. She was the "ideal companion" to a new generation of readers who were willing to experiment with cultural changes without falling prey to the "prejudices" of the past. She was "sophisticated," "conscious," "proud," "intelligent," and "beautiful."[26] For aesthetic and thematic inspiration, she found inspiration in *Marie-Claire* from France, *Constanze* from Germany, *Arianna* from Italy, and *Vogue* from the United States. For guidance, *Claudia* relied on her Latin American experiences, first in Argentina, where the magazine originally was published under the same name in 1957, and then in Brazil, where it was first published in Portuguese in 1961.[27]

As the historian Karina Felitti has argued, *Claudia* experienced a significant transformation, initially having difficulties overcoming its conservative roots during the 1960s, but eventually welcoming the more radical language of sexual liberation that emerged in the 1970s.[28] Counterintuitively, the change came under the leadership of a Catholic writer, Vicente Leñero, who published his first columns in *Claudia* in 1965 and became director of the magazine in 1970. He held this position for two years, when the much more progressive pages of the magazine reached as many as five hundred thousand monthly readers.[29]

The articles, editorial pages, and ads published during the first five years reinforced *Claudia*'s commitment to celebrate the nuclear family. Its pages were overwhelmingly concerned with giving practical yet mostly conservative advice to aspiring mothers and new wives. Not too different from magazines of an earlier era, readers were provided with the best suggestions on raising well-behaved children, having their homes clean, keeping their husbands satisfied, and maintaining a healthy and clean body. Similar to *Juventud* and *Señal*, moreover, the ideal image of the modern Mexican woman was represented with a light mestizo complexion and welcomed the latest fashion and technological innovations from Europe and the United States but remained loyal to her Catholic sensibilities.[30]

Claudia drastically evolved under the leadership of Leñero. While the magazine maintained its delicate balance between the cosmopolitan and the national, its pages welcomed greater dialogue with sexuality and the burgeoning liberation of women. Its pages featured influential female voices in journalism and academia, including those of Elena Poniatowska, Oriana Fallaci, Josefina King, Silva Cota, Carmen de Silva, Marta Acevedo, and María del Carmen Elu de Leñero. It published original articles and polls that addressed the needs and changing feminist ideas of the times.[31] The writers commented on current political events as well as on the ideological changes that were taking place within the church and the attitudes that a new and less conservative generation of women expressed toward the pill, divorce, the counterculture, and the nascent gay liberation movement. The more polarizing topic of abortion was also widely discussed, but it remained a taboo, as an overwhelming majority of women continued to condemn it for physical and moral reasons.[32]

The changes that *Claudia* experienced in the early 1970s were also evident in the articles, interviews, and innovative columns that Leñero published in the magazine. For example, with his extensive interviews with the actresses María Félix and Dolores del Río and the entertainment producers Ernesto Alonso and Raúl Velasco, he drew attention to a rapidly changing society that nostalgically looked to its golden age in cinema at a moment in which color television emerged as the more influential medium in urban Mexico.[33] Leñero also published a series of travelogues documenting the diverse regions and cultures of Mexico. Along with other journalists, he introduced his readers to local cuisines and customs as well as to changing generational attitudes that included diverse opinions on multiple topics that they felt concerned readers. These ranged from romantic relationships outside marriage to the right to enjoy sexual pleasure.

Similar articles discussed the feminist debates in academia that ensued after Betty Friedan's work was published in the United States, while other articles encouraged open discussions about lesbianism, no longer presented as a "psychological disease" but rather as a natural act of love.[34] Similarly, as the leading figure of *Claudia* in the early 1970s, Leñero welcomed interviews and opinion pieces by other journalists who wrote on the liberation of nuns in the aftermath of Vatican II, including their experiences as university students and their social work in factories and poor neighborhoods. For Sister María García Vallejo, who was enrolled at the Social Work School of UNAM, the Sixties pointed to "a marvelous era of renovation and change," one that demanded "greater individual expression" and called for a "meaningful dialogue."[35] Like other nuns of her generation who favorably responded to the 1965 decree *Perfectae caritis* (Perfect Charity) of Vatican II, she was "summoned to come out of the cloister and engage in real issues."[36]

Under Leñero's leadership, *Claudia* celebrated the "revolution" that simultaneously took place within the church. It was caught between the "anachronistic" ideas of *Humanae vitae*, which condemned all forms of contraception and reaffirmed the importance of married love between a man and a woman, on the one hand, and the excitement of Vatican II, on the other.[37] Leñero called for a productive dialogue between the church and advocated for women's liberation. Similarly, he pointed to Cuernavaca as the place that played a profound role in a fruitful engagement with psychoanalysis, which partly encouraged a new generation of Catholics to discuss pleasure in the broadest sense of the term. Leñero described the dioceses of Bishop Méndez Arceo as the "Netherlands of Mexico" and specifically referred to the *Dutch Catechism* (1966) as the most exciting theology of the times, including the attention it gave to sexuality, encouraging Catholics to explore "the erotic element" of love and hinting to homosexuality "as natural." In short, Leñero enthusiastically proclaimed that "the church has resuscitated," and like the Dutch, "we must also demystify its dogmas," including the antiquated yet still popular ideas associated with "the resurrection of Christ" and the so-called virginity of Mary. He concluded, "The objective sin [or immoral act] does not exist.... Our only goal should be the pursuit of true love," one without prejudices, fear of God, or the repression and ojectification of others.[38]

As the new director of *Claudia* in June 1970, Leñero embraced the "new path" of the magazine and "promised to defend it." For him, the change was evident in "a new effort to comprehend and celebrate the modern world of women." The modern woman questioned the intolerant views of the past and favorably responded to the emancipating language that had arrived from Europe, South America, and the United States. She embraced talent, maturity, and boldness and rejected the "shitty and prudish" fashions and customs of an earlier era. Yet *Claudia* did not simply represent "a magazine for women"; "more ambitiously," Leñero argued, her goal was to interpret and participate in the rising feminist movement that Mexico so desperately needed. For this, self-criticism and an honest engagement with opposite views were crucial. He explained that *Claudia* "welcomes criticism" and "is eager to participate in the liberation of women." She is the representation of the "new Mexican woman," one who has shaken off her "haggard nationalism [and] absurd chauvinistic attitudes" in favor of a productive, practical, and more inclusive "dialogue with the [modern] world."[39]

The Mocking of the "Gluttonous Snobs"

In reaching out to the nation's youth, Leñero supported the participation of a new generation of writers who embraced the reforms of Vatican II and wrote in favor of la onda. Emblematic of the progressive Catholics was the twenty-four-year-old Ignacio Solares, who later pointed to *Los albañiles* as one of the most influential novels for him. Eager to work with Leñero, Solares accepted an invitation to join the magazine, and similar to other young journalists who wrote for *Claudia*, he described them as foundational, not only for his writing career, but also for his understanding of his faith. Specifically, it was during this time when Leñero introduced him to several authors who shaped Ignacio's ecumenical view of Christianity. Unapologetic about their interest in exploring the most important social and political issues of the day from a Catholic perspective, these authors included Graham Greene and François Mauriac, British and French Catholic novelists, respectively, who criticized the conservativism of the church, celebrated the reforms of Vatican II, and spoke against European imperialism in Algeria and Vietnam.[40]

Representative of la onda was José Agustín. Only twenty years old at the time, he benefited from the early enthusiasm that Leñero expressed in his work. His first job with *Claudia* was in 1965, writing horoscopes. But more significantly, Agustín organized a writing group composed of a new generation of countercultural writers who were eager to discuss their work with Leñero and who were also invited to write for *Claudia*. They included Gustavo Sainz (author of *Gazapo* [1965]); Juan Tovar (author of the transgressive novel *El mar bajo tierra* [1967]); and Gelsen Gas (painter, playwright, and director of the countercultural film *Anticlimax* [1969]). In these meetings they commented on drafts of Agustín's *De Perfil* (1966) and gave feedback to Parménides García Saldaña on *Pasto verde* (1968). Arguably, these were the best books of la onda; they humorously mocked the traditional Catholicism of the nation and the generation of the Sixties, including its insecurities and nihilism, caught between the commercialism of the time, the sexual awakening of youth, and the authoritarianism of a patriarchal society. These themes were also introduced to the readers of *Claudia* in brief sections that featured rising figures in the counterculture and their respective work in film, painting, plays, and novels.[41]

Perhaps the much older Leñero did not entirely sympathize with the most radical elements of the counterculture, but he valued the ironic sensibility, irreverence, spontaneity, satirical touch, and outlandish fun. In 1970, he extended his collaboration with Agustín, Sainz, Tovar, Gas, and Solares to create the outrageous gazette, "Claudia en la Zona Rosa." The pink zone, or *zona rosa*, referred to the place where the fictitious character Claudia lived. The term was coined by Leñero in 1965 to describe the middle-class neighborhood in Colonia Juárez in southern Mexico City that welcomed the emergence of la onda. The Zona Rosa developed as the preferred hub for American tourists during the 1950s and 1960s, filled with boutiques, art galleries, fine restaurants, and movie theaters, and it eventually became one of the most gay-friendly areas in the city. In his hilarious description of the neighborhood, Leñero wrote, "She is too shy to be red and too daring to be white." She is "a cheap perfume in an elegant bottle, a provincial girl dressed in a chorus uniform. [The] daughter of *nouveau riche* [parents], she is pretty but silly; elegant but frivolous. [Above all], she is a gluttonous snob."[42]

Leñero published "Claudia en la Zona Rosa" on pink paper from 1970 to 1972 (see fig. 11). Its pages offered a fun space to mock what he saw as the pretentiousness and tackiness of an indulgent society that claimed to have all the answers but remained trapped in its authoritarian, pious, and conservative past. For example, in drawing a distinction between "Miss Mexico" and the "Beauty Queen of the Zona Rosa," the gazette made fun of those on the Left and the Right who took the concept of "free love" and the use of "the pill" too seriously. Similarly, in selected sections on "antique books," the contributors questioned the alleged radicalism and originality of the feminist movement by reproducing nineteenth- and early twentieth-century passages from famous books championing the liberation of women.

But perhaps the most hilarious section of the pink gazette was its selected "biographies" and "confessions of snobs." The contributors made fun of

FIGURE 11. *Claudia en la Zona Rosa.* The subsection at the bottom reads, "The Pink Zone Lives in Eternal Sin." From *Claudia de México* (October, 1970).

the popularity and often self-proclaimed militancy of the most celebrated intellectuals and artistic figures of the time, including Luis Buñuel, Carlos Fuentes, José Luis Cuevas, Alejandro Jodorowsky, and Carlos Monsiváis. Specifically, the snobs and other "natives" who presumably inhabited the Zona Rosa poked fun at the blurring of the lines that divided those who were "in" and those who were "out," according to the commentators of the time: between the *fresa* and the kitsch, the refined and the popular, the liberal and the conservative, the radical and the reformist, and the religious and the profane. The commercialization, silliness, nihilism, and lack of ingenuity of la onda was not spared, nor was the orthodoxy, demagoguery, and conservatism of a Left that claimed to have the answers for building a democratic nation but that often expressed a chauvinistic interpretation of the feminist movement. Silly representations were also made of traditional Catholics who demanded that the Zona Rosa be shut down, American tourists who discovered authenticity in kitsch products, devout Catholics who found pleasure in the sinful lives of artists, liberal intellectuals who saw the Zona Rosa as the aspirational site of a progressive future, the "native people" of the Zona Rosa who only consumed the counterculture on weekends, the boutique owners who profited from the commercialization of la onda, and the aspiring feminists who raised bigoted children.[43]

In short, no one was spared in the satirical columns of "Claudia en la Zona Rosa." In February 1972, *Claudia* published the last issue of its pink gazette. A month later Leñero resigned from the magazine and began his collaboration with his lifelong friend Julio Scherer García at the daily *Excélsior*.[44] By then, the radicalism and ingenuity of the counterculture was over; but its legacy in the rising feminist, environmentalist, and gay liberation movements remained relevant. In addition to his collaboration with Scherer García, Leñero delved further in the world of cinema. With Francisco del Villar, he made a series of films that addressed the liberation of women and homosexuality. His focus on these topics, albeit progressive for the times, remained confined to his identity as a heterosexual Catholic man. The limits of his progressive thinking were also evident in his role as director of *Claudia*. At the time of his resignation, the magazine had hired several women writers and reporters; but the editorial team of *Claudia* remained in the hands of a few men, with three minor but important exceptions: Lupita Morales and Ana Maria Novick, editorial assistants of the fashion section; and Ana Aguilar, coeditor with Ignacio Solares.

CINEMATIC DEPICTIONS OF HOMOSEXUALITY

Cinematic representations of male homosexuality date to the 1930s if not sooner. But, as Javier Valdovinos has documented in his extensive study of more than two hundred Mexican films, it was not until the 1970s that cinematic representations on the topic "came out of the closet."[45] These films were conscious of the social changes that characterized the period, namely, the emergence of a small but rising gay liberation movement, but they were not entirely successful in freeing themselves from the negative stereotypes of the past. The most demeaning of these representations were the popular *ficheras*, or sexploitation comedies with roots in the *cabaratera* (brothel) genre of the 1940s that consistently caricatured homosexual men as exclusively feminine, passive, and weak characters with the sole purpose of inciting cheap laughter. A different and more sophisticated interpretation emerged in the 1970s with the experimental work of younger directors, including Jaime Humberto Hermosillo and Arturo Ripstein, who rejected the blatant stereotyping of the past and intended to provide a nuanced and humane depiction of male homosexuality.[46]

In *La primavera de los escorpiones* (1970) and *El monasterio de los buitres* (1972), Francisco del Villar introduced Mexican audiences to the world of men romantically involved with and sexually attracted to other men. However, in both films homosexuality is mostly understood as a pathology or as a mirror of a national moment in crisis. The first of these pictures, written by Hugo Argüelles, for example, is the coming-of-age story of Daniel, a thirteen-year-old boy who is described as "odd," "alienated," and "complicated." His presumably homosexual father left him when he was only nine years old, despite his father's willingness to work out his "problems" with the help of a psychologist who "treated" him with electroshock therapy. Angry at his absent father and close to his overbearing mother, Isabel, the teenager expresses sympathy and curiosity for Julio and Andrés, two "friends" in their twenties who live in a motor home parked next to his mother's summer house. Daniel is depicted as a voyeur throughout the film. He spies on the couple with a telescope from his bedroom and puts on makeup in front of a mirror, all indicating the best intentions on the part of the director to explore Daniel's sexual awakening.[47]

But the story concludes tragically with a scene that made *La primavera de los escorpiones* one of the most controversial films in Mexican history. As the sensual Isela is preoccupied in a romantic adventure with Andrés (in their shared attempt to "cure" his homosexuality), Daniel is shown lying on the bed nearly naked with Julio. However, it is not clear if the arrogant and often violent Julio seduced the young boy, as most viewers would assume, or if Daniel, who is often portrayed as the most mature character in the film, is the one who actually took command of Julio's sexuality and initiated the relationship with the older man. Despite the film's flaws, it is this ambiguity that makes it fascinating. But it is also the allusion to pedophilia in relation to homosexuality that makes the grim ending of this film difficult to assess.

Also controversial was *El monasterio de los buitres*, a 1972 film written by Vicente Leñero based on Lemercier. As noted earlier, the protagonist of the film is Father Prior. He is a progressive priest who opened his monastery to a group of troubled monks hoping to overcome their "demons." Nearly all of them are "in love" with their liberal superior, including Marcos, a passive monk who is often overwhelmed by his greed, and Juan, the artistic and intellectual monk who is deprived by his vanity.

The same is true of Emilio, the central character of the film and the newest arrival to the monastery whose "impotence" haunts him to the point of depression. To overcome his sexual insecurity, Emilio forces himself to browse *Playboy* magazines in his cell. The magazines are covertly embedded between Bibles, which he gets from Camilo, an alcoholic monk of short stature, in charge of a library full of "religious texts" that include illustrations of male and female "saints." Akin to other films of the era, Emilio initiates a flirtatious relationship with the virginal Eusebia, an eighteen-year-old girl who buys textiles made at the monastery. In a conversation with Father Prior, Emilio confesses that he has always been "timid." He laments abandoning his studies after the premature death of his father and having to work with his mother, who made a living selling women's clothes. While his schoolmates repeatedly called him a *marica*, or sissy, he also expresses the pain he felt when his mother locked him in a room with an older woman, hoping that he would overcome "his issues." The progressive superior attempts to console him, insisting that God loves "all of his creatures." But it is only after Emilio talks to the monastery's psychoanalyst and loses his virginity to Amalia, the redeemed prostitute of the village, that he builds the courage to have a romantic relationship with Eusebia. In their first sexual encounter she makes fun of Emilio's "difficulties" but confesses that she has fallen in love with him. Still angry, the "delicate" Emilio threatens to return to Father Prior, who loves him, truly understands him, and does not make fun of his insecurities. But it is only after the Vatican excommunicates the prior that Emilio finally elopes with Eusebia. The founder of the monastery interprets the unwillingness of his flock to follow him not as a betrayal of their faith but as a sign that his methods of employing psychoanalysis actually worked.

Vicente Leñero continued to work with Francisco del Villar. In 1977 they cowrote the script of *Cuando tejen las arañas*, one of several films that touched on the topic of lesbianism. Although progressive at times in its representations of the liberation of women, they had difficulties presenting the love and sexual attraction between two women on screen.

When the Spiders Weave

Muchachas de uniforme was one of the earliest Mexican films to touch on the topic of lesbianism. Directed by Crevenna in 1951, it tells the story of

Manuela, a poor and illiterate orphan who lives in an authoritarian all-girls' Catholic boarding school, where she falls in love with her liberal teacher, Lucila. At the end of the film the young student commits suicide without ever receiving the love of her teacher, and Lucila becomes a nun. Two years later, Díaz Morales released *Juventud desenfrenada*. The film tells the story of Laura, a transgressive girl who enjoys dressing and behaving "like a man," and, like Manuela, she also dies at the end of the film. Had Laura been dressed as a young lady, her life would have been spared by the cop who shot her, mistakenly thinking she was a "rebel without a cause."[48] *La loba,* or the she-wolf, dies for the same reason. The villain in Roberto Rodríguez's *La culpa de los hombres* (1955), she is an aggressive lesbian who runs a women's prison with an iron hand and preys on the innocence of the young inmates until she is finally killed at the climax of the film.[49]

The representations of lesbians practically disappeared from Mexican pictures during the 1960s.[50] Instead, film directors paid attention to virginal nuns whose alleged repressed sexuality was often but discreetly depicted in relation to their presumed lesbianism. In these films the convent is generally portrayed as a refuge to those healing from a broken heart or attempting to escape from the sexual temptations and misogynist violence of the outside world.[51] Yet the convent often fails in its mission and instead becomes a space of corruption and depravity. While many of the nuns develop a masochistic relationship with Christ there, others are transformed into sexual objects of desire (for both men and women) or are depicted as victims of sexual assault. Yet as the counterculture influenced Mexican cinema and sexploitation generated significant success at the box office in the 1970s, the depictions of these nuns took on more aggressive, sacrilegious, and violent overtones. They are often portrayed as mad or vampire-like lesbians who have been possessed by the devil or who can only be "cured" of their alleged "depravity" with medical measures, ranging from psychoanalysis to the more aggressive electroshock therapy.[52]

An example of the latter is *Cuando tejen las arañas* (1977), a film directed by Roberto Gavaldón and cowritten by Vicente Leñero and Francisco del Villar. Released for "adults only," the film draws from the same tropes related to female youth rebellion examined in chapter 1 but takes a radical approach by placing lesbianism at the center of the story. The protagonist is Laura, a beautiful eighteen-year-old who returns to Mexico from a Catholic boarding school in Geneva, where she spent three years studying and dealing with the premature death of her beloved father. Unlike most people her age, she is conservative and has difficulties adapting to modern and secular Mexico. She is disgusted with her nymphomaniac and alcoholic mother, Julia. The mother is never dressed in black to mourn the memory of her husband, as depicted in nearly all Mexican films, but instead is portrayed as a hypersexualized woman who had an intimate relationship while married to Laura's father. Her lover is a hedonistic younger man from a lower class solely interested in Julia's wealth.

Claudia is Laura's best friend, a bisexual blonde whose view on life is undyingly reduced to her celebration of "free love." Always wearing trousers, she makes no effort to hide the physical attraction she feels for the virginal Laura. But it is what Laura discovers about her beloved father that pushes her first to a state of depression and then to a self-destructive lifestyle. Her father was not the idealized man that Laura so passionately admired as a child. A liberal professor at the university, he was a closeted homosexual who lived a double life and had multiple relationships with his male students. To overcome her despair, Laura follows Claudia's advice and starts to adopt the same rebellious behaviors she once detested. Like her adversarial mother, she starts drinking heavily and begins to cheat on her boyfriend, Sergio, a handsome and conservative university student who is boring and dull but always kind and respectful to Laura. Before getting married to Sergio, Laura explores her sexuality with Alex. He is an arrogant photographer who once had a relationship with Julia and who embodies the worst traits of the commercialized version of la onda. Aware of her mother's affairs, Laura loses her virginity to Alex, which she had kept as a sign of the intense love she had felt for her father, and eventually gets pregnant with her lover's baby.

During the night of her honeymoon with Sergio, she confesses that she had been cheating on him with Alex and had an abortion. But the new husband reaffirms his love for Laura and vows to respect her. Yet Laura remains in love with the childhood memory of her father. She clashes further with her mother and continues to cheat on Sergio with the repugnant photographer who claims to celebrate the liberation of women but who simultaneously enjoys humiliating Laura in public (to the point of watching her strip off her clothes in front of a group of strangers). Claudia is aware of her friend's misery. But as she begins "weaving" her trap, Claudia encourages this relationship, hoping that Laura will soon heal her broken heart.

Unlike Laura, Claudia is happy to be a "liberated woman." She flaunts her sexuality without reservation and enjoys the pleasure she has with her girlfriend, Lorena, an "exotic" Black model who frequently poses nude for Alex.

The beautiful and transgressive Claudia is depicted as the adversary of Alex. She is shown in command as she insists that soon Laura will come crawling to her. One night, Sergio finally breaks down and leaves Laura, promising never to return to her. Claudia throws an exuberant party to "celebrate" her divorce, which includes a live performance and an orgy with homosexual men and women voyeuristically celebrating their liberation. Lorena gives Laura "a sugar-like substance" that puts her in a state of ecstasy. The next morning, she wakes up naked with Alex and Lorena. With Laura having no recollection of the night, Claudia reminds her that she was also intimate with her. Enraged and still dazed by the drugs, Laura picks up a gun and shoots Alex in the back as he lays naked on the bed next to Lorena. The next day Julia is depicted paying a large sum of money to a lawyer who successfully makes a case for Laura. Instead of having to serve time in prison, she is required to enter a psychiatric hospital where she receives electroshock therapy. Once released, a "liberated" but "deranged" Laura moves in with the cunning Claudia. The film ends with a full-blown spider web over the ambivalent face of Laura.

CONCLUSION

The late 1970s marked a pivotal moment for the careers of Vicente Leñero and Francisco del Villar. Del Villar produced one of the best films of the era, *El lugar sin limites*, in 1977, and two years later, Leñero published a national interpretation of liberation theology, *El evangelio de Lucas Gavilán* (1979). In their respective projects they both addressed the social problems associated with homophobia and misogyny, and while the film used the character of the male transvestite Manuela to place these at the center of the story, the novel described these repressive characteristics of Mexico's conservative society as "structural sins" that a more progressive nation needed to overcome.

These positions did not emerge in a vacuum. The same year that Leñero published his book, a group of unionized workers at UNAM and the Metropolitan Autonomous University organized the March for Homosexual Dignity. This was an effort that began with the founding of the Homosexual Liberation Front of Mexico in 1971 and the declarations that openly gay intellectuals voiced in various outlets.[53] At the forefront of these figures was Nancy Cárdenas, who in 1972 organized the play of *The Boys in the Band* at UNAM. The play was based on the 1970 US film by Mart Crowley that many consider a milestone in the history of queer cinema. Two years later

Cárdenas accepted an invitation from Jacobo Zabludovsky to appear on his primetime show to speak favorably about her homosexuality, a first in Mexican television history. In 1975 she published the nation's first gay manifesto in the magazine *Siempre!* in collaboration with her friend and a leading figure in Mexico's New Left, Carlos Monsiváis, and one of the central figures in the 1968 student movement who later opened some of Mexico's first gay bars and libraries, Luis González de Alba. Also in 1975, Cárdenas organized a panel at the International Women's Conference on the topic of lesbianism.[54]

As the conservative tropes of the early Sixties gave in to the liberating language of the late Sixties, the characters in the writings of Leñero became more transgressive. For example, whereas male homosexuality was mostly described as a pathology in *El monasterio de los buitres* (similar to the other films directed by Del Villar during this period and not too different from the interpretation given in his earlier novel, *Los albañiles*), Leñero made a greater effort in *El evangelio* to draw attention to the violent tendencies and consequences of machismo.

In *El evangelio*, Leñero places Jesucristo Gómez in the contemporary context of modern Mexico, among the poorest sectors of society and those who were ostracized and repressed during the presidential years of Echeverría. Leñero tells the story of Mario Benítez, "the child of seven who was brought into this world by Eloísa Fajardo and Don Mario Benítez." Born and raised in the Cristero region of Guanajuato, Marito falls in love with music, learns to play the guitar, and sings proudly about his "feminine gestures." He finally comes out to his parents at eighteen. His father "nearly beats his son to death," demanding that he repent of his sins. But "with pride," Marito painfully remembers that "God made him that way." He recalls being labeled a "fag, faggot, sperm catcher, gay, inverted, bitch," and "covered in blood," he shouts at his father, "That is who I am, that is who I am."[55]

Once Marito is partially liberated, his father turns to alcohol and disregards his job. His younger sister is ostracized and denied the possibility of finding her dream job. Only Marito's mother, Eloisa, expresses sympathy for her son, hoping that if she prays hard enough to the saint of the Dominican order, Martin de Porres, God will "finally straighten" her boy.

At the climax of the story, Jesucristo Goméz meets Don Mario, who confesses to the Christ-like protagonist that his son is a "faggot," adding, "I do not deserve to be punished this way by God." Jesucristo responds, "God does not punish anyone. . . . The first step you have to take is to accept your own responsibility. You have to leave your son in peace. Do not make him feel abnormal or sick. It is not a sin [to be like him]. The only one who needs to straighten up is you."[56]

For Leñero, in short, the liberating power of Christ depended on love, compassion, and tolerance for people as individuals, as equals, regardless of class, race, gender, and sexual preference. For him, love was the most efficient agent for social change, the very presence of Christ on earth. Without this simple but powerful idea, Leñero argued in his novel, people are not capable of fulfilling a valuable life. At the end of the book, however, the same ecclesiastical authorities that preached resignation and obedience to the oppressed collaborate with the government authorities and have Jesucristo imprisoned, tortured, and killed. For them, he was not the Messiah but a political revolutionary who accused the church of neglecting the needs of the poor, abusing their power to enrich themselves, refusing to reform their authoritarian traditions to defend their hierarchical relationship with society, and thus ultimately responsible for the repression of the poor and the marginalized. What Mexico needed, Leñero concluded, were more revolutionaries whose activism was founded on the principle of love. But unlike other important Catholic intellectuals of the era, Leñero remained hopeful of the church, as he had done earlier in *Claudia* and *El pueblo rechazado*. In the last pages of *El evangelio*, the love of Jesucristo is embodied in a nameless priest who sees the Gospel of Gómez as the best and only path forward.

Ultraconservatives saw the novels of Vicente Leñero and the "pornographic" films of the 1970s as an aberration. They were equally critical of the most radical elements of the counterculture and, as the next chapter demonstrates, also of those who mocked the legacy of the Cristero Rebellion in the late Sixties when a group of revisionist historians instead celebrated them as symbolic leaders of the New Left.

NINE

Competing Interpretations of
Los Cristeros and Violent Reactions
to the Counterculture

The Spanish filmmaker Luis Alcoriza produced *Fé, esperanza y caridad* in 1974 in collaboration with Alberto Bojórquez and Jorge Fons, younger directors and recent graduates of the University Center for Cinematographic Studies. Composed of three independent shorts, the film ridicules the most important theological virtues of Catholicism. In *Faith*, Bojórquez centers the story on Regina, a pious woman who embarks on a long pilgrimage in search of a miracle to save her husband from a crippling disease. A group of men sexually assault her when she finally reaches the hill on which the Virgin stands. But on her way back home, she finds her husband has been miraculously cured of his illness, and her blind devotion to Catholicism is restored.

Hope is the more countercultural of the three films. Alcoriza tells the story of Gaby, a hippie-looking stunt man who consents to be nailed to a cross as part of a freak show at a circus with the hope of making enough money to buy a home for his pious mother (fig. 12). The voyeuristic show is a huge success. Hundreds of people representing the popular and wealthy sectors of society visit the spectacle simply to fetishize their masochist devotion to Christ. The women who take care of him find themselves sexually aroused, while those who stand in long lines to pay for the exhibition indulge in Gaby's pain, including tourists who appear fascinated with the paganism of Mexico. As the violent crucifixion turns into a pornographic view of Catholicism, Gaby's hope descends into despair. Everyone profits from the show, including his mother, who reinforces her love for God in the agonizing pain of her son. Gaby dies of an infection at the end of the film. In collaboration with a corrupt doctor, the owner of the circus had used cheap metal to nail Gaby to the cross instead of buying the more expensive gold nails that had been recommended by the health authorities.

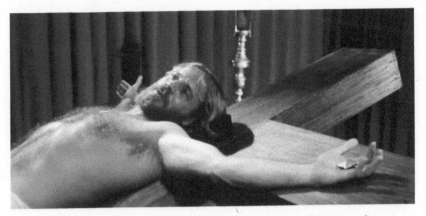

FIGURE 12. Gaby nailed to the cross. From *Esperanza* (dir. Luis Alcoriza, 1974).

Charity is the best of the three films in the eyes of the critics.[1] Fons features a series of tragic events that unfold after a wealthy woman drives to a shantytown to throw a handful of coins to a group of poor kids. A melee quickly unfolds as the kids try to grab the coins, ending up in the death of an innocent man. The widow finds it impossible to get help from the judicial and health authorities who work for an inept bureaucratic system that is more interested in collecting fees than in serving those in need.

Together, the three films depict a violent country caught in despair, inhabited by a wretched majority that is repressed by an authoritarian state and a corrupt version of Christianity. The criticisms of Catholicism they depict are emblematic of the leftist interpretations of religion during the 1970s.[2]

The first section of this chapter examines three of these leftist interpretations, with attention to the Cristero Rebellion, the 1926–29 war launched by militant Catholics in the name of Christ against the anticlerical government of Plutarco Elías Calles: *De todos modos Juan te llamas* (Marcela Fernández Violante, 1974); *La guerra santa* (Carlos Enrique Taboada, 1979); and *A paso de cojo* (Luis Alcoriza, 1979). These pictures were disliked by film critics and historians alike. Among them was the conservative French historian and author of *La Cristiada* (1972–74), Jean Meyer. But despite the criticisms, the films provided valuable commentary on the same authoritarianism and state repression that sparked the 1968 student movement.

The Cristero films of the 1970s were also disliked by ultraconservative Catholics whose views on the radicalism of the era are examined in the second section of this chapter. Among them was Antonio Rius Facius, a self-educated historian of the Cristero Rebellion and a regular contributor (and editor) of the traditionalist gazette *La Hoja de Combate* (1968–72). For the writers in this militant paper and the more violent *Réplica*, the Sixties pointed to a mad moment of despair and immorality. But as the historians Ibarrola Martínez and Herrán Ávila have argued, these traditionalists did not constitute a monolithic group. Following the 1971 excommunication of the anti-Semitic Jesuit priest Joaquín Sáenz Arriaga, these figures were largely polarized into two camps. On one side were those, like Rius Facius, who sympathized with Sáenz. In agreement with his book, *The New Montinian Church*, they saw the pope as an agent of Judaism who had taken advantage of the reforms of Vatican II to destroy Catholicism. On the other side were those who were critical of religious dialogue with modernity but remained loyal to Paul VI and the Holy See. The founder of Editorial Jus and central ideologue of the Sinarquista movement of the late 1930s and early 1940s, Salvador Abascal, represented this position.[3]

The rhetorical differences regarding the pope between Rius Facius and Abascal reached violent dimensions in the context of Vatican II. However, they agreed on the importance of keeping the memory of the Cristeros alive in response to the radicalism of the Sixties. They also shared the same reactions to the counterculture and armed struggle, interpreting them as two of the most significant threats to Mexico. In their respective publications, they encouraged their readers to come to the defense of Catholicism and specifically pointed to the Chilean director Alejandro Jodorowsky as a dangerous threat to the Hispanic identity of the nation and its Catholic youth. In his radical depiction of la onda, they argued, Jodorowsky had blurred the lines between the counterculture and militancy. Young sympathizers of Rius Facius and Abascal who were active in the universities agreed and violently protested the showing of one of Jodorowsky's most controversial films, *The Holy Mountain* (1972–73). President Luis Echeverría, who also viewed the artistic work of Jodorowsky with apprehension, had him expelled from the country in 1972.

Jodorowsky's expulsion from Mexico was not an isolated event. The French historian Jean Meyer suffered a similar fate in 1969 after having criticized the presidential administration of Gustavo Díaz Ordaz in the aftermath of the Tlatelolco massacre. Meyer returned to Mexico in the 1970s, but unlike the more radical Jodorowsky, he did not voice any public criticisms of the Echeverría administration, which welcomed a revisionist interpretation of the past, as part of the democratic opening of post-1968 Mexico.

REVISIONIST INTERPRETATIONS OF CATHOLICISM
AND THE MOCKING OF LOS CRISTEROS

On July 3, 1969, government agents knocked on the door of Jean Meyer's home and demanded that he present himself immediately to the French consulate.[4] They cited article 33 of the Constitution, which allowed the government to expel all foreigners from the country who were considered "undesirable" without the need for prior legal process. Labeled a "pernicious foreigner," Meyer was told that he had a week to pack his bags and return to Paris, where he was completing his doctoral dissertation on the Cristero Rebellion.[5] He later found out that the Díaz Ordaz administration had disapproved of an article he had published in *Esprit* on the student movements in Latin America, which included a brief section on Mexico, stating that it remained unclear who had committed the massacre at the Plaza of Tlatelolco. But in his description of the events, he argued that it was evident that the government was likely responsible for the crime.[6]

Jean Meyer described an irrational Mexican government that proved unwilling to engage in a productive dialogue with a democratic movement. When asked by the French ambassador why he had put his name on the *Esprit* article instead of publishing it anonymously, Meyer responded that he owed honesty to his students at El Colegio de México, where he had taught for four years.[7]

Before his arrival in Mexico in 1962, the then twenty-year-old Jean Meyer had sympathized with the Cuban Revolution, and with his friend Régis Debray he had protested the French occupation of Algeria. However, by the time he started teaching at El Colegio de México in the mid-1960s, Meyer had become an outspoken critic of Castro's Revolution and, unlike Debray, a harsh critic of armed struggle on the continent.[8] He continued to publish short articles on Latin America while residing in France, and in December 1971, he defended his doctoral dissertation, "La Christiade: Sociéte et ideologie dans le Mexique contemporaine, 1926–1929." A few months later, he returned to his teaching job at El Colegio de México and found the country different, less authoritarian. It all seemed more optimistic. The paranoia of Díaz Ordaz seemed to have faded away. New opportunities opened up for people in academia, film, and journalism. The leftist intellectual Carlos Fuentes was named ambassador to France. A new generation of historians spoke of the possibility of real change, including many of those teaching with him at El Colegio de México who called for a revisionist interpretation of the past, one that pushed against the official revolutionary narrative of the state.[9]

Within months of arriving in Mexico, Meyer published the three volumes of *La Cristiada* (1972–74). With a few exceptions, the reviews were overwhelmingly positive and celebrated the book as a foundational text that opened the academic door for those interested in religion. The historian of the Catholic Church Paul Murray wrote, "This is the most important book on any single aspect of Mexican Revolutionary history that I have read in the past forty years."[10] "What emerges," David Bailey similarly noted in an enthusiastic but less embellished tone, "is one of the most original and provocative works of Mexican history to appear in recent years." "A triumph of multidisciplinary scholarship," he added, "in both content and method, it is a magnificent contribution."[11] The French historian Christian Lalive d'Epinay also praised the originality of Meyer's work and added, "The Cristiada is an episode that has been, up to this point, embarrassing for Mexico's contemporary history and whose memory we have wanted to erase by eliminating witnesses and testimonies." He explained, "[The writing on the Cristero Rebellion] is troublesome for the Church, who treated the peasants in an underhanded manner; it is a point of contention for the post-revolutionary State, because it is compelled to ask who is revolutionary. But it is also a bother for Marxism: rebels in the name of Christ and peasants capable of organizing themselves!"[12] Lorenzo Meyer, a professor at El Colegio, agreed but concluded more cautiously, "Meyer wanted to destroy a myth, the black legend of the Cristeros, and he did it, but in such a unilateral way that he is risking the creation of a new one."[13]

La Cristiada was one of a number of books published in the aftermath of the Tlatelolco massacre that intended to provide a revisionist interpretation of the Mexican Revolution. In the words of the British historian Alan Knight, who first visited the Mexican archives in 1969, "It was time for *los de abajo* [the underdogs] to get their deserved attention." New archives were explored and became more accessible. Regional studies took priority. Oral, quantitative, and microhistories laid out the methodological work for alternative and more nuanced interpretations of history. European and US historians also became more interested in Latin America. Graduate programs grew exponentially, and the "vogue" of the decade sparked a new historical interest in revolutions and popular uprisings.[14]

Besides *La Cristiada*, the most influential (and leftist) revisionist monograph published after the 1968 student movement was John Womack's *Zapata and the Mexican Revolution* (1969). This was an "emblematic book of the New Left" that aimed to recover the collective experience of the militant peasants, which Jean Meyer described in 1971 as "remarkable" and a "beautiful example of the inextricable synthesis between event history and social history." Meyer explained in his review, "[*Zapata*] possesses the great merit [of its author] of liking his characters, the humble, those who are valued by the number, those whose habitual silence and immobility [have] misled [others] to believe that their minds were empty." Womack "did not mention the role of religion," Meyer lamented, but unlike other historians of the Revolution, "he recognized its full importance." But it was the detailed explanation that Womack presented in his book of how ordinary people "became sentimentally conscious of themselves and their situation vis-à-vis others" that made this a great book and an influential study that encouraged historians to revise their description of the masses, not as dupes manipulated by strong caudillos, but as active agents of their own history.[15] The Zapatista and Cristero campesinos described in the revisionist scholarship of Meyer and Womack, in short, had been reimagined in post-1968 Mexico as the "primitive rebels" of the New Left.[16]

Jean Meyer was less kind to the Cristero films made during the 1970s. These films were of poor quality and paid little attention to the revisionist scholarship, but as noted earlier, they effectively depicted the authoritarianism of the post-1968 era.

The "Irrational Authoritarianism" of Catholic Mexico "through the Eyes of a Young Girl"

De todos modos Juan te llamas is a 1974 film by Marcela Fernández Violante, the first woman graduate of the CUEC. Presented in English as *The General's Daughter*, it examines the history of the Cristero Rebellion "through the eyes of a young girl." It is an original cinematic project that aimed to "demystify" the official narrative of the church-state conflict in the broader political context of the Sixties, when a new generation of scholars reconsidered the significance of the Mexican Revolution from multiple perspectives that included innovative Marxist, regional, and microhistorical analyses.[17] In the context of the era, the film was also meant to be a "metaphor" for the Tlatelolco massacre.[18] The director explained in a 1983 interview, "I knew that I couldn't make a film about 1968, since it was so recent that I wouldn't have the proper perspective, but I asked what happens in the same situation when religion is the main source of the conflict?"[19]

The film centers on Guajardo, a Callista general who profits from the revolutionary war against the Cristeros.[20] He is a charismatic but corrupt man who once heroically fought against the American invasion of Veracruz in 1916 but who eventually profits from the Revolution. But as he climbs the social and political ladder, his family pays a price. His wife, Beatriz, is brutally killed in a church by an angry group of religious women who have been told by the anticlerical government of Guajardo that they can no longer practice their faith in public. His son joins a communist-inspired movement and is eventually imprisoned with the approval of his own father. But it is his young daughter, Armada, who is the most transgressive character in the film.[21] She is a teenager who engages in a romantic relationship with her distant cousin, Beltrán, a colonel in the Callista government who grows critical of Guajardo. Like her lover, she can see through the authoritarianism of her father, who has Beltrán killed. She retaliates by burning her father's stable. She leaves him behind, alone with his growing wealth. She takes a train to Mexico City, where her brother is imprisoned. Once liberated, she breaks ties from the authoritarianism of her father, and it is presumed that she will refuse to play the domestic role that she inherited after the death of her mother. At the end of the film, a shameless Guajardo is depicted standing in front of a church laughing out loud with Father Martí, the same priest who had instigated the mob that killed his wife.

Jean Meyer described *De todos modos Juan te llamas* as a mediocre and mostly technically flawed film but a welcome effort to bring the topic of the Cristeros to the big screen.[22] From the outbreak of the rebellion in the late 1920s to the end of the golden age of cinema in the late 1950s, filmmakers had only made a total of three feature films on the topic. It was unthinkable to do so throughout these years.[23] As the church strengthened its relationship with the government, the national film industry instead celebrated the accomplishments of the Revolution, in which police and religious authorities were equally presented as guardians of order and morality.[24]

Marcela Fernández Violante took advantage of the cinematic opening that characterized the administration of Echeverría. Five films on the Cristero Rebellion were produced during these years, not only to create a full feature film on the topic, but to be critical of the state and its alliance with the most conservative authorities of the church. However, Meyer lamented that these pictures had failed to meet the expectations of those who were eager to see fair treatment of the Cristero Rebellion on the big screen. In his interpretation and that of other critics, the directors had neglected to do research on the topic and did not bother to consult the revisionist interpretations on the Cristiada published during the 1960s and 1970s. Not too different from leftist interpretations on religion, moreover, they had simplistically depicted Cristeros as "dupes" or "folkloric silhouettes" who were manipulated by imperious priests and greedy landlords opposing agrarian reform.[25] A telling example of this is *La guerra santa*, which the critics disliked, but like *De todos modos Juan te llamas*, it too effectively commented on the authoritarianism of the era.

The Claustrophobic Horror of the Rebellion

La guerra santa (1979) is a fascinating film on the Cristero Rebellion that effectively draws from the gothic genre that made Carlos Enrique Taboada famous during the decade. His most ambitious and expensive project, it is a violent depiction of what the atheist director saw as an irrational war led by bloodthirsty fanatics, unremorseful priests, and ignorant dupes. Indicative of the political context of the post-1968 period, it is a suspenseful picture that successfully depicts the authoritarianism of the era as a horror story in need of genuine liberation, based not on utopian aspirations of Catholicism but on the emergence of a less authoritarian future, just as Marcela Fernández Violante envisioned with Armada in her film.[26] But unlike many of his other films, *La guerra santa* minimizes the role of the female protagonist.[27] For him, the terror of the war is a by-product of a man's world. For example, once the Cristeros liberate the pueblo from the "Satanist forces" of the anticlerical government of Calles, they commit the same atrocities they had claimed to be fighting against in the first place. They pillage the towns and violently assault the women. The religious authorities are not any better. With knowledge of their sins, a priest blackmails married women and asks them to restrain their husbands from their sexual pressure if their men refuse to join the war in defense of the Catholic nation.

La guerra santa is emblematic of the anticlerical interpretations written on the Cristero Rebellion. As Meyer has noted, it is unambiguously critical of Catholicism and the church and contains blatant "historical inaccuracies." It distorts the role of priests and is mostly unfair in its depiction of Cristeros. Meyer wrote, "Without a doubt, Taboada is a talented director . . . who does not spare the viewer from brutal images depicting the abuses committed by both sides of the conflict." Unfortunately, he minimizes "the systematic barbarity" of the federal government against the Cristeros, while the violence embraced by the latter and featured at greater length throughout the film is "simply shocking." But worse yet, the widespread and popular support Cristeros received is absent in the picture, while their Catholic faith is misconstrued and caricatured.[28]

Celso is the protagonist of the film. He is a poor and unintelligent potter whose simple life brings him joy. The ordinary love that he has for his wife and the Virgin of Guadalupe satisfy him, and so does his daily routine of making and selling kitsch pots. But his life is turned upside down when the local priest orders the people of his pueblo to join the "Cause" in defense of the Catholic nation. Celso ignores the call, but his wife convinces him to join the local militia, accepting, in the words of the priest, that "he who refuses to pick up arms, is giving his back to Christ."

Terrified, Celso sees no other choice but to join the religious battalion, which is led by Col. Ursino Valdés and Father Soler. The fanatic Ursino practices self-flagellation and has no patience for those with weak characters and irresolute Catholic faith. He is quick to order the execution of those who get drunk, disobey his orders, or fail to see the religious importance of their struggle. Father Soler is no different. He enjoys giving spiritual advice to the colonel and is not afraid to condemn him for his sins, including his unwillingness to prevent the brutal gang rape of a local woman at the hands of his troops, saying to the military leader, "Cruelty can be a useful weapon. That is not the case with unrelenting lust." Like Ursino, the priest has little sympathy for those who fail to see the value of their rebellion. He blesses the arms used for the fighting, approves of the execution of those who threaten to desert the battalion, and does not hesitate to use his imposing cross to avenge the death of martyred Cristeros. Riding on his horse, he confronts Callista soldiers with the crucifix in his right hand and kills them with a pistol in his left hand.

Once captured, the Callista soldiers are publicly humiliated and massacred. They are forced to walk barefoot over thorny cacti and are brutally whipped in front of the Cristero troops. Everyone is expected to participate in this punishment, as collective violence is represented as a purifying agent of their cause. An atheist socialist teacher suffers a similar fate. He is hung in front of his only child, to whom he says, "Do not look away. Make sure that you keep your eyes open and remember what these fanatics have done to your father." Celso is horrified and makes every effort to avoid participating in these violent acts. He hates the idea of having to use his rifle to kill anyone. Claustrophobia has replaced his ordinary life. He hides from Ursino and Father Soler while the others engage in the fighting. But his efforts are in vain. Colonel Ursino warns him that if he refuses to shoot at the enemy, he too will be executed. Horrified, Celso picks up his rifle and claims his first casualty. He has nightmares, but he eventually gets used to the killings and seems no longer concerned about losing his soul in the process.

Freed of the guilt that nearly cost him his life, Celso grows immune to the violence and the apocalyptic language around him. He is no longer shocked by the firing squads and is unfazed by the dead and mutilated bodies left hanging on the road and in front of churches. In a conversation with his friend, Celso asks, "Do you still believe in the existence of hell?," to which his friend responds, "Of course, where else would the devil hide?" A puzzled Celso briefly ponders that answer but no longer appears shaken by his irredeemable choices. On one occasion, his troop breaks into a house and Celso stays behind only to take sexual advantage of a young girl. At first he seems remorseful. But his "need to have a woman" convinces Celso to justify the assault. This is the same attitude that he embraces when he kills more Callista soldiers.

At the end of the film an airplane drops newspapers declaring the end of the war. Cristeros are encouraged to turn in their weapons to government authorities and return to their villages. Ursino prefers to join the faith of Father Soler (killed earlier in the film in front of a church), and still wearing the clothes smeared with the blood of the priest, he also chooses to die as a martyr. By contrast, Celso is thrilled to return to his simple life. However, he quickly discovers that his troops are no longer welcome in the village. The locals are afraid of the Cristeros and demand the presence of the federal troops for protection. The same priest who had manipulated them to join the rebellion at the beginning of the film gives orders to his flock to break ties with all the men who joined it. "They were once soldiers of God," he says to his followers, "but now they are criminals without a conscience. What began with the wings of angels, ended with the tail of the Devil." It is thus everyone's obligation "to denounce all [Cristeros] and deny them any more help." When the unarmed troops arrive at their pueblo, they are massacred in front of a church while an unremorseful priest watches Celso gasping for his last breath.

Celso never understood why he joined the Cristero Rebellion or what was at stake during the church-state conflict that ultimately led to his death. His faith is never explored in the film. With little concern to provide a historically accurate account of the Rebellion, Taboada is instead invested in documenting the toll that violence takes on ordinary people at the expense of their principles. In this sense, *La guerra santa* indirectly comments on the question of state repression that polarized the Left during the 1970s and forced many, including militant Catholics, to pick up arms against the government.[29] But more concretely (and similar to *De todos modos Juan te llamas*), the horror depicted in his Cristero film draws attention to the persistence of authoritarianism, a period of despair haunted by the traditionalism of the past despite the liberationist movement of the era.[30] The film is thus a clear condemnation of all forms of violence and particularly critical of those who justified their militancy in religious language. The same is true of *A paso de cojo*, a Buñuelesque film on the Cristero Rebellion by Luis Alcoriza. Unlike Taboada's preference for suspense and horror, however, the Spanish director relies on the tools of the counterculture, as he had done in his short in *Fé, esperanza y caridad* (1974). He mocks the war and pokes fun at the religiosity of the Cristeros and their alleged manipulation by opportunistic priests.

The Grotesque Empowerment of the Underdogs

A paso de cojo is the least celebrated film made in the 1970s on the Cristero Rebellion. Overwhelmingly disliked by the critics, it is a satirical picture that tells the story of a group of handicapped indigents who come together in the name of St. Ignacio to defend the church from the tyrannical forces of President Calles. The people who join the battalion are not representative of "los de abajo," the underdogs celebrated in the revisionist scholarship. Moreover, their depravity is not meant to symbolize the sins of humanity that Christ hoped to redeem, as depicted by Catholic novelists at the time.[31] Instead, they are blind, deaf, epileptic, crippled, or dwarfed in size. Many are portrayed as beggars. They are terrified of dying. They suffer from poor self-esteem, and nearly all of them are starving and dressed in dirty clothes. Others are even less fortunate and are missing limbs or are intellectually challenged.

What the downtrodden have in common is a deep desire to be seen as "normal." Religion fails them. Their leaders are the one-armed Emilio, a self-proclaimed veteran of the Mexican Revolution who has a fanatical devotion to his Catholic faith, and Aurelio, an opportunistic and cowardly Spanish priest who entices people to join the rebellion but only accompanies the battalion after he is taken hostage as a chaplain. Once part of the battalion, the priest finds multiple ways to take advantage of his followers. He is more interested in drinking good wine and having tasty meals than providing spiritual guidance to the Cristeros. For legitimacy, the members of the battalion draw on the legacy of St. Ignacio, the sixteenth-century military man, crippled during battle, who underwent a spiritual conversion that ultimately led him to a divine life that culminated in the foundation of the Jesuit order. Like St. Ignacio, the indigents aim for religious enlightenment and social acceptance, but similar to the Cristeros in Taboada's film, they lose their souls in the process. They are penniless and lack weapons, horses, and strategic plans. Selfishness, thirst, hunger, and public humiliation only make their existence more miserable and their appearance more pathetic. But once armed and organized by a new leader with some military experience, the Cristeros pillage villages, assault the women, get drunk to celebrate their conceived victories, and do not think twice about betraying one another.

It is through their criminal behavior and despicable demeanor, not their consciousness-raising or discovery of liberation, that they find a distorted sense of empowerment. To their satisfaction, they engage in battle with the enemy only briefly, in the last minutes of the film, when they massacre a wrecked military battalion. But more revealing, at the end of the film the defeated soldiers of God embody the grotesque nature of violence that characterized their rebellion, in the eyes of the film director. Their search for "dignity and honor" is a futile one, with the exception perhaps of Emilio. He is a fraud whom the viewer discovers never participated in the Mexican Revolution but walks away in disillusionment from the Cristeros and perhaps his own Catholic faith. Not only do the men he leaves behind become the same "coward and bloodroot beasts" they were fighting against, but they also return to their "incomplete" selves at the end of the war. By contrast, Father Aurelio joins a parish that he always dreamed of, complete with a convent with good wine, abundant food, and a team of obedient and beautiful nuns at his disposal. In this sense, the ending is not very different from those in *De todos modos* and *La guerra santa*.

A paso de cojo is an absurd and often hysterical film on the Cristero Rebellion, dismissed by its critics as his "most opportunist and least caustic" of his films, "dispersed in its approach, chaotic in its outcome, and completely detached from historical accuracy."[32] It should not be so easily dismissed, however. It is a telling product of its time that provides intriguing commentary on the Sixties. In this case, it is an experimental picture caught between the anticlerical view of the Left that persisted during these years and the cynical irreverence that remained of the counterculture. Like Taboada and Fernández Violante, Alcoriza hoped to provide commentary on the effects that violence and authoritarianism had on ordinary people, but his film appeared more invested in mocking not only what he saw as the hypocrisy and corruption of Catholicism, as further emphasized in his collaboration with Alberto Bojórquez and Jorge Fons in *Fé, esperanza y caridad*, but also and more originally the academic celebration of "los de abajo." The representation of the downtrodden is profoundly silly to the point of ridicule, precisely at a moment when scholars writing on their struggle were celebrating their political agency and religious consciousness as "primitive rebels" (in the words of Eric Hobsbawm) of an earlier era and thus relevant icons for the New Left. In this sense, *A paso de cojo* is both silly and original. Film critics, including Meyer, differed in their evaluation of the film and instead called it an aberration and a cheap imitation of the finest anticlerical work of Buñuel.[33] Ultraconservative writers who achieved significant success during the Sixties, such as the Cristero novelist Antonio Rius Facius, also viewed these films, and the counterculture of the era as a whole, with disgust and as exemplary of the moral decay of the nation.

"PANIC" AND REACTIONARY VIOLENCE TO THE COUNTERCULTURE

Antonio Rius Facius published the first edition of *Méjico Cristero* in 1960. Presented as the second of two volumes detailing the history of the Catholic Association of Mexican Youth, this widely advertised book was an unapologetic account of the Cristero Rebellion, replete with gruesome photographs of the executions of martyred Catholics. The second edition was published in 1966. Unlike the revisionist work of Jean Meyer (among others), this book placed the heroism of middle-class youth at the center of the story. By the time it was distributed in the early 1960s, all institutions of the church were invited to support the "Christianity Yes; Communism No!" campaign that expanded across the country, while a broad range of ultraconservative leaders encouraged the creation of violent Catholic student organizations in the universities. In this context, the book dwelled on the state violence of the past and encouraged its readers to defend the Hispanic nation and its Catholic identity from all the tyrannical forces that remained during the Sixties. *Juventud* published a review of *Méjico Cristero* in 1961, describing it as "the most accurate" account of the "biggest and purest epic" event in "our history." The author of the review encouraged young readers to learn from Rius Facius, whom he described as a hero with an "objective" and "healthy Cristero heart" and whose lifelong commitment to fight atheist forces was admirable. He wrote, "Let us become familiarized" with our collective "struggles" of the past. After all, the Cristero Rebellion "has important lessons for today." These lessons were "key for understanding the socio-religious evolution" of contemporary Mexico and the current polarization of its people.[34]

Born in Mexico City to Spanish parents in 1918, Rius Facius emerged as one of the most prolific ultraconservative writers of the Sixties. His books were published by Patria and Editorial Jus, and his columns appeared to a broader audience in the dailies *El Sol de México* and *El Universal* and in the more obscure gazette *La Hoja de Combate*. In the 1940s and 1950s, he had been a strong supporter of the PAN, a key figure in Catholic Action, one of the original founders of the MEP, and a regular anticommunist contributor to *Lectura* and *Juventud Católica*, where *Méjico Cristero* was widely advertised.[35]

The ideological positions of Rius Facius moved even further to the Right in the aftermath of Vatican II in response to what he saw as the "Marxification of Christianity." In particular, he pointed to the diocese of Cuernavaca and its international connections with "self-described progressives" in the Catholic universities of Louvain and South America as mostly responsible for the social, moral, and political deterioration of Mexico during the Sixties. He accused them of hiding behind vague notions of "social justice," "dialogue," "de-colonialism," "liberation," "love," and "psychoanalysis," with the sole purpose of creating "a propitious climate for revolution." In agreement with similar authors of the era, Rius Facius understood the term "revolution" as an umbrella for chaos and anarchy encompassing those who sympathized with the armed struggle and minimized the threat of the counterculture. For him, the followers of the radical priest Camilo Torres were just as damned as those who expressed enthusiasm for rock music and the sexual liberation of women. Like the Cristeros of an earlier era, in short, the young activists of the post–Vatican II period had the moral and political obligation to defend Catholic Mexico.[36]

The "Threat of Mendezarceismo"

La Hoja de Combate spent a significant number of its pages responding to student activism, la onda, and the liberation of women. Founded in 1967 by the conservative ideologue of the Sinarquista movement, Salvador Abascal, this publication placed the counterculture in the broader context of the Cold War era and saw the aesthetic and sexual revolution of the Sixties as a Marxist conspiracy against "Méjico" (spelled with "j").[37] For many of its writers, Marxism did not make its way to the nation exclusively from the Soviet Union. It also emerged from the International (and for some, "Jewish") forces that originated in the United States and in the progressive churches that expanded across the world in the aftermath of Vatican II. Both were ultimately interested in destroying the Hispanic identity and Catholic institutions of the nation.[38]

In the broader context of the era, *La Hoja de Combate* blamed all of the social ills associated with modernity on what its writers termed "Mendezarceismo." The phrase was loosely employed in reference to those who sympathized with the bishop of Cuernavaca, Sergio Méndez Arceo. It included a vast list of enemies that ranged from liberals and Freemasons to progressive priests and lay activists who welcomed the teaching of Vatican II. In addition to Iván Illich, the Austrian director of CIDOC, and Gregorio Lemercier, the Belgian abbot responsible for the school of psychoanalysis, the list contained Catholic priests who published in *Señal*, *Contacto*, and *Christus*, including the Jesuits Martín de la Rosa, Luis del Valle, and Enrique Maza; the Claretian priest Enrique Marroquín; and the Dominican friars at UNAM, Alex Morelli and Agustín Desobry.[39] Their magazines were worse than *Excélsior*, *Siempre!*, and *Claudia* because they "pretended" to be Catholic. In particular, they accused them of hiding behind vague notions of social justice and liberation, but in reality, they were interested in dividing and ultimately destroying the church. In their magazines, they had "normalized" homosexuality, the consumption of drugs (most notably LSD), and sex outside marriage.[40]

The ultraconservative writers were equally critical of those teaching at UNAM and the Ibero-American University and regularly accused their Jesuits and Dominican teachers of corrupting the nation's youth. The immoral exhibitions of European cinema and the teachings of Sartre, Marcuse, and Camus at these schools not only had blurred the lines between Marxism and the counterculture, but they were also used to lure students into the rank and file of the Left. Worse yet, for the founder of *La Hoja de Combate*, Salvador Abascal, young women had no place in the schools and should instead be educated at home, free from the immorality of television and distant from the erotic cinema of the times. Many of the contributors to this publication agreed and specifically identified the cine clubs at the universities and their "a-go-go masses" as "pornographic" and "contaminating" spaces where young people were exposed to the "orgies" of foreign artists and to the Marxist literature of "terrorists" who cared more about Maoist China and the "butchery" of Castro than the stability and respect of Méjico.[41]

But in their multifaceted and blurred critique of the counterculture, the liberation of women, student activism, and the militancy of the Left, the writers also pointed to what they saw as a weak ("liberal/Masonic/anti-clerical") government. In its hesitation to fully repress the counterculture and censor the cinema of the times, they argued, the state had failed to see the direct link between the "sexual deviancy" of la onda and the "terror" imposed on the nation by urban guerrilla uprisings that had proliferated in Mexico in the early 1970s. Young people who joined one or both of these movements were "self-indulgent" and "destructive" and should thus be disciplined with all the force available at the hands of those in power.[42]

When it came to the counterculture, one of the writers for *La Hoja de Combate* who spent significant ink on the subject was Juan Bosco Abascal. The eldest son of Salvador Abascal, he was born in 1943 at Colonia Santa María Auxiliadora. This was the same commune that witnessed the growth of the Sinarquista movement under the leadership of his father in Baja California. In his teens Bosco became familiar with the editorial work of Jus and enrolled at the Jesuit Ibero-American University, where he pursued a degree in psychology and was introduced to theology. As a university student he protested the European films shown to students, and like his elders, he demanded an end to the incorporation of jazz instruments during the liturgy. During this period, Bosco also started his writing career in the pages of *La Hoja de Combate*, where he published a series of short articles on la onda and with his siblings encouraged his readers to take the battle to the trenches of the counterculture. His columns were written for "adult readers only" and provided specific details on the fashion, music, aesthetics, and "sinful habits" of la onda. Mexican Catholics, he argued, needed to be familiarized with the "Satanist" phenomenon of the counterculture and with the leaders of the church who tolerated it.[43]

Starting in 1971, Bosco departed from his more traditionalist father by taking his fight to a broader audience. He appeared on television shows to explain the conservative opposition of his family to the radicalism of the times. The most discussed of these took place on November 12, 1971, on Jorge Saldaña's *Anatomías* talk show. The five Abascal siblings engaged in a roundtable discussion during the show with six young women who endorsed the sexual revolution and the aesthetics of la onda. Dressed in suits, ties, and proper dresses (which fell below the knees), the Abascal family stood in sharp contrast to the appearance of their counterparts, "wearing miniskirts" and "hot pants," "smoking cigarettes," and defending their right to liberate themselves from patriarchal society. The siblings pointed to the counter-culture as a selfish and dangerous movement disguised behind the facade of peace and highlighted the medical and psychological repercussions associated with "free love." They argued that the audience should not be fooled and fall prey to what they saw as the "Americanization" of the Catholic nation. They encouraged viewers to defend the Hispanic identity of the country and its Catholic institutions and avoid all sinful habits that insulted traditional Catholicism. They insisted that sexual encounters should only take place after marriage between a man and a woman. Rock music and foreign entertainers who insulted national sensibilities had no place in Méjico. Selected television shows and films, approved by a strict censoring agency and completely free of immoral language and sexual depravity, should be limited to adult audiences only. The future of the nation, in short, no longer relied on a passive defense of the country but instead required an action-driven approach against the multiple foreign figures invested in putting an end to Christianity.[44]

The violent magazine *Réplica* also emerged as a sharp critic of foreign artists and their influence on the counterculture. Founded with the support of the Tecos in Guadalajara as a harsh critic of Rome, the fascist magazine specifically pointed to the Beatles and the Chilean leader of the panic movement, Alejandro Jodorowsky, as the most dangerous enemies of the nation. In drawing a comparison to Charles Manson, the authors frequently referred to Jodorowsky as the "antichrist." They demanded his immediate deportation and called on their readers to launch an aggressive and violent campaign against him.[45]

The most extreme columns and pamphlets published during this period described the commercialization of the godless nihilism celebrated by the Beatles as an international Jewish conspiracy against the nation. The writers called their readers to see their music for what it was, a tool of Marxism brought to Mexico to manipulate the minds and politics of the nation's youth. Rius Facius and the journalist Manuel Magaña Contreras made similar arguments in relation to the 1971 Avándaro festival.[46] As evidence, they pointed to specific lyrics of some of the most famous songs of the British band, including, among others, "Norwegian Wood," allegedly responsible for "normalizing" lesbianism; "Back to the USSR," which supposedly celebrated the communism of the Soviet Union; "Eleanor Rigby," which mocked Christianity; and "Yellow Submarine" and "Lucy in the Sky with Diamonds," which openly celebrated the consumption of drugs. Like they did with Alejandro Jodorowsky, they called for the banning of rock music and the repression of those who consumed the most radical elements of la onda.[47]

Shared Panic and the Climbing of The Holy Mountain

In the eyes of ultraconservatives, *The Holy Mountain* represented one of the most serious threats to the nation and its Catholic identity. Written and directed by Alejandro Jodorowsky and produced by Allen Klein (American businessman and record producer of the Beatles and the Rolling Stones), the 1972 film presented an outrageous and sacrilegious expression of la onda that involved the collaboration of some of the most "treacherous" countercultural figures of the Sixties.[48]

The origins of the film date to 1960, when Jodorowsky moved to Mexico City and first developed his "panic movement." Originally understood as an interdisciplinary theatrical response to the commercialization of surrealist art, his panic movement (named after the Greek gods of terror and laughter) meant to "take the theater out of the theater" by breaking its dividing lines with poetry, dance, and the visual arts for the ultimate goal of achieving enlightenment. Drawing inspiration from Antonin Artuad's theater of cruelty and Samuel Beckett's theater of the absurd, Jodorowsky understood the performance of violence, anarchy, and chaos as the first step to transcend traditional norms, passivity, and traumas associated with the status quo and with the religious upbringing of his generation. For him, panic theater, in its most salacious expression, was a therapeutic "collective festivity." It was primarily meant to free people from their individuality, solitude, anguish, and restrained notions of morality disguised by vague notions of "dignity, respect, and decency." Faced with absurdity, terror, euphoria, humor, and spontaneity, audiences were provoked with nonconformist sexual acts, violent destruction of material objects that most people found valuable, and gory religious images that included blood, live animals, and nude performers.[49]

Forced to confront their panics, the audiences witnessing the theatrical performances of Jodorowsky had the potential to heal their souls and find spiritual liberation. By the late Sixties, his movement had presented more than one hundred plays that blurred the lines between reality and fantasy. But while living in Mexico he also produced surrealist comic strips lasting more than two hundred weeks, as well as three films that eventually forced the Chilean artist out of the country, *Fando y Lis* (1968), *El Topo* (1970), and *The Holy Mountain* (1972–73).[50] Liberals and their ultraconservative foes found them offensive to the sensibilities of the country, and so did the surveillance agents of the government who lamented the popularity of the "morbid" Chilean artist among university students and called for censoring Jodorowsky.[51]

The Holy Mountain brings Jodorowsky's panic movement of the Sixties to the big screen. It is based on *Ascent of Mount Carmel*, a sixteenth-century spiritual Spanish treatise in which St. John of the Cross provided a detailed account of his relentless pursuit of a mystical union with the son of God. Similarly, Jodorowsky tells the story of a Christ-like thief who embarks on a spiritual journey in search of the secret to immortality and enlightenment.[52] During his journey, the nameless thief encounters an alchemist who turns his excrement into gold and introduces him to seven figures representing the different planets in the solar system and what Jodorowsky sees as some of the worst threats faced by humanity that brought a despairing end to the Sixties. These include manufactured weapons of mass destruction, the brainwashing of a passive society carried out by a powerful market-ing industry invested in promoting a cult of celebrity and beauty, rampant consumerism, militarism, and the exploitation of Third World cultures by the West.

The thief engages in a wide range of outrageous and sacrilegious scenes that includes his near-crucifixion by a group of children only to be rescued by an amputee dwarf. Together they smoke a joint and experience a series of outlandish yet at times beautiful and hilarious cinematic adventures with men in drag, transvestites, fascists, tourists, and religious fanatics. These scenes blur the lines, not only between reality and fiction, but also between the decent and the depraved, the beautiful and the grotesque, the ordered and the chaotic, the sacred and the commercialized, the normal and the de-viant, and the religious and the profane.

Writers in *Réplica* described the film as a "homosexual nightmare" and were especially offended by what they saw as horrific depictions of the Mexi-can army.[53] The Christian Anticommunist League criticized the "satanic film" for its anti-Catholic message, insisting that the "Jewish degenerate" had insulted the Mexican church, "the most loyal to Rome in Latin America."[54]

This was a view shared by many writers in *La Hoja de Combate* who cared less about the image of the army and were instead critical of all institutions affiliated with the government.

In November 1972, the Christian Anticommunist League wrote a letter to all Mexican bishops that included clippings from newspapers that provided detailed denunciations of the film and photographs of the most outrageous scenes in *The Holy Mountain*.[55] In the letter, the authors wrote that their "patience was not divine and it had now been exhausted." Claiming to speak on behalf of all Catholics, the authors were enraged at the religious authorities who allegedly allowed the Chilean director to film inside a Mexican church and "transform it" into a "theater of sexual orgies and debauchery."[56]

Ultraconservatives were equally outraged at the scenes that explicitly addressed the Tlatelolco massacre. In them, Jodorowsky draws attention to what he sees as a complicit society that included a national church and its loyal flock. In addition, the film places blame on an international tourist community visiting Mexico during the Olympic Games and an ordinary group of citizens who passively consumed the student massacre as an uproarious spectacle. To add further insult to injury, the scenes depicting the massacre take place outside the Metropolitan Cathedral in the first twenty-five minutes of the film.

Jodorowsky first references the massacre by showing a passing truck carrying dead bodies. The truck then drives in front of a group of Indigenous women sitting on the sidewalk washing the bloody clothes of the students. The thief walks by the corpses and laughs hysterically, still intoxicated by marihuana. The panic continues as the film shows a battalion wearing gas masks shooting at a group of young male and female students with tape over their mouths.[57]

The escalating chaos of the film unfolds with two contrasting scenes. The first shows a group of soldiers carrying crucified bodies of lambs on their bayonets, a clear religious reference to the students killed in the Plaza of Tlatelolco. The contrasting scene depicts a group of devout upper-class Catholics praying with their arms, pointing to the sky, and walking on their knees toward the church, completely oblivious to the presence of the marching soldiers. A bus full of American tourists wearing sombreros then arrive at the plaza taking pictures of everything they see, including a second shot of the dying students laying on the ground bleeding, tied with ropes around their wrists, and still wearing tape over their mouths. Birds fly out of the bodies of the massacred students as the tourists continue to take pictures, laughing hysterically at the spectacle of violence. A soldier arrives and grabs one of the female tourists and proceeds to assault her as a group of bystanders loudly cheer at the violation of the blonde American woman. The transvestite husband, wearing a long native dress, films the soldier raping his wife, hands over the 8mm camera to the thief so that the husband can also appear in his picture, and gives the thief a one dollar tip for his services.

But it was a different set of scenes that proved even more offensive to Catholics, prompting them to demand the complete censoring of Jodorowsky and his final expulsion from the country.[58] This set of scenes begins by showing a group of morbidly obese Roman soldiers and a man in drag wearing a nun's habit standing in front of a store with a sign that reads, "Christs for sale." As they carve the meat of a dead animal, the Romans see the thief walking by and demand that he carry a large, heavy wooden cross. They get him drunk and use his body as a mold to make hundreds of statues of Christ. He wakes up only to see multiple clay representations of his crucified body. The thief screams in agony, retaliates against his repressors, destroys many of the Christ figures, and holds one of them in his arms as he stares at the image of the son of God with love and tender eyes.

Jodorowsky then daringly takes the film inside the Parish of Our Lady of Guadalupe, where the viewers see a group staring at a bloody image of Christ composed of a chimpanzee and twelve female prostitutes of different backgrounds and ages, including one who is just a child, no more than thirteen or fourteen years old (fig. 13). The women walk out and stand in front of the church as they wait to be picked up by passing men. An old man resembling a priest arrives and pulls the child closer to him. He kisses her hand, removes his glass eye, and gives it to her. The group of women leaves the old man behind and encounters the thief carrying one of the crucified clay figures made earlier by the Romans.

The thief continues to walk on the streets until he climbs to the top of a tall red tower with a rope where he meets an alchemist (played by Jodorowsky) who promises to heal him. The alchemist tells him that he is a piece of "excrement [who] can change himself into gold" and sends him to meet the seven figures representing the different planets in the solar system, including Axon, the chief of police responsible for the student massacre. Representing Neptune (a planet typically represented by the female gender), Axon is depicted as a science fiction warrior whose strength and survival depend on the voluntary and ritualistic castration of hundreds of young men whom he trains as future soldiers, skilled in the art of brutal killing.

FIGURE 13. Staring at Christ at the Parish of Our Lady of Guadalupe. From *The Holy Mountain* (dir. Alejandro Jodorowsky, 1972–73).

Clearly, *The Holy Mountain* was a film that broke all the cinematic rules. It went well beyond the countercultural films of an earlier era and pushed the boundaries of artistic expression in Mexico. For Jodorowsky, nothing was sacred, not even the counterculture. In the final scene, the thief reaches the mountain and presumably achieves immortality. Yet the alchemist tells him that it is all a facade. He orders the camera crew to zoom out and says to the viewer who can see the production set of the film that "real life awaits us." The viewer then sees that the film, and by extension the countercultural pursuit for enlightenment, is nothing but a sham.

The Holy Mountain was featured at the Cannes film festival in 1973. It soon became a cult sensation in Western Europe, the United States, and Brazil. In Mexico, an edited version, which eliminated more than twenty minutes from its original footage, was first shown in private parties and in select cine clubs in 1975.[59] By then, the democratic opening of Luis Echeverría had proven to be part of a dual state strategy to co-opt the Left while simultaneously repressing its most militant and defiant leaders. But the cynical and violent overtones of the film resonated outside Mexico. As the film scholar Alessandra Santos has argued, *The Holy Mountain* is a "dystopian film," which echoed the pessimistic environment that marked the end of the Sixties. By its release in 1973, the Vietnam War had reached its most violent phase and the increasingly militant sectors of the Left questioned the peaceful strategies of the antiwar movement in most of the Western world. Police brutality against young people made the option of armed struggle further feasible across Europe and in the United States, while in Latin America the military dictatorships extended their dirty wars against all democratic movements that challenged their authority and moved their countries to a neoliberal path.[60] Mexico appeared no different in this regard, and the state repression that marked the administration of Luis Echeverría also contributed to the end of the Sixties.

CONCLUSION

On May 9, 1972, five young men waited at the airport for the bishop of Cuernavaca, Sergio Méndez Arceo, who was returning from Chile where he had attended the Christians for Socialism Conference. On his way to the car, they threw red paint and acetic acid at him, while on different occasions others did the same to Iván Illich and the Dominican friars of UNAM. Alejandro Jodorowsky was also a frequent target of similar groups. In reaction to a performance organized at the San Carlos Academy in 1964, a group of students demanded the Chilean artist be banned from all educational institutions in Mexico. Four years later, a similar group participated in a riot that erupted during the Acapulco Film Festival in response to the showing of his film, *Fando y Lis* (1967). This was the tale of a young couple on a quest to find the mythical paradise of Tar, in which Jodorowsky included sacrilegious scenes that poked fun at the rituals of Catholicism.[61]

By the early 1970s, a group of students had allegedly sent Jodorowsky numerous death threats and had violently attacked theaters and movie houses that dared to feature his "pornographic" films.[62] The Echeverría government became equally intolerant of his films and eventually forced him out of the country. Jodorowsky recalled, "One morning, there was a loud knock at my door. Three huge detectives, looking like professional thugs, said: A large number of complaints have been lodged against you. You cannot get away with attacking our institutions, our religion, or [our] army. If you don't want something unpleasant to happen to you or to your family, then you must remove every religious image and every military or other official uniform from your film."[63]

According to the surveillance documents that monitored the activities of Alejandro Jodorowsky since his arrival in Mexico, the archbishop of Guadalajara, José Garibi Rivera, was the central person behind the complaints against the Chilean artist.[64] As examined in chapter 4, Garibi Rivera had been one of the most powerful ecclesiastical figures who supported Díaz Ordaz during the 1968 student movement. In the early 1970s he expressed criticism of the leftist tendencies of Luis Echeverría, but according to the documents, he primarily spent most of his energy targeting the "Red Bishop" of Cuernavaca. The espionage documents in Jodorowsky's file also reference the different interpretation of the Chilean artist by the leader of CENCOS, José Álvarez Icaza. According to him, Jodorowsky had received permission from Abbot Guillermo Schulemburg to film inside the Cathedral, but Garibi Rivera used the scandal as an opportunity to tarnish anyone who sympathized with progressive Catholicism. For Álvarez Icaza, the real scandal was the tolerance that many had shown for the growth of ultraconservative voices during the Sixties. For him, their demand to censor the arts diminished democracy and only made Mexico more reactionary. He was right.

For cinema, state censorship only intensified during the presidential administration of José López Portillo (1976–82).[65] According to film scholars, this period quickly devolved into "the darkest chapter" of the national cinema as partly evident in the censorship of several films that touched on Catholicism, including, among others, *Nuevo mundo* and *La viuda negra*. *Nuevo mundo* was a 1978 film directed by the 1968 activist Gabriel Retes that told the story of Fray Pedro, a sixteenth-century Machiavellian priest who successfully manufactured the myth of the Virgin of Guadalupe with the sole purpose of bringing an end to a long and violent history of Indigenous uprisings.

La viuda negra (1977), written by Francisco del Villar, told the story of Feliciano, a misogynist priest who had a sexual relationship with the younger Matea inside the church. But the real "scandal" happened at the end of the film, when an emasculated Matea officiates a Sunday Mass in front of a group of sinners who hysterically laugh at her "madness." This reactionary interpretation was shared even by progressive Catholics who had welcomed the liberation of women but who were not necessarily ready to have them in the role of priests.

The censorship of these and other films took place under the leadership of Margarita Portillo, wife of the president of Mexico. During this period, the Directorate of Radio, Television, and Cinema was consolidated under her management, and with it, the government took initiatives to privatize the film industry and push the militant movements of an earlier era to the margins. Portillo weakened the film syndicates. She sharply reduced government subsidies and called for stricter censorship of political and religious films. A commercial, low-quality cinema instead took over the film industry.[66] This marked the end of the most exciting countercultural cinema and the end of films on the Cristero Rebellion. These cinematic representations would have to wait until the 1990s, when the PRI finally lost its grip on the nation to the conservative opposition.[67] But, as this chapter has argued, the sense of despair that brought an end to the utopian aspirations of the Sixties was also evident in the enablement of the Far Right.

Conclusion

Arabella arrived in Paris with her family in the summer of 1961 at the age of twenty-one. Seven years earlier, the Eisenhower administration had sponsored a CIA coup in Guatemala that put a violent end to the democratic presidency of her father, Jacobo Arbenz. Her family sought political refuge, first in Mexico City and then in Toronto, where she continued her studies. In Canada, Arabella quickly excelled her classmates and learned various languages, including French and German. In Paris, she reunited with her parents, and from there, they moved to Prague and Moscow, where the family remained monitored by US agents. Her parents hoped to return to Latin America, and while they moved temporarily to Montevideo and then settled in Havana, Arabella went back to Paris. By then, she had become an outspoken critic of the leftist politics of her parents and their understanding of the world. She had also grown irritated by the continuous hostility of the US government to her family and annoyed at the bombastic words Fidel Castro and Che Guevara had used to contrast the reformist politics of her father with the radicalism of the Cuban Revolution.

While living in France, the young Arabella dove into the counterculture that swept young Parisians in the early Sixties. She modeled clothes for distinguished designers and became fascinated with French cinema. While she studied acting and pursued a career in the film industry, she openly expressed her bisexuality and freely experimented with drugs. At a party hosted by her wealthy Latin American friends she met Emilio Azcárraga Milmo, who was impressed by her intelligence and beauty. The television magnate began a romantic relationship with the ten years' younger Arabella and promised her a bright future in Mexico. In 1962, the aspiring actress arrived in Mexico City and met some of the nation's most influential figures, including the novelist Carlos Fuentes, who invited her to play the leading role in the film *Una alma pura*. She accepted the invitation, but she quickly got into trouble with the artistic community while residing in the Zona Rosa. After the 1964 release of the film, she was accused of having an inappropriate relationship with the younger nephew of Emilio Azcárraga who was in his late teens at the time. There were rumors of other romantic adventures she had while making the film, including with the openly gay ranchera singer Chavela Vargas and with her costar, Enrique Rocha, who was then dating the actress and stepdaughter of Carlos Fuentes, Julissa. Truth or myth, following the intervention of the Azcárraga family, the Mexican government allegedly ordered the "pernicious actress" to leave the country. Her parents encouraged Arabella to reunite with them in Cuba, but she refused and instead she left for Colombia with Jaime Bravo Arciga. The Mexican bullfighter proved to be the love of her life. After he was injured while performing in the ring, she begged him to give up the violent career that he loved. He refused but maintained his frenzied relationship with her. On October 5, 1965, Arabella met with Jaime one last time. Tormented by his unwillingness to leave the country with her, she pulled a gun from her purse and shot herself in front of him. Her body was sent to Mexico, and she was buried there by her parents, who were finally allowed to enter the country after several attempts that were denied by Díaz Ordaz. Jacobo Arbenz, who had a conflicted but profound love for his daughter, was found dead in a bathtub in Mexico City, the victim of a suicide, six years later.[1]

The rebellious but tragic life of Arabella Arbenz has a remarkable parallel to the central story of the only film in which she starred, *Una alma pura*. Written by Carlos Fuentes and directed by Juan Ibáñez, the 1964 film marked a rupture in Mexican cinema, caught between the stagnation, lack of artistic creativity, conservatism, and authoritarianism of an earlier era and the more independent and exciting cinema that matured in the aftermath of the 1968 student movement and eventually provided new opportunities to a younger generation of political and countercultural filmmakers. Representative of this talent was the twenty-five-year-old Ibáñez, who continued to collaborate with Fuentes on other projects, and with the novelist's support, he made one of the best films on youth rebellion during the Sixties, *Los caifanes* (1967).[2]

Una alma pura tells the controversial story of the incestuous love between Claudia and her brother Juan Luis. Born to conservative and wealthy Catholic parents in Mexico City, the siblings are tormented by their forbidden love.

They do their best to remain emotionally close to each other but do what is necessary to stay physically apart. In this effort, the brother hires prostitutes and gets drunk to get the courage to hit on other people, including an inebriated man at a bar. But his love for Claudia only intensifies when he feels alienated from the urban and consumerist life of the city. He hates the idea of ending up like his parents, consumed in a materialist and moralistic world while seeking redemption in their Catholic faith. Hoping for a brighter future and determined to put behind him the prohibited love for his sister, he leaves for New York to work as an intern with the United Nations. He has sexual relationships with multiple partners at Columbia University. But Claudia continues to write to him, begging him to come back to her. The film is a series of flashback reenactments of the love letters the siblings send to each other, describing past and present adventures with and without one another.

The turning point of the film takes place when Juan Luis meets Clara, who has a remarkable resemblance to Claudia. The new girlfriend gets pregnant, but following his sister's advice, Juan Luis successfully convinces his girlfriend to have an abortion. His sister informs their parents of his decision. They label their son a criminal, and Claudia tells him that their parents no longer welcome him at their house. Clara is devastated after the abortion and is confused by the unwillingness of her boyfriend to embrace the routine life of a relationship. She takes a bottle of pills and dies of an overdose inside a movie theater. In her purse is a letter from Claudia where she confesses to Clara her deep love for her brother. Juan Luis finds the letter in the purse and is distraught. As he runs away from the same moving camera used to make the film, Juan Luis leaps into the Hudson River and commits suicide. A callous Claudia takes a plane to New York to bring her brother's body back to Mexico.

Una alma pura draws direct inspiration from Jean-Luc Godard's *A bout de souffle* (*Breathless*), the 1960 film that marked the birth of la nouvelle vague (the French New Wave). Like the original, Ibáñez's remarkable film places the alienation of youth at the center of its story. It dramatizes the sense of despair that ultimately brought an end to the most utopian aspirations of the Sixties with astonishing detail and points to the alleged "depravity" that many conservatives often associated with the liberation of women. While Claudia shares the same remorselessness as Godard's protagonist, Juan Luis lives in modern but claustrophobic Mexico. His generation is trapped in an authoritarian, yet commercialized world that celebrates the material success of a privileged middle class but is haunted by Christian morality and the lack of honest dialogue. Juan Luis detests the hypocrisy of his parents and their blind involvement in the patriarchal order. He is equally critical of their passive authoritarianism and their lack of true love for each other. His forbidden relationship with Claudia points to his feeling of entrapment, as well as to the most radical expressions of the sexual revolution that created a moral panic in Catholic Mexico. These growing tensions are further evident in the techniques used by Ibáñez that made la nouvelle vague so influential during this period, including the violent jump cuts, the expressive close-ups in tight spaces, and the long takes with a hand-held camera, which often plays the voyeuristic role of a protagonist, "a confidant of sin," as so accurately noted by the film scholar Israel Rodríguez. As Rodríguez explained, "The film has no happy ending." After the abortion and suicide of Clara, "Juan Luis is hunted by the camera, which hounds him in condemnation until the protagonist decides to escape from the movie by taking his own life."[3]

The alienation of youth and the entrapment of a consumerist but moralistic Mexico were two themes at the center of the liberationist cinema of the Sixties, but so were the more positive aspirations of love. Other films examined in this book transgressed rigid boundaries by addressing these topics. They rejected the cinematic tropes of the golden age and brought once tabooed topics to the big screen, including homosexuality, sex outside marriage, abortion, drug consumption, and suicide. Most of these films did not enjoy mass audiences. They were primarily made by male directors and often dismissed by film critics as mediocre and of poor cinematic value. But they were crucial nonetheless. Similar to the innovative spaces of debate and the myriad magazines also discussed in this book, these films successfully captured the excitement, frustration, and disapproval that many people expressed in response to the radicalization of the counterculture. They effectively documented the everyday cultural changes that the nation experienced, from a traditional Catholic past to a more global, liberating, and secular era, when the polarizing context of the Cold War strengthened the once-fragile relationship between government and ecclesiastical authorities. They successfully captured the consolidation of this power, which only strengthened with the founding of the PRI in 1946 and provided evidence for the changing perceptions of youth rebellion thereafter. Whereas the films produced in the 1950s prioritized the conservative views of parents and those of the government and ecclesiastical authorities, those made between about 1962 and 1968 expressed a more conscious effort to portray youth rebellion from the perspectives of young people. They were not entirely successful, but they offered valuable commentary on the evolving interpretations of Catholicism in the aftermath of Vatican II. The year 1968 marked a defining moment in the production of these films. From then on, they assertively criticized the authoritarianism of the era and more effectively captured the desire for competing notions of liberation, caught between aspiring conceptions of love and frustrating realities of despair.

As film scholars have pointed out, the University Center for Cinematographic Studies played a foundational role in producing the liberationist films of the Sixties. Its founders took advantage of the democratic opening of Luis Echeverría to form a new generation of filmmakers. Primarily young men, these directors successfully revived national cinema. Many of them saw it necessary to include a discussion of Catholicism in their depictions of the counterculture, including those who did not conceive of themselves as religious but valued the need to discuss the importance of faith in their films.

But Catholics had also plenty to say on the shifting cultural changes of the era. They did not universally see religion as inherently at odds with modernity, as often assumed in a scholarship that has prioritized the perspectives of secular actors and like the state, has inaccurately reduced all religious figures to "reactionaries." In promoting a dialogue with the secular world, a group of liberal Catholics saw film as a great opportunity to "decolonize" the traditional ethos of the Mexican church.[4] Like some actors on the Marxist Left, they too created innovative spaces for the celebration (and consumption) of youth culture. These shaped the significance of la onda, the Mexican counterculture that challenged but did not entirely defy the traditionalism of the past and that came to an end with its commercialization and repression in the 1970s.

While lay activists and priests found relevance in the world of cinema, others saw the broader world of the arts as an opportunity to establish a fruitful interaction with the nation's youth, or saw the counterculture as convenient for discussing national aspects of Catholicism. This engagement with competing interpretations of modernity that characterized the Cold War era included original depictions of the legacies of the Cristero Rebellion that underwent a revisionist phase in the aftermath of the Cuban Revolution and the Tlatelolco massacre. Unlike the scholarly work published on the subject, these films mocked the Cristeros to provide intriguing commentary on the authoritarianism of post-1968 Mexico and critique the alliance that state and ecclesiastical authorities had established since the 1940s.

For many of the actors depicted in the book, the most utopian elements of la onda represented "a sign of the times," that is, a genuine expression of liberation, in the language of Vatican II. On the oppositive side of youth rebellion was an increasing sense of despair that brought so many to apathy, disillusionment, alienation, frustration, violence, and suicide. In the broader countercultural context of the Sixties, "the dream was over" as early as 1970, as John Lennon famously put it in his single, "God." In the Mexican countercultural scene this was evident in the sense of frustration that came with the state repression and commercialization of la onda in the aftermath of the 1971 Avándaro rock festival.

Not everyone saw benefit in the language, aesthetics, and ideas of the counterculture, however, and instead became invested in the world of politics. They too interpreted the Sixties as an effervescent time of liberation and concientización, ripe for radical change. The overwhelming majority of them articulated their utopian desire for change in the name of love. In paying greater attention to the politicization of youth, they drew inspiration from Guevara, Torres, Teilhard de Chardin, Freire, and many others. They relied on new tools in sociology and recognized the importance of creating new combative spaces of change. These gave rise to a more assertive activism that effectively protested the repression of the state. This activism successfully challenged the traditional politics of the PAN and the paternalism and charity projects of Catholic Action. While most of the actors discussed here demanded radical change, only a minority envisioned this change outside the capitalist system, as evident in the pages of *Corporación*, *Palestra*, *Juventud*, *Rumbo*, and *Diálogo*. Those in positions of power expressed little interest in making these distinctions and often interpreted all political (and countercultural) challenges to the status quo as a foreign attack on the nation. This led to further state repression and to the expulsion of a small but defiant group of "pernicious foreigners."

The vast majority of religious authorities in positions of power supported the government and found it futile to protest the authoritarianism of the PRI, even in the aftermath of the Tlatelolco and Corpus Christi massacres. For a number of Catholics who welcomed the progressive language of Vatican II, however, these two events marked decisive moments in their lives. The 1968 movement coincided with the Medellín conference in Colombia in giving greater legitimacy to the preferential option for the poor and the importance of ecumenism as a viable expression of love. This language gave rise to small but important popular movements in Mexico's own liberation theology. Their work only materialized after the First National Congress of Theology, held in Mexico City in 1969. Participants made an effort to bridge the gaps between "faith and development," when many religious movements first demanded autonomy from the ecclesiastical authorities and adopted a more progressive relationship with the marginalized.

The 1971 Corpus Christi massacre pushed others toward more radical paths. These actors gave greater urgency to the need to create "new/integrated" men and women. In 1972, this was evident in the pages of *Contacto*, *SPES*, *Víspera*, and *Liberación* and in the participation of a small but influential group of priests and lay Catholics at the Christians for Socialism conference in Chile, in the creation of Priests for the People, in the participation of radical Jesuits in Monterrey and Nezahualcóyotl, and in the torture and silencing of priests. The same was true of the successful efforts of their peers to give full autonomy to the National Center of Social Communications and the Carlos Septién García School of Journalism. The latter created a defining space for the training of Catholic reporters, intellectuals, and activists, and so did the cultural center that a group of Dominican friars established at UNAM.

Catholic Action and the more autonomous Mexican Social Secretariat also experienced significant changes during the Cold War. The most radical groups were those working with the nation's youth who saw it necessary to champion a dialogue between Christianity and Marxism. The same was true of those who welcomed the Latin Americanization of the Movement of Professional Students and rejected the conservativism and more national approach of the Corporation of Mexican Students. A minority of young people who participated in these groups lost faith in nonviolence (including critical pedagogy, promoción social, and the Revision of Life method) in the 1970s and saw no other option but to pick up arms. The majority welcomed a dialogue with leftist actors, but for the most part, they fell short in fully collaborating with them, except on rare occasions. This lack of unity was also caused by the fact that leftist student activists often described their Catholic peers as reactionary, even during the most radical years of the Sixties. Many progressive Catholics sympathized with the humanist and anti-imperialist goals of the Cuban Revolution, but they overwhelmingly disapproved of its leaders' growing relationship with the Soviet Union.

Most of the actors examined in the book had remained hopeful after the Tlatelolco massacre and were only further radicalized during the democratic opening of Luis Echeverría, which many journalists, intellectuals, and priests writing in various Catholic publications saw with apprehension, and even, according to some Catholics writing for *Señal* and *Christus*, as detrimental, and as others insisted in *La Nación*, more harmful than the authoritarianism of Díaz Ordaz. Many of these actors felt betrayed by the liberal Left and the conservative majority that composed the Mexican church.

Those on the Far Right were critical of liberal religious authorities and simultaneously saw the populist policies of Echeverría as the culmination of the radicalism of the Sixties, as a time of despair, often with little distinction between the most utopian elements of the counterculture, student activism, the populist policies of the government, and the reformist Christianity after Vatican II. They too opened new spaces of engagement, like *La Hoja de Combate* and the more aggressive *Réplica*, in which authors specifically pointed to the diocese of Cuernavaca and the universities as the epicenters of political and countercultural subversion. A few of them welcomed violence as necessary, as was the case of those who supported the University Movement of Renovated Orientation. The Sixties not only encouraged many of these actors to see beyond the shadows that remained of the Cristero legacy but also made them relevant players in the conservative movements that eventually contributed to the demise of the PRI. Their reactionary movements against free love, the liberation of women, abortion, and homosexuality grew after this era, and so did their campaigns against "pornography," a catchphrase that many of them loosely used in reference to the counterculture and the arts.

Like Arabella Arbenz, the majority of the actors described in this book conceived of themselves as part of a larger world that was interconnected and within closer reach to push for significant change during the Sixties. At times, these actors operated in transnational networks, within but also frequently outside leftist and rightist boundaries. They often framed the importance of their movement beyond the nation in a broader, Latin Americanized and Catholic world, as a new generation of Southern Cone activists insisted. Many of them benefited from and were shaped by the interactions they successfully established in prerevolutionary Havana and Lima, where the International Catholic Cinema Office (OCIC) opened its Spanish-speaking offices; in Montevideo, where a group of university students created the Latin American Secretariat; and in various cities in Colombia, Chile, and Argentina, where the most radical Catholicism emerged across the continent. Some drew inspiration from the Bandung Conference (1955) and the Cuban Revolution (1959), and nearly all of them welcomed the progressive language that followed Vatican II (1962–65) and the Medellín conference (1968). Liberal (*Miranda prorsus*, 1957), conservative (*Humanae vitae*, 1968), progressive (*Gaudium et spes*, 1964) and radical (*Populorum progressio*, 1967) papal encyclicals and documents were foundational in their radicalization.

The most significant changes of the era did not happen dramatically or in the aftermath of revolutionary events. Instead, they took place in incremental and everyday fashion and mostly in media outlets, in small grassroots movements (often led by sympathizers with liberation theology), and especially in the culture industry, as evident in the shifting, less authoritarian, and even radical understandings of gender and sexuality. Over the years, the radicalism of the counterculture blended into the mainstream culture of consumerism, and it was this transition that brought significant changes to Mexico.

In the world of politics, secular Mexico remained authoritarian, economically violent, and repressive in the aftermath of the Sixties. But the work that ecumenical priests, a new generation of lay activists, and militant writers did in questioning the contradictions of capitalism was of utmost importance. The same was true of outspoken Catholic intellectuals. All played important roles in criticizing state repression and in transforming Mexico into a more democratic nation. They also contributed to the creation of a combative journalism and the growth of Christian base communities. In the context of the Cold War, they remained committed to the preferential option for the poor, expressed interest in youth activism, and called for the defense of human rights.

To conclude, *Love and Despair* has brought together two scholarships of modern Mexico that have all too often remained disengaged from one another. The first is a secular body of work, mostly written from the perspective of the Left, that has all too often caricatured Catholicism as monolithic, unified, and strictly reactionary, or progressive, but almost exclusively in relation to liberation theology. The second is a Catholic body of work that has prioritized an institutional history of the church and its national ecclesiastical authorities with little attention to gender, the counterculture, and lay activists who found inspiration in the arts, film, and global networks. The stories depicted here mattered in the internationalization of everyday life that largely characterized the Cold War era in Latin America. But the role of religion cannot continue to be ignored in expanding our understanding of the Global Sixties in the region.

Cinematic Representations of Youth Rebellion (1941–ca. 1964)

Films Listed in Alphabetical Order	Main Topics Highlighting the Crisis of Youth	
	Sex and/or Sexuality	Ideas Presented as Foreign
¿A dónde van nuestros hijos? (Benito Alazraki, 1956) Classification: B-2	–Intimate relationships out of wedlock –Abortion	–Communism –Authoritarian parents –Social pressure –Rapid growth of Mexico City
El caso de una adolescente (Emilio Gómez Muriel, 1957) Classification: B-2	–Intimate relationships out of wedlock –Abortion –Vanity	–The American Way of Life –Materialism –Lack of communication with parents –Alcohol consumption –Motorcycles
¿Con quién andan nuestras hijas? (Emilio Gómez Muriel, 1955) Classification: B	–Pregnancy conceived in a convertible –Sexual promiscuity	–The American Way of Life –Women's work and college life –Drugs and alcohol –Modernity: city streets as a backdrop for seduction –Lack of parental love
Cuando los hijos se van (Bustillo Oro, 1941) Classification: Unknown	–Intimate relationships out of wedlock	–Modernity –Urbanization –Parental abandonment –Greed and materialism
La edad de la tentación (Alejandro Galindo, 1958) Classification: C	–Abortion –Pornographic magazines –Pregnancy conceived in convertibles –The pill –Prostitution	–The American Way of Life –Materialism –US football –Hedonism –Consumerism –Authoritarian, distant, and divorced parents –Drug consumption –Urbanization

Films Listed in Alphabetical Order	Main Topics Highlighting the Crisis of Youth	
	Sex and/or Sexuality	Ideas Presented as Foreign
Ellas también son rebeldes (Alejandro Galindo, 1959) Classification: B	–Intimate relationships out of wedlock	–The American Way of Life: leather jackets associated with youth delinquency –Yellow journalism, obsessed with vanity, sexual misconduct, and crime –Divorced and materialistic parents
Juventud desenfrenada (José Díaz Morales, 1956) Classification: C-2	–Abortion –Lesbianism –Prostitution	–The American Way of Life –Rock 'n' roll –Drugs –Parental absence and selfishness
Juventud Rebelde/jóvenes y rebeldes (Julián Soler, 1961) Classification: A	–Intimate relationships out of wedlock	–The American Way of Life –US football –Youth delinquency
Juventud sin Dios/Siempre hay un mañana (Miguel Morayta, 1961) Classification: A		–The American Way of Life –US football –Hedonism –Authoritarian and alcoholic parents
La juventud sin ley (Gilberto Martínez Solares, 1965) Classification: B	–Intimate relationships out of wedlock –Abortion	–The American Way of Life –Rock 'n' roll; materialism –Youth delinquency –Divorce –Indifferent and authoritarian parents –Drugs –Yellow journalism, obsessed with vanity, sexual misconduct, and crime
Maldita ciudad (Ismael Rodríguez, 1954) Classification: C-2	–Pregnancy conceived in convertibles	–The American Way of Life –Modernity: rapid urbanization –Multifamily housing –Youth delinquency –Physical abuse and greediness of parents/adults
Muchachas de uniforme (Alfredo B. Crevenna, 1951) Classification: C-1	–Intimate relationships out of wedlock –Abortion –Lesbianism	–Liberalism –Secularization

Films Listed in Alphabetical Order	Main Topics Highlighting the Crisis of Youth	
	Sex and/or Sexuality	Ideas Presented as Foreign
Peligros de juventud (Benito Alazraki, 1959) Classification: B	–Prostitution –Intimate relationships out of wedlock	–The American Way of Life –US football –Hedonism –Materialism –Youth alienation –Alcoholism
Quinceañera (Alfredo B. Crevenna, 1958) Classification: A		–Greed –Materialism –Divorce
La rebelión de los adolescentes (José Díaz Morales, 1957) Classification: C	–Intimate relationships out of wedlock	–The American Way of Life –Hedonism –Motorcycles –Rock 'n' roll –Drug trafficking
Señoritas (Fernando Méndez, 1958) Classification: A	–Abortion	–Modernity: rapid urbanization –Divorce
Una calle entre tú y yo (Roberto Rodríguez, 1952) Classification: B-2	–Intimate relationships out of wedlock	–The American Way of Life –US football –Hedonism –Materialism
Una familia de tantas (Alejandro Galindo, 1948) Classification: B-2	–Pregnancy out of wedlock	–The American Way of Life –New modern values and ideas about female liberation –Modernity: rapid urbanization

Other films consulted for the book (in chronological order): *Su adorable majadero* (Alberto Gout, 1938); *Mil estudiantes y una muchacha* (Juan Bustillo Oro, 1942); *Cortesana* (Alberto Gout, 1948); *Azahares de tu boda* (Julián Soler, 1950); *La edad peligrosa* (José Díaz Morales, 1950); *Los olvidados* (Luis Buñuel, 1950); *Dicen que soy comunista* (Alejandro Galindo, 1951); *The Wild One* (László Benedek, 1953); *Y mañana serán mujeres* (Alejandro Galindo, 1954); *Blackboard Jungle* (Richard Brook, 1955); *East of Eden* (Elia Kazan, 1955); *La culpa de los hombres* (Roberto Rodríguez, 1955); *Al compás del rock and roll* (José Díaz Morales, 1956); *Los amantes* (Benito Alazraki, 1956); *Rebel without a Cause* (Nicholas Ray, 1956); *Tu hijo debe de nacer* (Alejandro Galindo, 1956); *Los hijos del divorcio* (Mauricio de la Serna, 1957); *La virtud desnuda* (José Díaz Morales, 1957); *Les Amants* (Louis Malle, 1958); *Chicas casaderas* (Alfredo B. Crevenna, 1959); *Estos años violentos* (José Díaz Morales, 1959); *Mis padres se divorcian* (Julián Soler, 1959); *Suddenly Last Summer* (Joseph L. Makiewicz, 1959); *La Dolce Vita* (Federico Fellini, 1960); *Mañana serán hombres*

(Alejandro Galindo, 1960); *The Subterraneans* (Ronald MacDougall, 1960); *Teresa* (Alfredo B. Crevenna, 1960); *Viridiana* (Luis Buñuel, 1961); *El Ángel exterminador* (Luis Buñuel, 1962); *Cuando los hijos se pierden* (Mauricio de la Serna, 1962); *Lolita* (Stanley Kubrick, 1962); *La sombra de los hijos* (Rafael Baledón, 1963); and *El pecador* (Rafael Baledón, 1965).

Cinematic Representations of Youth, Liberation, the Counterculture, and Progressive Catholicism (ca. 1961–ca. 1978)

	Main Topics		
Films Listed in Alphabetical Order	Sexuality and the Counterculture	Catholicism/ Liberation	Reaction/ Repression
A paso de cojo (Luis Alcoriza, 1979)		–The Cristero Rebellion as irrational/ violent	–Death
Una alma pura (Juan Ibáñez, 1964)	–The liberation of women –Alienation –Abortion –Incest	–Repressive Catholicism	–Suicide
Cambio (Alfredo Joskowicz, 1971)	–Alienation –Environmental disaster		–State repression/ death –Allegory of the Tlatelolco massacre
Cinco de chocolate y uno de fresa (Carlos Velo, 1967)	–The liberation of women –Drugs	–Progressive Catholicism	–State repression
Crates (Alfredo Joskowicz, 1970)	–The liberation of women –Alienation –Environmental disaster	–Progressive Catholicism	–Suicide
Cuando tejen las arañas (Roberto Gavaldón, 1977)	–The liberation of women –Abortion –Bisexuality –Drugs		–Death –Electroshock therapy

Films Listed in Alphabetical Order	Main Topics		
	Sexuality and the Counterculture	Catholicism/ Liberation	Reaction/ Repression
De todos modos Juan te llamas (Marcela Fernández Violante, 1974)		–The Cristero Rebellion as irrational/ violent	–Death –Allegory of the Tlatelolco massacre
Fé, esperanza y caridad (Alberto Bojorquez, Luis Alcoriza, and Jorge Fons, 1974)		–Repressive Catholicism	–State repression –Corruption
La guerra santa (Carlos Enrique Taboada, 1979)		–The Cristero Rebellion as irrational/ violent	–Death
Hasta el viento tiene miedo (Carlos Enrique Taboada, 1968)	–The liberation of women	–Repressive Catholicism	–State repression –Death/suicide
El infierno de todos tan temido (Sergio Olhovich, 1979)	–Alienation –Drugs	–Repressive Catholicism	–Electroshock therapy –Allegory of the Tlatelolco massacre
El monasterio de los buitres (Francisco del Villar, 1973)	–The liberation of women –Male homosexuality –Psychoanalysis	–Vatican II reforms –Repressive Catholicism	
La montaña sagrada/ The Holy Mountain (Alejandro Jodorowsky, 1972–73)	–Drugs –Liberation	–Repressive Catholicism	–State repression –The Tlatelolco massacre
Los perversos (a-go-go) (Gilberto Martínez Solares, 1965)	–The liberation of women –Youth rebellion –Abortion	–Vatican II reforms –Repressive Catholicism	–Death
La primavera de los escorpiones (Francisco del Villar, 1970)	–Male homosexuality		
La viuda negra (Arturo Ripstein, 1977)	–The liberation of women	–Repressive Catholicism	

Additional films consulted for the book (in chronological order): *Los jóvenes* (Luis Alcoriza, 1961); *El tejedor de los milagros* (Francisco del Villar, 1961); *El cielo y la tierra* (Alfonso Corona Blake, 1962); *8½* (Federico Fellini, 1963); *The Gospel according to St. Matthew* (Pierre Paolo Pasolini, 1964); *Simón del desierto* (Luis Buñuel, 1965); *Los cuervos están de luto* (Francisco del Villar, 1965); *Blow-Up* (Michelangelo Antonioni, 1966); *Los caifanes* (Juan Ibáñez, 1967); *Fando y Lis* (Alejandro Jodorowsky, 1968); *El grito* (Leobardo López Aretche, 1968); *Los recuerdos del porvenir* (Arturto Ripstein, 1968); *Sor Ye Yé* (Ramón Fernández, 1968); *Teorema* (Piere Paolo Pasolini, 1968); *Patsy, mi amor* (Manuel Michel, 1969); *Las pirañas aman en cuaresma* (Francisco del Villar, 1969); *Las reglas del juego* (Mauricio Wallerstein, 1970); *El Topo* (Alejandro Jodorowsky, 1970); *Ángeles y querubines* (Rafael Cordiki, 1971); *Frida Kahlo* (Marcela Fernández Violante, 1971); *Mecánica nacional* (Luis Alcoriza, 1971); *Los meses y los días* (Alberto Bojórquez, 1971); *El castillo de la pureza* (Arturto Ripstein, 1972); *El festín de la loba* (Francisco del Villar, 1972); *La verdadera vocación de Magdalena* (Jaime Humberto Hermosillo, 1972); *Satánico Pandemonium/La sexorcista* (Gilberto Martínez Solares, 1973); *El llanto de la tortuga* (Francisco del Villar, 1974); *Alucarda, la hija de las tinieblas* (Juan López Moctezuma, 1975); *Las fuerzas vivas* (Luis Alcoriza, 1975); *La lucha con la pantera* (Alberto Bojórquez, 1975); *La otra virginidad* (Juan Manuel Torres, 1975); *El Apando* (Felipe Cazals, 1976); *Canoa* (Felipe Cazals, 1976); *Lo mejor de Teresa* (Alberto Bojórquez, 1976); *El lugar sin límites* (Arturo Ripstein, 1977); *Prisión de mujeres* (René Cardona, 1977); *Tres mujeres en la hoguera* (Abel Salazar, 1977); *Cadena perpetua* (Arturo Ripstein, 1978); and *Mundo Nuevo* (Gabriel Retes, 1978).

NOTES

INTRODUCTION

1. Guevara, "Socialism and Man in Cuba"; Torres and Gerassi, *Revolutionary Priest*, 245–49, 367–69; Freire, *Pedagogia del oprimido*, 33–34, 65–81; Gutiérrez, *Caridad y amor humano*, 9; Câmara, *Spiral of Violence*, 41–83; and the Beatles, "All You Need Is Love."

2. For earlier interpretations of love in the case of Mexico, see Caso, "La existencia como economía."

3. Booth, "Rethinking Latin America's Cold War."

4. Joseph, "What We Now Know and Should Know," 4.

5. Andes and Young, *Local Church, Global Church*.

6. Sarlo, *La batalla de las ideas*.

7. Gilman, *Entre la pluma y el fusil*; Zolov, "Introduction: Latin America in the Global Sixties"; Marchesi, *Latin America's Radical Left*; Vaughan, *Portrait of a Young Painter*; and Field, Krepp, and Pettinà, *Latin America and the Global Cold War*.

8. In this sense, Mexico successfully capitalized on its revolutionary past to leverage a strong position with Cuba, the Soviet Bloc, and the nonaligned countries, and often at odds with the interests of the United States. See, e.g., Keller, *Mexico's Cold War*; Zolov, *The Last Good Neighbor*; and Thornton, *Revolution in Development*.

9. Zolov, "Expanding Our Conceptual Horizons"; and Gilman, *Entre la pluma y el fusil*.

10. Gosse, "A Movement of Movements," 292. See also the important work of Chávez, *Poets and Prophets of the Resistance*; Hernández Sandoval, *Guatemala's Catholic Revolution*; Londono-Ardila, "Consciousness-Raising and Liberation"; and García Mourelle, *La experiencia de la Juventud Obrera Católica*.

11. See relevant cases in Dunn, *Contracultura*; and Markarian, *Uruguay: 1968*.

12. As is well known in the scholarship, the archbishop of Mexico City, Luis María Martínez, was a key figure responsible for improving the relationship between the church and the state in the aftermath of the Cristero Rebellion.

13. Pacheco Hinojosa, *Iglesia católica*.

14. Loaeza, *Clases medias*; and Andes, *The Mysterious Sofía*.

15. See, e.g., Pettinà, *Historia mínima de la Guerra Fría*; and the national case studies in Joseph and Spenser, *In from the Cold*.

16. Westad, *The Global Cold War*; and Harmer, *Beatriz Allende*, 4.

17. Vaughan, *Portrait of a Young Painter*, 8.

18. Fernández, "Oral History of the Chilean Movement," 284.

19. McLeod, *The Religious Crisis of the 1960s*, 1. See also Horn, *The Spirit of Vatican II*.

20. Latin American Catholics had expressed more ambivalent positions toward the Soviets during the 1950s. See, e.g., Rupprecht, "Latin American *Tercermundistas*."

21. Torres and Gerassi, *Revolutionary Priest*, 245–369.

22. Mestman, *Las rupturas del 68 en el cine de América Latina*.

23. Gutiérrez, interview with the author. See also Bidegain, "La organización de movimientos de juventud"; and Andes and Young, *Local Church, Global Church*.

24. *Mater et magistra*, encyclical of Pope John XXIII on Christianity and social progress, May 15, 1961; *Pacem in terris*, encyclical of Pope John XXIII on establishing universal peace in truth, justice, charity, and liberty, April 11, 1963; *Gaudium et spes*, Pastoral Constitution on the Church in the Modern World, promulgated by Pope Paul VI, December 7, 1965; and *Populorum progressio*, encyclical of Pope Paul VI on the development of peoples, March 26, 1967. All can be found at *La Santa Sede*, https://www.vatican.va/content/vatican/it.html; last accessed January 6, 2022.

25. Pettinà, *Historia mínima de la Guerra Fría*.

26. García, "La Iglesia mexicana desde 1962."

27. As cited in Annett, *Cathonomics*, 36.

28. Gutiérrez, interview with the author.

29. *Populorum progressio*. In his "Message to the Tricontinental" (1966), Guevara no longer spoke of "revolutionary love" as instrumental in bringing about radical change, as noted earlier, but rather he emphasized the importance of "hatred" in defeating the legacies of colonialism.

30. CELAM, "Documentos finales de Medellín," September 1968, https://www.ensayistas.org/critica/liberacion/medellin/, last accessed January 6, 2022; and Gilman, *Entre la pluma y el fusil*, 51.

31. De Guiseppe, "Italian Catholics"; and García, "La Iglesia mexicana desde 1962."

32. Pensado, "Silencing Rebellious Priests"; and Bissio, "Bandung in Latin America."

33. Sociedad Teológica Mexicana, *Memoria del Primer Congreso*.

34. This was the position expressed, among others, by the representatives of the Episcopal Union of Mutual Help, the Theological Mexican Society, and the National Center of Indigenous Missions.

35. Carassai, *The Argentine Silent Majority*; and Cowan, *Securing Sex*.

36. Pensado, *Rebel Mexico*, 22.

37. *Heraldo Cultural* and *Señal*, May–September 1968.

38. See, among others, Díaz, *Departamento vacío* (1965); Fuentes, *Los jóvenes* (1968); and Careaga, *Mitos y fantasías* (1974).

39. Glantz, *Onda y escritura*; and Monsiváis, *Días de guardar*.

40. Randall, *Hippies*.

41. See also Agustín, *La nueva música clasica*.

42. Agustín, "Cuál es la onda"; Price, "José Agustín"; and García Saldaña, *En la ruta de la onda*.

43. José Agustín, Prólogo to Marroquín, *La contracultura como protesta*.

44. See, e.g., Feixa, "De las bandas."

45. Zolov, *Refried Elvis*, 114, 134, 140, 177, 217–24.

46. Dunn, *Contracultura*, 5–9.

47. Barr-Melej, *Psychedelic Chile*, 4–5; Manzano, *The Age of Youth in Argentina*; Markarian, *Uruguay: 1968*; and Luke, *Youth and the Cuban Revolution*.

48. Chávez, "Operación amor"; and Barr-Melej, *Psychedelic Chile*.

49. See, e.g., Appelbaum, *St. Francis of America*, 110–35.

50. Vaughan, *Portrait*, 27; Cosse, *Mafalda*; Manzano, *The Age of Youth in Argentina*; Frazier and Cohen, *Gender and Sexuality in 1968*; Salgado, "Making Friends"; and Langland, *Speaking of Flowers*.

51. Salgado, "Making Friends," 301–2.

52. Vaughan, *Portrait of a Young Painter*, 23.

53. Salgado, "Making Friends," 303.

54. Salgado, "Making Friends," 303.

55. Cano, "Mexico: The Long Road to Women's Suffrage." See also Espino Armendariz, "Feminismo católico en México."

56. Valdovinos Torres, "La homosexualidad en el cine mexicano"; Macías González, "Los homosexuals como sujetos peligrosos"; and Rubenstein, "A Sentimental and Sexual Education."

57. Vaughan, *Portrait of a Young Painter*, 3; and Passerini, *Autobiography of a Generation*.

58. Langland, "Transnational Connections of the Global Sixties," 25. See also the chapters in Andes and Young, *Local Church, Global Church*.

59. Some people gave me permission to use their names; others preferred that I use pseudonyms, and I have indicated this in the notes and bibliography.

60. Wilkie, "Postulates of the Oral History Center"; and Fernández, "Oral History of the Chilean Movement," 286.

61. Pérez, *Confessional Cinema*, 3–4.

1. BEAUTY, CINEMA, AND FEMALE YOUTH REBELLION

1. Aspe Armella, *La formación social y política de los católicos mexicanos*; Loaeza, "Mexico in the 1950s"; and Sanders, "Women, Sex, and the 1950s."

2. Padilla Rangel, "Mujeres e Iglesia católica."

3. Torres Septién, "Cuerpos velados, cuerpos femeninos." See also Blancarte, *Historia de la iglesia*; and Mcintyre, *Protestantism and State Formation.*

4. See, e.g., the representations by Marlon Brando and James Dean in *The Wild One* (Benedek, 1953) and *Rebel without a Cause* (Ray, 1955), respectively.

5. Andrés Ruszkowski, "Los criterios nacionales y la encíclica 'Miranda Prorsus,'" *OCIC*, June 20–21, 1958, ASLA-FLP, OCIC file.

6. Ziegler, letter to Penichet, February 14, 1957, ASLA-FLP, OCIC file.

7. Ziegler, letter to Ruszkowski, June 6, 1957, ASLA-FLP, OCIC file.

8. In addition, Ziegler spoke against the "artistic nudes" that appeared in films such as *La virtud desnuda* (Díaz Morales, 1957).

9. Yvonne Hemptinne was also influential in the life of Emma Ziegler, mostly from her office with the OCIC in Belgium.

10. Monsiváis, "Notas sobre cultura popular"; and Zolov, *Refried Elvis.*

11. See chaps. 6 and 7.

12. On this point, see the important work of Torres Septién, "Cuerpos velados, cuerpos femeninos"; Tuñón, *Mujeres de luz y sombra*; and Porter, *From Angel to Office Worker.*

13. Andes, *The Mysterious Sofía*, xxi.

14. Sanders, "Women, Sex, and the 1950s," 274.

15. Emma Ziegler, "Ha muerto uno de nuestros asistentes," *Juventud* (January 1969).

16. *Juventud* (October 21–28, 1951).

17. Tuñón, *Mujeres de luz y sombra*, 142.

18. "Enemigos del Hogar," *Juventud* (May 1942).

19. Sofía del Valle, "Patria en Peligro," *Juventud* (July 1942).

20. Emma Galán, "Actuación cívica de la mujer," *Juventud* (June 1947).

21. On universal suffrage, see Cano, "Mexico: The Long Road to Women's Suffrage."

22. Andes, *The Mysterious Sofía.*

23. Emma Ziegler, "La caridad: Sello de las asambleas," *Juventud* (September 1942).

24. Emma Ziegler, "Faro de Paz," *Juventud* (August 1946).

25. The supporting work of Andrés Ruszkowski in South America and Yvonne Hemptinne in Belgium was instrumental in this success.

26. Edelmiro Traslosheros, letter to Msgr. Chanoine Brohée, April 21, 1936, KADOC, SIGNIS Collection, BE/942855/325/45.

27. "OCIC: Naturaleza y fines," 1951; ¿Qué es la OCI?," *Cencos* (1965); and Black, *The Catholic Crusade against the Movies.*

28. Ramírez Llorens, "Noches de sano esparcimiento," 66–67; and Ruszkowski, "Testimonio."

29. Ruszkowski, "Testimonio," 36.

30. América Penichet, letters to Yvonne Hemptinne, February 15, 1958, and Msgr. Julián Mendoza Guerrero, March 7 and November, 21, 1961, KADOC, SIGNIS Collection, BE/942855/1429/825.

31. *Juventud* (March 1934).

32. Manuel Vidal, letter to OCIC, September 3, 1937, KADOC, SIGNIS Collection, BE/942855/325/45.

33. Zermeño Padilla, "Cine, censura y moralidad en México"; and Penichet, letter to Ziegler, 1951, 6–7; OCIC, "Education to the Cinema, Conclusions from the Study Days in Madrid," 1952; "Congreso Nacional para la Moralización," 1953; OCIC, "The Moral Classification of Films," 1954; and "Manifiesto de la Comisión Nacional para la Moralización del Ambiente," 1956, 2–28, ASLA-FLP, OCIC file.

34. "Informe que rinde la Srta. Victoria Martínez Vigil, Presidente Diocesana de la JCFM, 1953–1956" (1956), 9–30, AACM.

35. Zermeño Padilla, "Cine, censura y moralidad en México," 84.

36. Zermeño Padilla, "Cine, censura y moralidad en México," 86–87.

37. Peredo Castro, "Catholicism and Mexican Cinema."

38. Costa, *La "apertura" cinematográfica*, 55; and Zermeño Padilla, "Cine, censura y moralidad en México."

39. "Conclusiones de la Primera Reunión de Latinoamérica de la OCIC" (March 10, 1951); Penichet, letters to Ziegler, June 7 and July 19, 1951; and Ziegler, letter to Andrés Ruszkowski, April 4, 1960, ASLA-FLP, OCIC file. See also Rosario Escudero, "Semana cultural del cine," *Juventud* (February 1957); and "Algo de cine," *Juventud* (September 1957).

40. Torres Septién, "Los fantasmas de la Iglesia."

41. Ziegler, letter to De la Fuente, April 25, 1957, ASLA-FLP, OCIC file.

42. Andrés Ruszkowski, "Los criterios nacionales y la encíclica 'Miranda Prorsus,'" *OCIC* (June 20–21, 1958), ASLA-FLP, OCIC file.

43. Ziegler, letter to Ruszkowski, June 6, 1957, ASLA-FLP, OCIC file.

44. Torres Septién, "Los fantasmas de la Iglesia"; and Ziegler, letter to Penichet, February 14, 1957, ASLA-FLP, OCIC file.

45. Penichet, letter to Ziegler, September 9, 1957; "Centro Pío XI, Informe de las actividades de agosto de 1958 a agosto de 1959," August 25, 1958, ASLA-FLP, OCIC file; and Emma Ziegler, "¿Qué nos pide el Papa?," *Cine-Temas* 2:1 (1958), AACM.

46. Ayala Blanco, *La Aventura del cine mexicano*; and Mora, *Mexican Cinema*.

47. Fox, "Pornography and 'the Popular' in Post-Revolutionary Mexico."

48. A similar alliance takes place in response to comic books. See Rubenstein, *Bad Language, Naked Ladies*.

49. Tierney, *Emilio Fernández*.

50. See, e.g., Hershfield, *Mexican Cinema/Mexican Woman*.

51. Ayala Blanco, *La Aventura del cine mexicano*.

52. Ayala Blanco, *La Aventura del cine mexicano*.

53. Ayala Blanco, *La búsqueda del cine mexicano*, 223–47.

54. Other representative examples from the early era but with little attention to youth culture are *Mil estudiantes y una muchacha* (Bustillo Oro, 1942), *La edad peligrosa* (Díaz Morales, 1950), and *Una calle entre tu y yo* (Rodríguez, 1952).

55. A notable but limited exception is *Maldita ciudad* (Rodríguez, 1954).

56. Vaughan, *Portrait of a Young Painter*.

57. For a representative sample of these films, see appendix 1.

58. Ciuk, *Diccionario de directores del cine mexicano*; and Galindo, *El cine mexicano*. See also the similar case regarding comic books in Rubenstein, *Bad Language, Naked Ladies*.

59. Torres Septién, "Los fantasmas de la Iglesia."

60. See appendix 1 for other films by these directors that touched on the social dangers associated with youth rebellion.

61. Martínez (pseudonym), interview with the author.

62. See similar examples in appendix 1.

63. The Constitution had guaranteed equality for women in divorce proceedings since 1917.

64. The Onix prizes were institutionalized at the Ibero-American University after the Havana conference.

65. Romero Pérez, letter to Darío Miranda, October 25, 1961, ASLA-FLP, OCIC file.

66. CCCO, "Ellas también son rebeldes," 1961, AACM.

67. Alba, S.A., Distribuidores del Sector Católico—Películas Sonoras de 16 mm, Censuradas por la Autoridad Eclesiástica, Catálogo Complementario, 1958; and "Comisión de Moralización," *ACM, Boletín de la Junta Central* 22:5–6 (September–October 1958), AACM.

68. OCIC, *¿Con quién andan nuestras hijas?* (1956), AACM.

69. "¿Con quién andan nuestras hijas?," *La Nación*, no. 756 (April 8, 1956): 17.

70. See other examples in appendix 1.

71. In these films, the convertible is frequently represented as one of the places where young women are introduced to alcohol (typically a cocktail from the United States such as the highball) and lose their virginity. See appendix 1.

72. On the repression of homosexuality, see Macías González, "The Transnational Homophile Movement," 137.

73. The Port of Acapulco is frequently depicted in these films as a place of sin, drug use, and prostitution. See also, among other examples, *Señoritas* (Méndez, 1958).

74. This is a central "lesson" also evident in *Juventud sin Dios* (Morayta, 1961).

75. Rentería Díaz, *El aborto: Entre la moral y el derecho*.

76. Instead, it received a B-2 classification.

77. The motorcycle as a vehicle associated with the deaths of young men was first introduced in *The Wild One* (Bebedek, 1953).

78. For other films that treated the topic of abortion in a similar fashion, see appendix 1.

79. As the Spanish historian Jorge Pérez noted, "Nuns functioned fairly autonomous from men—though not from patriarchy." Pérez, *Confessional Cinema*, 119.

80. "Muchachas de uniforme," *La Nación* (June 11, 1951).

81. Ziegler, letter to Penichet, June 20, 1951, ASLA-FLP, OCIC file.

82. Penichet, letter to Ziegler, July 19, 1951, ASLA-FLP, OCIC file.

83. Penichet, letter to Ziegler, July 19, 1951, ASLA-FLP, OCIC file.

84. See the examples in appendix 1.

85. See, e.g., Verónica de la C., "Las bases de un matrimonio feliz—el noviazgo," *Juventud* (June 1956).

86. She starred in *Maldita ciudad* (Rodríguez, 1954), *Con quién andan nuestras hijas* (Gómez Muriel, 1955), *El caso de una adolescente* (Gómez Muriel, 1957), and what many consider her best film, *Quinceañera* (Crevenna, 1958).

87. See Torres Septién, "Belleza reflejada."

88. Sanders, "Women, Sex, and the 1950s," 287.

89. See, e.g., Graciela Benítez M., "La profesión ante la moral católica," *Palestra* 15 (January–February 1957); and "Presencia de la joven en el medio estudiantil," *Palestra* 26 (June–August 1961).

90. A notable example is *A dónde van nuestros hijos* (Alazraki, 1956).

91. See, e.g., María L. Garcinava, "Estudiantes," *Juventud* (May 1945); and "Hogar y política: La mujer en la familia," *Juventud* (October 1953).

92. On other films by Alazraki addressing youth rebellion, see appendix 1.

93. See also *Dicen que soy comunista* (Galindo, 1951).

94. "La vida del padre Lambert," *Esto* (June 7, 1953).

95. América Penichet, "Del territorio de Cuba Libre," letter to the Centros Nacionales y a todos los amigos del OCIC, January 14, 1959, ASLA-FLP, OCIC file. My emphasis.

96. América Penichet, letters to Yvonne Hemptinne, April 18, May 20, and December 6, 1961, KADOC, SIGNIS Collection, BE/942855/1429/825.

97. Penichet, letters to Ziegler, March 14 and June 14, 1961, ASLA-FLP, OCIC file.

98. Emma Ziegler, "Chispazos," *Cine Temas* 3:6 (1959); and Emma Ziegler, "El cine soviético, arma política," *Juventud* (October 1960). See also Miguel Angel Portillo Solis, "La dulce vida, ni es dulce ni es vida," *Juventud Católica* (May 1961).

99. Emma Ziegler, "Los católicos frente al cine," *Cine Temas* 3:9 (1959); and "Chispazos," *Cine Temas* 4:3 (1960).

100. Manuel E. Cal and Emma Ziegler, "Juicio moral de la película 'La Dulce Vida,'" *ACM Circular*, no. 168-1 (April 1961). *Suddenly, Last Summer* (Mankiewicz, 1959), *The Subterraneans* (MacDougall, 1960), and *Les Amants* (Malle, 1958) touched on the themes of homosexuality, existentialism, and sexual promiscuity, respectively.

101. Penichet, letter to Ziegler, June 14, 1961; and Ruszkowski, letter to Ziegler, August 28, 1961, ASLA-FLP, OCIC file.

102. Ziegler, letter to Cebollada, January 11, 1962, ASLA-FLP, OCIC file.

103. Ziegler, letter to Penichet, July 31, 1963, ASLA-FLP, OCIC file.

104. A film that received harsh criticism from Ziegler and was censored in Guadalajara due to the involvement of a group of Catholic parents was *Lolita* (Kubrick, 1962). Garcinava and Ziegler, letter to the Juntas Diocesanas de la ACM, June 20, 1963, AACM.

105. CCOC, "Viridiana," 1961, AACM.

106. *El Ángel Exterminador* (Buñuel, 1962) makes a similar argument.

107. See chap. 3.
108. Ziegler, letter to Penichet, March 18, 1964, ASLA-FLP, OCIC file.

2. STUDENT ACTIVISM DURING THE COLD WAR

1. Pensado, "A 'Third Way' in Christ," 165.
2. Bissio, "Bandung in Latin America."
3. Rupprecht, "Latin American *Tercermundistas*," 232–35.
4. I published my initial findings on these organizations in Pensado, "A 'Third Way' in Christ"; and Pensado, "El Movimiento Estudiantil Profesional (MEP)."
5. See, among many others, DFS, Exp. 63-1-63, L-23, H-225.
6. Female activists affiliated with the Corporation participated in the Women's Union of Catholic Students (UFEC).
7. Bermeo, interview with the author.
8. Bermeo, interview with the author.
9. Bermeo, interview with the author
10. Calderón Vega, *Cuba 88*.
11. Mabry, *Mexico's Acción Nacional*, 21.
12. Calderon Vega, *Cuba 88*; and Espinosa, *Jesuit Student Groups*.
13. The first and most active presidents of the Corporation were Gabriel de Alba (1947–50), José Audifred (1950–53), José Manuel Covarrubias (1953–56), Jorge Bermeo (1956–57), and Joaquin López Campuzano (1957–60).
14. Sanabria and Beuchot, *Historia de la filosofía cristiana*; and UFEC, *David Mayagoitia*.
15. He also created the National Union of Professionals (UNP) where members of the Corporation and their female counterparts in UFEC continued their movement after graduating from college.
16. Bermeo, interview with the author.
17. Bermeo, interview with the author.
18. Bermeo, interview with the author.
19. Zavala, interview with the author.
20. "Vida de la Corporación de Estudiantes Mexicanos," *Corporación* (March 1950).
21. David Mayagoitia, "*¡Definámonos! ¿católicos o comunistas?*" (1951) and "El deber cívico" (1952); and David Mayagoitia and Jorge Bermeo, "Ideario" (1951), AACM. See also "La pirámide invertida o que es el comunismo," *Corporación* (March–April 1951); and David Mayagoitia, "Informe sobre las actividades de la Corporación durante el presente año de 1959," October 14, 1959, AACM. Isaac Guzmán, "El estudiante universitario y los problemas sociales," *Corporación* (July 1950); Grupo de la Facultad de Derecho de la UNAM, "Crisis de la revolución," *Corporación* (July 1950); "El deber cívico," *Corporación* (December 1951); and Jorge Demetriades, "El corporativista y su misión de jefe," *Corporación* (March 1958).

22. "Vida de la Corporación de Estudiantes Mexicanos," *Corporación* (March 1950); José Audifred, "Estructuración, organización y formación," *Corporación* (December 1957); David Mayagoitia, "Notas sobre la fundación de la Corporación de Estudiantes Mexicanos," *Corporación* (July 1958); and Octavio Márquez, Archbishop of Puebla, "Comisión Episcopal para el Apostolado de los Seglares," October 5, 1961, AHAM.

23. "Participación estudiantil en el gobierno universitario," *Corporación* (May 1950).

24. See, e.g., Luis Calderón Vega, "Reflexiones universitarias," *Corporación* (March–April 1951); and "En torno a la autonomía de la UNA," *Corporación* (May, 1954).

25. Luis Calderón Vega, "Gente de Casa," *Reforma Universitaria* (September 15 and 30, 1958).

26. Luis Calderón Vega, "Cuba 88," *Corporación* (October 1957); "Editorial, Diez años de servicio," *Corporación* (December 1957); and David Mayagoitia to Miguel Miranda y Gómez, "Situación actual de las universidades oficiales mexicanas," June 10, 1964, AACM.

27. Costa (pseudonym), interview with the author.

28. Costa, interview with the author.

29. Corporación, "Diez años de servicio," *Corporación* (March 1958); and "Avance comunista en las filas estudiantiles," *Corporación* (May 1959). See similar sentiments expressed by the National Confederation of Students (CNE) in "El movimiento estudiantil en el DF contra el alza de tarifas de los autobuses de servicio urbano"; Horacio Guajardo, "Este Orden," *Reforma Universitaria* (August 31, 1958); and "Nuevos choques estudiantiles en la Ciudad de Guadalajara," *Reforma Universitaria* (November 15, 1958).

30. "Anarquía universitaria," *Corporación* (July–August 1960).

31. "Faltan más maestros que estudiantes," *Reforma Universitaria* (September 30, 1958); and Ignacio de la Concha, "En torno a los problemas de la Universidad," *Reforma Universitaria* (September 30, 1958).

32. José Audiffred, "La Conferencia Nacional de Estudiantes," *Corporación* (December 1951); and "La acción cívica estudiantil: Ponencia presentada por la Corporación en el XX Congreso de la CNE," *Corporación* (May 1953).

33. Marín (pseudonym), interview with the author.

34. Costa, interview with the author.

35. Bermeo, interview with the author.

36. Adrián García Cortés, "Vida del estudiante universitario: Casa, vestido, sentido," *Corporación* (July 1950); "Instituto Nacional de la Juventud Mexicana," March 3, 1957; "Informe sobre actividades de la Corporación de Estudiantes Mexicanos durante el presente año de 1959," AACM; and "Realización de la vocación social del estudiante católico universitario," *Corporación* (January–February 1961).

37. "Editorial: Participación estudiantil en el gobierno universitario," *Corporación* (May 1950); Mayagoitia, "Notas sobre la fundación"; "Misión de la universidad frente al movimiento intelectual actual," *Corporación* (December 1959); and

Diego H. Zavala, "Responsabilidad del profesional católico en la vida de los universitarios mexicanos," *Corporación* (March 1960).

38. Marín, interview with the author.

39. "Realización de la vocación social del estudiante católico universitario," *Corporación* (January–February 1961).

40. Costa and Bermeo, interviews with the author.

41. "Editorial: Una conciencia universitaria vigorosamente católica," *Corporación* (September–October 1950); and Mayagoitia, "Informe sobre las actividades de la Corporación durante el presente año de 1959," AACM.

42. David Mayagoitia to Miguel Miranda y Gómez, "Situación actual de las universidades," AACM; Antonio Obregón Padilla, "IX asamblea nacional de la Corporación," *Corporación* (March 1958); and David Mayagoitia, "Memorándum sobre un sondeo respecto del ateísmo en el medio universitario (maestros y alumnos), profesional y de investigación," August 1967, AHAM.

43. Costa, interview with the author.

44. Bermeo, interview with the author.

45. These sentiments were also shared by the National Confederation of Students (CNE). See, e.g., "La vida del estudiante de medicina en el DF," *Reforma Universitaria* (November 15, 1958); "Primera reunión regional de dirigentes estudiantiles de la zona norte del país, realizada por la CNE," *Reforma Universitaria* (December 15, 1958); "Dirigir, enseñar, profesar," *Reforma Universitaria* (January 15, 1959); and "Educación de la voluntad," *Reforma Universitaria* (March 31, 1959).

46. Mayagoitia and Bermeo, "Ideario," AACM.

47. See chaps. 3 and 5.

48. CELAM, *40 años*; Carlos McGrath, letter to Franz Hengback, November 1, 1966; and Alberto Meyer, letter to Bosco Silva, November 5, 1966, ASLA-FLP, Universidades file.

49. Pelegrí, *JECI MIEC*; "¿Qué es Pax Romana?," *Pax Romana, Boletín* (October 1948).

50. "Welcoming Remarks by Attorney General Robert F. Kennedy to the Opening Session of the Inter-Federal Assembly of Pax Romana, Georgetown University, Washington, D.C., Monday, July 20, 1964."

51. "Welcoming Remarks."

52. Bidegain, "La organización de movimientos de juventud"; and Londono-Ardila, "Consciousness-Raising and Liberation."

53. Also important is the 1964 meeting in Petrópolis, Brazil. Organized by Iván Illich, the meeting brought together leading figures of what later would be termed "liberation theology," Juan Luis Segundo, Gustavo Gutiérrez, and Lucio Gera.

54. McLeod, *The Religious Crisis of the 1960s*; and Horn, *The Spirit of Vatican II*.

55. Juan Madrigal, "Seminario sobre Revisión de Vida," April 1968, ASLA-FLP, MIEC-JECI file.

56. Jarque, *Pax Romana*.

57. Jarque, *Pax Romana*; and Gutiérrez, interview with the author.

58. Jarque, *Pax Romana*; and Vasquez (pseudonym) and Gutiérrez, interviews with the author.

59. See, e.g., Ribeiro, "La Universidad necesaria," *Gaceta de la Universidad*, Suplemento (1957–73).

60. Jarque, *Pax Romana*; and Pelegrí, *JECI MIEC*.

61. Secretariado Latinoamericano, "Quinta Sesión Mundial de JEC Internacional: La vocación del estudiante ante el subdesarrollo," 1967, ASLA-FLP, MIEC-JECI file; and Luis Carriquiry, "Buga, la nueva reforma," *Víspera* 2:5 (April 1968).

62. Luis Sereno Coló, "A Long Walk through Latin America," *Convergence*, no. 3–4 (1981). Emphasis in the original.

63. Gutiérrez, interview with the author.

64. García and Bermeo, interviews with the author.

65. Vasquez, interview with the author; and "Presentación matrimonial," *El Porvenir* (November 13, 1967).

66. Sereno, letter to Adveniat, May 7, 1962, AA.

67. Luis Sereno Coló, "Características del medio universitario como condicionante de la Acción"; and A. Mitre, "Prensa estudiantil," MEP, IV Convención Nacional de Estudiantes de A.C., Septiembre de 1963, ASLA-FLP, MIEC-JECI file.

68. Glenda Bee, "Los grupos naturales en la sociedad," ASLA-FLP, MIEC-JECI file.

69. Vasquez, interview with the author.

70. "IV Convención Nacional de Estudiantes," *ACM: Boletín de la Junta Central* 27:12 (October 15, 1963); and Vasquez, interview with the author.

71. Guillermo Sedano, "Características de la respuesta," MEP, IV Convención Nacional de Estudiantes de A.C., Septiembre de 1963, ASLA-FLP, MIEC-JECI file.

72. On the importance of the Dominican friars, see chap. 7.

73. Sereno, "Características"; and Vasquez, interview with the author.

74. Vasquez, interview with the author; and Londono-Ardila, "Consciousness-Raising and Liberation."

75. See, e.g., the pages of *Palestra*, the central magazine of the UFEC from 1957 to 1965.

76. MEP, "IV Convención Nacional de Toluca," September 1963, ASLA-FLP, MIEC-JECI file.

77. On the influence of these intellectuals and the importance of the *Dutch Catechism*, see chaps. 4 and 7, respectively.

78. Sedano, "Características"; and Calderón O., "¿Qué es un dirigente?," MEP, IV Convención Nacional (September 1963), ASLA-FLP, MIEC-JECI file.

79. Sedano, "Proyección social."

80. Sedano, "Características."

81. Manzano, interview with the author.

82. Sereno Colo, letter to the Latin American Secretariat, April 20, 1965, AA.

83. Londono-Ardila, "Consciousness-Raising and Liberation."

84. Bidegain, Vasquez, and Manzano, interviews with the author.

85. Bidegain, interview with the author; and Tirado Mejía, *Los años sesenta*.

86. Bidegain, interview with the author.

87. "Aproximación a la realidad latinoamericana: Iglesia-Movimiento," *SPES* (October 19, 1972).

88. Rosendo, Bidegain, and Gutiérrez, interviews with the author.

89. Bidegain, interview with the author; and Londono-Ardila, "Consciousness-Raising."

90. "CELAM, "La misión de la universidad católica en América Latina," *Víspera* 1:1 (1967); "Los MECs del Cono Sur," *Víspera* 1:3 (October 1967); Benoit Dumas, "La Rebelión de Mayo," *Víspera* 1:6 (July 1968); "América Latina: La situación actual," "Movimiento estudiantil en Estados Unidos," and "La JEC Internacional," *SPES* 1:1 (1969); "Brasil: Encuentro nacional de JUC" and "Movimiento estudiantil en América Latina," *SPES* 1:3 (1969); "Noticias del Movimiento," *SPES* 1:4 (1969); Pierre Furter, "La Universidad según Darcy Ribeiro," *Víspera* 3:11 (July 1969); JECI, sesión mundial," *SPES* 1:9 (1970); and "Marco de constantes generales" and "La sesión mundial de la JECI," *SPES* 2:17 (1971).

91. Mike Lenaghan, "Ecumenismo y Nueva Izquierda," *Víspera* 1:2 (August 1967); Charles West, "The Last Happening," *Víspera* 1:6 (July 1968); Jorge Poggi, "Psicoanálisis, ética de la libertad," *Víspera* 1:7 (October 1968); "Marcuse: Todo es utopía," *Víspera* 2:8 (January 1969); "Algo sobre espiritualidad," *SPES* 1:4 (1969); "Dos años después de Medellín," *SPES* 1:9 (1970); Juan Damián, "Canción, protesta y consumerismo," *Víspera* 5:23 (May–June 1971).

92. "La situación dominicana" and "Dentro del nacionalismo revolucionario," *Víspera* 1:1 (1967); Héctor Borrat, "Los cinco dólares del Presidente Johnson," *Víspera* 1:6 (July 1968); Gustavo Matías, "Aspectos militares de la guerra de Vietnam," *Víspera* 1:7 (October 1968); Enrique Maza, "El movimiento estudiantil y sus repercusiones para la Iglesia," *Cuadernos de Documentación, MIEC-JECI* 3:11 (1969); "Desde Santo Domingo," *SPES* 1:2 (1969); Luis H. Péasara, "Nixon: Law and Order," *Víspera* 2:8 (January 1969); Asunción: Los sucesos de octubre," *SPES* 1:3 (1969); Paulo Schilling, "Militares y militarismo en el Brasil: Mitos y realidades," *Víspera* 3:11 (July 1969).

93. On the importance of Câmara, see chap. 5.

94. H. Zambrano, "Mi amigo Camilo Torres," and J. L. Segundo, "Camilo Torres, sacerdocio y violencia," *Víspera* 1:1 (1967); Alberto Methol Ferré, "La Revolución verde olive, Debray y la OLAS," *Víspera* 1:3 (October 1967); "La muerte del Che" and "Reflexiones pacíficas sobre la revolución," *Víspera* 1:4 (January 1968); Alberto Methol Ferré, "Precisiones sobre la crítica al foquismo," *Víspera* 1:5 (April 1968); "La represión y el compromiso del cristiano," *SPES* 1:8 (1970); "A qué Iglesia nos referimos," *SPES* 1:9 (1970); and "Colombia, cartas de militantes," *SPES* 2:11 (1970).

95. "Adviento en América Latina" and "El P. Carbone y la justicia argentina," *SPES* 1:10 (1970); "Chile: Iglesia y socialism," *SPES* 2:13–14 (1971); and "Aproximación a la realidad latinoamericana," *SPES* 3:19 (1972).

96. J. Gaido, "Parroquia universitaria Cristo Obrero," *Víspera* 1:1 (1967); and "La sesión mundial de la JECI," *SPES* 2:15–16 (1971).

97. "América Latina, Patria Grande"; "Montevideo: La partida del Secretariado," *Víspera* 6:26 (March 1972); and "Mi fe creció en la prisión," *SPES* 2:19 (1972).

98. "Mi fe creció en la prisión," *SPES* 2:19 (1972).

99. Gutiérrez, interview with the author.

100. Gutiérrez, *Teología de la liberación* (1971).

101. Nessan, *The Vitality of Liberation Theology*, 43–48; and Salazar Palacio, *La guerra secreta del Cardenal.*

102. Lernoux, *Cry of the People*, 306.

103. The other teachers were Ramón Martínez Silva, Penella, Alfonso Zahar Vergara, and Adolfo Menéndez Samará.

104. See, e.g., David Mayagoitia, "Hace veinticinco años," *Rumbo* (March–April 1968); Jorge Rendón Alarcón, "Martin Luther King," *Rumbo* (May–June 1968); and Francisco Riñon G., "Unas palabras para el diálogo marxista cristiano," *Rumbo* (March–April 1971).

105. See chap. 5.

106. Pérez, interview with the author.

107. Costa and Bermeo, interviews with the author.

108. Gutiérrez, interview with the author.

3. COMBATIVE JOURNALISM AND DIVISIONS WITHIN THE CHURCH

1. Other key books published during these early years included Ortiz, *Jueves de Corpus*; and Tirado et al., *El 10 de junio y la izquierda radical.*

2. "Sangriento jueves de corpus," *La Nación* (July 1, 1971); "La procuraduría y el 10 de junio, II," *La Nación* (August 15, 1971); and "El equipo de 'los halcones': ¿Cinismo oficial o remordimiento?," *La Nación* (September 15, 1971).

3. "Murió uno de los periodistas y políticos más temidos y respetados: El panista Gerardo Medina," *Proceso* (August 20, 1994).

4. In comparison to its Latin American counterparts, the PAN did not officially embrace a Christian identity. It established an ambiguous relationship with ecclesiastical authorities and failed to associate itself with the international Christian Democratic movement. See Loaeza, "The National Action Party."

5. See Mabry, *Mexico's Acción Nacional.*

6. See chaps. 1 and 2.

7. Pacheco Hinojosa, *Iglesia católica*; Pérez Rosales, "La revista Señal"; and Torres Septién, "Estado contra Iglesia / Iglesia contra Estado."

8. See, e.g., Gillingham, *Journalism, Satire, and Censorship in Mexico.*

9. Leñero, *Los periodistas.*

10. See, e.g., Freije, *Citizens of Scandal.*

11. Noted exceptions include Smith, *The Mexican Press and Civil Society;* and Pérez Rosales, "La revista Señal."

12. An analogous but radical turn to the Left was also evident in the history of the Mexican Social Secretariat and the National Center of Social Communications (CENCOS).

13. See chap. 2.

14. Pérez Miranda, *El parlamento de los pueblos*, 15–18.

15. Pérez Miranda, *El parlamento de los pueblos*, 15–18; and González Torres, letter to Díaz de Urdanivia, January 30, 1950, in CEDISPAN.

16. Pérez Miranda, *El parlamento de los pueblos*, 18–30.

17. He was particularly famous for his columns on bullfighting.

18. See chap. 9.

19. Hernández Vicencio, *Revolución y constitución*.

20. Pérez Miranda, *El parlamento de los pueblos*; Mügemburg, *La cruz*; and *La Nación* (1958–63).

21. Pérez Rosales, "La revista Señal.

22. Velázquez, *Pedro Velázquez*.

23. Pérez Rosales, "La revista Señal."

24. Torres Septién, "Estado contra Iglesia / Iglesia contra Estado," 67. See also Loaeza, *Clases medias*.

25. Leñero, *Gente así*; "Murió uno de los periodistas"; and Bermeo, interview with the author.

26. Serrano Álvarez, *Prensa y oposición política en México*.

27. Leñero, *Gente así*; "Murió uno de los periodistas."

28. See, e.g., Gerardo Medina, "Politécnicos y normalistas, sin darse cuenta... están siendo utilizados por el PC," *La Nación* (May 13, 1956).

29. Mabry, *Mexico's Acción Nacional*; and Mügemburg, *La cruz*.

30. Under the supervision of Tomás Montero Torres, these photographers were Antonio Velázquez and Fernando Delgado, among others.

31. For a description of the importance of photography in newspapers during the 1968 student movement, see Del Castillo Troncoso, *Ensayo sobre el movimiento estudiantil de 1968*.

32. Pensado, *Rebel Mexico*, 36; and *La Nación* (1956–61).

33. See chap. 2.

34. Mügemburg, *La cruz*.

35. Among others, these young panistas were Hugo Gutiérrez Vega, Carlos Arriola, Manuel Rodríguez Lapuente, and Emilio Tiessen.

36. Mügemburg, *La cruz*; Mabry, *Mexico's Acción Nacional*; and Gómez Peralta, "Los orígenes de la Democracia Cristiana en el Partido Acción Nacional."

37. Pensado, "Silencing Rebellious Priests."

38. *La Nación* (1961–68).

39. *La Nación* (1961–68); and Mabry, *Mexico's Acción Nacional*.

40. *La Nación* (1961–68); and Mügemburg, *La cruz*.

41. Among others, they included Salvador Flores Llamas, Luis Leñero Otero, Manuel Ignacio Ulloa, Jaime Cabeza de Vaca, and Luis Felipe Coello Macías.

42. See chap. 2.

43. Salvador Flores Llamas, "Frente al peligro comunista," "Ahora, calemos hondo," "Hoy como ayer," "Lucha sin tregua," and "Preparémonos para la lucha"; Luis Leñero Otero, "La evolución social," "Política y sociedad," "La Revolución Social," "¿La Paz?," "La realidad social y su conocimiento," and "El crecimiento en México"; Mario Rodríguez de la Vega G., "Anticomunismo, la propaganda," "Misión social del empresariado," "¿De quién es culpa?," "Anticlericalismo," "¡Entusiasmo!," and "Relaciones Humanas"; Jaime Cabeza de Vaca, "Una nueva actitud," "Desde abajo," and "La Revolución es para México y no México para la Revolución; Manuel Ignacio Ulloa, "Los imperialismos" and "Cristianismo y Revolución Mexicana"; and Luis Felipe Coello, "Ante el peligro," *Señal*, June 11, 1961 to February 18, 1962.

44. Salvador Flores Llamas, "Ahora calemos hondo," *Señal* (July 30, 1961).

45. This was the case of Luis Leñero Otero, the brother of the Catholic novelist Vicente Leñero.

46. These were the respective cases of Manuel Ignacio Ulloa, Jaime Cabeza de Vaca, and Salvador Flores Llamas.

47. See chap. 9.

48. Pensado, "To Assault with the Truth"; and Santiano Jiménez, "Anticomunismo."

49. Luis Felipe Coello, "Ante el peligro"; and Rius Facius, *¡Excomulgado!*

50. Pensado, "To Assault with the Truth."

51. See chap. 9.

52. See chap. 2.

53. Mügemburg, *La cruz*; and Guerrero Olivares, *Una generación desconocida*.

54. See chap. 7.

55. On Leñero, see chap. 8.

56. See, e.g., "La mordida," *Señal* (March 5, 1970); "Los cómics, el medio olvidado," *Señal* (October 22, 1970); and "La corrupción en México," *Señal* (April 15, 1972).

57. Miguel Ángel Granados Chapa, "Tensiones en la Universidad," *Señal* (February 6, 1968).

58. Miguel Ángel Granados Chapa, "Crisis en las Universidades," *Señal* (May 9, 1968); and "Una educación humanista," *Señal* (September 12, 1968).

59. Miguel Ángel Granados Chapa, "El conflicto estudiantil: Sentido y alcance de la autonomía," *Señal* (August 13, 1968); and "Los intereses no estudiantiles," *Señal* (August 29, 1968).

60. Miguel Ángel Granados Chapa, "Trasfondo de la crisis," *Señal* (September 26, 1968); "¿Camino a la solución?," *Señal* (October 10, 1968); "Ante el retorno a clases," *Señal* (December 5, 1968); "Erupciones estudiantiles," *Señal* (June 5, 1969); "La UNAM hoy," *Señal* (August 14, 1970); "Los 'porristas,' delincuentes," *Señal* (September 10, 1970); "Hacia la nueva universidad," *Señal* (February 8, 1971); and "Las porras," *Señal* (August 28, 1971).

61. Miguel Ángel Granados Chapa, "¿Podemos aceptar el socialismo? Definitivamente sí," *Señal* (November 6, 1970).

62. By 1969 Vekemans had published several books on these topics, including, among many others, *Integración latinoamericana y solidaridad internacional* (1968).

63. See also Guerrero Olivares, *Una generación desconocida*.

64. Loaeza, "The National Action Party," 218.

65. See the similar case that the writer for *Atisbos* and *El Sol de México* and graduate of the School of Journalism, Manuel Magaña Contrera, made in his 1971 book, *Troya juvenil*.

4. RESPONSES TO THE TLATELOLCO
AND CORPUS CHRISTI MASSACRES

1. "Elvia Alcaraz Astudillo contraerá matrimonio," *Novedades* (October 1, 1968); Mireya Cuéllar, "Una boda teñida de sangre," *La Jornada* (October 2, 2001); and Poniatowska, *Massacre in Mexico*, 211, 229–35, 274.

2. Trejo, cited in Juan Arvizu, "México 68: El arte de la represión," *El Universal* (October 1, 2008); and Morales (pseudonym), interview with the author.

3. Brewster, *Responding to Crisis in Contemporary Mexico*, 51; and Fuentes, *Tiempo mexicano*, 153.

4. Del Castillo Troncoso, *La matanza del jueves de corpus*; and Ovalle, *Tiempo suspendido*.

5. González, "Algunos grupos radicales de izquierda y de derecha."

6. I presented some preliminary findings in Pensado, "The Anonymous Dead of 1968 Mexico."

7. "Carta Pastoral sobre integración y desarrollo del país," March 26, 1968, *Christus* (May 1, 1968).

8. Pensado, *Rebel Mexico*, 206.

9. "Al pueblo mexicano," September 10, 1968, AHAM.

10. García, interview with the author.

11. Velázquez, *Pedro Velázquez*.

12. Méndez Arceo, cited in Fazio, *No quiero ser perro mudo*.

13. García and Reygadas, interviews with the author.

14. Ernesto Corripio Ahumada, "Mensaje Pastoral," October 9, 1968, AHAM; and García, interview with the author.

15. See also the case of the Dominican director of *Contacto*, Alex Morelli, in chap. 5.

16. Aspe Armella, *Cambiar en tiempos revueltos*.

17. "Carta del padre Arrupe a los Provinciales de América Latina," December 12, 1966, in Del Valle, *Siempre humano*, 147–56; and Arrupe, *Essential writings*.

18. "Carta a los Jesuitas de América Latina, Río de Janeiro," May 6–14, 1968, in Del Valle, *Siempre humano*, 140–46; "Carta del Padre General Pedro Arrupe a todos padres jesuitas miembros de los CIAS de América Latina," *Contacto* (May and June 1968); and "Declaración del P. Provincial de los jesuitas mexicanos," *Christus* (April 1972).

19. These included Miguel Ángel Granados Chapa (from *Señal, Crucero,* and *Excélsior*), Froylán López Narvaez (from *Excélsior*), Pablo Latapí (from *Christus* and the Center of Educational Studies), Alejandro Avilés (from *La Nación*), and Tomás Alláz (from *Siempre!* and the University Cultural Center at UNAM).

20. Hélder Cámara, "Carta a los jóvenes," *Christus* (June 1968); Hernán Larraín, "Los jóvenes, ¿nuevo poder?" *Christus* (February 1969); Martín de la Rosa, "Conclusiones (de Medellín): El Establishment," *Christus* (December 1970); Enrique Marroquín, "Avándaro interpela a la Iglesia," *Christus* (November 1971); and Luis del Valle, "En búsqueda del método," *Christus* (November 1972).

21. "Fallece Enrique Maza, fundador de Proceso," *Proceso* (December 24, 2015); Julio Scherer García, "De la vida profunda de Enrique Maza," *Proceso* (January 8, 2018); and García, interview with the author.

22. See chap. 7 for similar descriptions of the concept of dialogue by the Dominican friars at UNAM.

23. Enrique Maza, "Los sacerdotes también necesitamos dialogar," "Que se debe decir al pueblo," "La actitud postconciliar," "Sobre la justicia social," "Un nuevo tipo de religioso y sacerdote," "Nuestro silencio es complice," "La situación social de México," and "Iglesia mexicana," *Christus* (November 1966, November 1967, September 1968, April 1969, March 1970, August 1970, April 1971, and June 1971).

24. Enrique Maza, "El movimiento estudiantil y sus repercusiones para la Iglesia," *Christus* (December 1968); Aspe Armella, *Cambiar en tiempos revueltos,* 134–49; and Enrique Maza, "México: 'Iglesia y movimiento estudiantil," MIEC-JECI, *Documentos* 3:11 (1969).

25. Maza, "El movimiento estudiantil."

26. Fazio, *No quiero ser perro mudo.*

27. Fazio, *No quiero ser perro mudo,* 31–40. See also "Homilía en la Basílica de Guadalupe," CIDOC, Doc. 71:319 (1971). My emphasis.

28. Gerardo Medina, "Huichilobos vuelve a Tlatelolco," *La Nación* (October 15, 1968); and *¿Por Qué?,* Special Number (October 1968).

29. *Diario de los debates,* September 1, 1969, 25.

30. Medina Valdés, *Operación 10 de junio.* See also chap. 2.

31. See, e.g., Elena Poniatowska, "El movimiento," *Contacto* (September 1971).

32. See chap. 3 for the case of Granados Chapa in *Señal.*

33. Gabriel Zaid, "Carta a Carlos Fuentes," *Plural* (September 2, 1972); Fernando García Ramírez, "Gabriel Zaid, ¿Crítica, para qué?"; and Castillo Troncoso, *La matanza del jueves de corpus,* 46, 54–57.

34. Besides Zaid, other Catholics who collaborated with Elizondo included Miguel Ángel Granados Chapa and Vicente Leñero.

35. García Ramírez, "Gabriel Zaid"; Gabriel Zaid, "Gaspar, cultura y fe," *La Jornada* (June 18, 1997); and *Informaciones Católicas Internacionales,* 1968–72.

36. Zaid, "Carta a Carlos Fuentes"; and Cosío Villegas, *El estilo personal de gobernar.*

37. Blancarte, *Historia de la iglesia católica en México,* 299–305; and Pensado, "Silencing Rebellious Priests."

38. Blancarte, *Historia de la iglesia católica en México*, 299–305.

39. Solis Mimendi, *Jueves de Corpus*; and Del Castillo Troncoso, *La matanza del jueves de corpus*, 56. On Echeverría's commitment to human rights, see Quezada, "The Revolution in Crisis."

40. Pensado, "Silencing Rebellious Priests."

5. THE THORNY QUESTIONS OF ARMED STRUGGLE AND SOCIALISM

1. Leñero, *Compañero*.

2. Leñero, *Teatro documental*; Leñero, *Vivir del teatro*; and Hartch, *The Prophet of Cuernavaca*.

3. Leñero, *Teatro documental*.

4. González (pseudonym), interview with the author. See also Kunzle, *Chesucristo*.

5. Leñero, *Viaje a Cuba*.

6. Leñero, *Vivir del teatro*, 62.

7. Luis Suárez, "Fray Alberto de Ezcurdia," *Siempre!* (September 1962).

8. Rodríguez Araujo, "Católicos contra el capitalismo."

9. García, interview with the author.

10. "Reunión de responsables," unspecified DFS document, 1966, 11–27.

11. Pacheco Hinojosa, *Iglesia católica;* and González, "Algunos grupos radicales de izquierda y de derecha."

12. Pensado, "El Movimiento Estudiantil Profesional (MEP)."

13. Álvarez Gutiérrez, "De católico a guerrillero"; and Guerrero Olivares, *Una generación desconocida.*

14. Álvarez Gutiérrez, "La OCU."

15. Álvarez Gutiérrez, "La OCU," 186–88.

16. Álvarez Gutiérrez, "La OCU," 197; and González, "Algunos grupos radicales de izquierda y de derecha."

17. Álvarez Gutiérrez, "La OCU," 98; Álvarez Gutiérrez, "De católico a guerrillero," 128; and García, interview with the author.

18. Del Valle, *Siempre humano*, 49, 266–69; and De la Rosa, *Promoción popular*, 71–79.

19. "Sobre el 10 de junio," *Liberación* (July 1971).

20. José Luis Sierra, "El sistema mexicano ante los hechos del 10 de junio," *Contacto* (September 1971).

21. Pensado, "El Movimiento Estudiantil Profesional (MEP)"; and Del Valle, *Siempre humano*, 269–70.

22. Ovalle, *Tiempo suspendido*.

23. Tirado et al., *El 10 de junio y la izquierda radical*.

24. Martín de la Rosa, "La revolución no se hace en la cafetería," *Contacto* (September 1971): 96–97.

25. Laffay, "Le pére Morelli," 298–300; and Malley and Chambon, *Le Pére Morelli*, 29–41.

26. Malley and Chambon, *Le Pére Morelli*, 29–41; and Monreal, "Dominicos de Toulouse en Montevideo."

27. Monreal, "Dominicos de Toulouse en Montevideo."

28. Monreal, "Dominicos de Toulouse en Montevideo"; Laffay, "Le pére Morelli," 320–24; and Malley and Chambon, *Le Pére Morelli*, 47–60.

29. See chap. 7.

30. Morelli, *Hacia una iglesia popular*, 7–10.

31. Malley and Chambon, *Le Pére Morelli*, 157–158.

32. Malley and Chambon, *Le Pére Morelli*; and Morelli, *Hacia una iglesia popular*, 8–11.

33. Velázquez, interview with the author.

34. This was also true of *Christus*, as described in chap. 4.

35. *Contacto* (October 1972, June 1971, and December 1974).

36. Morelli, *Hacia una iglesia popular*, 11–12.

37. Alex Morelli, "Sobre el 10 de junio," "Medellín, piedra de escándalo," "La larga marcha," and "Hacia un nuevo orden internacional," *Contacto* (September 1971, October 1973, April 1974, and January–April 1975).

38. Guevara, "Message to the Tricontinental."

39. Alex Morelli, "Reflexión espiritual," "La no violencia revolucionaria," "¿Violencia o no violencia para América Latina?," "Proposiciones para una revolución no violenta," "Liberación y violencia," and "Nuevos elementos para una Teología de Liberación," *Contacto* (January–February 1968, November–December 1968, February 1972, and October 1972).

40. De la Rosa, "La teología de Camilo Torres," *Liberación* (February 1972); and *Christus* (May 1972).

41. De la Rosa, *Promoción popular*; Oliveros de Miranda, "José Porfirio Miranda"; and Álvarez Gutiérrez, "De católico a guerrillero," 106–7.

42. Del Valle, *Siempre humano*, 263.

43. Álvarez Gutiérrez, "De católico a guerrillero," 107.

44. Enrique Maza, "¿Por qué me hice sacerdote?," *Christus* (December 1969); and "¿Un nuevo tipo de religiosos y de sacerdote?," *Christus* (March 1970).

45. Martín de la Rosa, "El drama de los cristianos revolucionarios," *Christus* (November 1972).

46. On the role of progressive priests in Nezahualcóyotl, see also Yee, *Informal Metropolis*, chap. 8.

47. Malley and Chambon, *Le Pére Morelli*, 88–91, 128.

48. Malley and Chambon, *Le Pére Morelli*, 83.

49. Malley and Chambon, *Le Pére Morelli*, 87–88.

50. See also Yee, *Informal Metropolis*, chap. 8.

51. Malley and Chambon, *Le Pére Morelli*, 88.

52. Malley and Chambon, *Le Pére Morelli*, 129.

53. Malley and Chambon, *Le Pére Morelli*, 129, 152–53.

54. Malley and Chambon, *Le Pére Morelli*, 137–43.

55. Malley and Chambon, *Le Pére Morelli*, 145–49.

56. Malley and Chambon, *Le Pére Morelli*, 80–81.

57. Reygadas, interview with the author.

58. See chap. 7.

59. Reygadas, interview with the author.

60. See chap. 7.

61. Reygadas, interview with the author. Quoted passages in the next paragraph also from this interview.

62. Specifically, with the Family Christian Movement.

63. Prior to *Pedagogía del oprimido*, Freire published the Spanish version of *Educación como práctica de la libertad* in Chile in 1965.

64. Guzmán and Dosil, "Paulo Freire." See also Yee, *Informal Metropolis*, chap. 8.

65. Guzmán and Dosil, "Paulo Freire"; and Reygadas, interview with the author. See also De la Rosa, *Alfabetizar concientizando*.

66. Reygadas, interview with the author.

67. García, interview with the author.

68. See chap. 7.

69. "Marx y la Biblia, a propósito de un libro," *Contacto* (September 1971): 86. The book was also discussed on Saldaña's popular television show, *Anatomías*, in July 1971.

70. See respectively, Álvarez Gutiérrez, "La OCU"; and Álvarez Gutiérrez, "De católico a guerrillero," 138–141.

71. André Gunder Frank, "Dependencia económica, estructura de clases y política del subdesarrollo en Latinoamérica"; Immanuel Wallerstein, "El ascenso y futura desaparición del sistema capitalista. Conceptos para un análisis comparativo"; "Carta abierta de Iván Illich a su santidad. El silencio de Paulo VI"; "Pide el Obispo Méndez Arceo plegarias para que se reflexione sobre los sucesos del jueves"; "Contra el acarreo a misa y manifestaciones públicas se pronunció Mons. Méndez Arceo"; "Se Explica con los periodistas Méndez Arceo"; "Socialismo democrático para el desarrollo Latinoamericano"; Daniel Berrigan, "Carta a los Jesuitas"; Xavier Leon-Dufour, "La violencia según la biblia"; Harvey Cox, "Religión: de la esclavitud a la liberación"; Germán Guzmán Campos, "Ideario del padre Camilo Torres sobre la violencia"; Martin de la Rosa, "La teología de Camilo Torres"; José P. Miranda, "La moral de los secuestros (en América del Sur)"; "Carta: segundo aniversario de la masacre de Tlatelolco"; and El Secretariado para el Apostolado de los Seglares declara en torno a los sucesos del jueves 10 de junio." All in *Liberación* (December 1969–December 1972).

72. Reygadas and García, interviews with the author.

73. García, interview with the author; and "Movimiento base del movimiento Sacerdotes para el Pueblo," *Contacto* (December 1972).

74. "Documento del primer Congreso del movimiento 'Sacerdotes para el Pueblo,'" *Contacto* (February 1972); García, "La Iglesia mexicana desde 1962";

and Luis del Valle, "Encuentro de Sacerdotes para el Pueblo," *Christus* (August 1973).

75. Del Valle, *Siempre humano*, 280–83.

76. Malley and Chambon, *Le Père Morelli*, 164–65.

77. Jo, "Movimiento 'Sacerdotes para el Pueblo.'"

78. García, interview with the author; De la Rosa, *Promoción popular*; and Del Valle, *Siempre humano*.

79. See chap. 2.

80. Manzano, letter to Salas, February 4, 1969; Salas Obregón, letter to the MEP, May 30, 1969; and Hernández, letter to Manzano, September 23, 1969, ASLA-FLP, MIEC-JECI file.

81. Hernández, letter to Buenaventura, July 18, 1970; and Ignacio Salas Obregón, "El problema del hombre," n.d., ASLA-FLP, MIEC-JECI file.

82. Bertand, *Hacia la puerta*; and Álvarez Gutiérrez, "La OCU."

83. García, interview with the author.

84. Del Valle, *Siempre humano*, 69, 265–66.

85. Hernández, letter to Montevideo, January 10, 1969, ASLA-FLP, MIEC-JECI file.

86. Hernández, letter to Montevideo, January 10, 1969, and letter to Adveniat, January 20, 1969, ASLA-FLP, MIEC-JECI file. On Adveniat and the Latin American Secretariat, see chap. 2.

87. Hernández, letter to Manzano, March 13, 1969, ASLA-FLP, MIEC-JECI file.

88. Hernández, letter to "Estudiantes en Cristo," May 26, 1969, ASLA-FLP, MIEC-JECI file.

89. Hernández, letter to Manzano, September 23, 1969, ASLA-FLP, MIEC-JECI file.

90. Hernández, letter from Morelia, "Reflexión sobre el medio estudiantil y la iglesia," January 2, 1970, ASLA-FLP, MIEC-JECI file.

91. Hernández, letter to Merino, February 24, 1972; and letter to Manzano, March 6, 1972, ASLA-FLP, MIEC-JECI file.

92. García, Reygadas, and Marroquín, interviews with the author.

93. Vasquez (pseudonym), interview with the author. See the similar account given by in Del Valle, *Siempre humano*, 269.

94. Pensado, "El Movimiento Estudiantil Profesional (MEP)."

95. Vasquez, interview with the author.

96. Manzano, interview with the author.

97. Quezada, "The Revolution in Crisis."

98. Pensado, "Silencing Rebellious Priests."

99. Pensado, "Silencing Rebellious Priests."

100. Francisco Merino, letter to Pregardier, July 17, 1972, AA.

101. Londono-Ardila, "Consciousness-Raising and Liberation."

102. Luis Sereno Coló, letter to Pregardier, May 26, 1976; Hoffacker, letter to Luis Sereno Coló, May 25, 1975; Luis Sereno Coló, letter to Stehele, September 8,

1977; and Luis Sereno Coló, "Proyecto para el trabajo de American Latina del Secretariado del MIIC, para el año de 1979," December 23, 1978, AA.

103. Luis Sereno Coló, letters to Bernardo Syeber, February 27, May 18, and July 2, 1979; Luis Sereno Coló, letter to Bernardo Syeber, July 27, 1979; Bernardo Syeber, letter to Luis Sereno Coló, August 2, 1979; Luis Sereno Coló, letter to Pax Romana, February 2, 1980; and Luis Sereno Coló, letter to Bernardo Syeber, February 10, 1982, AA.

104. Vasquez, interview with the author. Specifically, she referred to the leftist magazine *Proceso* and the lay organization headed by CENCOS.

105. Luis Sereno Coló, letter to Bernardo Syeber, February 10, 1982; letter to Pregardier, April 12, 1982; and "Encuentro Latinaomericano del MIIC en Ecuador, September 2, 1982, AA.

106. Almanza Villarreal and Torres González, interviews with the author.

107. Almanza Villarreal, interview with the author.

108. Torres González, interview with the author.

109. Torres González and Almanza Villarreal, interviews with the author.

110. Pensado, "Silencing Rebellious Priests."

111. Almanza Villarreal and Torres González, interviews with the author; "Torres González Héctor," DFS, Versión Pública, 169 pp.; "Almanza Villarreal, Eufemia Belén," DFS, Versión Pública, 25 pp., AGN.

112. Almanza Villarreal and Torres González, interviews with the author.

113. Bertand, *Hacia la puerta*.

114. Carassai, *The Argentine Silent Majority*.

115. Bertand, *Hacia la puerta*; and Oliveros de Miranda, "José Porfirio Miranda."

116. Torres González, interview with the author.

117. See, e.g., the accounts given in Guerrero Olivares, *Una generación desconocida*.

118. Luis Sereno Coló, "Características del medio universitario como condicionante de la acción católica universitaria," n.d.; "IV Convención Nacional de Estudiantes," *ACM: Boletín de la Junta Central* 27:12 (October 15, 1963); "Panorama estudiantil internacional," *MEP: Información Estudiantil* 1:2 (January 15, 1963); and Mario Zarduño, S.J., "Subdesarrollo político," *MEP: Documentos*, no. 2 (May 1965), AHAM.

119. Sereno Coló, "Características" and "El Militante," *MEP: Documentos*, no. 3 (June 1965), AHAM.

120. Sereno Coló, "Características"; and MEP, "Ambiente universitario: Visita realizada a la Ciudad de Guadalajara," September 2, 1969, ASLA-FLP, MIEC-JECI file.

121. MEP, "Equipo Coordinador," n.d.; and Anaya, "Opiniones y declaraciones: Poder juvenil," ASLA-FLP, MIEC-JECI file.

122. MEP, "Conclusiones, seminario, realidad nacional" (March 1967), ASLA-FLP, MIEC-JECI file.

123. Manzano, interview with the author.

6. *LA ONDA* AS LIBERATION AND THE MAKING
OF *LA CONTRACULTURA COMO PROTESTA*

1. Marroquín, interview with the author.

2. Marroquín, interview with the author.

3. Marroquín, interview with the author; and Marroquín, *Historia y profecía*, 34–49.

4. Marroquín, interview with the author.

5. García, interview with the author.

6. Marroquín, interview with the author; and Marroquín, *La contracultura como protesta*, 22.

7. Marroquín, interview with the author; and King, *Angel with Drumsticks*, 58–63.

8. On the Zona Rosa, see chap. 8.

9. Zolov, *Refried Elvis*; and Randall, *Los Hippies*.

10. Zolov, *Refried Elvis*; Dawson, "Salvador Roquet, María Sabina, and the Trouble with *Jipis*"; and Estrada, *Huautla en tiempos de hippies*.

11. By the late 1960s Benítez published these findings in two books that became influential in the Mexican counterculture, *La tierra mágica del peyote* (1969) and *Los hongos alucinantes* (1970). See Estrada, *Huautla en tiempos de hippies*; and Marroquín, *La contracultura como protesta*, 35.

12. Estrada, *Huautla en tiempos de hippies*.

13. On *Claudia*, see chap. 8.

14. These were written by José Agustín, Gustavo Sainz, Parménides García Saldaña, and Margarita Dalton, respectively.

15. Glantz, *Onda y escritura*.

16. Debroise and Medina, *La era de la discrepancia*.

17. "Todas a San Luis Potosí a nuestro segundo encuentro cultural," *Juventud* (November 1966); and "Queremos vivir y hacer vivir el amor," *Juventud Católica* (November 1966).

18. "La psicología moderna y la vida sexual," *Cencos* (April 28, 1967).

19. "Consideraciones del Episcopado mexicano acerca de la 'Humanae Vitae,'" August 9, 1968, AACM; Felitti, "De la 'mujer moderna' a la 'mujer liberada'"; and Espino Armendariz, "Feminismo católico en México."

20. See, e.g., JCFM, "V Encuentro Cultural in Puebla," August 7–9, 1970, AACM.

21. M. Lara, "El amor libre, visto por muchachas de hoy," *Señal* (November 17, 1970). See similar comments in "La mujer en el presente," *Juventud Católica* (December 1970).

22. See chap. 1.

23. "III Encuentro Cultural de la Juventud" and "V Encuentro Cultural," JCFM Pamphlets, November 22–24, 1968, and August 7–9, 1970, AACM.

24. Javier Duplá, "La ola de sexo" and "Liberación sexual de la mujer," *Señal* (January 1, 1971).

25. See, e.g., Julio Chávez Montes, "La píldora," Pedro Richards CP, La píldora II," *Señal* (January 29, 1970); and "La píldora de feminiza a la mujer," *Señal* (May 7, 1970).

26. Gaspar Elizondo, "Llegaron los hippies," *Señal* (February 15, 1968).

27. Joaquín Antonio Peñalosa, "Una clase sobre hippies," *Señal* (July 11, 1968); Joaquín Antonio Peñalosa, "Tanto tienes, tal te drogas," *Señal* (October 9, 1970); and Joaquín Antonio Peñalosa, "¿Por qué los jóvenes nos drogamos?" *Señal* (March 10, 1973).

28. Key national figures participated in the forum, including the comic actor Mario Moreno Cantinflas, the chronicler Carlos Monsiváis, and the cartoonist Abel Quezada.

29. "II Foro Internacional de la Juventud: Violencia, drogas, erotismo," *Señal* (February 19, 1970); Carlos Aparicio Martínez, "Los que propicia la afición a las drogas es el medio insano que los adultos hemos creado," *Señal* (February 26, 1970); and Carlos Aparicio Martínez, "Cuatro armas contra la mariguana," *Señal* (April 9, 1970). See also "Las drogas y sus males," *Juventud Católica* (December 1970).

30. Alberto Barranco Chavarría, "¿Por qué usamos el pelo largo?," *Señal* (May 22, 1971); "¿Qué quiere la juventud?," *Señal* (October 23, 1971); and "El profesor Alejandro Avilés . . . ," *Señal* (November 20, 1971).

31. See appendix 2.

32. Other films that touched on the changing relationship between priests and society in the aftermath of Vatican II include *Las chicas malas del Padre Méndez* (Fernánez Unsáin, 1970) and *El oficio más antiguo del mundo* (Alcoriza, 1970)—as described in Janzen, *Unholy Trinity*.

33. Nuns played similar roles in *El cielo y la tierra* (Corona Blake, 1962) and *Sor Ye Yé* (Fernández, 1968).

34. See chap. 1 and the films listed in appendix 1.

35. Also worth noting is *Patsy, mi amor* (Michel, 1969). On *Los caifanes*, see Solorzano-Thompson, "Vicarious Identities."

36. On the cinematic representations of nuns in Spanish cinema, see Pérez, *Confessional Cinema*, 118–52.

37. See *Cinco de chocolate y uno de fresa* (dir. Carlos Velo, 1967), https://en.wikipedia.org/w/index.php?curid=14722423.

38. See chap. 1 and the films listed in appendix 1.

39. She also starred in *La verdadera vocación de Magdalena* (Hermosillo, 1972).

40. Greene, *Rock, Counterculture and the Avant-Garde*; and Cottrell, *Sex, Drugs, and Rock 'n' Roll*.

41. Zolov, *Refried Elvis*.

42. Marroquín, interview with the author.

43. *Juventud* (March 1967); Jesús Pavlo Tenorio, "La fauna—un conjunto jesuita para el mundo joven," *Señal* (October 23, 1971).

44. Cuetos, interview with the author; and Hernández Vicencio, "Sergio Méndez Arceo."

45. See chaps. 3 and 9.

46. Jesús Pavlo Tenorio, "La drogadicción: Un vicio burgués y reaccionario," interview with Enrique Marroquín, *Christus* (November 1974).

47. Marroquín, interview with the author.

48. Marroquín, interview with the author; Marroquín, *Historia y profecia*, 89–116.

49. See the introduction and chap. 5.

50. This is one of the central arguments of *La contracultura como protesta*.

51. "Un acercamiento Episcopal al fenómeno de las drogas," Jesús Pavlo Tenorio, "La drogadicción," "Síntesis de una entrevista a varios párrocos del D.F acerca del problema de las drogas," and Arnaldo Zenteno, "Tere, una chica de 16 años: Tres meses de mariguana y policía," all in *Christus* (November 1974); Marroquín, interview with the author; and Huxley, *Island*.

52. Marroquín, interview with the author; and Estrada, *Huautla en tiempos de hippies*.

53. Marroquín, interview with the author; Marroquín, *Historia y profecia*, 89–117.

54. Levi, *Aquarian Gospel of Jesus the Christ*; De la Ferreire, *Yug, yoga, yoghismo*; and Huxley, *Island*.

55. Marroquín, interview with the author; and Santos, *The Holy Mountain*. On Jodorowsky, see chap. 9.

56. Marroquín, interview with the author. This is a position shared in Enrique Maza, "El espíritu santo y la mujer," *Christus* (June 1975).

57. Marroquin, interview with the author; and Marroquín, *La contracultura como protesta*, 173.

58. Marroquin, interview with the author. See also Dawson, "Salvador Roquet, María Sabina, and the Trouble with *Jipis*"; and Estrada, *Huauhtla en tiempos de hippies*.

59. Marroquin, interview with the author.

60. Enrique Marroquín, "¿Por qué no intentar de nuevo la presentación de Hair?," *Piedra Rodante* (August 1971).

61. Marroquín, interview with the author; Juan Bosco Estrada, "Jesucristo superestrella," *Christus* (June 1974); and Thompson, *The Rocky Horror Picture Show*.

62. Castillo Bolaños and Maza Reducindo, *La escuela imposible*.

63. Maza Reducindo, interview with the author.

64. See chap. 5 for similar comments by Martín de la Rosa and Alex Morelli.

65. Maza Reducindo, interview with the author.

66. Marroquín, *La contracultura como protesta*.

67. Zolov, *Refried Elvis*, 221.

68. *Piedra Rodante* (May 1971–January 1972).

69. Marroquín, "¿Por qué no intentar de nuevo la presentación de Hair?," *Piedra Rodante* (August 1971).

70. Enrique Marroquín, "Discos (John Lennon)," *Piedra Rodante* (August 1971).

71. Pérez Miranda, *El parlamento de los pueblos*, 28, 134. On the importance of the countercultural magazine *El Corno Emplumado*, see Randall, "Testimonio."

72. See his articles cited in notes 43, 46, and 51.

73. Enrique Marroquín, "Dios quiere que llueva para unirnos," *Piedra Rodante* (October 30, 1971); and Enrique Marroquín, "Cultura pop y represión," *Piedra Rodante* (November 15, 1971).

74. Enrique Marroquín, "Drogas y conciencia trascendental," *Piedra Rodante* (January 1972).

75. Or sentence him to the death penalty, as the conservative journalist Blanco Moheno encouraged in his popular columns in *Siempre!* and *Impacto*.

76. This was the position taken by the chronicler Carlos Monsiváis, the militant writer of *¿Por que?*, Horacio Espinoza, and the cartoonist Eduardo del Rio ("Rius").

77. Zolov, *Refried Elvis*, 222.

78. Marroquín practiced the preferential option for the poor in Christian base communities that he helped build in Mexico City and Puebla from 1972 to the mid-1980s.

79. Among others, he frequently cites Huxley's *Island* (1962); *Gaudium et spes* (Joy and Hope, 1965); and Madows's computerized report on population growth, *The Limits to Growth* (1972).

80. Marroquín, *La contracultura como protesta*, 186–87.

7. DIALOGUE AS LOVE AND COUNTERCULTURAL CINEMA AT UNAM

1. García Riera, *Historia documental del cine mexicano*, vol. 13, 218–19.

2. See chap. 1 for a similar story depicted in *Muchachas de uniforme*.

3. *Hasta el miedo tiene miedo* (Taboada, 1968).

4. Aguirre (pseudonym), interview with the author.

5. In this sense, the CUC differed from the more political Polytechnic Center of Development and University Cultural Workshop, founded respectively by the Marist priests in Mexico City in 1964 and the Jesuits in Monterrey in 1966.

6. Kassman Sack, *America's Teilhard*.

7. Kassman Sack, *America's Teilhard*, 152; and Cerf, "Objetivos, medios y normas," 1967–75, ACUC.

8. Sánchez (pseudonym), interview with the author.

9. Aguirre, interview with the author; and Marcuse, *One-Dimensional Man*.

10. Sánchez and Hernández (pseudonym), interviews with the author.

11. Aguirre, interview with the author; and Cerf, "Objetivos, medios y normas," ACUC.

12. Aguirre, interview with the author.

13. Among others, these friars were Agustín Desobry, Hernando Flores Arazayo, José Sedano, Juan Pablo, Tomás Aláz, and Benito Marín.

14. Sánchez, interview with the author; and "Mujer para un mundo nuevo," *Diálogo* (September–October 1967).

15. See the various pamphlets from 1963 to 1969, ACUC.

16. Sánchez, interview with the author.

17. Sánchez, interview with the author; and Cerf, "Objetivos, medios y normas," ACUC. On Leñero, see chap. 8.

18. Sánchez, interview with the author.

19. Sánchez, interview with the author; and Cerf, "Objetivos, medios y normas," ACUC.

20. Aguirre and Sánchez, interviews with the author.

21. Cerf, "Objetivos, medios y normas," ACUC.

22. Aguirre, interview with the author.

23. Sánchez, interview with the author.

24. See the attempts made by the Corporation of Mexican Students and the MEP, discussed in chap. 2.

25. Cuetos, interview with the author; "Una nueva Universidad para América Latina," in Reunión del Departamento Pastoral Universitario del CELAM, Lima, Peru August 31, 1964, ASLA-FLP, CELAM file; and Duque, letter to all university parishes in Latin America, March 15, 1965, ASLA-FLP, MIEC-JECI file.

26. Cuetos, interview with the author; "Nouvelles de Centre," *Copilco* (June 1964), KADOC, SIGNIS Collection; and McLeod, *The Religious Crisis of the 1960s.*

27. Luis Suárez, "Fray Alberto de Ezcurdia," *Siempre!* (October 1962); Gutiérrez, *Teología de la liberación*; and Horn, *The Spirit of Vatican II.*

28. Suárez, "Fray Alberto."

29. See chap. 3.

30. "De la Sorbonne a l'UNAM," *Copilco* (March 1964), KADOC, SIGNIS Collection.

31. "Por primera vez en México: Católicos y comunistas entablan un diálogo," *Siempre!* (October 1962); Antonio Rodríguez, "La renovación en la iglesia es reprimida y camina sin Dios," *Siempre!* (October 1970); and Saldaña Magdalena, "En Tetelpan descansa fray Alberto de Ezcurdia," *Excélsior* (July 3, 1973).

32. "De la Sorbonne a l'UNAM," *Copilco* (March 1964), KADOC, SIGNIS Collection.

33. This missionary effort was due to a shortage of priests in Latin America combined with the idea that rapid urbanization, Protestantism, and Marxism had created a crisis on the continent.

34. See chap. 5 for the similar case of Alex Morelli.

35. "Registro de la Fundación del CUC," May 25, 1962, ACUC; Cuetos, interview with the author; and "Entrevista con el R.P. Agustín Desobry," *Diálogo* (May–June 1965).

36. Fernández-Cobián, "Psicoanálisis, religión y arquitectura"; and "La cite universitaire," *Copilco* (June, 1964), KADOC, SIGNIS Collection.

37. Concha Malo, interview with the author.

38. Hernández, interview with the author; and Carolina Álvarez de la Cadena Rivero, testimony, in Castañeda Iturbide, *Los años por contar*, 119–21.

39. See chap. 2.

40. Desobry, letter to Estudiantes, October 23, 1961, ACUC; Desobry, letter to Pax Romana, September 8, 1963; and Marcos G. McGrath, letter to Agustin Desobry, August 5, 1964, ASLA-FLP, CELAM file.

41. CUC, *Libro de Oro*, ACUC.

42. These were offered by the Dominican friars, Vicente Eguiguren, Alberto de Ezcurdia, and Laudelino Cuetos, respectively.

43. Luis Suárez, "Sobre fray Tomás Aláz contra el MURO," *Siempre!* (January 1964); and Agustín Desobry, "Los pistoleros de la Parroquia Universitaria," *Diálogo* (July–August 1964).

44. Gutiérrez, Marroquín, and García, interviews with the author.

45. See chap. 1.

46. Cuetos, interview with the author; and Luis Buñuel, in CUC, *Libro de Oro*, ACUC.

47. Aguirre, Cuetos, and Sánchez, interviews with the author.

48. Aguirre, interview with the author; Desobry, letter to Estudiantes, March 2, 1965, ACUC; "Cine clubs y cine forums," *Diálogo* (September–October 1967); and *Teorema* (Pasolini, 1968).

49. Cuetos, interview with the author; and *Teorema*.

50. Hernández, interview with the author.

51. "Brevísima historia del cine en el CUC" and "Nuestros consentidos," in *Cine Arte y CUC: Aniversario, 1974–1979*, KADOC, SIGNIS Collection.

52. Other Dominicans in charge of the cuquitos included Rafael Gerard and Julián Pablo Fernández.

53. "Nace el Proyecto cuquitos en las 9 prepas," 1963; "Cuquitos (para las preparatorias)," *Diálogo* (July–August 1964); "Lo que pensamos: Formación de un Centro de Formación Cristiana Universitaria," *Diálogo* (March–April 1965); "Se crea la Escuela de Dirigentes," CUC, 1964; and Desobry, letter to Estudiantes, March 2, 1965, ACUC.

54. Desobry, Letter, February 2, 1967, ACUC.

55. As examined in chapter 2, this was a goal that the leaders of the Corporation of Mexican Students had similarly expressed in the 1950s.

56. Luis Leñero Otero, "Jornadas para el desarrollo," 1964, ACUC.

57. Desobry, Letter, February 2, 1967; Laudelino Cuetos, "Centro de Acción Social," 1966; and CUC, "Escuelas de dirigentes, programas detallados," 1964–69, ACUC.

58. CUC, "Solicitudes a la escuela de dirigentes," 1968 and 1969, ACUC.

59. Raúl Vera López, testimony, in Castañeda Iturbide, *Los años por contar*, 93–94.

60. Olivia Jiménez Valdés, Yolanda Estrada García, Rebeca Arrieta Soto, Elvia Díaz de León D'Hers, and Carolina Álvarez de la Cadena Rivero, testimonies, in Castañeda Iturbide, *Los años por contar*, 85–121.

61. Sánchez, Hernández, and Aguirre, interviews with the author.

62. "Lo que pensamos. Diálogo ¿Por qué?," *Diálogo* (July–August 1964); "Carta de Desobry a un muy estimado señor sobre la revista *Diálogo*" (July 1964); and Desobry, letter to Estudiantes, March 2, 1965, ACUC.

63. See also "Reflexiones de un pagana sobre el arte de amar," *Diálogo* (May–June 1965).

64. On these conservative magazines, see chaps. 1 and 2.

65. "Diálogo con la ciencia," *Diálogo* (September–October 1966); "La veterinaria y su función social," *Diálogo* (March–April 1966); "El estudio de las humanidades" and "Sentido de la historia," *Diálogo* (July–August 1966); "En torno a la Ingeniería," *Diálogo* (October–November 1966); "Función social del comercio y la administración," "Pop Art, nueva dimension de la estética," and "La persona como vocación," *Diálogo* (September–October 1967).

66. *Diálogo* (May–June 1967).

67. "Para comprender la enciclica," *Diálogo* (May–June 1967); and *Populorum progressio*.

68. See "Actividades del CUC," *Díalogo* (1966–67).

69. "Fellini, *8½*," *Diálogo* (March–April 1965); and *8½* (Fellini, 1963).

70. "Nuestros consentidos," *Cine Arte y CUC: Aniversario, 1974–1979*, ACUC; *The Gospel according to St. Matthew* (Pasolini, 1964); and *Blow-Up* (Antonioni, 1966).

71. "Vietnam en cifras," *Diálogo* (September–October 1967); and Alberto de Ezcurdia, "Marxismo y cristianismo," *Siempre!* (September 1967).

72. Jardón, *1968, el fuego de la esperanza*, 56; Zermeño, *México, una democracia utópica*, 195–97.

73. Desobry, "Declaración de la Parroquia Universitaria," October 1968, ACUC; and Cuetos, interview with the author.

74. Agustín Desobry, "Declaración: La PU no tiene relación con MURO," September 16, 1968, ACUC.

75. Laudelino Cuetos, "¿Que es el CUC?," ACUC.

76. Pérez Torrent, "Crises and Renovations," 100.

77. Vázquez Mantecón, *El cine súper 8 en México*.

78. Costa, *La "apertura" cinematográfica*.

79. Burton, *Cinema and Social Change in Latin America*.

80. Ciuk, *Diccionario de directores del cine mexicano*, 349–50; and Filmoteca UNAM, *El Grito, memoria en movimiento*.

81. Desmond, *Cynics*, 24.

82. Appelbaum, *St. Francis of America*, 110–35.

83. Appelbaum, *St. Francis of America*, 110–35.

84. See chap. 1.

85. *Juventud Católica* (May 1958); Ruszkowski, letter to Ziegler (November 30, 1959); Romero Pérez, letter to Miranda (October 25, 1961); *OCIC—Informaciones*, no. 3 (March–April 1962); *OCIC—Informaciones*, no. 11 (November–December 1963); and "CENCOS, cursos de capacitación e iniciación cinematográfica" (June 9, 1966), ASLA-FLP, OCIC file.

86. See also the similar case that Andrés Ruszkowski made in Lima, Peru, during the late 1950s and early 1960s, as discussed in chap. 1.

87. Romero Pérez, *El cine, arma de dos filos*.

88. Braun, "Protest of Engagement."

8. SEXUAL LIBERATION AND THE
REDEMPTION OF HOMOSEXUALITY

1. *El monasterio de los buitres* (Del Valle, 1973); and Gallo, *Freud's Mexico*, 117–151.

2. De la Torre, *Vivir del cine*, 61; and Leñero, "El monasterio de los buitres," film script, 1973, CDF-UNAM.

3. In 1976, Jorge Fons directed a film with the same title.

4. Leñero, *Los albañiles*.

5. Franco Leñero, *Rosario Castellanos*.

6. See, e.g., Leñero, *Viaje a Cuba*.

7. Niño, "Religión y sociedad en la obra de Vicente Leñero"; and Anderson, *Vicente Leñero*.

8. De la Torre, *Vivir del cine*; Cheren, "Entrevista inedita a Vicente Leñero"; and Day, "Entrevista con Vicente Leñero."

9. *Cadena perpetua* (Ripstein, 1978).

10. Leñero, *Los periodistas*.

11. An exception, which I rely on in this chapter, is Ramírez Berg, *Cinema of Solitude*.

12. Valdovinos Torres, "La homosexualidad en el cine mexicano."

13. Cárdenas, interview with the author.

14. Cheren, "Entrevista inedita a Vicente Leñero"; and Franco, "Mi vida con Vicente."

15. Pax Romana, "Memoria de la II Reunión," Havana, April 1955, ASLA-FLP, MIEC-JECI file.

16. Among others, his teachers included the director of *La Nación*, Alejandro Avilés, and the founder of the PAN, Luis Calderón Vega.

17. De la Torre, *Vivir del cine*; Cheren, "Entrevista inedita a Vicente Leñero."

18. See chap. 2.

19. He traveled to Spain with a scholarship from the Institute of Hispanic Culture in Madrid. Once in Mexico, he also completed his career in engineering and received the first prize at the annual National Contest of University Writers for his first novel *La polvadera* (1958).

20. Vicente Leñero, "Pero que allá," *Señal* (January 12, 1958).

21. Vicente Leñero, "Mayor felicidad conyugal," *Señal* (September 1, 1959).

22. Vicente Leñero, "Rebeldes sin causa, I," *Señal* (October 25, 1959); "Rebeldes sin causa, II," *Señal* (November 1, 1959); and "Rebeldes sin causa, III," *Señal* (November 8, 1959).

23. Vicente Leñero, "El drama de las colonias proletarias," *Señal* (April 26, 1959); "Mexico en pie. Puebla: ¡Cristianismo sí! ¡Comunismo No!," *Señal* (June 11, 1961); and "Habla la Juventud—la evolución social," *Señal* (June 18, 1961).

24. Niño, "Religión y sociedad en la obra de Vicente Leñero."

25. Ernesto was the cousin of the famous novelist Luis Spota.

26. *Claudia de México* (September 1965).

27. Felitti, "De la 'mujer moderna' a la 'mujer liberada.'"

28. Felitti, "De la 'mujer moderna' a la 'mujer liberada.'" See also Cosse, "*Claudia*, la revista de la mujer moderna"; and Salgado, "'A Small Revolution,'" which points to the analogous Chilean magazine, *Paula*.

29. Felitti, "De la 'mujer moderna' a la 'mujer liberada.'"

30. See chap. 1.

31. See, e.g., "Entrevista a Oriana Fallaci," *Claudia de México* (October 1967); Josefina King, "La píldora, una victoria para el amor," *Claudia de México* (July 1968); Josefina King, "¿Qué sabe usted de la reforma educativa?," *Claudia de México* (February 1969); Silvia Costa, "La castidad," *Claudia de México* (July 1969); María del Carmen Elu de Leñero, "Una encuesta nacional—el verdadero perfil de la mujer mexicana," *Claudia de México* (August 1969); Carmen de Silva, "Prohibido Prohibir," *Claudia de México* (November 1969); Silvia Cota, "El matrimonio ya no es una cárcel," *Claudia de México* (May 1970); Carmen de Silva, "¿Por qué teme al sexo?," *Claudia de México* (April 1971); and Elena Poniatowska, "El despertar de la mujer mexicana a la cultura," *Claudia de México* (August 1971).

32. See, e.g., "¿A dónde va la familia mexicana? Una encuesta nacional," *Claudia de México* (April 1969); and Ignacio Solares, "¿El derecho de no nacer? Las consecuencias sociales y morales del aborto," *Claudia de México* (February 1972).

33. *Claudia de México* (May 1966, September 1966, December 1966, and March 1968).

34. See, e.g., "El amor y la revolución de los jóvenes," *Claudia de México* (July 1968); "El Papa dijo sí al ritmo," *Claudia de México* (January 1969); and Jesús Castillo, "La mujer tapatía en busca de su libertad," *Claudia de México* (December 1970).

35. Alicia Azuela de la Cueva, "Las monjas se liberan," *Claudia de México* (November 1971).

36. Pérez, *Confessional Cinema*, 125.

37. Niño, "Religión y sociedad en la obra de Vicente Leñero."

38. Vicente Leñero, "La iglesia ha resucitado," *Claudia de México* (July 1969).

39. Vicente Leñero, "México es un país donde las mujeres leen Claudia," *Claudia de México* (October 1970).

40. Solares, "Sobre Vicente Leñero."

41. "Gaceta: Claudia en la Zona Rosa," *Claudia de México* (August 1970–February 1972); Alfonso Perabeles Morel, "¡Huy, los hippies!," *Claudia de México* (May 1968).

42. Vicente Leñero, "La Zona Rosa," *Claudia de México* (October 1965).

43. "Gaceta: Claudia en la Zona Rosa," *Claudia de México* (August 1970–February 1972).

44. He also served as director of *Revista de Revistas* (the cultural magazine of *Excélsior*) from 1973 to 1976.

45. Valdovinos Torres, "La homosexualidad en el cine mexicano."

46. Valdovinos Torres, "La homosexualidad en el cine mexicano"; and Schulz-Cruz, *Imágenes gay en el cine mexicano*.

47. *La lucha con la pantera* (Bojórquez, 1975) also dared to touch on the topic, albeit less effectively.

48. See chap. 1.

49. For a discussion of this film, see Legido, *Escondidas en el cine.*

50. An exception is *Lola de mi vida* (Barbachano-Ponce,1964), which was not consulted for this chapter.

51. Vilchis Arriola, "La invisibilidad de la narrativa lésbica en el cine mexicano."

52. See, e.g., *Las reglas del juego* (Wallerstein, 1970); *Ángeles y querubines* (Cordiki, 1971); *Satánico Pandemonium/La sexorcista* (Martínez Solares, 1973); *Alucarda, la hija de las tinieblas* (López Moctezuma, 1975); *El Apando* (Cazals, 1976); *Prisión de mujeres* (Cardona, 1977); and *Tres mujeres en la hoguera* (Salazar, 1977). See also *Los meses y los días* (Bojórquez, 1971), which touches on lesbianism in relation to the decadence of the era.

53. Simonetto, "La otra internacional."

54. Simonetto, "La otra internacional"; and Monsiváis, "Envío a Nancy."

55. Leñero, *El evangelio,* 135–37.

56. Leñero, *El evangelio,* 137–41.

9. COMPETING INTERPRETATIONS OF LOS CRISTEROS AND VIOLENT REACTIONS TO THE COUNTERCULTURE

1. See, e.g., García Riera, *Historia documental del cine mexicano,* vol. 16, 112–16.

2. See also *Crates* (Joskowicz, 1970), discussed in chap. 7.

3. Ibarrola Martínez, "Rupturas en el integrismo católico mexicano posconciliar"; and Herrán Ávila, "Las falsas derechas."

4. Meyer, interview with the author.

5. On the expulsion and naturalization of "pernicious foreigners" in postrevolutionary Mexico, see Yankelevich, "Extranjeros indeseables en México."

6. Jean Meyer, "Le movement étudiant en Amérique latine," *Esprit* (May 1969).

7. Meyer, interview with the author.

8. See, e.g., Jean Meyer, "Cuba's enfermé dans sa révolution," *Esprit* (March 1967); and Jean Meyer, "Camilo Torres: In Memoriam," *Esprit* (May 1966).

9. Meyer, interview with the author.

10. Paul V. Murray, Book review, *Catholic Historical Review* 61:5 (October 1975): 596–98.

11. David C. Bailey, Book review, *Hispanic American Historical Review* 56:1 (February 1976): 145–47.

12. Christian Lalive d'Epinay, "La Christiade ou l'irréductible religion," *Archives de sciences sociales des religions* 21:42 (July–December 1976): 173–77.

13. Lorenzo Meyer, Book review, *English Historical Review* 92:365 (October 1977): 871–72.

14. Knight, "Interpreting the Mexican Revolution"; Matute, "El 68 y la historiografía en México"; and Bailey, "Revisionism and the Recent Historiography of the Mexican Revolution."

15. Jean Meyer, "A propos d'un livre et d'un cinquantenaire: La mort de Zapata," *Annales: Histoire, Sciences Sociales* 26:6 (1971): 1198–1202.

16. San Miguel, "Mito e historia en la épica campesina."

17. San Miguel, "Mito e historia en la épica campesina."

18. See additional examples in appendix 2.

19. Horton, "'We Are Losing Our Identity.'"

20. See also Thornton, "Re-Framing Mexican Women's Filmmaking."

21. See also Thornton, "Re-Framing Mexican Women's Filmmaking."

22. Meyer and Iñiguez Mendoza, *La cristiada en imágenes*, 87–97.

23. Meyer and Iñiguez Mendoza, *La cristiada en imágenes*; García Muñoz, "La guerra cristera en la cinematografía mexicana"; and De la Vega, "La cruz y la canana."

24. See, e.g., the films discussed in chap. 1. On filming the revolution, see Thornton, *Revolution and Rebellion in Mexican Films*.

25. Meyer and Iñiguez Mendoza, *La cristiada en imágenes*, 77–119.

26. As noted earlier in the book, this is the same argument Taboada makes in *Hasta el viento tiene miedo* (Taboada, 1968).

27. García Bogliano, "Las mujeres en el cine de Carlos Enrique Taboada."

28. Meyer and Iñiguez Mendoza, *La cristiada en imágenes*, 98–109.

29. See chap. 5.

30. A telling example is *Canoa* (Cazals, 1977), which has received greater attention from historians. See, e.g., Mraz, *Looking for Mexico*, 206–14. On the broader impact of violence, see also the important work of Kloppe-Santamaría, *In the Vortex of Violence*.

31. See, e.g., the case of Vicente Leñero in chap. 8.

32. De la Vega, "La cruz y la canana," 151–52.

33. Meyer and Iñiguez Mendoza, *La cristiada en imágenes*, 110–18.

34. Rius Facius, *Méjico Cristero*; and Salvador Flores Llamas, "Méjico Cristero," *Juventud* (February 1961).

35. Rius Facius, *Un joven sin historia*, 467–93.

36. Rius Facius, *La Hoja de Combate*; and Ibarrola Martínez, "Rupturas en el integrismo católico mexicano posconciliar." See also the cases of Coello and Müggenburg in chaps. 2 and 3.

37. Young, "Fascist, Nazis, or Something Else?"

38. Other key writers included Salvador Borrego (Holocaust denier and author of the fascist *Derrota Mundial*, 1954), Celerino Salmerón (right-wing historian and author of *En defensa de Iturbide*, 1974), and Gloria Riestra (ultraconservative Catholic poet and author of *Tormenta sobre la iglesia*, 1971).

39. See, e.g., Salvador Abascal, "Unión solapa las herejías de Iván Illich"; Salvador Abascal, "La traición de la Universidad Iberoamericana"; Antonio Rius Facius, "En Cuernavaca se desconocen principios teológicos"; Antonio Rius Facius, "El obispo

de Cuernavaca y la Doctrina eucarística and "Discurso del Padre Martín de la Rosa," *La Hoja de Combate* (October 18, 1967; January 4, 1968; February 4, 1968; August 12,1969; and August 12, 1970).

40. See, e.g., "El homosexualismo está 'in,'" "Paraíso juvenil," and "Lo secunda Señal," *La Hoja de Combate* (June 12,1969); and "'Christus' contra Cristo," *La Hoja de Combate* (July 12, 1969).

41. See, e.g., Salvador Borrego, "Noticias de Fondo"; Celerino Salmerón, "La misa con música a-go-go"; and Salvador Abascal, "La traición de la Universidad Iberoamericana," *La Hoja de Combate* (October 4, 1968; December 12, 1968; and August 12, 1969).

42. Antonio Rius Facius, "La historieta de Don Sergio," and Salvador Borrego, "Noticias de Fondo"; Celerino Salmerón, "Soviet en el Estado de Nuevo León"; Salvador Borrego, "Lázaro Cárdenas: Balance con hechos, no con adjetivos"; Salvador Borrego, "Guerrilla urbana"; and Celerino Salmerón, "Teatro, circo, y subversión en Cuernavaca," *La Hoja de Combate* (April 12, 1970; July 12, 1970; November 12, 1970; and April 12, 1971).

43. Juan Bosco Abascal, "Estragos del progresismo en el ITESO," "Importante aclaración," "A corrupción de lo mejor," "Lemercier, mito y complejo," "¿Fue cristo un guerrillero o un revolucionario?," "Avándaro: Los Diez Mandamientos," and "Fiestas y costumbres paganas," *La Hoja de Combate* (June 12, 1970; July 12, 1970; September 12, 1970; April 12, 1971; August 12, 1971; and October 12, 1971).

44. Antonio Rius Facius, "Los Abascal," *El Universal* (November 12, 1971); and "Polemica sobre moral," *La Hoja de Combate* (December 12, 1971).

45. "Esoterismo de trovadores y hippies" and José Chávez Chávez, "Un mariguano más: Jodorowsky," *Réplica* (April 1971). See also Luis Vega Díaz, "Hippies: Hipocresía y holguera," and José Chávez Chávez, "La rebelión de la juventud," *Réplica* (August 1969); Santiago J. Illescas, "La nueva moral inmoral," *Réplica* (September 1969); Diego Marcos, "La industria de protesta," *Réplica* (October 1969); Ernesto del Castillo, "Las drogas," *Réplica* (April 1971).

46. See, e.g., Magaña Contreras, *Troya juvenil* (1971) and *Marx en sotana* (1974).

47. Silvano Hernández Hernández, "Rock y Revolución," *Réplica* (January 1972).

48. Jodorowsky, *The Spiritual Journey of Alejandro Jodorowsky;* and Esteban Aguila F., "Jodorowsky se atreve insultar al Ejército Mexicano," *Réplica* (September 1972).

49. Jodorowsky, *Teatro* pánico, 11–19. See also Vaughan, *Portrait of a Young Painter*, 167–68.

50. Jodorowsky, *The Spiritual Journey of Alejandro Jodorowsky*; and Santos, *The Holy Mountain*.

51. DFS, Alejandro Jodorowsky, Versión pública, Box 240, AGN.

52. See the similar story of Crates examined in chap. 7.

53. Esteban Aguila F., "Jodorowsky se atreve a insultar al Ejército Mexicano," *Réplica* (September 1972); and Chávez Chávez, "Un mariguano más," *Réplica* (April 1971).

54. Liga Anticomunista Cristiana, "A los Excmos. Sres. Arzobispos y Obispos de la Iglesia Católica en México," November 1972, AHAM.

55. The Christian Anticommunist League was one of several ultraconservative groups that splintered from the fascist MURO, described in chap. 2.

56. "II Foro Internacional de la Juventud sobre drogas y erotismo," *La Hoja de Combate* (April 12, 1970).

57. This scene is a clear reference to the September 13 march when thousands of students silently protested in the streets against state violence and the lack of freedom of expression.

58. DFS, Alejandro Jodorowsky, Versión pública, Box 240, AGN.

59. Santos, *The Holy Mountain*, 2.

60. Santos, *The Holy Mountain*, 2.

61. *Fando y Lis* (Jodorowsky, 1968); and Jodorowsky, *The Spiritual Journey of Alejandro Jodorowsky*.

62. See, e.g., Jiménez, *El Yunque*, 114–20.

63. Jodorowsky, *The Spiritual Journey of Alejandro Jodorowsky*, 225–27.

64. DFS, Alejandro Jodorowsky, Versión pública, Box 240, AGN.

65. See, among others, Ramírez Berg, *Cinema of Solitude*; and Pensado and Ochoa, *México Beyond 1968*.

66. González Moreno, "Cine mexicano en la década de los setenta."

67. See the examples in Meyer and Iñiguez Mendoza, *La cristiada en imágenes*, 129–93.

CONCLUSION

1. "El cine mexicano encara un tema espinoso: el incesto," *Life en Español* (August 16, 1965); "No amo a mi marido como figura sino como hombre. Dice Arabella Arbenz," *El Tiempo* (September 27, 1965); "Comprobado suicido de Arabella Arbenz," *El Tiempo* (October 8, 1965); "Hoy será sepultada Arabella en México," *El Tiempo* (October 10, 1965); and Isabel Garma, "La muerte fue el exilio definitive de Arabella Arbenz," *Crónica* (October 6, 1995).

2. Solorzano-Thompson, "Vicarious identities."

3. Rodríguez, "An auteur Cinema for Mexico," 141; and Menne, "A Mexican Nouvelle Vague'."

4. Marroquín, interview with the author.

BIBLIOGRAPHY

ARCHIVES AND PRIMARY SOURCES

Archives

AA	Adveniat Archives, Essen, Germany
AACM	Archivo de Acción Católica Mexicana, Mexico City, Mexico
AAPA	Antonio Aguilar, Private Archive, Mexico City, Mexico
ACUC	Archivo del Centro Universitario Cultural, Mexico City, Mexico
AGN	Archivo General de la Nación, Mexico City, Mexico
AHAM	Archivo Histórico del Arzobispado Mexicano, Mexico City, Mexico
ASLA-FLP	Archivo del Secretariado Latinoamericano, Fondo Leonidas Proaño, Quito, Ecuador
ASSM	Archivo del Secretariado Social Mexicano, Mexico City, Mexico
AUHAM	Archivo Histórico de la UNAM, Mexico City, Mexico
CDF-UNAM	Centro de Documentación de la Filmoteca de la UNAM, Mexico City, Mexico
CEDISPAN	Centro de Estudios, Documentación e Información sobre el Partido de Acción Nacional (PAN), Mexico City, Mexico
CIDNE	Centro de Información y Documentación de Nezahualcóyotl, State of Mexico, Mexico
CONDUMEX-FRF	Centro de Estudios de Historia de México, Fondo Rius Facius, Mexico City, Mexico
CUA	Catholic University Archives, Washington, DC
DFS	Dirección Federal de Seguridad, Archivo General de la Nación, Mexico City, Mexico
FU	Filmoteca UNAM, Mexico City, Mexico

IISUE	Instituto de Investigaciones sobre la Universidad y la Educación, Mexico City, Mexico
KADOC	Documentation and Research Centre on Religion, Culture and Society, SIGNIS Collection, Louvain, Belgium
UNDA	University of Notre Dame Archives, South Bend, IN

Libraries

Biblioteca Central Universitaria BUAP, Puebla, Mexico
Biblioteca de la Universidad de Lima, Lima, Peru
Biblioteca Francisco Xavier Clavigero, Universidad Iberoamericana, Mexico City, Mexico
Biblioteca Miguel Lerdo de Tejada, Mexico City, Mexico
Biblioteca Nacional, Buenos Aires, Argentina
Biblioteca Nacional de México, Mexico City, Mexico
Biblioteca Pública Carlos E. Restrepo, Bogotá, Colombia
Biblioteca Pública del Estado de Jalisco, Juan José Arreola, Guadalajara, Mexico
Burk Library at Union Theological Seminary, Columbia University, New York
Center for Research Libraries, Chicago, IL
Daniel Cosío Villegas, El Colegio de Mexico, Mexico City, Mexico
Hemeroteca Nacional, UNAM, Mexico City, Mexico
Hesburgh Library, University of Notre Dame, South Bend, IN
Instituto Mexicano de Doctrina Social Cristiana (IMDOSOC), Mexico City, Mexico
Princeton University Library, Princeton, NJ
Regenstein Library, University of Chicago, Chicago, IL

Surveillance Documents, Dirección Federal de Seguridad (DFS)

Almanza Villarreal, Eufemia Belén
Borrego, Salvador
CENCOS (Centro Nacional de Comunicación Social)
CIDOC (Centro Intercultural de Documentación)
Coello Macías, Luis Felipe
Comisión Nacional para la Moralización del Ambiente
Escuela de Periodismo Carlos Septién García
Frente Popular Anticomunista
Granados Chapa, Miguel Angel
Illich, Iván
Jodorowsky, Alejandro
López Arretche, Leobardo
Méndez Arceo, Sergio
Los Procesos

Revista *La Nación*
Sierra Villarreal, José Luis
Torres González, Héctor
Universidad Nacional Autónoma de México

Interviews with the Author

Aguirre, Francisco (pseudonym). March 13, 2014, Mexico City.
Almanza Villarreal, Eufemia Belén. March 9, 2016, Mexico City.
Bermeo, Jorge. December 11, 2015, Mexico City.
Bidegain, Ana María. April 4, 2018, University of Notre Dame.
Cárdenas, Cuauhtémoc. April 1, 2013, University of Notre Dame.
Concha Malo, Miguel. January 23, 2016, Mexico City.
Costa, Manuel (pseudonym). December 9, 2015, Mexico City.
Cuetos, Laudelino. June 18, 2016, Mexico City.
García, Jesús. January 19, 2016, Mexico City.
Gómez del Campo, Mercedes. December 9, 2015, Mexico City.
González, Dario (pseudonym). December 9, 2015, Mexico City.
Gutiérrez, Gustavo. December 4, 2015, University of Notre Dame.
Hernández, María Eugenia (pseudonym). March 15, 2014, Mexico City.
Manzano, Rosendo. July 8, 2021, University of Notre Dame, via Zoom.
Marín, Víctor (pseudonym). December 9, 2015, Mexico City.
Marroquín, Enrique, October 19, 2016, Guadalajara, Mexico.
Martínez, Fernanda (pseudonym). December 9, 2015, Mexico City.
Maza Reducindo, Jorge. December 5, 2014, Mexico City.
Meyer, Jean. April 17, 2017, University of Notre Dame.
Morales, Pedro (pseudonym). March 9, 2016, Mexico City.
Pérez, Mario. December 2, 2015, Mexico City.
Reygadas, Rafael. October 27, 2020, University of Notre Dame, via Zoom.
Sánchez, Edith (pseudonym). March 15, 2014, Mexico City.
Torres González, Héctor. March 9, 2016, Mexico City.
Vasquez, María (pseudonym). March 7, 2017, Mexico City.
Velázquez, Manuel. June 18, 2012, Mexico City.
Zavala, Diego. December 9, 2015, Mexico City.

Magazines, Journals, and Newspapers

ACM, Boletín de la Junta Central
ACM, Circular
Annales: Histoire, Sciences Sociales
BIDI: Boletín Iberoamericano de Información del MIEC
Boletín MEP/EJUC
Cencos

Christus
Cine Guía
Cine-Temas
Claudia de México
Contacto
Convergence
Copilco
Corporación
Crónica
Cuadernos de Documentación, MIEC-JECI
Esprit
Excélsior
Diálogo
Heraldo Cultural
La Hoja de Combate
Impacto
Informaciones Católicas Internacionales
JEC: International Bulletin
Juventud
Juventud Católica
Liberación
Life en Español
MEP Bulletín
MEP. Documentos
MEP: Información Estudiantil
La Nación: Órgano de Acción Nacional
OCIC Informaciones
Palestra
Pax Romana, Boletín
Pax Romana: Órgano del MIEC
Piedra Rodante
¿Porqué?
El Porvenir
Proceso
Puño
Reforma Universitaria: Periódico de la Confederación Nacional de Estudiantes
Réplica
Rumbo
Señal
Siempre!
SPES
El Tiempo
El Universal

Víspera
YCS: International Bulletin

Encyclicals and Other Important Church Documents

CELAM. "Documentos finales de Medellín," September 1968.
Pope John XXIII. *Mater et magistra*, Christianity and Social Progress, May 15, 1961.
———. *Pacem in terris*, Peace in Truth, Justice, Charity, and Liberty, April 11, 1963.
Pope Leo XIII. *Rerum novarum*, Of Revolutionary Change, May 15, 1891.
Pope Paul VI. *Gaudium et spes*. Pastoral Constitution on the Church in the Modern World, December 7, 1965.
———. *Populorum progressio*, The Development of Peoples, March 26, 1967.
———. *Humane vitae*, Of Human Life, July 29, 1968.
Pope Pius XI. *Casti connubii*, Of Chaste Wedlock, December 31, 1930.
Pope Pius XII. *Miranda prorsus*, On the Communication Fields: Movies, Television, and Radio, September 8, 1957.
Sociedad Teológica Mexicana. *Memoria del Primer Congreso Nacional de Teología: Fe y Desarrollo*. Mexico City: Ediciones Alianza, 1970.

SECONDARY SOURCES

Aguirre Cristiani, María Gabriela, and Nora Pérez Rayón Elizundia. *Los proyectos católicos de nación en el siglo XX: Actores, ideologías y prácticas*. Mexico City: Universidad Autónoma Metropolitana, 2020.
Agustín, José. "Cuál es la onda," *Diálogos: Artes, Letras, Ciencias Humanas* 10:1 (January–February 1974): 11–13.
———. *La nueva música clásica*. Mexico City: Editorial Universo México, 1985.
Álvarez Gutiérrez, Ana Lucía. "De católico a guerrillero: El caso de Ignacio Salas Obregón." BA thesis, University of Guanajuato, 2015.
———. "La OCU: Una historia contada a través de diversas perspectivas." MA thesis, El Colegio de San Luis, 2019.
Anderson, Danny J. *Vicente Leñero: The Novelist as Critic*. Frankfurt: P. Lang, 1989.
Andes, Stephen J. C. *The Mysterious Sofía: One Woman's Mission to Save Catholicism in Twentieth-Century Mexico*. Lincoln: University of Nebraska Press, 2019.
Andes, Stephen, and Julia Young, eds. *Local Church, Global Church: Catholic Activism in the Americas before Vatican II*. Washington, DC: Catholic University of America Press, 2016.
Annett, Anthony M. *Cathonomics: How Catholic Tradition Can Create a More Just Economy*. Washington, DC: Georgetown University Press, 2022.
Appelbaum, Patricia. *St. Francis of America: How a Thirteenth-Century Friar Became America's Most Popular Saint*. Chapel Hill: University of North Carolina Press, 2015.

Arrupe, Pedro, and Kevin F. Burke. *Essential Writings*. Maryknoll, NY: Orbis Books, 2004.

Aspe Armella, María Luisa. *La formación social y política de los católicos mexicanos: La Acción Católica Mexicana y la Unión Nacional de Estudiantes Católicos, 1929–1958*. Mexico City: Universidad Iberoamericana, 2008.

———. *Cambiar en tiempos revueltos: Una mirada al debate interno de la Provincia Mexicana de la Compañía de Jesús a través de Pulgas (1963–1972)*. Mexico City: Asociación Mexicana de Promoción Cultural Social, 2016.

Ayala Blanco, Jorge. *La búsqueda del cine mexicano (1968–1972)*. 2 vols. Mexico City: Universidad Nacional Autónoma de México, 1974.

———. *La aventura del cine mexicano (1931–1967)*. Mexico City: Universidad Nacional Autónoma de México, 2021.

Bailey, David C. "Revisionism and the Recent Historiography of the Mexican Revolution." *Hispanic American Historical Review* 58:1 (1978): 62–79.

Barr-Melej, Patrick. *Psychedelic Chile: Youth, Counterculture, and Politics on the Road to Socialism and Dictatorship*. Chapel Hill: University of North Carolina Press, 2017).

The Beatles. "All You Need Is Love." In *All You Need is Love/Baby You're a Rich Man*. Capitol Records, 1967.

Benitez, Fernando. *Los hongos alucinantes*. Mexico City: Ediciones Era, 1964.

———. *En la tierra mágica del peyote*. Mexico City: Ediciones Era, 1969.

Bertand, Hermann Von. *Hacia la puerta: En búsqueda del destino*. Mexico City: Castellanos Editores, 2004.

Bidegain, Ana María. "La organización de movimientos de juventud de Acción Católica en América Latina: Los casos de los obreros y universitarios en Brasil y en Colombia entre 1930–1955." PhD diss., Université Catholique de Louvain, 1979.

Bissio, Roberto. "Bandung in Latin America: The Hope for Another World." *Inter-Asia Cultural Studies* 17:1 (2016): 19–26.

Black, Gregory D. *The Catholic Crusade against the Movies, 1940–1975*. Cambridge: Cambridge University Press, 1997.

Blancarte, Roberto. *Historia de la iglesia católica en México (1929–1982)*. Mexico City: Fondo de Cultura Económica, 2012.

Booth, William A. "Rethinking Latin America's Cold War." *Historical Journal* 64:4 (2021): 1128–50.

Braun, Herbert. "Protest of Engagement: Dignity, False Love, and Self-Love in Mexico during 1968." *Comparative Studies in Sociology and History* 39:3 (1997): 511–49.

Brewster, Claire. *Responding to Crisis in Contemporary Mexico: The Political Writings of Paz, Fuentes, Monsiváis, and Poniatowska*. Tucson: University of Arizona Press, 2005.

Burton, Julianne. *Cinema and Social Change in Latin America: Conversations with Latin American Filmmakers*. Austin: University of Texas Press, 1986.

Calderón Vega, Luis. *Cuba 88*. Mexico City: La Esfera, 1959.

Câmara, Hélder. *Spiral of Violence*. Denville, NJ: Dimension Books, 1971.

Cano, Gabriela. "Mexico: The Long Road to Women's Suffrage." In *The Palgrave Handbook of Women's Political Rights*, ed. Susan Franceschet et al., 115–27. London: Palgrave Macmillan, 2019.

Carassai, Sebastián. *The Argentine Silent Majority: Middle Classes, Politics, Violence, and Memory in the Seventies*. Durham, NC: Duke University Press, 2014.

Careaga, Gabriel. *Mitos y fantasias de la clase media en México*. Mexico City: Joaquín Mortiz, 1974.

Caso, Antonio. "La existencia como economía, como desinterés y como caridad." In *Obras Completas*, vol. 3. Mexico City: UNAM, 1972.

Cosío Villegas, Daniel. *El estilo personal de gobernar*. Mexico City: Joaquín Mortiz, 1974.

Castañeda, Carlos. *The Teachings of Don Juan: A Yaqui Way of Knowledge*. Berkeley: University of California Press, 1968.

Castañeda Iturbide, Francisco. *Los años por contar*. Mexico City: Centro Universitario Cultural, 2000.

Castillo Bolaños, Fernando, and Jorge Maza Reducindo. *La escuela imposible: La Preparatoria Popular de 1968*. Mexico City: Lecuona, 2002.

Chávez, Joaquín M. *Poets and Prophets of the Resistance: Intellectuals and the Origins of El Salvador's Civil War*. Oxford: Oxford University Press, 2017.

———. "Operación amor: Hippies, Musicians, and Cultural Transformation in El Salvador." In *The Routledge Handbook of the Global Sixties: Between Protest and Nation-Building*, ed. Chen Jian et al., 159–67. London: Routledge, 2018.

Cheren, Silvia. "Entrevista inédita a Vicente Leñero." *Revista de la Universidad de México* 131 (January 2015): 17–28.

Ciuk, Perla. *Diccionario de directores del cine mexicano*. Mexico City: Conaculta, 2000.

Collado Herrera, María del Carmen, ed. *Las derechas en el México contemporáneo*. Mexico City: Instituto Mora, 2020.

Cosse, Isabella. "*Claudia*: La revista de la mujer moderna en la Argentina de los años sesenta (1957–1973)." *Mora* 17:1 (2011). http://www.scielo.org.ar/scielo.php?script=sci_arttext&pid=S1853-001X2011000100007.

———. *Mafalda: Historia social y política*. Mexico City: Fondo de Cultura Económica, 2013.

Costa, Paola. *La "apertura" cinematográfica: México, 1970–1976*. Puebla: Universidad Autónoma de Puebla, 1988.

Cottrell, Robert C. *Sex, Drugs, and Rock 'n' Roll: The Rise of America's 1960s Counterculture*. New York: Rowman & Littlefield, 2015.

Cowan, Benjamin A. *Securing Sex: Morality and Repression in the Making of Cold War Brazil*. Chapel Hill: University of North Carolina Press, 2016.

Dawson, Alexander S. "Salvador Roquet, María Sabina, and the Trouble with *Jipis*." *Hispanic American Historical Review* 95:1 (February 2015): 103–33.

Day, Stuart A. "Entrevista con Vicente Leñero." *Chasqui* 33:2 (November 2004): 17–26.

Debroise, Olivier, and Cuauhtémoc Medina. *La era de la discrepancia / The Age of Discrepancies: Arte y cultura visual en México / Art and Visual Culture in Mexico, 1968–1997*. Mexico City: Turner, 2014.

De Guiseppe, Massimo. "Italian Catholics and Latin America during the 'Long 68.'" In *Global 1968: Cultural Revolutions in Europe and Latin America*, ed. Anthony P. Monta and A. James McAdams, 37–72. Notre Dame, IN: University of Notre Dame Press, 2021.

De la Rosa Medellín, Martín. *Alfabetizar concientizando*. Tijuana: Promoción Popular Urbana, 1986.

———. *Promoción popular y lucha de clases: Análisis de un caso*. Mexico City: Servicios Educativos Populares, 1979.

De la Vega Alfaro, Eduardo de la Cruz. "La cruz y la canana (la rebelión cristera en el cine mexicano)." *Comunicación y Sociedad* (January–February 1990): 119–56.

Del Castillo Troncoso, Alberto. *Ensayo sobre el movimiento estudiantil de 1968: la fotografía y la construcción de un imaginario*. Mexico City: Instituto Mora, 2012.

———. *La matanza del jueves de corpus: Fotografía y memoria*. Mexico City: Instituto Nacional de Estudios Históricos de las Revoluciones de México, 2021.

Del Valle Noriega, Luis. *Siempre humano, siempre en proceso*. Aguascalientes: Centro de Estudios Jurídicos y Sociales Mispal, Centro de Reflexión Teológica, 2011.

Desmond, William. *Cynics*. London: Routledge, 2014.

Díaz, Abel Santiago. *Departamento vacío: La novela de los estudiantes*. Mexico City: B. Costa Amic, 1965.

Dunn, Christopher. *Contracultura: Alternative Arts and Social Transformation in Authoritarian Brazil*. Chapel Hill: University of North Carolina Press, 2016.

Espino Armendariz, Saúl. "Feminismo católico en México: La historia del CIDHAL y sus redes transnacionales (c. 1960–1990)." PhD diss., El Colegio de México, 2019.

Espinosa, David. *Jesuit Student Groups, the Universidad Iberoamericana, and Political Resistance in Mexico, 1913–1979*. Albuquerque: University of New Mexico Press, 2014.

Estrada, Álvaro. *Huautla en tiempos de hippies*. Mexico City: Grijalbo, 1996.

Fazio, Carlos. *No quiero ser perro mudo: Don Sergio Méndez Arceo y el 68*. Mexico City: Equipo Celebrando a don Sergio, 1998.

Feixa, Carles. "De las bandas a las culturas juveniles." *Estudios sobre las Culturas Contemporáneas* 5:15 (1994): 139–70.

Felitti, Karina. "De la 'mujer moderna' a la 'mujer liberada': Un análisis de la revista *Claudia de México* (1965–1977)." *Estudios Mexicanos* 67:3 (2018): 1345–93.

Fernández-Cobián, Esteban. "Psicoanálisis, religión y arquitectura: Fray Gabriel Chávez de la Mora y el monasterio de Santa María de la Resurrección." *EdA: Esempi di Architettura* (January 2021): 1–34.

Fernández, David. "Oral History of the Chilean Movement 'Christians for Socialism,' 1971–73." *Journal of Contemporary History*, 34:2 (1999): 283–94.

Field, Thomas C., Stella Krepp, and Vanni Pettinà, eds. *Latin America and the Global Cold War*. Chapel Hill: University of North Carolina Press, 2020.

Filmoteca UNAM. *El Grito, memoria en movimiento*. Mexico City: Universidad Nacional Autónoma de México, 2018.

Fox, Claire F. "Pornography and 'the Popular' in Post-Revolutionary Mexico: The Club Tívoli from Spota to Isaac." In *Visible Nations: Latin America Cinema and Video*, ed. Chon A. Noriega, 143–73. Minneapolis: University of Minnesota Press, 2000.

Franco Leñero, Estela. "Mi vida con Vicente." In *"Los católicos": Vicente Leñero en torno a la fe*, 17–50. Mexico City: Ediciones Proceso, 2016.

———. *Rosario Castellanos, semblanza psicoanalítica: Otro modo de ser humano y libre*. Mexico City: Plaza & Janés, 1985.

Frazier, Lessie Jo, and Deborah Cohen, eds. *Gender and Sexuality in 1968: Transformative Politics in the Cultural Imagination*. London: Palgrave Macmillan, 2009.

Freije, Vanessa. *Citizens of Scandal: Journalism, Secrecy, and the Politics of Reckoning in Mexico*. Durham, NC: Duke University Press, 2020.

Freire, Paulo. *La educación como práctica de la libertad*. Bogotá: Editorial América Latina, 1965.

———. *Pedagogía del oprimido*. Barcelona: Biblioteca Nueva, 1969.

Fuentes, Carlos. *Tiempo mexicano*. Mexico City: Joaquín Mortiz, 1971.

Fuentes, V. *Los jóvenes*. Mexico City: Siglo XXI, 1968.

Galindo, Alejandro. *El cine mexicano: Un personal punto de vista*. Mexico City: Edamex, 1985.

Gallo, Rubén. *Freud's Mexico: Into the Wilds of Psychoanalysis*. Cambridge, MA: MIT Press, 2010.

García, Jesús. "La Iglesia mexicana desde 1962." In *Historia general de la Iglesia en América Latina*, Tomo V, ed. Alfonso Alacá, 361–493. Mexico City: Ediciones Paulinas, 1984.

García Bogliano, Adrián. "Las mujeres en el cine de Carlos Enrique Taboada." In *Taboada*, ed. Pablo Guisa, 13–44. Mexico City: Jus, 2011.

García Mourelle, Lorena. *La experiencia de la Juventud Obrera Católica Femenina en Uruguay (1944–1960)*. Montevideo: Observatario del Sur, Centro de Documentación, Investigación y Promoción Social, 2010.

García Muñoz, Gerardo. "La guerra cristera en la cinematografía mexicana: Entre el melodrama y el anticlericalismo." *Colorado Review of Hispanic Studies* 8 (Fall 2010): 183–200.

García Riera, Emilio. *Historia documental del cine mexicano*. Vols. 5–17, 1949–1976. Mexico City: Instituto Mexicano de Cinematografía, 1993.

García Saldaña, Parménides. *En la ruta de la onda*. Mexico City: Editorial Diógenes, 1972.

Gillingham, Paul, Michael Lettieri, and Benjamin T. Smith. *Journalism, Satire, and Censorship in Mexico*. Albuquerque: University of New Mexico Press, 2018.

Gilman, Claudia. *Entre la pluma y el fusil: Debates y dilemas del escritor revolucionario en América Latina*. Mexico City: Siglo XXI, 2012.

Glantz, Margo. *Onda y escritura en México: Jóvenes de 20 a 33*. Mexico City: Siglo XXI, 1971.

Gómez Peralta, Héctor. "Los orígenes de la Democracia Cristiana en el Partido Acción Nacional (1952–1964)." *Estudios Políticos* 25 (January–April 2012): 107–29.

González, Fernando M. "Algunos grupos radicales de izquierda y de derecha con influencia Católica en México (1965–1975)." *Historia y Grafía* 29 (2007): 57–93.

González Moreno, Obed. "Cine mexicano en la década de los setenta: Un espejismo." *Toma Uno* 6 (2018): 43–61.

Gosse, Van. "A Movement of Movements: The Definition and Periodization of the New Left." In *A Companion to Post-1945 America*, ed. Jean-Christopher Agnew and Roy Rosenzweig, 277–302. Cambridge: Blackwell, 2002.

Greene, Doyle. *Rock, Counterculture and the Avant-Garde, 1966/1970: How the Beatles, Frank Zappa and the Velvet Underground Defined an Era*. Jefferson, NC: McFarland, 2016.

Guerrero Olivares, Maria Teresa, ed. *Una generación desconocida: Movimiento social demócrata cristiano, 1962–1970: Testimonios*. Chihuahua: Instituto Chihuahuense de Cultura, 2014.

Guevara, Ernesto Che. "Message to the Tricontinental." Marxist Internet Archive. Executive Secretariat of the Organization of the Solidarity of the Peoples of Africa, Asia, and Latin America (OSPAAAL). Havana, April 16, 1967. https://www.marxists.org/archive/guevara/1967/04/16.htm.

———. "Socialism and Man in Cuba." Marxist Internet Archive. First published under the title, "From Algiers, for Marcha," March 12, 1965. https://www.marxists.org/archive/guevara/1965/03/man-socialism.htm.

Gutiérrez, Gustavo. *Caridad y amor humano*. Lima: UNEC, 1966.

———. *Teología de la Liberación: Perspectivas*. Lima: Centro de Estudios y Publicaciones, 1971.

Guzmán, María de Jesús, and Xavier Dosil. "Paulo Freire: Otro volcán en Cuernavaca." *Kavilando* 9:1 (2017): 116–20.

Harmer, Tanya. *Beatriz Allende: A Revolutionary Life in Cold War Latin America*. Chapel Hill: University of North Carolina Press, 2020.

Hartch, Todd. *The Prophet of Cuernavaca: Ivan Illich and the Crisis of the West*. Oxford: Oxford University Press, 2015.

Hernández Sandoval, Bonar L. *Guatemala's Catholic Revolution: A History of Religious and Social Reform, 1920–1968*. Notre Dame, IN: University of Notre Dame, 2018.

Hernández Vicencio, Tania. *Revolución y constitución: Pensamiento y acción política de tres mexicanos en la primera mitad del siglo XX*. Mexico City: Instituto Nacional de Antropología e Historia, 2014.

———. "Sergio Méndez Arceo y su visión internacionalista." *Política y Cultura* 38 (2012): 89–117.

Herrán Ávila, Luis. "Las falsas derechas: Conflict and Convergence in Mexico's Post-Cristero Right after the Second Vatican Council." *The Americas* 79:2 (April 2022): 321–50.

Hershfield, Joanne. *Mexican Cinema/Mexican Woman, 1940–1950*. Tucson: University of Arizona Press, 1995.

Horn, Gerd-Rainer. *The Spirit of Vatican II: Western European Progressive Catholicism in the Long Sixties*. Oxford: Oxford University Press, 2014.

Horton, Andrew. "'We Are Losing Our Identity': An Interview with Mexican Director Marcela Fernández Violante." *Film Quarterly* 15:1 (1987): 2–7.

Huxley, Aldous. *Island*. London: Chatto & Windus, 1962.

Ibarrola Martínez, María del Carmen. "Rupturas en el integrismo católico mexicano posconciliar: Una mirada desde el caso de Antonio Rius Facius." In *Intelectuales católicos conservadores y tradicionalistas en México y Latinoamérica (1910–2015)*, ed. Laura Alarcón Menchada et al. 165–80. Zapopan: El Colegio de Jalisco, 2019.

Janzen, Rebecca. *Unholy Trinity: State, Church, and Film in Mexico*. Albany: State University of New York Press, 2021.

Jardón, Raúl. *1968, el fuego de la esperanza*. Mexico City: Siglo XXI, 1998.

Jarque, Joan E. *Pax Romana. Congreso mundial de Montevideo: La responsabilidad social de la universidad*. Barcelona: Editorial Estela, 1962.

Jian, Chen, et. al., eds. *The Routledge Handbook of the Global Sixties: Between Protest and Nation-Building*. London: Routledge, 2018.

Jiménez Jiménez, Lauro. *El Yunque: La ultraderecha en Querétaro*. n.p.: Published by author, 2008.

Jo, Young-Hyun. "Movimiento 'Sacerdotes para el Pueblo' y la transformación socio-eclesiástica en México." *Revista Iberoamericana* 21:1 (2010): 81–104.

Jodorowsky, Alejandro. *The Spiritual Journey of Alejandro Jodorowsky: The Creator of El Topo*. South Paris, ME: Park Street Press, 2008.

———. *Teatro pánico*. Mexico City: Ediciones Era, 1965.

Joseph, Gilbert M. "What We Now Know and Should Know: Bringing Latin America More Meaningfully into Cold War Studies." In *In from the Cold: Latin America's New Encounter with the Cold War*, ed. Gilbert M. Joseph, Daniela Spenser, and Emily Rosenberg, 3–46. Durham, NC: Duke University Press, 2008.

Joseph, Gilbert M., Daniela Spenser, and Emily Rosenberg, eds. *In from the Cold: Latin America's New Encounter with the Cold War*. Durham, NC: Duke University Press, 2008.

Kassman Sack, Susan. *America's Teilhard: Christ and Hope in the 1960s*. Washington, DC: Catholic University of America Press, 2019.

Keller, Renata. *Mexico's Cold War: Cuba, the United States, and the Legacy of the Mexican Revolution*. Cambridge: Cambridge University Press, 2017.

King, Pamela. *Angel with Drumsticks: The Rock That Shook the Foundations of the Vatican*. New South Wales: Ferrai, 2014.

Kloppe-Santamaría, Gema. *In the Vortex of Violence: Lynching, Extralegal Justice, and the State in Postrevolutionary Mexico*. Oakland: University of California Press, 2020.

Knight, Alan. "Interpreting the Mexican Revolution." Texas Papers on Mexico, 1988.

Kunzle, David. *Chesucristo: The Fusion in Image and Word of Che Guevara and Jesus Christ*. Berlin: De Gruyter, 2016.

Laffay, Augustine. "Le père Morelli (1919–1979)." In *La Province dominicaine de Toulouse, XIX–XX siècles: Une histoire intellectualle et spiritualle*, ed. Henry Donneaud et al., 297–324. Paris: Karthala, 2015.

Langland, Victoria. *Speaking of Flowers: Student Movements and the Making and Remembering of 1968 in Military Brazil*. Durham, NC: Duke University Press, 2013.

———. "Transnational Connections of the Global Sixties as Seen by a Historian of Brazil." In *The Routledge Handbook of the Global Sixties: Between Protest and Nation-Building*, ed. Chen Jian et al., 15–26. London: Routledge, 2018.

Legido, Rosi. *Escondidas en el cine: Censura y personajes sáficos*. Madrid: LES, Editorial Murcia, 2021.

Legión Mexicana de la Decencia. *Apreciaciones: Catálogo de los espectáculos censurados por La Legión Mexicana de la Decencia de 1931 a 1958*. Mexico City: Legión de la Decencia, 1959.

Lennon, John. "God." In *John Lennon/Plastic Ono Band*. Apple/EMI, 1970.

Leñero, Vicente. *Los albañiles*. Madrid: Biblioteca Breve, 1963.

———. "Compañero." *Diálogos: Artes, Letras, Ciencias Humanas* 6:2 (March–April 1970): 14–27.

———. *El evangelio de Lucas Gavilán*. Barcelona: Seix Barral, 1979.

———. *Gente así*. Madrid: Alfaguara, 2007.

———. *Los periodistas*. Mexico City: Joaquín Mortiz, 1978.

———. *El pueblo rechazado*. Mexico City: Joaquín Mortiz, 1969.

———. *Teatro documental*. Mexico City: Editores Mexicanos Unidos, 1985.

———. *Viaje a Cuba*. Mexico City: Fondo de Cultura Económica, 1974.

———. *Vivir del teatro*. Mexico City: Fondo de Cultura Económica, 2012.

Lernoux, Lenny. *Cry of the People: United States Involvement in the Rise of Fascism, Torture, and the Murder and the Persecution of the Catholic Church in Latin America*. New York: Doubleday, 1980.

Levi, H. Dowling. *The Aquarian Gospel of Jesus the Christ: The Philosophic and Practical Basis of the Religion of the Aquarian Age of the World*. Los Angeles: DeVorss, 1964.

Loaeza, Soledad. *Clases medias y política en México: La querella escolar, 1959–1963*. Mexico City: El Colegio de México, 1988.

———. "Mexico in the Fifties: Women and Church in Holy Alliance." *Women's Studies Quarterly* 33:3–4 (2005): 138–60.

———. "The National Action Party (PAN): From the Fringes of the Political System to the Heart of Change." In *Christian Democracy in Latin America: Electoral Competition and Regime Conflicts*, ed. Scott Mainwaring and Timothy R. Scully, 196–246. Stanford, CA: Stanford University Press, 2003.

Londono-Ardila, Sandra. "Consciousness-Raising and Liberation: The Latin American Progressive Catholic Student Movement and the Regional Version of the Revision of Life Method (1955–1968)." *Journal of World Christianity* 9:2 (2019): 151–70.

Luke, Anne. *Youth and the Cuban Revolution: Youth Culture and Politics in 1960s Cuba*. Lanham, MD: Rowland & Littlefield, 2018.

Mabry, Donald. J. *Mexico's Acción Nacional: A Catholic Alternative to Revolution*. Syracuse, NY: Syracuse University Press, 1973.

Macías González, Víctor. "The Transnational Homophile Movement and the Development of Domesticity in Mexico City's Homosexual Community, 1930–70." *Gender & History* 26:3 (2014): 519–44.

———. "Los homosexuales como sujetos peligrosos en la ciudad de México (1940–1960)." In *Hampones, intocables y pecatrices: Sujetos peligrosos de la Ciudad de México (1940–1960)*, ed. Susana Sosenski, 84–119. Mexico City: Fondo de Cultura Económica, 2019.

Magaña Contreras, Manuel. *Marx en sotana*. Mexico City: Rodas, 1973.

———. *Troya Juvenil*. Mexico City: Ideal, 1971.

Malley, François, and Albert Chambon. *Le Pére Morelli, de Dachau a Netza*. Paris: Cerf, 1986.

Manzano, Valeria. *The Age of Youth in Argentina: Culture, Politics, and Sexuality from Perón to Videla*. Chapel Hill: University of North Carolina Press, 2014.

Marchesi, Aldo. *Latin America's Radical Left: Rebellion and Cold War in the Global 1960s*. Cambridge: Cambridge University Press, 2019.

Marcuse, Herbert. *One-Dimensional Man: Studies in the Ideology of Advanced Industrial Society*. New York: Beacon Press, 1966.

Markarian, Vania. *Uruguay: 1968. Student Activism from Global Counterculture to Molotov Cocktails*. Berkeley: University of California Press, 2017.

Marroquín, Enrique. *La contracultura como protesta: Análisis de un fenómeno juvenil*. Mexico City: Joaquín Mortiz, 1975.

———. *La cruz mesiánica: Una aproximación al sincretismo católico indígena*. Mexico City: Palabra Ediciones, 1989.

———. *Historia y profecia: Memoria de 50 años de ministerio*. n.p.: Published by author, 2014.

Matute, Alvaro. "El 68 y la historiografía en México: Alcances y limitaciones." In *Estudios Historiográficos*, ed. Alvaro Matute, 87–95. Cuernavaca: Centro de Investigación y Docencia en Humanidades del Estado de Morelos, 1997.

Mcintyre, Kathleen. *Protestantism and State Formation in Postrevolutionary Oaxaca*. Albuquerque: University of New Mexico Press, 2022.

McLeod, Hugh. *The Religious Crisis of the 1960s*. Oxford: Oxford University Press, 2010.

Meadows, Donella H, Dennis L. Meadows, Jorgen Randers and William W. Behrens III. *The Limits to Growth: A Report for the Club of Rome's Project on the Predicament of Mankind*. New York: Universe Books, 1972.

Medina Valdes, Gerardo. *Operación 10 de junio*. Mexico City: Ediciones Universo, 1972.

Menne, Jeff. "A Mexican 'Nouvelle Vague': The Logic of New Waves under Globalization." *Cinema Journal* 47:1 (Autumn 2007): 70–93.

Mestman, Mariano. *Las rupturas del 68 en el cine de América Latina: Contracultura, experimentación y política*. Buenos Aires: Ediciones Akal, 2016.

Meyer, Jean, and Ulises Iñiguez Mendoza. *La cristiada en imágenes: Del cine mudo al video*. Guadalajara: Universidad de Guadalajara, 2006.

Monreal, Susana. "Dominicos de Toulouse en Montevideo: Una comunidad controvertida en un periodo bisagra (1953–1970)." *Cuadernos del Claeh* 38:109 (2019): 63–84.

Monsiváis, Carlos. *Días de guardar*. Mexico City: Ediciones Era, 1971.

———. "Envío a Nancy, activista ejemplar." *Debate Feminista* 10 (September 1994): 257–63.

———. "Notas sobre cultura popular en México." *Latin American Perspectives* 5:1 (Winter 1978): 98–118.

Mora, Carl J. *Mexican Cinema: Reflections of a Society, 1896–1980*. Berkeley: University of California Press, 1982.

Morelli, Alex. *Hacia una iglesia popular*. Mexico City: Centro de Estudios Ecuménicos, 1980.

Mraz, John. *Looking for Mexico: Modern Visual Culture and National Identity*. Durham, NC: Duke University Press, 2010.

Mügemburg, Federico. *La cruz: ¿Un ariete subversivo?* Mexico City: Libro Rojo, 1970.

Nessan, Craig. *The Vitality of Liberation Theology*. Eugene, OR: Pickwick Publications, 2012.

Niño, Miguel Angel. "Religión y sociedad en la obra de Vicente Leñero," PhD diss., Michigan State University, 1977.

Oliveros de Miranda, María Adela. "José Porfirio Miranda de la Parra: Una vida entre Marx y la Biblia." *Signos Filosóficos* 7 (2002): 297–306.

Ortiz, Orlando. *Jueves de Corpus*. Mexico City: Editorial Diógenes, 1979.

Ovalle, Camilo Vicente. *[Tiempo suspendido]: Una historia de la desaparición forzada en México, 1940–1980*. Mexico City: Bonilla Artigas Editores, 2019.

Padilla Rangel, Yolanda. "Mujeres e Iglesia católica en los años cuarenta: La gestación de una nueva moral." *Caleidoscopio* 2 (1997): 123–47.

Pacheco Hinojosa, María Martha. *Iglesia católica en la sociedad mexicana, 1958–1973: Secretariado Social Mexicano, Conferencia de Organizaciones Nacionales*. Mexico City: Instituto Mexicano de Doctrina Social Cristiana, 2005.

Pani, Erika. *Conservadurismo y derechas en la historia de México*. Vol. 2. Mexico City: Fondo de Cultura Económica, 2009.

Passerini, Luisa. *Autobiography of a Generation: Italy, 1968*. Middletown, CT: Wesleyan University Press, 2004.

Pastor Escobar, Raquel. "Vaticano II en el laicado mexicano: José Álvarez Icaza y la puesta en práctica del concilio ecunemico." PhD diss., Universidad Nacional Autónoma de México, 2004.

Pelegrí, Buenaventura. *JECI-MIEC: Su opción, su pedagogía*. Montevideo: Centro de Documentación del MIEC-JECI, 1972.

Pensado, Jaime M. "The Anonymous Dead of 1968 Mexico: A Comparative Study of Counterrevolutionary Violence and Protest with Uruguay and Brazil." In *Global 1968: Cultural Revolutions in Europe and Latin America*, ed. James McAdams and Anthony P. Monta, 341–82. Notre Dame, IN: University of Notre Dame Press, 2021.

———. "El Movimiento Estudiantil Profesional (MEP): Una mirada a la radicalización de la juventud católica mexicana durante la Guerra Fría." *Mexican Studies/ Estudios Mexicanos* 31:1 (Winter 2015): 156–192.

———. *Rebel Mexico: Student Unrest and Authoritarian Political Culture during the Long Sixties.* Stanford, CA: Stanford University Press, 2013.

———. "Silencing Rebellious Priests: Rodolfo Escamilla García and the Repression of Progressive Catholicism in Cold War Mexico." *The Americas* 79:2 (April 2022): 263–89.

———. "A 'Third Way' in Christ: The Project of the Corporación de Estudiantes Mexicanos (CEM) in Cold War Mexico." In *Local Church, Global Church: Catholic Activism in the Americas before Vatican II*, ed. Stephen Andes and Julia Young, 165–84. Washington, DC: Catholic University of America Press, 2016.

———. "'To Assault with the Truth': The Revitalization of Conservative Militancy in Mexico during the Global Sixties." *The Americas* 70:3 (January 2014): 489–521.

Pensado, Jaime M., and Enrique C. Ochoa, eds. *México beyond 1968: Revolutionaries, Radicals, and Repression during the Global Sixties and Subversive Seventies.* Tucson: University of Arizona Press, 2018.

Peredo Castro, Francisco. "Catholicism and Mexican Cinema: A Secular State, a Deeply Conservative Society and a Powerful Catholic Hierarchy." In *Moralizing Cinema: Film, Catholicism, and Power*, ed. Daniel Bilteÿreyst and Daniela Treveri Gennari, 66–68. London: Routledge, 2015.

Pérez, Jorge. *Confessional Cinema: Religion, Film, and Modernity in Spain's Development Years, 1960–1975.* Toronto: University of Toronto Press, 2018.

Pérez Miranda, Manuel. *El parlamento de los pueblos: Historia de la Escuela de Periodismo Carlos Septién García (1949–2011).* Mexico City: Ediciones Septién, 2012.

Pérez Rosales, Laura. "La revista Señal: La cuestión social y el enemigo comunista en México a mediados del siglo XX." *La Cuestión Social: Documentos, Ensayos, Comentarios y Reseñas de Libros acerca de lo Social* 20:4 (2012): 378–97.

Pérez Torrent, Tomás. "Crises and Renovations (1965–1991)," In *Mexican Cinema*, ed. Paulo Antonio Paranaguá, 94–115. London: British Film Institute, 1995.

Pettinà, Vanni. *Historia mínima de la Guerra Fría en América Latina.* Mexico City: El Colegio de México, 2018.

Poniatowska, Elena. *Massacre in Mexico.* Columbia: University of Missouri, 1991.

Porter, Susie S. *From Angel to Office Worker: Middle-Class Identity and Female Consciousness in Mexico, 1890–1950.* Lincoln: University of Nebraska Press, 2018.

Price, Brian L. "José Agustín and the New Classical Music of Counterculture." *Revista de Estudios Hispánicos* 49:2 (2015): 243–65.

Quezada, Ariana. "The Revolution in Crisis: A History of Human Rights in Mexico, 1970–1980." PhD diss., University of Oklahoma, 2016.

Randall, Margaret. *Hippies: Expresión de una crisis.* Mexico City: Siglo XXI, 1968.

———. "Testimonio: Recordando *El Corno Emplumado.*" *Revista Casa de las Américas* 280 (July–September 2015): 100–118.

Ramírez Berg, Charles. *Cinema of Solitude: A Critical Study of Mexican Film, 1967–1983.* Austin: University of Texas Press, 1992.

Ramírez Llorens, Fernando. "Noches de sano esparcimiento: Estado, católicos y empresarios en la censura al cine en Argentina (1955–1973)." PhD diss., Escuela Nacional de Realización y Experimentación Cinematográfica, 2016.

Raymund de la Ferreire, Serge. *Yug, yoga, yoghismo: Una matesis de psicología.* Bogotá: Menorah, 1961.

Rentería Díaz, Adrián. *El aborto: Entre la moral y el derecho.* Ciudad Juárez: Universidad Autónoma de Ciudad Juárez, 2001.

Rius Facius, Antonio. ¡Excomulgado! Trayectoria y pensamiento de Joaquin Sáenz Arriaga. Mexico City: Costa Amic, 1980.

———. *Méjico Cristero.* Mexico City: Editorial Patria, 1960.

———. *Un joven sin historia.* Mexico City: Editorial Tradición, 1973.

Rodríguez Araujo, Octavio. "Católicos contra el capitalismo." *Cuadernos Americanos* (January–February 1968): 16–23.

Rodríguez, Israel. "An Auteur Cinema for Mexico." In *Desafío a la Estabilidad/Defying Stability: Procesos artísticos en México/Artistic Processes in Mexico, 1952–1967,* ed. Rita Eder, 133–43. Mexico City: Turner, 2014.

Romero Pérez, J. *El cine, arma de dos filos.* Mexico City: Editorial Patria, 1957.

Rubenstein, Anne. *Bad Language, Naked Ladies, and Other Threats to the Mexican Nation: A Political History of Comic Books in Mexico.* Durham, NC: Duke University Press, 1998.

———. "A Sentimental and Sexual Education: Men, Sex and Movie Theaters in Mexico City, 1910–2010." *Estudios Mexicanos/Mexican Studies* 36:1–2 (Winter–Summer 2020): 216–42.

Rupprecht, Tobias. "Latin American *Tercermundistas* in the Soviet Union: Paradise Lost and Found." In *Latin America and the Global Cold War,* ed. Thomas C. Field et al., 221–40. Chapel Hill: University of North Carolina Press, 2020.

Ruszkowski, Andrés, "Testimonio." In *El cine en el Perú: 1950–1972. Testimonios,* ed. Giancarlo Carbone, 35–40. Lima: Universidad de Lima, 1993.

Salazar Palacio, Hernando. *La guerra secreta del Cardenal López Trujillo.* Bogotá: Ediciones Temas de Hoy, 1996.

Salgado, Alfonso. "Making Friends and Making Out: The Social and Romantic Lives of Young Communists in Chile (1958–1973)." *The Americas* 76:2 (April 2019): 299–326.

———. "'A Small Revolution': Family, Sex, and the Communist Youth of Chile during the Allende Years (1970–1973)." *Twentieth Century Communism* 8:8 (2015): 62–88.

Salvador Treviño, Jesús. "The New Mexican Cinema." *Film Quarterly* 32:3 (1979): 26–37.

San Miguel, Pedro L. "Mito e historia en la épica campesina: John Womack y la Revolución Mexicana." *Secuencia* 76 (January–April 2010): 135–56.

Sanabria, José Rubén, and Mauricio Beuchot. *Historia de la filosofía cristiana en México*. Mexico City: Universidad Iberoamericana, 1994.

Sanders, Nichole. "Women, Sex, and the 1950s Acción Católica's Campaña Nacional de Moralización del Ambiente." *Estudios Mexicanos/Mexican Studies* 36:1–2 (Winter–Summer 2020): 270–97.

Santiano Jiménez, Mario. "Anticomunismo católico: Origen y desarrollo del Movimiento Universitario de Renovadora Orientación (MURO), 1962–1975." In *Las derechas en el México contemporáneo*, ed. María del Carmen Collado Herrera, 187–255. Mexico City: Instituto Mora, 2020.

Santos, Alessandra. *The Holy Mountain*. New York: WallFlower Press, 2017.

Sarlo, Beatriz. *La batalla de las ideas*. Buenos Aires: Emecé, 2007.

Schulz-Cruz, Bernard. *Imágenes gay en el cine mexicano: Tres décadas de joterío 1970–1999*. Mexico City: Fontamara, 2008.

Serrano Álvarez, Pablo. *Prensa y oposición política en México, La Nación, 1941–1960*. Mexico City: Instituto Nacional de Estudios Históricos de las Revoluciones de México, 2012.

Simonetto, Patricio. "La otra internacional: Prácticas globales y anclajes nacionales de la liberación homosexual en Argentina y México (1967–1984)." *Secuencia* 107 (May–August 2020): 1–37.

Smith, Benjamin T. *The Mexican Press and Civil Society, 1940–1976: Stories from the Newsroom, Stories from the Street*. Chapel Hill: University of North Carolina Press, 2018.

Smyth, Kevin. *A New Catechism: Catholic Faith for Adults*. Freiburg im Breisgau: Herder and Herder, 1967.

Solares, Ignacio. "Sobre Vicente Leñero." In *"Los católicos": Vicente Leñero en torno a la fe*, ed. Miguel Mier Meza, 77–100. Mexico City: Ediciones Proceso, 2016.

Solis Mimendi, Antonio. *Jueves de Corpus: Sensaciones revelacionales de un Halcón*. Mexico City: Offset, 1975.

Solórzano-Thompson, Nohemy. "Vicarious identities: Fantasies of Resistance and Language in Juan Ibáñez's *Los Caifanes* (1966)." *Film & History* 34:2 (2004): 38–45.

Thompson, Dave. *The Rocky Horror Picture Show: Music on Film Series*. London: Rowman & Littlefield, 2012.

Thornton, Christy. *Revolution in Development: Mexico and the Governance of the Global Economy*. Oakland: University of California Press, 2021.

Thornton, Niamh. "Re-Framing Mexican Women's Filmmaking: The Case of Marcela Fernández Violante." In *Latin American Women Filmmakers: Production, Politics, Poetics*, ed. Deborah Martin and Deborah Shaw, 197–216. London: Tauris, 2017.

————. *Revolution and Rebellion in Mexican Films*. London: Bloomsbury, 2018.

Tirado, Manlio, et al. *El 10 de junio y la izquierda radical*. Mexico City: Editorial Heterodoxia, 1971.

Tirado Mejía, Alvaro. *Los años sesenta: Una revolución en la cultura*. Madrid: Debate, 2014.

Torre de la, Fernando. *Vicente Leñero: Vivir del cine*. Guadalajara: Universidad de Guadalajara, 2007.

Torres, Camilo, and John Gerassi. *Revolutionary Priest: The Complete Writings & Messages of Camilo Torres*. New York: Random House, 1971.

Torres, Fernando. "La ruptura del amor eficaz Camilo Torres, el movimiento estudiantil y la Teología de la liberación." *Caminos: Revista Cubana de Pensamiento Socio Teológico*, no. 51 (2009): 38–51.

Torres Septién, Valentina. "Belleza reflejada: el ideal de la belleza femenina en el discurso de la Iglesia, 1930–1970." *Historia y Grafía*, no. 19 (2002): 55–87.

————. "'Bendita sea tu pureza': Relaciones amorosas de los jóvenes católicos en México (1940–1960)." In *Amor e historia: Expresión de los afectos en el mundo de ayer*, ed. Gonzalbo Aizpuru y Bazant, 385–413. Mexico City: El Colegio de México, 2012.

————. "Cuerpos velados, cuerpos femeninos: La educación moral en la construcción de la identidad católica femenina." *Historia y Grafía*, no. 9 (1997): 167–90.

————. "Estado contra Iglesia/Iglesia contra Estado: Los libros de texto gratuito. Un caso de autoritarismo gubernamental, 1959–1962?" *Historia y Grafía* 19:37 (July–December 2011): 45–77.

————. "Los fantasmas de la Iglesia ante la imagen cinematográfica: 1953–1965." *Historia y Grafía*, no. 16 (2001): 111–43.

Tuñón, Julia. *Mujeres de luz y sombra en el cine mexicano: La construcción de una imagen, 1939–1952*. Mexico City: El Colegio de México, 1998.

Unión Femenina de Estudiantes Católicas, *David Mayagoitia, S.J.: Apóstol intelectual*. Mexico City: Unión Femenina de Estudiantes Católicas, 2001.

Valdovinos Torres, Javier. "La homosexualidad en el cine mexicano." BA thesis, UNAM, 1990.

Vaughan, Mary Kay. *Portrait of a Young Painter: Pepe Zúñiga and Mexico City's Rebel Generation*. Durham, NC: Duke University Press, 2017.

Vázquez Mantecón, Álvaro. *El cine súper 8 en México (1970–1989)*. Mexico City: Filmoteca UNAM, 2012.

Vekemans, Roger, and Ismael Silva Fuenzalida. *Integración latinoamericana y solidaridad internacional*. Brussels: Centro para el Desarrollo Económico y Social de América Latina, 1968.

Velázquez, Manuel. *Pedro Velázquez: Apostol de la justiciar. Vida y pensamiento*. Mexico City: Secretariado Social Mexicano, 1978.

Vilchis Arriola, Sugeily. "La invisibilidad de la narrativa lésbica en el cine mexicano." In *Miradas panorámicas al cine mexicano: Teoría, historia y análisis*, ed. Laura Zavala, 183–94. Aguascalientes: Universidad Autónoma de Aguascalientes, 2020.

Westad, Odd Arne. *The Global Cold War: Third World Interventions and the Making of Our Times.* Cambridge: Cambridge University Press, 2005.

Wilkie, James W. "Postulates of the Oral History Center for Latin America." *Journal of Library History* 2:1 (January 1967): 45–55.

Yankelevich, Pablo. "Extranjeros indeseables en México: Una aproximación cuantitativa a la aplicación del Artículo 33 constitucional." *Historia Mexicana* 53:3 (January–March 2004): 693–744.

Yee, David. *Informal Metropolis: Life on the Edge of Mexico City: 1940–1976.* Lincoln NE: University of Nebraska Press, forthcoming.

———. "Shantytown Mexico: The Democratic Opening in Ciudad Nezahualcóyotl, 1969–1976." *The Americas* 78:1 (January 2021): 119–47.

Young, Julia G. "Fascist, Nazis, or Something Else? Mexico's Unión Nacional Sinarquista in the US Media, 1937–1945." *The Americas* 79:2 (April 2022): 229–61.

Zermeño, Sergio. *México, una democracia utópica: El movimiento estudiantil del 68.* Mexico City: Siglo XXI, 1987.

Zermeño Padilla, Guillermo. "Cine, censura y moralidad en México: En torno al nacionalismo cultural católico, 1929–1960." *Historia y Grafía*, no. 8 (1997): 77–102.

Zolov, Eric. "Expanding Our Conceptual Horizons: The Shift from an Old to a New Left in Latin America." *A Contracorriente* 5:2 (2008): 47–73.

———. "Introduction: Latin America in the Global Sixties." *The Americas* 70:3 (January 2014): 349–62.

———. *The Last Good Neighbor: Mexico in the Global Sixties.* Durham, NC: Duke University Press, 2020.

———. *Refried Elvis: The Rise of the Mexican Counterculture.* Berkeley: University of California Press, 1999.

INDEX

Granados Chapa, Miguel Ángel, 86, 99–105, 128
El Grito (film), 214
Guajardo Elizondo, Horacio, 86, 90, 94–95, 96, 101
La guerra santa (film), 247–50, 280
guerrilla movements/warfare, 74–75, 126, 128–29, 133, 152, 255. See also armed struggle
Guevara, Ernesto "Che," 129fig.; and Compañero, 127–28; and hatred, 10, 284n29; as influential, 7; on love and hatred, 1, 136, 284n29; and Morelli, 134, 136; the Secretariat's views of, 74; on Vietnam, 9
Gutiérrez, Gustavo: and Chenu, 201; conference presentations, 67; and CUC, 205; on love, 1; MIEC and JECI alliance, 65; at Pax Romana 1962, 80; Petrópolis liberation theology meeting, 292n53; and prisoned youth, 75; on Sereno Coló, 68; Teología de la liberación, 201

Hair (musical), 185, 186, 188
Halcones/Hawks, 110, 119, 120–21, 125, 132–33
happiness, 16
Harmer, Tanya, 6
Hasta el viento tiene miedo (film), 194–95, 280
hatred, 10, 136, 284n29
Hays Code, 33
health care, 141
hedonism, 14, 24, 276–77
Hengbach, Franz, 63
Hernández, Javier "Kiko," 130, 149–54, 157, 165, 166–67, 179
Hernández, María Eugenia, 197, 208–9
Hernández Chávez, Jesús, 77, 78
Herrán Ávila, Luis, 242
Herrasi, Pedro, 146
hierarchy of church: and Christian Democrats, 85; and the Corporation, 78; and Guevara, 75; and identity, 79; and middle class morality, 5; and PRI, 5; priests challenging, 113–14; and "Youth Speaks," 97; and Ziegler and JCFM, 53
hierarchy of student movement, 102

hippies. See xipitecas/hippies
Hippies: Expresión de una crisis (Randall), 13
La Hoja de Combate (journal), 253–55
Hollywood, 24, 37, 38, 39, 47, 214
The Holy Mountain (film), 242, 257, 258–61, 261fig., 280
homosexuality: and A. Arbenz, 266; in Dutch Catechism, 199; and ficheras, 232–33; in film, 43, 45–46, 220–21, 232–39; and film classifications, 34tab.; gay liberation, 17, 232, 237–39; and The Holy Mountain, 258; lesbianism as love, 228; as natural, 228; Zone Rosa, 230
Hope (film), 240, 241fig.
horror films, 194–95
Humane vitae (encyclical), 12, 17, 171, 183, 228
humanism, 62, 66, 201, 218
Of Human Life (encyclical). See Humane vitae
human rights, 154–56
hungry coyote. See Nezahualcóyotl

Ibáñez, Juan, 175–76, 266–68, 279
Ibero-American University (UIA), 39, 57, 131, 132, 151, 217–18
identity, 36, 190, 256, 295n4. See also Corporation of Mexican Students
Illich, Iván, 71, 127, 205, 221, 262, 292n53
illiteracy, 31, 144–45, 151, 158, 207
imperialism, 10, 54, 73, 74, 97
Indigenous Peoples, 14, 36, 143, 183, 263
inequality, 70
El infierno de todos tan temido (film), 280
Informaciones Católicas Internacionales (ICI) (journal), 123
Institute and School of Cultural Cinema, 217–18
Institutional Revolutionary Party (PRI). See Partido Revolucionario Institucional
integrated man, 1, 149
Intercultural Center of Documentation (CIDOC), 221
International Catholic Cinema Office (OCIC), 24–25, 30, 34, 52
internationalization, 3
International Movement of Catholic Intellectuals, 155

International Movement of Catholic
Students (MIEC), 63–66, 67, 69, 71, 72
International Relief, 27
International Student Conference, 54, 58
International Young Catholic Students
(JECI), 65–66
Ituarte Servín, Alfonso, 92

JCFM (Juventud Católica Femenina
Mexicana): overview, 23; and cinema,
32; and femininity, 52; on *Muchachas de
uniforme*, 46; and sex discussions,
171–72; and Ziegler history, 26–28, 53.
See also *Juventud*
Jesus Christ, 5, 128, 260. *See also* Christianity; God
Jesus Christ Superstar (musical), 186
Jesus Movement, 187–88
Jewish faith, 198
Jiménez, Manuel, 143
Jiménez Valdés, Olivia, 208
Jodorowsky, Alejandro, 183, 242, 256, 257,
262–63. See also *The Holy Mountain*
Joskowicz, Alfredo, 214–15. See also *Crates*
journalism: combatting repression, 92,
93*fig.*, 95–96, 101–2, 116, 126; during
Corpus Christi massacre, 119; and
covert instigators, 120; critiquing
government, 91; and ethics, 89;
Granados Chapa views on, 100; and
human rights, 154; MURO against, 99;
removal of defiant priests, 104; scholarship of Mexican, 87; schools of, 88;
universities as undemocratic, 102–3. *See
also* Carlos Septién García School of
Journalism; Medina Valdés, Gerardo;
individual magazines and newspapers
Los jóvenes (film), 176
Joy and Hope (Vatican II encyclical), 9, 66,
196
Juenesse Etudiante Catholique Internationale (JECI), 65–66, 67, 71, 72, 75
Jueves de Corpus Sangriento (Solis
Mimendi), 125
Julissa, 186
Jus, 89
Juventud (magazine): overview, 23, 26; on
boycotting films, 32; demands of

women, 28–29, 47–48; on flirting, 171;
interest in counterculture, 193; on the
pill, 172
Juventud desenfrenada (film), 43–44, 235,
276
Juventud Rebelde/jóvenes y rebeldes (film),
276
Juventud sin Dios/Siempre hay un mañana
(film), 49–50, 276
La juventud sin ley (film), 276

Kennedy, John F. *See* Alliance for Progress
Kennedy, Robert F., 64, 81
King, Martin Luther, Jr., 136
Knight, Alan, 244

labor organizing, 158
Lalive d'Epinay, Christian, 244
Langland, Victoria, 18
Larraín, Hernán, 114
Larraín, Manuel, 65
Latin American Episcopal Council, 8–9,
65, 67, 75, 136, 149
Latin American Secretariat in South
America (the Secretariat): overview,
65–66; closing of, 153; repression of,
74–75, 76, 80; Sereno and Vasquez, 155;
Víspera and *SPES*, 73–74
Latin American unity, 67
laws, 28, 33, 225
League of Mexican Decency, 24, 25, 30,
32–35, 46
Leary, Timothy, 178–79
Lebret, Louis-Joseph, 134
the Left (general): and CENCOS, 296n12;
Cerf's views, 199; and *Claudia de
México*, 231; and CUC, 159; and Echeverría, 125–26; false narratives of PRI,
121; and human rights, 154; and
morality, 60; newspapers views of, 105;
sharing concerns with Catholics, 55–56;
students protesting on campus, 56–57;
in *El 10 de junio y la izquierda radical*,
133. *See also* anticommunism; communism; Marxism; socialism
Lemercier, Gregorio, 220, 221
Leñero, Vicente: overview, 221–22, 223–26;
Los albañiles, 198, 221; and *Cadena*

131. *See also* Corpus Christi massacre; priests and protests; repression; student movement 1968

psychedelic drugs, 14, 170, 176, 177, 181–84, 185

psychoanalysis, 220

El pueblo rechazado (play), 220, 221

punks, 14

pure writing, 13

Quezada, Ariana, 154–56

Quinceañera (film), 277

El Quinqué Mágico, 182

Rábago González, Manuel Salvador, 78, 131, 159

racism, 10

radicalism: Adveniat concerned with, 63; of *Claudia de México*, 228–29; and consumerism, 273; and *Contacto*, 135; Cultural University Workshop, 78; Echeverría's role in, 153; and encyclicals, 66, 76; labor priests, 101; and love, 156; massacres role in, 153, 157; and Morelli, 139; nonviolence as, 136; panistas, 95; and the Secretariat publications, 73; of UNAM teachers, 77. *See also* armed struggle; critical pedagogy; la onda movement/counterculture; Marroquín, Enrique; Marxism; militancy; Movement of Professional Students; socialism; xipitecas/hippies

Radio UNAM, 202

Ramos Zavala, Raúl, 131, 133

Randall, Margaret, 13

La rebelión de los adolescentes (film), 277

Refried Elvis (Zolov), 15

Réplica (magazine), 256

repression: after Avándaro festival, 190, 192; of Aug. 1968 protests, 212; of Catholic Workers, 139; of Christians for Socialism Conference, 76; counterculture film list, 279–80; journalism combatting, 92, 93*fig.*, 95–96, 101–2, 116, 126; during labor uprisings, 119; long history of, 119; during medical student strikes, 119; and Monterrey bank robbery 1972, 158; and MURO, 98–99, 102, 104, 208; and la

onda, 15; poverty as, 140; during presidential elections, 119; and PRI, 5; of priests, 155; priests parts in, 141; of the Secretariat, 74–75; visibility of, 120; of xipitecas, 185. *See also* Corpus Christi massacre; disappeared; Tlatelolco massacre; torture

Research Center for the Development and Integration of Latin America, 76

Retes, Gabriel, 263

Revision of Life, 10, 66, 67, 70, 150, 156

Revista Internacional de Cine (magazine), 30

revolution, 16, 253. *See also* Cuban Revolution; Mexican Revolution

Revolution dans la revolution? (Debray), 128

"The Revolution Is Not Made in the Cafeteria" (de la Rosa), 133

Revueltas, José, 187

Reygadas, Rafael, 130, 143–46, 148, 155

Ribeiro, Darcy, 67, 71

Ripstein, Arturo, 222

Rius Facius, Antonio, 242, 252–53

rock music: Avándaro festival, 14, 15, 189–92, 191*fig.*, 256; in films, 178; as insulting, 256; in JCFM performances, 172; and local parishes, 179–81, 180*fig.*; and Marroquín, 168–70, 178–81, 185, 186, 188–90; and la onda roots, 13–14, 15–16, 43; *Señal* on, 174; youth rebellion film list, 275–77. *See also* Beatles

The Rocky Horror Show (musical), 186

Rodríguez, Israel, 268

Rodríguez, Roberto, 235

Rolling Stones, 168

Romero, Jesús, 39–40

Romero Pérez, Jesús, 35, 217–18

de la Rosa, Martín, 114, 130, 131–32, 137–38, 147, 149

Ruiz, Samuel, 87, 111

rumberas, 25

Rumbo (magazine), 76–77, 77*fig.* See also *Corporación*

Ruszkowski, André, 30–31, 33–34, 35, 52

Sabina, María, 169–70

Sada, Garza, 158, 159

Sáenz Arriaga, Joaquín, 242

Safa, Patricia, 138

ultraconservatism. *See* conservatism; Far Right; fascism

Una alma pura (film), 266–68, 279

Una calle entre tú y yo (film), 277

Una familia de tantas (film), 37, 277, 279

UNAM (Universidad Nacional Autónoma de México): arts influence, 134–35; Cerf, 196–99; Chávez's resignation, 99, 102; CUEC, 200, 213–14, 217, 245, 269; and La Fauna, 180; Granados Chapa at, 100–101; lectures on revolution, 70; March for Homosexual Dignity, 237; Marxism workshops, 151; and military, 111; Morelli at, 134–35; and MURO, 86; "Our teachers" cartoon, 77, 77*fig.*; politicking at, 60; Radio UNAM, 202; School of Leaders, 207–9; sex discussions, 171. *See also* Corporation of Mexican Students; University Cultural Center

underdevelopment, 10

Unión Femenina de Estudiantes Católicas (UFEC), 290n15

unions, 158

United States: and alcohol in films, 288n71; Alliance for Progress, 74, 75, 136, 143–44; Americanization and materialism, 49, 74; American tourists, 230, 231; Chicano movement, 136; CIA, 75, 139, 265; Civil Rights movement, 15; classification of films, 33; hippies and Christianity, 16; and Mexican Revolution, 283n8; and middle class Mexico, 26; and Pan-American Catholicism, 33; as predatory, 58, 72; Summer of Love, 178–79; youth rebellion film list, 275–78. *See also* Hollywood; imperialism

Universal Declaration of Human Rights, 154

universities (general), 4, 58–59, 96. *See also* Corporation of Mexican Students; Movement of Professional Students; students; *various institutions*

University Anticommunist Front, 98

University Center for Cinematographic Studies (CUEC), 200, 213–14, 217, 245, 269

University Cultural Center (CUC): overview, 200; and Cerf, 196, 197; Desobry at, 202–13; *Diálogo*, 209–12, 210*fig.*; Europe and friars at, 218; European films at, 199; impressions of guests at, 204; as pivotal to 1968 movement, 212–13; School of Leaders, 207–9; *Teorema* shown at, 206

University Cultural Workshop, 150, 159

University Movement of Renovated Orientation (MURO), 86, 98–99, 102, 104, 208

University of Puebla, 98

Urán, Carlos, 72–73

urbanization, 36, 309n33

Urraza, Esther Alicia, 138

Uruguay, 74

utopia, 6, 73

Valdovinos, Javier, 232

Valle, Sofía del, 27

Vasquez, María, 68, 70, 76, 81, 153, 155–56

Vatican II: overview, 8–11; aggiornamento, 9, 174–75; as challenging conservatives, 167; dangers of, 220; as destroying Catholicism, 242; and Granados Chapa, 86; and human rights, 154; and liberation of nuns, 228; as Marxification of Christianity, 253; and Movement of Professional Students, 63; and *Señal*, 99–100; and Sereno Coló, 69; state referencing *Gaudium et spes*, 66; and Teilhard de Chardin, 144; in "Youth Speaks" in *Señal*, 97. *See also* the church; *individual encyclicals*

Vaughan, Mary Kay, 6, 38

Vázquez Corona, Rafael, 151, 152

Vázquez Mantecón, Alvaro, 213–14

vegetarianism, 182

Vekemans, Roger, 75–76, 105, 136

Velázquez, Manuel, 112

Velázquez, Pedro, 27, 87, 111, 112, 135

Velo, Carlos, 178. See also *Cinco de chocolate y uno de fresa*

Vera López, José Raul, 208

Vértiz, Julio, 56

Vietnam War, 9, 15, 261

Founded in 1893,
UNIVERSITY OF CALIFORNIA PRESS
publishes bold, progressive books and journals
on topics in the arts, humanities, social sciences,
and natural sciences—with a focus on social
justice issues—that inspire thought and action
among readers worldwide.

The UC PRESS FOUNDATION
raises funds to uphold the press's vital role
as an independent, nonprofit publisher, and
receives philanthropic support from a wide
range of individuals and institutions—and from
committed readers like you. To learn more, visit
ucpress.edu/supportus.